CONTEXTUAL DESIGN

Defining Customer-Centered Systems

Contextual Design: Defining Customer-Centered Systems
is the premier title in the Morgan Kaufmann Series in
Interactive Technologies.

Stuart Card, Jonathan Grudin, Mark Linton, Jakob Nielsen,
Tim Skelly, Series Editors

CONTEXTUAL DESIGN

Defining Customer-Centered Systems

HUGH BEYER

KAREN HOLTZBLATT

INCONTEXT ENTERPRISES

MORGAN KAUFMANN PUBLISHERS

An Imprint Of Elsevier

SAN FRANCISCO   SAN DIEGO   NEW YORK   BOSTON
LONDON   SYDNEY   TOKYO

Senior Editor	Diane Cerra	Text Design	Ross Carron Design
Production Manager	Yonie Overton	Copyeditor	Ken DellaPenta
Production Editor	Elisabeth Beller	Proofreader	Jennifer McClain
Cover Design	Ross Carron Design	Compositor	UpperCase Publication Services
Cover Photo	Will Crocker/	Illustrator	Cherie Plumlee
	THE IMAGE BANK	Indexer	Valerie Robbins
		Printer	Courier Corporation

Designations used by companies to distinguish their products are often claimed as trademarks or registered trademarks. In all instances where Morgan Kaufmann Publishers is aware of a claim, the product names appear in initial capital or all capital letters. Readers, however, should contact the appropriate companies for more complete information regarding trademarks and registration.

Permissions may be sought directly from Elsevier's Science and Technology Rights Department in Oxford, UK. Phone: (44) 1865 843830, Fax: (44) 1865 853333, e-mail: permissions@elsevier.co.uk. You may also complete your request on-line via the Elsevier homepage: http://www.elsevier.com by selecting "Customer Support" and then "Obtaining Permissions".

ACADEMIC PRESS
An Imprint Of Elsevier
525 B Street, Suite 1900, San Diego, CA 92101-4495, USA
http://www.academicpress.com

Academic Press
Harcourt Place, 32 Jamestown Road, London NW1 7BY, United Kingdom
http://www.hbuk.co.uk/ap/

Morgan Kaufmann Publishers
340 Pine Street, Sixth Floor, San Francisco, CA 94104-3205, USA
http://www.mkp.com

Library of Congress Cataloging-in-Publication Data
Beyer, Hugh
    Contextual design : defining customer-centered systems / Hugh
Beyer, Karen Holtzblatt.
        p. cm.
    Includes bibliographical references and index.
    ISBN-13: 978-1-55860-411-7   ISBN-10: 1-55860-411-1 (pbk.)

    1. System design.   2. System analysis.   I. Holtzblatt, Karen.
II. Title.
QA76.9.S88B493   1998
004.2'1--dc21   97-35927
                                                          CIP

This book is printed on acid-free paper.

Acclaim for *Contextual Design*

If necessity is the mother of invention and you don't know what users need, you can't invent. Karen and Hugh present a step-by-step way to uncover, understand, and use those needs. If developers are not already using techniques like those presented here, they should read this book carefully to see what they are missing.

—DAN BRICKLIN
cocreator of VisiCalc

Hugh Beyer and Karen Holtzblatt are widely recognized as the foremost experts on contextual inquiry, and they have packed what they know into a book of both substance and intelligence. It has been a long wait but worth it. The book lucidly shows how to capture the real requirements of customers and how to tailor designs to fit their needs. If you care about your customers and want to create products they need as well as want, then you need to understand contextual inquiry and contextual design. You need this book.

—LARRY CONSTANTINE
Principal Consultant, Constantine & Lockwood, Ltd.
Professor of Computing Sciences, University of
Technology, Sydney (Australia)
Author of *Constantine on Peopleware* and *Software for Use*

For many years, Beyer and Holtzblatt have been pioneers in the field of human-computer interaction, showing how the context of computer use can be (and needs to be) the central focus of analysis and design. This book conveys the understanding and wisdom that they have gained from their experience in contextual design in a form that is accessible to students and design practitioners. It will serve as a guide and handbook for the next generation of interaction designers, and as a result we can expect the usabilty and appropriateness of computer systems to be greatly improved.

—TERRY WINOGRAD
Stanford University

Foreword

Marshall McClintock

It's almost passé now for forewords to books on the human-computer interaction (HCI) to begin with stating how computers were once the domain of specialists and are now mass consumer products. Today people are likely to use computers at work and school as well as while shopping and playing, and numerous other ways. Now computers are simply part of daily life in the developed world, and nothing suggests that this trend will stop. However, it's not the ubiquity of computers that's particularly surprising; rather it's the ways we've found to integrate them (often rather successfully) into our lives.

Computer interaction has come a long way since punched cards. Moreover, in the process, we have learned much about human-computer interaction, much of which HCI research has substantiated. However, designing computer software still remains a rather mysterious art. Newspapers and magazines abound with stories of computer systems and products that are delivered late and over budget and that do not perform as expected. Anyone who has had to wait while a store clerk struggles with a new, "easy-to-use" computer system can attest to this.

While numerous books exist on software and computer system design, they primarily focus on the engineering aspect. Usually there is a brief chapter (or a few pages, more likely) on defining requirements, and then you are into a detailed discussion of object modeling and data flow diagrams. Missing is a discussion of and a set of methods for deciding what to build and how what you build will affect all the other related activities. In filling that gap, this book is a landmark.

Design of any complex product, by its nature, is a multidisciplinary group process. Any attempt to bring some structure to design, of necessity, must span numerous fields. The authors do an admirable job of weaving techniques from industrial engineering, anthropology, human factors, software design, and group process together. While each of these various techniques has its own pedigree, this book's value is the way the authors have integrated them into a coherent design methodology.

In addition, the authors have considerable experience in applying this methodology to real problems in real software development projects with real development teams across a wide array of businesses. These have not been "toy projects" conducted with graduate students. The examples in the book are numerous and practical. The diagrams are clear and illustrate the important use of rough models to capture design thinking.

All this praise notwithstanding, I would not be the jaded skeptic I am if I did not offer a few caveats. The complete contextual design methodology may not fit all organizations or all design projects equally well. Some parts may have more benefit in some situations than other parts. You may have to adjust it some for your own work process. However, without understanding the whole methodology, you cannot make these trade-offs.

As I said earlier, one of the strengths of this book is that it has been written by people who have a great deal of experience in software product development. It is also an ambitious book. It is not the complete solution, but it is, I believe, the beginning of the solution. Good software design will not come from a few specialists. It must be informed by the work of many people involved in designing products. I believe this book provides a sound basis for everyone who is now, or will be in the near future, involved in creating useful and usable software products.

Contents

Part 3   Seeing across Customers   *137*

Preface

When Hugh and I first started our consulting business, we wondered if we should write a book right away. Every consulting firm needs a book, we thought. But Larry Constantine, our mentor in the consulting business, said, "Wait awhile, until your experience is richer." Five years later, Contextual Design, while still evolving and improving, is robust in ways we would not have imagined because of the questioning of our teams and the demands of their corporate contexts. And we are more seasoned, more insightful, more realistic, and more humble.

I do not think we in the industry realize how amazing it is that software and software/hardware systems get built and shipped at all. I remember the first time I looked into the guts of a really big computer. I saw thousands of electrical connections, any one of which might shut down the system or produce incorrect calculations. How could we ever get it right—let alone achieve the targeted reliability? The design and shipping of anything is a phenomenon and a tribute to our creative and organizational skills. Remember, we were the same kids who fought to be in the front seat, not the back; who got mad if someone told us what to do; who were graded on individual achievement and contribution—not the stuff of collaboration.

We were taught that we should and could create, change, and shape the future of the world with our technology. Despite all our complaints about usability and engineering-driven organizations, all the rework we do throughout the life cycle, all the times we signed the requirements docs only to be told we built the wrong thing, all the low expectations of first versions, all our frustrations and work-arounds—

we have changed the face of everyday work life for the better. As an industry we should pause to applaud ourselves.

But we know it is not enough. Commercial and IT organizations alike know that to be competitive and to achieve the goals of our businesses we must drive an understanding of our customer right into the center of our development processes: how customers work, how they buy, and what they will be doing in the future. We know that the future success of our businesses necessitates a commitment to understanding the customer and understanding business. Making these two things real within organizations is what Contextual Design and InContext's work is all about.

Hugh and I (and many of you) are part of a larger movement. Any field seems to move in a direction pushed by its participants and pulled by sources hard to identify. Ten years ago, when I started working with computers and usability, customers were drawn into the design process to check the design at the tail end—but not to drive it. In most commercial companies, marketing wrote marketing messages to convince a market they would benefit from the product idea engineering thought up with little input from customers. Design conversations barely touched on how to match the structure of user work to the structure of the system. Today's challenge is in front-end design— the idea that the voice of the customer must be heard before we start to build.

But it is a struggle. Any change is a struggle. Engineers used to making what they are interested in feel constrained by having to think about what is useful and can sell. We all have to hold back the voice that tells us that producing code is progress—even if we cancel the project, even if it is the wrong code, even if we don't know what would be useful to code. How does understanding work produce code? It is a struggle of personalities as we try to work in cross-functional teams to produce a shared direction. It is hard to remember that one smart guy working alone probably doesn't have the whole answer. We simply have to realize that design is about people working together, and that's what makes it hard.

I remember the first design team I worked with. I barely knew what a computer was, but I jumped in to help a team designing a very large and expensive computer. They were stuck, not on the guts of the engine, but on the control panel! So I listened to six engineers arguing about how to lay out the switches: "Won't we crash the system by accident if the remote selection is on the same switch as off?" "Oh, they'll only do that once." And whether or not there should be a key in the switch: "Security is important." "No, it isn't." "Yes, it is." As I listened, I realized that the team simply had no ground for their decisions. There was no way that reasoning and argument could get them to an answer. So I collected some data on how the panel was used: "Are you kidding? We won't touch the remote. Someone might crash it." "We turn the knob very, very slowly." "Someone crashed it once, and the whole business stopped. No one touchs that knob now." And on security: "The computer is in a locked room; we don't need it locked." "Locking is a pain. We keep losing the key." "We keep the key taped to the computer so we can find it." "I catch my clothes on that lock; it sticks out." The design was done in a day. We had a new switch for on and off and stopped agonizing about the key. I recently ran into a member of that team. He said he still talks about what happened 10 years later. The power of simply having data.

Contextual Design was developed to be sure we make the right thing for customers, but it was also developed to help people stop agonizing and move on. Designers and engineers want to do the right thing, and they agonize to try to figure out what it is. But there is no direction without customer data—data about how work is structured, what matters to people, and real characterizations of a market. Data is the only reliable outside arbitrator for people. This fact is the beginning and the end of Contextual Design. Data is the language of sharing that allows communication. Data breaks the deadlock. Data is the source of invention because it defines the need. If we get the right data, if we know how to roll it up to see the customer population (not just the single person we talked to), if we know how to pull design implications from the data, if we reuse data from project to project— data pushes us forward to successful design within an engineering time frame.

But what about internal systems? Classic systems design includes the step of going to talk to the customer, much as a contractor must go to talk to the person contracting them. To those trained in classic systems design, it may sound foolish to make such a big deal about starting by talking with those who will use the systems. If you are hired by someone to make something, certainly you must go ask what they want. But asking what they want presumes that they can really tell you. I wanted windows in my new den, but what I really meant was I wanted a lot of light and to see the garden. Windows come in many types and technologies. To get light I had to listen to my contractor, not just tell him what to do. And in the basement I just had it wrong. He said that a built-in buffet where I wanted it would toss everyone near it into the supporting poles. The fact was I didn't hire my contractor to do what I said, I hired him (I found out) to partner with me in figuring out what I should build. Data about work practice and knowledge of technology is the shared conversation of customers and systems designers. I believe that this is what participatory design is really all about. Ten years ago the user movement in IT was the Joint Application Development (JAD) session. But classic JAD focuses on the contracting aspects of the relationship—not the co-design aspect of the relationship. Today, JAD sessions are getting to be more like design meetings but often without the necessary contextual work practice data. And today, contextual data is filtering into business analysis.

But in some ways, IT is too close to its customer because the customer pays their bills. Meeting the needs of the department paying your bill is not the same thing as helping the business as a whole move forward. Object modeling, enterprise modeling, and process reengineering are trying to address seeing and designing the corporate practices as a whole. But how do you see a whole process from the point of view of everyday life experience, and how do you do it with enough detail so that the big decisions turn into reasonably usable software once it hits the worker's desk? This is what we are faced with today.

Contextual Design grew up, and is growing up, inside these historical and organizational forces. It is the reflection of these forces, and it is one of the forces pushing us toward customer-centered organizations—not just customer-centered systems. In the end, real invention fills a need, and figuring out how to fill that need with technology can seize the imagination of an engineer. Meeting a real need makes money directly through selling products or indirectly through supporting efficient businesses. So being customer-centered means change, but it also brings all corporate goals together.

Contextual Design is about how to use data for design in organizations that make things. This book is about what we now know. Ten years ago, as far as I knew, no one thought we needed field data to do design. (All my papers on field techniques got rejected!) Now, most think we do—and now we need to know how to get it and what to do with it. This book is the result of our dialogue with the forces in the industry and the real people on our teams. And as you take it and use it, in whole or in part, you will change it again—because that is what industry change is about: creating our own reality by stealing and transforming ideas from others.

ACKNOWLEDGMENTS

Many thanks to the following people:

John Whiteside, who started me off in this industry and had the foresight to know that we needed to do something else to get real product transformation

Sandy Jones, my first partner in making my ideas about field data real and coauthor along with Steve Knox and John Bennett of the first Contextual Inquiry (CI) course

The whole original SUE group at DEC—Sandy, Dennis, Chauncy, Michael, Tom, Elliot, and Alana—who listened, learned, spread the word, transformed, and pushed CI

John Bennett, my first mentor, who pushed me into the CHI community and helped me write my first published words about a contextual perspective

Jonathan Grudin—always a champion, without whose challenge there would never have been the much republished and used CI paper (I admit I respond to dares)

Lou Cohen, who introduced me to all the concepts and processes of quality from which I stole shamelessly and who nagged me into making the first CI course

Russ Doane, who was the best internal marketer for CI I ever met

Alfonsio DiIanni, for being himself

Every team at Digital who used, argued with, and transformed what eventually became Contextual Design (CD)

Martin Dickau, who said, "—huh?" when I first explained how to think about work practice. I went home and developed the work models.

Larry Constantine, our consulting business mentor, who helped us learn to write, publish, and believe in our work

Those first clients and our champions: Irene Wong, Deb Fromholtzer, Dennis Allen, and the guys from Fluke

Every client we have ever had—those we liked and those we didn't—for trying what we told them and making it work, and for getting stuck and making us face what wasn't good enough

Mike C., for asking us to make our process fit his organization, for wishing for CD Lite. (We think we have it now—see the last chapter.)

Every coach we trained, for every question you asked and every clarification you wanted. Forgive us our impatience.

Every consultant and designer who ever took our ideas, used them, and spread them in many different forms. All we ask is acknowledgment!

Every academic who had their class read our stuff—even if you don't think it is perfect.

Every process consultant, designer, or academic who we ever stole an idea from (we hope we referenced you all). Do more so we can steal more.

Diane Cerra, our editor, for her nagging and encouragements—and great dinners

Every reviewer of this manuscript who made this book usable (we hope!)

To our spouses—Les and Ivy—and children—Ari and Shoshie, Charlie, Lily, Frankie and Lucy—who lost lots of attention over the last year

To all of you, we give our heartfelt thanks and appreciation—and ask amends for any past neglect, abuse, mistakes, and arrogance.

And finally—from me to you, partner—for every word, for tying our ideas to the page.

Karen Holtzblatt

Introduction   1

Developing software has never been easy. But over the last 20 years the requirements for software development have gotten far more stringent. Once computers were used by experts in glass rooms; now everyone on the street expects to use a computer to get their jobs done. Once computer users knew and liked technology; now users want their computers to be as invisible as a ballpoint pen so they can focus on their jobs. Once applications supported a single, bounded task—compute compound interest for a bank's loans, perhaps; now they are expected to support the whole work of the business, from electronic funds transfers with the Federal Reserve to the company's email system. It's no longer enough to be a good software engineer. To be successful in today's world, those who define and build hardware and software systems[1] must know how to fit them into the fabric of everyday life.

Commercial software vendors recognize the reality of the new situation when they emphasize "solutions" over products. Traditionally, new products were most often defined by an engineer getting a bright idea, building it, then looking for a market for it. But the new demands of the market suggest that the new product won't be accepted if it doesn't fit with customers' other systems and existing ways of working. Customers are looking for an integrated set of products that solve whole work problems, not point products that don't work with anything else, that don't seem to solve the problems they have, and that are too hard to use.

The challenge of system design is to fit into the fabric of everyday life

Commercial product vendors are one major segment of the software development industry; the other is the Information Technology

---

[1] For simplicity's sake, we use "system" to refer to any combination of hardware and software used to deliver a product, application, or computer platform.

(IT) departments, building the systems that run a company. Their customers[2] are the people actually doing the work of the business. The new user expectations have hit IT departments just as hard as commercial vendors. Taught by the ubiquitous desktop systems, their customers expect that all systems will be as easy to use. They expect to be able to access and manipulate corporate data from the PC on their desk as easily as they access their own desktop files. When they can't get the systems they want, these customers decide that the IT department is out of touch, has far too long a response time, and too often delivers systems that can't be used. Then the customers change direction, cancel the IT project, and buy some desktop solution off the shelf—which they expect the IT department to maintain. The IT department responds with processes designed to help them manage the demands on them: Joint Application Development (JAD) sessions to clarify requirements, formal sign-off to control changes, and enterprise modeling to recapture some of the initiative. But in the end it's the customers' system, and there's a limit to how much these processes can keep them from changing their minds.

The problems both kinds of organization are struggling with have the same root. Requirements engineering—front-end design—systems analysis—whatever the term used to describe the activity, the hard underlying problem is determining what to build to help people do their work better and specifying it at a level of detail that developers can code to. Customer-centered design promises a solution, but taking advantage of it leads quickly to questions about the nature of systems development and the organizations that practice it. What is the right way to define new systems? What's the relationship between those who say what to build and those who build it? How do we make sure the system specification defines something the customers really want? And how do the different parts of an organization work together to invent and deliver

> *Contextual Design is a backbone for organizing a customer-centered design process*

---

[2] We'll use "customer" to refer to anyone who uses or depends on a system—it's a more inclusive term than "user," which we'll use only for those who interact with the system directly. There's some dispute as to whether the "customer" or the "user" should be primary in the design process. Some worry that the term "customer" leads the design team to focus too much on those who pay for a system, rather than those who use it. We recognize that danger, but also recognize that a system must meet the needs of *all* those who depend on it, and so prefer the more inclusive term.

a coherent system? An approach to system design that hopes to have an impact on real organizations must be able to answer these questions. (See "Readings and Resources" for additional perspectives on the problem.)

Contextual Design (CD) is an approach to defining software and hardware systems that collects multiple customer-centered techniques into an integrated design[3] process. Contextual Design makes data gathered from customers the base criteria for deciding what the system should do and how it should be structured. It makes deciding how customers will work in the future the core design problem and uses those decisions to drive the use of technology. It unifies all an organization's actions into a coherent response to the customer. And it defines activities focused on the customers and their work, rather than leaving team members to argue with each other based on personal opinion, anecdotes, or unverifiable claims about "what customers would like."

THE CHALLENGES FOR DESIGN

Making customer-centered design practical for real engineering organizations depends on striking a balance among multiple considerations. For customer-centered design to be possible at all, the process needs to include techniques for learning about customers and how they work. This means that we must discover the everyday work practice of people. But anyone's real work practice is intricate and complex; understanding it in depth

Collect and manage complex customer data without losing detail

leads to an overwhelming amount of immensely detailed information. One typical response to such large quantities of data is to "reduce" it—perhaps by summarizing the top five issues in all the data and just responding to those. Another typical response is to decide that the problem is too big to address—and instead to deal with one customer

---

[3] Throughout this book, we use "design" in the ordinary English sense of conceiving and planning a system. This is how Mitch Kapor uses the word (Kapor 1991). The technical software engineering usage of "design" is different; it applies to the design of the implementation only. Since our topic is customer-centered *design,* we have reappropriated the term; Chapter 11 discusses how this activity fits into the development life cycle.

problem or issue at a time, respond to that one issue, and ignore the rest. One team found 100 different user needs, grouped them into 20 application areas, and assigned each to a different team—resulting in 20 unintegrated point solutions. None of these approaches give the design team the ability to respond to the customers' whole work practice with a coherent set of systems. The trick is to give the team tools that let them see the breadth of data without being overwhelmed, to see the common structure and pattern without losing the variation, and to understand the wealth of detail without losing track of its meaning.

Seeing customer data is critical, but so is understanding how to design a response. In customer-centered design there are three levels of design response that matter. First, and most impor-

Design a response that is good for the business and the customers

tant, is the design of work practice. If the team is to define a new system that fits into the fabric of its customers' lives, then the team—in partnership with the users themselves—needs to see and redefine that fabric. This allows them to define a new work life that hangs together for the user. Second comes the design of the corporate response that delivers the new work practice. It is not enough to design the system alone. A custom software system's internal users need to integrate organizational roles, business procedures, and the system (perhaps including software, hardware, and communications connections) that supports them. A commercial product depends on the definition of the market message, associated services, delivery mechanisms, and the product itself. All these different aspects must be planned and delivered together to create a viable business. Third, when the nature of the corporate response has been defined at a high level, the team can design the structure of the system itself. Whether software only or software and hardware combined, the system creates an environment for its users to work in; it's up to the team to ensure that that environment fits the flow of their work. The challenge for customer-centered design is to provide for all three levels of design in a process that guides the design team's daily actions and fits within the constraints of the organization.

It's people who create a design and people who have to work together to make it happen. Putting a team to work on a problem, rather than one person, means an organization can handle larger and more complex problems. A team has multiple skills and points of view to bring to bear on a problem. A cross-functional team drawn from the departments that have to cooperate to produce a system can account for the issues and needs of each department. Designing effectively together depends on techniques that manage the interaction between people in a room so that they can create a unified corporate response. But pulling a cross-functional team together means breaking down some of the walls between parts of the organization. Given the extreme pressure all organizations are under to produce results quickly, the different groups must be able to work in parallel once the corporate response is defined, while still maintaining the coherence of the total effort.

> *Foster agreement and cooperation between stakeholders*

Contextual Design deals with the issues of gathering data, driving design, and managing the team and organizational context. It has evolved over the last 10 years through intensive work with teams producing products and internal systems, and designing organizational processes. This grounding in real experience has ensured that Contextual Design takes the needs of working design teams into account, providing methods to develop insights and shared direction among team members at each point. Contextual Design provides complete support for the design process, from the initial customer data gathering through the transition to object-oriented design (or whatever other implementation model you favor). The process brings together the techniques needed to design a system that meets its customers' needs, while addressing the challenges of making a design process work in real-world situations.

> *Make the process practical given real time-driven organizations*

THE CHALLENGE OF FITTING INTO EVERYDAY LIFE

Federal Express has changed how businesses work on a daily basis by providing an affordable, reliable way of getting packages to another location overnight. Spreadsheets have made elaborate numerical models commonplace, where once they were the domain of a specialist. And even such a simple thing as the mouse and windowing user interface (UI) has helped move computers from specialized tools to an integral part of everyday work. These products and services are important because they make new ways of working possible.

These examples suggest that the critical aspect of a new product or service is the new way of working that it enables. But what does it mean to enable a new way of working? How is it that a system might support or disrupt work practice?

Consider the true story of one user trying to do a simple task: A user of a standard office system needs to print a label. From her point of view, this should be simple. She should write her letter, putting the address at the top. She should tell the computer to print an address label, and put a label in the printer. The computer should get the address from the letter and print it on the label. This is her *user work model* for the task: these are the concepts she uses and the strategy she takes for granted to get her label printed. If they were built into her systems, her work would be straightforward.

Instead, the system offers its own *system work model,* which imposes new distinctions and a style of work foreign to her. She writes the letter, with the address at the top, but she can't just print the label from that address. First, she must create a separate document containing only the address so it will print properly on her labels. She copies the address from the letter to this separate document.

Support the way users want to work

She tells the system to print the document, remembering to say that it should use the manual feeder. It will use the sheet feeder if she forgets, even if she's put a label in the manual feeder (it's easy to forget). She waits for the system to realize that it has to ask for the next sheet. (She must not insert the label before the system asks, or the printer will spit it out without printing on it.) When the dialog box comes up saying the "print manager" (the what?) has a problem, she dismisses the dialog box and switches to the print manager application. She cannot tell the print manager to continue without switching to it. She goes to the printer (which is across the room), takes it offline, inserts the label, and puts the printer back online. (If she inserts the label without taking the printer offline, it spits it out without printing on it.) She goes back to the computer and dismisses the dialog box requesting a new sheet of paper to print on. (It will not sense that she put a label in.) Finally, she switches back to her application.

Printing a label is a conceptually simple task. But this system presents an enormously complex model for it. It introduced many new steps, driven by the concepts of technology, not by the needs of the work. It introduced new concepts that the user must understand to get her job done: What's the print manager, and how is it different from an application? How do you switch applications? If the print manager can put up a dialog box asking the user to switch to it, why can't it also say what's wrong? If the system can tell there's no label in the printer, why can't it tell when there *is* a label in the printer? What's the distinction between on- and offline? How is that different from on and off? The system's model is hard to understand because it makes no sense in terms of the work people are trying to do. And the net result, of course, was that this user never did use the computer to print labels. The new work practice was so foreign and cumbersome she preferred to continue writing labels by hand.

This system supports work poorly. It is poor not because functions are missing but because the system imposes a work model that does not make the job more efficient and does not match the user's expectations. The designers of this system had no choice about imposing a way of working. *Any* system imposes a model of work. The only choice designers have is whether they will design that work model explicitly to support the

Don't increase work and frustration with automation

user or whether they will allow it to be the accidental result of the technical decisions they make. This model of work was created by the interaction of multiple tools designed by multiple groups in several organizations. No job, even one as simple as printing a label, is accomplished with a single tool. Design has become difficult because systems now support almost every aspect of work life. It's up to the design team to understand the environment their tool will be used in because it is the combination of tools that controls their customers' work practice. (See Terwilliger and Polson [1997] for related research.)

CREATING AN OPTIMAL MATCH TO THE WORK

Does this mean that a new system must match its customers' existing work practice exactly? Certainly not—that would be a sure path to failure. But systems must match the user's model closely enough that the user can make the transition. History is littered with excellent innovations solving real problems that have never been adopted because it is simply too hard to switch models. The Dvorak key layout *will* increase your typing speed—if you are willing to retrain your fingers and accept incompatibility with virtually every keyboard in existence. Switching to DC current in your home *will* eliminate the risk of electrocution to you and your family—if you are willing to install a converter and replace every appliance you own. Neither idea has gone anywhere because the cost of change is too high.

Then how can a design innovate successfully? By taking one step at a time, always considering the interaction between the new ideas and the current work practice. Consider the history of the word processor. Originally, everyone used typewriters, and typing became the work model users understood. Early word processors stayed close to the typewriter model. They just provided better typing and better correction. Then word processors introduced cut and paste—metaphors taken from the physical operations of cutting with scissors and pasting with glue, something everyone had to do already. These features were an easy extension of the model. Then word processors introduced multiple buffers and multiple documents open at a time, making it easy to share and transfer text across documents. Then they introduced automatic word-wrapping and multiple fonts, and desktop publishing was born. Each step was an easy increment over the previous, and each step walked the user community a little further away from the typewriter model. Now word processing has little but the physical act of typing in common with using a typewriter.

Innovate through step-by-step introduction of new work practice

The history of word processing illustrates how work can be revolutionized over time. A good design provides an *optimal* match between the users' current way of working and the work practice introduced by the new system; it changes the work enough to make it more efficient but not so much that people cannot make the transition. Innovative designs that succeed are those that offer new ways of working and new advantages while maintaining enough continuity with people's existing work that they can make the transition.

Determining what makes an optimal fit is a decision for the design team; there's no absolute right answer. It's part of the design process to decide how to integrate an innovation into the customers' work practice so smoothly that they can successfully adopt it. In customer-centered design, we seek a framework for the discussion so that the decision is based on customer data, and a way to check the decision with the customer.

KEEPING IN TOUCH WITH THE CUSTOMER

If designing from an intimate understanding of the customer is so basic, why is it so hard to achieve? As product development companies grow, they create organizations that have the effect of keeping designers away from their customers. A start-up expects their developers to help make the sale by talking to potential clients. But, as it grows, it develops a sales organization to handle the customer interface; it puts account representatives in place to control the sales organization; and it puts marketing and product management organizations in place. All this tends to keep developers away from even the salespeople. A start-up puts developers on the customer support line. But, as it grows, a whole organization takes over the customer support function, with a formal interface for providing feedback to development. Developers are isolated from immediate customer feedback about how they are doing. We've talked to developers so isolated from their customers and so powerless to make changes that they didn't even want to talk to customers because they didn't think they could fix any problems they found.

Organizational growth isolates developers from customers

IT departments have difficulty staying close to their customers for a different reason. They, too, tend to become isolated from their customers as the company grows, but the different solutions available to them each come with attendant problems. They create new roles—business, systems, or requirements analysts—to translate between customers and developers, but find that customers still believe the IT department doesn't understand their business. The additional layer doesn't create a close working relationship with the customers, and it doesn't create a clean handoff to development.

Sitting with the users makes cross-departmental projects hard

To control shifting requirements, IT departments put sign-off processes in place, but customer priorities and requirements still change. Then they situate developers with the people in the businesses they support, so they are closely involved with the work of the business. This improves the client relationship, but it means the IT department can't share resources or expertise and can't take a strategic role looking across the whole company's information systems. So they decide they are too fragmented and pull everyone back together again, reintroducing the problems of isolation.

This kind of oscillation is typical in IT departments, but in the end it misses the point. Any arrangement of people comes with its attendant problems—the only solution is to recognize the problems and address them. The IT department needs some distance from the customers to see across the stovepipes created by the different departments and plan systems that address the business as a whole (along with a way to fund such systems). At the same time, they need mechanisms that keep them in close partnership with their customers.

This is the challenge for Contextual Design: to make a design team's understanding of their customer explicit and give them enough distance to see the work practice as a whole, across the business or across a market. Yet at the same time, the process must keep the design team thoroughly grounded in the knowledge of what's real for their customers.

THE CHALLENGE OF DESIGN IN ORGANIZATIONS

Who gets to say what a system will do? Is it really the marketing department or systems analysts saying, "Build this," with the engineering team just following their specification? Or do marketing or the analysts really only say, "Make this *kind* of a thing," with the engineers actually deciding what they will build and how the system will work? In fact, both sides have a role to play in saying what a new system will look like—the creation of a system in real organizations is the outcome of their cooperation.

The underlying problem is inescapable. Today's systems are too large to be built by a single person. So organizations divide the process of defining and building a system into parts and assign each part to a group of people. The people in each group specialize in their own part and lose contact with what all the rest are doing. There are four questions to answer in the course of developing a system, and these questions tend to define natural breaks in the development process, so it's easy to assign one group to answer each question. The questions are, *What matters in the work—* what aspects of work should be addressed? *How should we respond—*

Breaking up work across groups creates communication problems

what kind of a system should a team respond with? *How should the system be structured*—what exact function, arrangement of function, and system structure best meets the needs of the work? And *how are we doing*—does the system as designed actually work for the customers?

The first question (what matters?) asks what aspects of the customers' work practice a new system should address, what issues or problems should be overcome, what roles and tasks are important to support. The group tasked with answering this question is typically marketing or business analysts. When management changes an organization, they often define what matters for its information systems in directives. "Too much overhead goes into approving purchases," they say. "Give every group a credit card and authority to use them." Or, "Our chemical databases are our lifeblood—tie together all the databases across the company." Or marketing might tell their engineering group, "Design a product to support business planning," or "Put this product on the Web." These directives say at a very high level what work issue the system should address, but don't really define the system. What aspects of a product are affected by putting it on the Web? Does tying databases together mean one database, replicated databases, or a way to search across multiple databases? From the point of view of those setting direction, these questions are details; it's not their job to answer them.

Different organizational functions focus on different parts of a coherent process

Answering these questions means saying what the response will be: how the corporation will coordinate to respond to the issues with system designs, processes, services, and delivery strategies. Marketing may be part of defining the response unless the company is very engineering-driven. Requirements analysts may do this unless they are very nontechnical, in which case developers will drive it. The customers themselves should be involved with an internal system, since it defines how they work. A research or architecture group may drive defining a response. Marketing and analysts may have the formal charter to "develop the specification for the system," but in our experience they don't really define system behavior to the level of detail needed to write code. "They give us a specification," the developers tell us. "But there's always lots that we have to decide, and they usually ask us for things that are really impractical. So it's give-and-take."

Deciding how to structure the system means deciding exactly what function to include, exactly how the system will behave, and how it will appear on windows, menus, or screens. This is nearly always done by developers, which means they need to understand the whole work context in which the system will be used. Otherwise they cannot make decisions that are appropriate for the customer. Developers don't get customer data at this level of detail from their marketers or systems analysts. Working out the detailed system structure depends on an additional level of customer data that developers have to get themselves—or design the system based on what feels right to them. Some companies have gone so far as to put the development group in a different state from their users and analysts, to create a group focused on its development work. But that just creates a greater need for communication and causes more serious isolation when travel budgets are cut.

Every function needs customer data, but it has to be the right kind of data

The final question for design asks, How are we doing? This question checks the progress of the system with the customer to ensure that it's still the right system, and low-level changes haven't made it unusable. This question is often separated out and given to a usability or Quality Assurance group to test. Answering the question looks at the system itself (for bugs and fit to the specification) and tests the system with users. But in either case, dealing with the results is the job of the developers. So they have to receive, understand, and believe in the feedback—which means they have to buy into the process of getting it and trust the group that collects it. And often, when there's been no real design from data so far, the flaws discovered at this point are so fundamental they cannot really be addressed at this stage of development.

Data showing what is wrong is frustrating if builders can't fix it

All these different parts of defining what a system will be have to come together if the system and design process are to work. The people defining the response have to respond to real work problems; the people building the system have to build the response they agreed to. But keeping each part isolated to its own group creates communication problems across the organization. The formal documents in engineering processes capture the evolving design, but also are intended to manage the communication and disagreement between groups. "You signed off on this specification. That means you're committed to it." "Yes, but we've reorganized and don't need that anymore." Or, "Yes, but we talked to this important customer and there's just no point in shipping if we can't meet this need." Or, "Yes, but it's not possible to implement that given the technology we have."

Design in organizations is about developing a coherent direction across all the groups: agreement on the corporate response they intend to deliver. It's not that changes will never happen—it's that when changes happen, the whole organization can respond appropriately across all functions, rather than turning the changes into an argument between two groups. In turn, a coherent view depends on taking account of all the different perspectives during the development of the corporate response. Marketing and analysts need the technical perspective to see opportunities for new kinds of systems. Engineering needs the marketing perspective to see why some directions make a good product and others don't. They need the analyst's perspective to see the work issues they might address. An IT team needs the customer's perspective to ensure their proposed changes to working procedures are reasonable and will be accepted. After they've developed a corporate response, they can work in parallel for efficiency without losing the single direction. But in up-front design, a cross-functional team works best.

Cross-functional design teams create a shared perspective

TEAMWORK IN THE PHYSICAL ENVIRONMENT

Creating a cross-functional team that does design work together runs into some surprising problems in real organizations. Consider the most basic question: where is such a team to meet? A quick look at the physical structure of most organizations would make you think they are designed to keep people apart. The most common work environment for a developer is the cubicle—an area big enough for one person to work in comfortably, containing a terminal and a desk. But it is not big enough for several people to work together comfortably, and it does not have the wall space to support group work. Meeting rooms do exist, but a meeting room's key characteristic is that it is shared and booked by the hour. Because it is booked by the hour, the only work that it supports is that which can be completed in a short time—a half day at most. Start booking rooms for longer than that on a regular basis, and you get dirty looks

Organizations have no real spaces for continuing team work

from your coworkers. After all, you are hogging a shared resource. Not only that, but because the room is shared, you can't leave much stuff in it. Every conversation has to restart from scratch, and every meeting has to start with spreading out all the design diagrams again.

So the only work a meeting room supports is work that can be completed in a few hours and that does not require much physical support—no hardware, no charts, no diagrams, nothing you cannot roll up in a few minutes and take with you. Maybe there's a network hookup—but to which LAN? And is it still good? And how do you hook this laptop PC to it anyway? Given these constraints, is it any wonder that designers and engineers consider meetings a waste of time? The very physical structure of a typical large corporation announces plainly that real engineering happens alone in cubicles and that when people gather in a meeting room, they are not doing real work. There's nothing in the usual structure of organizations to support the face-to-face needs of initial system design.

MANAGING FACE-TO-FACE DESIGN

Working together effectively means having workplaces where real work, done by multiple people working face-to-face, can happen. It also

Face-to-face work depends on managing the interpersonal

means giving these people the interpersonal skills and process to make their sessions effective. One division manager addressed a particular thorny problem by booking rooms at a local hotel, sending his five senior architects there, and telling them they were fired if they didn't come up with a solution in a week. He got a result, but we find people are usually happier, more creative, and produce results more quickly if they have a reasonable process to work in. The typical response to having a process—even from people who "hate" process—is, "Thank you. Now I finally know what to do."

Working together is a new skill; it is not something taught in schools and is rarely taught on the job. Working together effectively means understanding how to keep a design conversation on track, how to focus on the work issue and not each other, how to manage everyone's personal idiosyncrasies, and how to uncover and address the root causes of disagreements. Unless teams learn to do this, their designs suffer because the models people have for handling disagreements trade off coherence of the design for keeping people happy.

One primary model people have for handling disagreement is horse trading: "I think you're wrong on that. But I'll let you have it if you'll give me this other thing that is really important to me." Horse trading leads to a system that is a patchwork of features, with no coherent theme. And horse trading causes everyone on the team to disinvest from the design because everyone has had to agree with at least one decision they thought was fundamentally wrong.

Other models for handling disagreement exist, but most don't work any better. There's the compromise model, which says, "You say we should design everything as dialog boxes. I think everything should be buttons. So we'll implement both and make everyone happy." Everyone is happy except the user, who has a dozen ways of doing each function and no clear reason to choose one way rather than another. Or there is the guru model, which says, "The guru is smart and knows everything. We'll all do what the guru says." That is fine, except the population of gurus who are infallible on technical architecture, GUI design, user work practice, marketing, project planning, and the host of other skills necessary to get a product out is vanishingly small.

Disagreements can lead to an incoherent design

Contextual Design defines a process for developing systems that takes the interpersonal issues into account. It defines procedures for deciding among design alternatives based on data, not arguments or horse trading. It defines roles for people to take on during design sessions that keep the discussion on track. It does this not only to make the design process more efficient, but because when people argue and have no process for making decisions, it pulls the system apart.

Customer-centered design keeps user work coherent by creating a well-working team

Front-end system design forces us to address interpersonal issues because it's in this part of the design process that bringing different functions face-to-face matters so much. Traditional design draws less heavily on the skills of working together. Committing to keeping the customer work coherent despite the different perspectives and skills on the team makes knowing how to work together critical. We find that when people have a clear process and clear roles to play, when they become sensitive to the individual styles that cause them to clash in the room, and when they have concrete data to base decisions on, they can overcome the barriers to working together effectively.

This is what it means to be customer-centered: not only does customer data drive design, but the design process leads to a system that keeps the users' work coherent in the system, from invention through implementation. The challenge for Contextual Design is to build in techniques that recognize the issues around working together and provide ways to do so effectively.

THE CHALLENGE OF DESIGN FROM DATA

Design is a cognitive activity. It is thought work. It begins with a creative leap from customer data to the implications for design and from

Learn how to see the implications of customer data

implications to ideas for specific features. A clear understanding of the customer doesn't *guarantee* any kind of useful system gets designed and delivered. Design depends on being able to see the implications of data. In many of the classic stories about the development of new systems in the computer industry, inventors were responding to their unarticulated sense of what was important based on their own experience. Ken Olsen was an engineer building digital circuitry. He knew other engineers would buy smaller computers if they were available and invented the first minicomputers. Dan Bricklin learned accounting while getting his MBA. He knew accountants would use automated spreadsheets and invented VisiCalc. These entrepreneurs responded to their experience with potential customers by designing systems to meet their needs.

These pioneers also knew how to see how the implications of their customer knowledge and the possibilities of technology could trans-

Recognize that designing from customer data is a new skill

form the way people work. But companies are now designing larger systems and systems that support people who are "not like us" and whose work "we do not do." That's a harder problem. Seeing how knowledge of *other* people's work should change a design is a skill and a new way of thinking for many people. Even hiring a customer into the development team doesn't guarantee the skill—most customers don't have in-depth knowledge of the technology. Just as moving from procedural to object-oriented design is a new skill requiring a new way of thinking, just as moving from forms interfaces to windowing interfaces is a new skill, moving to customer-centered, data-based design is a new skill. Coders who are new to object-oriented languages and UI designers new to windows tend to continue operating out of their old way of thinking—they create code or user interfaces that still reflect the old structures. In the same way, people who aren't used to designing from data don't find it natural to see design implications in data. Much of Contextual Design—and much of this book—is intended to help designers see design implications in customer data.

The idea that design isn't inherent in data tends to be lost when we talk of requirements *gathering* or *elicitation.* When someone checks his answering machine as soon as he walks in the office in the morning, this action says he wants to know at once who has tried to reach him. For a communications tool, this piece of data might suggest that an immediately visible notification of waiting messages is critical, perhaps by putting a blinking red light on the box. But nothing in the customer's environment declares a requirement for a blinking light. Requirements and features don't litter the landscape out at the customer site. Designers have to make this leap from fact to implication for design. And because design is implied by the customer data, what designers see in data changes based on what they are designing—a maker of office chairs would be more interested in whether the customer sat down before playing his messages. Making the shift to data-based design asks designers to learn to draw design implications out of the work, rather than implementing enhancement requests.

> *Don't expect to find requirements littering the landscape at the customer site*

THE COMPLEXITY OF WORK

A design team reacts to their understanding of the customer by designing a solution. This isn't primarily a design for technology—how to structure and deliver a particular tool that will improve work in some way. It's the design of a new way of working that is supported by technology. We saw in the label story above that when technology is the focus for design, the work practice falls apart, and the user has to run back and forth

> *The complexity of work is overwhelming, so people oversimplify*

between computer and printer to print a label. Instead, a customer-centered design process makes work practice the focus for design. All the rest of the design elements fall out of this. But it's a difficult transformation for the engineer who is used to looking for ways to apply neat technology.

Designing work practice is a daunting task because any real work is complex and intricate. What's really involved in writing a letter? When do people decide to start fresh, and when do they start from a previous letter they wrote? How do people choose the style of a letter, and how do they maintain it throughout? What's involved in keeping an address book, choosing an address from it, and inserting it into the letter? "Writing a letter" is one simple aspect of office work, yet who really understands what's involved? But to support these customers well, designers must understand work at this level. Unless they can see and manage the complexity of real work, they can't keep it coherent for the user.

MAINTAINING A COHERENT RESPONSE

If work is to remain coherent, the system work model had better hang together. It's not good enough to get the five top issues or the three key market requests and respond to each separately. After five years of that, companies are saying to us that they no longer know what all the systems they have do or how they might fit together. To keep from losing control of the systems like this, designers have to respond to work issues not with individual features but with a *systemic response*. Such a response keeps the system work model coherent even when delivery is broken into multiple products and versions.

Furthermore, it's no longer enough to design single systems in isolation. Computer systems are now supporting so much of people's work that understanding how they fit together is critical—but because work is complex, the web of systems that supports it is also complex. Currently, most work is supported by a combination of systems so complex that no one really understands it. Consider office work again, supported by word processors, spreadsheets, financial packages, layered on operating systems extended by add-on utilities, running on hardware from several

A systemic response—not a list of features—keeps user work coherent

vendors. Just try to get someone to explain to you why you can't fax from your word processor using the third-party PC-card modem you bought last week. It's too hard, even for the developers who control all the parts.

The team needs to see the work practice of its users and see the system structure as a whole. Revealing both work practice and system structure calls for a representation that makes the important issues stand out. Team members can interact over this representation, using it to present their thoughts and capture their conversation. It's this coherent representation that ensures the system hangs together, supports the customer, and gives the whole organization a single focus for parallel efforts. It's this coherent representation that continually reminds each developer how her part fits into the system as a whole and supports the overall work flow of her users. It discourages developers from focusing on one part to the exclusion of all others, inducing them to keep the system in proportion.

Diagrams of work and the system help a team think systemically

Keeping a system coherent also depends on the organization that delivers it. When development groups break the work into pieces that they can understand individually and support each piece separately, they produce a multitude of systems that don't hang together. They do this for the best of reasons: they have to ship something. Development cycles of two years and up are no longer acceptable; many teams are moving to delivering in six-month windows. The challenge is to accept this reality of the engineering world and still keep the system coherent—to recognize the overall work situation and envision the integrated solution, but deliver in small pieces that are useful on their own but can grow up into a single solution to the whole problem.

The core of any design process is supporting design thinking: the invention and development of ideas for a coherent system, based on an understanding of customers' work practice. Design thinking maintains system coherence in the face of the breadth of complexity and variety and the depth of detail in both the work and system. The challenge for Contextual Design is to support design thinking through techniques that lead to developing a coherent understanding of the work and the system's response, making both work and system concrete, explicit, and sharable and dealing with the tendency of organizational structures to pull the design apart.

THE EVOLUTION OF CONTEXTUAL DESIGN

Contextual Design grew over many years of working with design teams on different problems. As we recognized places in the process that teams had difficulty with, we modified the process or introduced new steps to address the problem. Here's a summary of how the process grew.

Contextual Inquiry (CI) was the first part of the process. Karen Holtzblatt developed it as a response to a challenge from John Whiteside: design a process that would lead to new kinds of systems rather than iterating existing systems (Holtzblatt and Jones 1995). Prototyping and usability testing could iterate an existing system, but couldn't suggest wholly new directions. CI meets the challenge by putting designers and engineers directly in the customers' work context, thereby giving them the richest possible data to invent from. From this beginning, interpersonal issues were central; cross-functional CI teams developed a shared understanding of the customer from the beginning to alleviate the transition to development. The core process for CI was worked out with Sandy Jones by working with several engineering projects.

Contextual Inquiry produces vast amounts of detail, and managing the quantity of information became difficult. So Holtzblatt adapted the affinity diagram process to reveal the order and structure in the data collected during contextual interviews. This became the classic CI process taught for many years at places such as the Conference on Computer-Human Interaction (CHI).

Paper prototyping to test a design is an adaptation of Participatory Design methods, especially those developed at Aarhus University (Ehn 1988; Greenbaum and Kyng 1991), combining them with the style of interviews used in CI. Paper prototypes were introduced to iterate designs with customers without the need to commit anything to code. In this way, a design could be tested with minimal investment.

Working intensively with design teams revealed that when designing for the customer, there wasn't a good way to represent design alternatives. The Pugh matrix process provided a way to envision several design alternatives and combine them to produce new alternatives, while keeping team members from butting heads (Pugh 1991). This process, much modified, became the visioning process in Contextual Design.

In sketching out system designs, we tended to get into unwanted arguments in the teams. UI sketches tended to divert the team into UI design prematurely, and no other formalism existed to show the structure of the system from the user's point of view. We developed the User Environment formalism as a way to capture in standard form the sketches we wanted to represent our early designs. One of the first uses of the formalism was to represent a complex design integrating nine point products, showing each product team their place in the overall design.

But we discovered that teams still had a hard time seeing design implications in the hierarchical structure of an affinity diagram. An affinity doesn't show the structure or pattern of work; it reveals issues but doesn't show how to structure a solution. Work models are a formalization of informal sketches of customer work. As we used these models in different design situations, we became more confident that they did represent the key aspects of work for most design problems, and we standardized the five that Contextual Design now includes.   ➪

Finally, we found that it was too hard to lead a team through the transition from consolidated models to User Environment Design; it was still too much like magic. So we introduced an explicit visioning step to create the new design. At first we had people work out the details in redesigned sequence models, but then found they preferred to think pictorially in storyboards.

At each point in the evolution of Contextual Design, we had a process that worked well enough for the problems at hand. But at each point we recognized problems we did not have a good way to solve. Contextual Design grew by taking a problem and using our principles of design to redesign the process to address it. Solving that problem would then reveal the next, and so on, until the process got reasonably stable. The result of this evolution is the process you now have. ❑

CONTEXTUAL DESIGN

Contextual Design is a customer-centered process responding to these issues. It supports finding out how people work, so the optimal redesign of work practice can be discovered. It includes techniques that manage the interpersonal dimension of designing in cross-functional teams and keep designers focused on the data. And it leads the team through the process of discovering design implications for redesigning work practice, developing a corporate response, and structuring a system in support of the redesign.

Contextual Design provides explicit steps and deliverables for the front end of design, from initial discovery through system specification. As such it works well for organizations putting ISO 9000 or SEI-compliant processes in place: well-defined steps and measurable deliverables support the requirements of those standards for defined, repeatable processes. Though optimized for large, complex projects, Contextual Design has been successfully used on small projects as well. And because Contextual Design provides a complete structure for the front end, teams have used it very effectively as a scaffolding into which they incorporate additional techniques and processes as the need arises.

In our approach to process design, we recognize that much of what we do is to make explicit and public things that good designers do implicitly. Each of the parts of Contextual Design reflects a part of the design process that has to happen anyway—either informally in one person's head or publicly as an explicit design step. Making a step explicit makes it something that a team can do together and makes it possible to share the thinking process and results with others. It may also make the step take longer, but if you're currently going through a lot of argument in design and rework, making that step explicit may well reduce the time it takes. And if your customers are complaining about usability and integration across applications, taking the time may be what's required. Make sure, when you look at your processes, to take into account not just the formal time a step takes, but the amount of time it really takes in your organization. If your engineering team is still arguing over what functions should be included in a release two weeks before test, you are still in the requirements analysis phase no matter what your project calendar says or how much code you've written. Deciding how you will use a design process—which steps are critical, which can be omitted—is an important first step for any project. (Chapter 20 gives guidance on how to tailor Contextual Design to specific situations.)

CD externalizes good design practice for a team

The parts of Contextual Design, and the parts of the book that cover them, are as follows:

Contextual Inquiry: The first problem for design is to understand the customers: their needs, their desires, their approach to the work. Even the hacker coding in the basement has some notion of who he thinks the customers are and what they want. A customer-centered process makes an explicit step of understanding who the customers really are and how they work on a day-to-day basis. Contextual Design starts with one-on-one interviews with customers in their workplace while they work. These are followed by team interpretation sessions in which everyone can bring their unique perspective to bear on the data. This supports the team in developing a shared view of all the customers they interview. We'll describe Contextual Inquiry and how to apply it in Part 1.

Talk to the customers while they work

Work modeling: Understanding the customer is good, but customer work is complex and full of detail. At the same time it's intangible; work practice is not naturally a concrete thing to be manipulated. Designers might be able to get away without an explicit representation of a simple work domain they are familiar with. But what happens when the work domain is complex and unfamiliar? What happens when it crosses multiple departments in an organization? How do you communicate and share knowledge of a way of working? For these sit-uations, Contextual Design provides a concrete representation. *Work models,* built during interpretation sessions, provide a concrete representation of the work of each customer interviewed. There are five kinds of work model, each providing a unique per-spective on the customer. Each perspective is complete, showing the whole work practice, yet focused on a single set of issues. These work models are described in Part 2.

Represent people's work in diagrams

Consolidation: Systems are seldom designed for a single customer. But designing for a whole *customer population*—the market, depart-ment, or organization that will use the system—means being able to see the common structure inher-ent in the work different people do. Studying different customers will give designers a feel for the common approaches to work across the population, but it takes special techniques to make that "feel" explicit so that a team can see the common pattern without losing individual variation. The consolidation step of Contextual Design brings data from different customers together and looks across multiple customers to produce a single picture of the population a system will address. This is done through an *affinity diagram* (Brassard 1989), bringing individual points captured during interpretation sessions together into a wall-sized, hierarchical diagram showing the scope of issues in the work domain, and *consolidated work models,* showing the underlying pattern and structure of the work the design will address. Together, they show what matters in the work and guide how to struc-ture a coherent response. Consolidation is described in Part 3.

Pull individual diagrams together to see the work of all customers

Work redesign: Any system is put in place because its designers hope to improve their customers' work practice. That improvement is often implicit, presented as the result of adopting some technological solution. In Contextual Design, the team uses the consolidated data to drive conver-sations about how work could be improved and what technology could be put in place to support the new work practice. The team invents improved ways to structure the work rather than focusing on technical solu-tions. This *vision* drives changes to the organizational structure and

Create a corporate response to the customers' issues

procedures, as well as driving the system definition. Using *storyboards,* the team develops the vision into a definition of how people will work in the new system and ensures that all aspects of work captured in the work models are accounted for. (Storyboards act like stories of the future in the sense used by Rheinfrank and Evenson [1996].) This process is described in Part 4.

User Environment Design: The new system must have the appropriate function and structure to support a natural flow of work. This

Structure the system work model to fit the work

structure is the system work model—the new way of working implicit in the system. It's the floor plan of the new system, hidden behind user interface drawings, implemented by an object model, and responding to the customer work—but typically not made explicit in the design process. In Contextual Design, the system work model has an explicit representation in the User Environment Design. As a floor plan for the system, the User Environment Design shows the parts and how they are related to each other from the user's point of view. The User Environment Design shows each part of the system, how it supports the user's work, exactly what function is available in that part, and how it connects with other parts of the system, without tying this structure to any particular UI. With an explicit User Environment Design, a team can make sure the structure is right for the user, plan how to roll out new features in a series of releases, and manage the work of the project across engineering teams. Basing these aspects of running a project on a diagram that focuses on keeping the system coherent for the user counterbalances the other forces that would sacrifice coherence for ease of implementation or delivery. Building and using a User Environment Design for development is described in Part 5.

Mock-up and test with customers: Testing is an important part of any systems development, and it's generally accepted that the soon-

Test your ideas with users through paper prototypes

er problems are found, the less it costs to fix them. Rough paper prototypes of the system design test the structure and user interface ideas before anything is committed to code. Paper prototypes support continuous iteration of the new system, keeping it true to the user and giving designers a data-based way of resolving disagreements. In prototyping sessions, users and designers redesign the mock-up together to better fit the user's work. The results of several of these sessions are used to improve the system and drive the detailed UI design. Paper prototyping is described in Part 6.

Putting into practice: In the last chapter, we look at practical issues of putting a new design process in place. You'll encounter resistance, you'll have to work with the limitations of the organization you have, and you'll have to build on the skills you have in place. Altering Contextual Design to fit your organization and your specific design problems means recognizing which parts are critical and which are less necessary in each case. What works for a two-person team won't work for a fifteen-person team; what works to design a strategy for a new market venture won't work for the next iteration of a 10-year-old system. We'll discuss common project situations, how to tailor the process to them, and how to ensure you don't lose the key features of the process along the way.

Tailor Contextual Design to your organization

Each part of the book has a similar structure: the first chapter focuses on the organizational situation and issues driving that phase of the design process. If you're looking for an overview of Contextual Design and the thinking behind it, concentrate on the first chapter of each part. The second chapter of the part describes what makes this phase of the design process customer-centered. It discusses how to make customer considerations central given the needs and constraints of this phase of design. And the third chapter of each part describes how to do the work, covering particular procedures and techniques that guide a team through the process.

This book is intended to capture our experience designing customer-centered processes to meet a wide variety of team situations and design problems. As we describe in Part 3, there's a broad commonality of work practice across any industry, so we expect the solutions we've developed to be generally useful; there will be a lot here that you can pick up and apply in your own situation. However, every situation is unique, and you should expect that you will tailor the things you pick up to your problem, team, and organization. Treat Contextual Design as a coherent design process but also as a collection of techniques and a framework for thinking. Where you have other techniques you've found to be valuable, slide them into the appropriate place in the process. This is a starting point. What you do with it is up to you.

ALAN'S STORY

I'm the project manager for a network management application. We'd done a lot of good engineering work on the application, converting it to C++ and cleaning up the architecture. We also had pretty good software development processes—we specified new features before building them instead of coding by the seat of our pants, down to the point of dealing with error conditions. But when we presented our last version to customers, they liked it but were not excited. I decided we didn't really understand our customers well enough and that we should do something about it.

Our UI designer had some experience with Contextual Design and talked me into trying it for our next version. I was told it would take 15 days, so I agreed to put four engineers on it, including myself. Then when I talked to the coach who would lead us through the project, I found out it would actually take four to six months. This was a shock. But I decided it was important, and we went ahead with three engineers and three documentation people.

We did 16 contextual interviews in all. Even during the initial interviews, I learned more about the customers' real needs. It wasn't so much that we came up with new features as that my whole understanding of the real priorities changed: things that I thought were priority 100 I realized we had to do in this release, and some cool technical features that were priority 1 moved down to 100. Throughout the project, I changed priorities of different tasks and reassigned people as I understood better what our customers needed.

We built an affinity and consolidated our models, which crystallized our understanding of customer priorities. Then we did the visioning and storyboards based on the vision. This frankly scared me; I thought if we had data from 50 or 60 people I could rely on it better. Also at this point, some of the UI designers pulled out. They were bothered by working as a team on a part of the design they used to do alone and said they didn't see the need for all this customer data. We went forward with the redesign, but then I began to get uncomfortable; some of the team didn't want to be tied to reality. They wanted to design from scratch.

I decided to cut and run. I told the team we had two weeks to develop final designs for changes to be delivered in the next release—that made everyone get very concrete. We cleaned up our ideas, and the team's architect and I wrote six specifications capturing the new design. I assigned the specifications to developers to flesh out and code on their own. Issues did come up later during development, and we would go back to the consolidated models and affinity to resolve them. Often when engineers were arguing over two alternatives, the models would suggest some third alternative that they hadn't even thought of.

We finished the release and showed it around the company. People were excited, but the real test came when we demonstrated it at our worldwide users' group meeting. For each new part of the system, I explained what we saw customers trying to do, how the new system would help them do it better, and then showed them the product actually doing it.

Our customers gave us a standing ovation. That's never happened before.

Looking back over the project, what strikes me is that we achieved this with no extra engineering effort. We didn't take longer to ship this release, or work longer hours than on any other, and we didn't have more developers. We were just better focused because we knew what was important to the customer. I'm using more of the process on my current release and am finding that's still true: the additional insight we are gaining is still worth the effort.   ❑

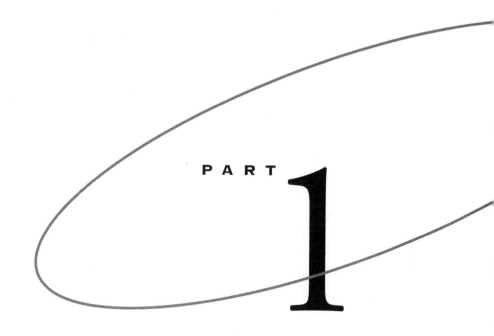

PART 1

Understanding the Customer

Gathering Customer Data 2

Ask a developer if he designs from customer data, and he will sure-ly say he does. Sue went to a users' group meeting and talked to people there; Joe showed a demo at an industry show; Mary makes a point of meeting with internal customers at least once a month. These are traditional methods of maintaining customer contact. What is driving the widespread desire in the industry to go beyond these methods, to enable designers to learn more about their customers and involve customers more fully in the design?

"Design" in our sense is the intentional structuring of a system so that the parts work together coherently to support the work of people. There is plenty of formal and informal evidence that getting the design right is a major difficulty in the industry. Informally, products ship late or not at all because people cannot agree on what to build; Information Technology (IT) groups feel that the departments they serve can never make up their minds

Getting the design right for the work is the major challenge

about what they want. Formally, studies show that most problems in software systems can be traced back to problems in the requirements, and the later in development a problem is caught, the more it costs to fix.[1] Studies also show that the more customer contact a project has, the more likely it is to be successful (Keil and Carmel 1995). The literature and experience on requirements engineering demonstrate that gathering good customer data is hard. The exact combination of approaches to use on a particular project calls for careful consideration

[1] This has become folk wisdom in the industry; see, for example, Daley (1977) or Boehm (1976).

and design. Simply following the organization's usual methods for gathering data will generally not produce the data a design team needs. The methods used by commercial and IT organizations are different, and we will consider them separately to show how they fall short of providing a complete view of the customer.

Marketing doesn't provide design data

Developers writing commercial software usually depend on a marketing department to provide guidance on what to build. Marketing is a discipline with a long history and extensive literature—certainly longer and more extensive than software development. People have worked out effective ways of understanding a market to sell products to it. Yet, when marketing comes to a design team to tell them what to build, there's a mismatch.

"Marketing never tells us any of the things we need to know," say product designers. But the people in marketing say, "We give them all kinds of data! They just refuse to use it." In fact, understanding a market is fundamentally different from understanding what to design into a system, and the data traditionally collected for marketing has limited usefulness for product design. Marketing needs to understand what people will buy and how people make buying decisions; designers need to understand what will help people do their work better while fitting into their lives and matching their culture. There is only a limited overlap between these questions.

Marketing asks: what should we make?

Marketing has developed many different techniques for finding out what people will buy. Important factors in the answer include how much money the target market has, what hardware (or mix of hardware) and other infrastructure they are committed to, what they think their big problems are, and what technology is currently "hot." This way of thinking about a market leads to asking certain questions. Given a story about how hard it is to print a label (such as the example in Chapter 1), a marketing expert might ask: Are you in a home office, small office, or large office? What kind of computer and printer do you have? Are they from the same manufacturer? What word processor are you using? How often do you do this task? How much is it worth to you to have the problem fixed?

The designer's basic question is different: how can I structure a system to make people's work more efficient? This question leads to asking about the structure of the work people do: What are the parts of a letter? How is a label different from an envelope? Does anyone understand the difference between "on" and "online"? Can you reach your printer and your keyboard at the same time? A system impacts work; designing a system requires understanding work at this level. From marketing's point of view, these questions are irrelevant; none of them affect who will buy a product. Marketing wants to be able to say, "There is a market here for a product addressing these concerns. Customers in this market are companies of this kind, and they would be willing to spend this much money." That's the designer's starting point. Given that starting point, designers need to dive into the work as the people in the market perform it. They need to discover the detailed structure of existing work to see how their product can enable a new, better way of working.

Designers ask: how should it be structured?

Because marketing and design have different goals, techniques useful to marketing tend not to be useful to designers. Marketing techniques tend to characterize and scope the market, rather than describing the structure of its work. As a result, marketing techniques tend to be quantitative. When you want to scope a market, it may be useful to ask, "How much money do you expect to spend on equipment next year?" and average the results across all respondents. Designers must build on more qualitative data. "What are the parts of a letter, and how are they used?" The answer to this question is a description of work practice, not any sort of number. Even if a question looks like it has a numeric answer ("How far is your printer from your keyboard?"), appearances are deceiving. For a designer, the true answer isn't a number, it's "Too far to keep dashing back and forth between them."

Marketing techniques generally assume you know what the questions are. When characterizing a market, this assumption may be reasonable—there are a few dimensions that matter, and they tend to repeat from problem to problem. Accordingly, marketing techniques structure the interaction and control the

Traditional marketing techniques can't collect design data

resulting data. For example, surveys and structured interviews both start with a list of questions that explicitly or implicitly drive the interaction and define what is important. But as soon as design starts, no one knows what the questions are. No one knows what will turn out to be important. "Installation is the #1 problem" reports a customer satisfaction survey (a marketing technique). But what is wrong with installation (a design question)? When do installations happen, and who does them? What information is available when they do them? Which of the many alternative fixes is best?

Even the customer doesn't necessarily know what the questions are:

> Users of an X-ray machine kept asking for more and more exact speed controls on their X-ray machines, trying to run the image at exactly $1/4$ second per frame. It was not until someone studied the work they were doing that they realized the users just needed a timer—they were trying to run the tape at an exact speed so they could measure elapsed time. The customers requested a technical fix to the existing system, but the real issue was in the structure of the work they were doing.

This is true in general with wish lists and other customer requests; the customer will focus on a narrow fix, but understanding the context of the work that drove the request will result in more insight and better solutions. The customer acts as though the question were, "What simple tweak or addition to the system as it is will overcome the problem I'm having?" The designer wants to know, "What new concepts or features would make the system radically more appropriate to the job at hand?" Answering this question requires an open-ended technique.

None of this is to say that designers don't need to worry about what people will buy. It's only within the context of a market with

Qualitative and quantitative techniques build on each other

needs to be met and money to spend that design makes sense. But once marketing techniques have identified a market and shown that there is money to be made there, designers must look in depth at how people in the market work[2] to determine what

---

[2] For simplicity's sake, we'll refer to the activities that customers are engaged in as "work" everywhere. Of course, a consumer product might support general life tasks, and a game supports play; these same techniques have been successfully applied to both environments.

to build. Quantitative techniques using predefined questions can identify the market and show designers where it is interesting to explore. Understanding the work of the market requires a qualitative technique that explores the customers' work practice and makes new discoveries about how people work and what they need. The discoveries may then lead to new strategies for addressing the market and new market messages for selling to it. They will confirm whether the identified market will really have a significant impact on the work. Then, quantitative techniques may again be useful to show that the work practice to be supported is sufficiently widespread to make a good business. The two disciplines, marketing and design, build on each other with complementary goals and techniques, to result in a whole-product definition. (Hansen [1997] reports on the effectiveness of different mechanisms for gathering customer feedback in a start-up.)

THE ROCKY PARTNERSHIP BETWEEN IT AND ITS CLIENTS

The job of an IT department is to support the business practice of the organization so people can get their work done efficiently. They must understand the work people do and know how to work with them to make their procedures more efficient with technology. IT departments have the luxury of building for a captive customer base. They know who their customers are and can talk to them directly. Their customers know the system is being built for them; they have often specifically requested it. Close working relationships should be easy to create.

In truth, however, the relationship between IT departments and their customers is often antagonistic. "They can never give us what we want in a reasonable period of time. Everything takes two years and even then it's late," say customers. But the IT developers respond, "Of course it's late. They changed the requirements five times, and then when they saw the system they decided they wanted a whole new subsystem added." Instead of creating a trusting partnership with the customer departments, IT is perceived as constantly failing. The customers—the people actually running the business—end up feeling that they cannot rely on IT to

Having customers on site doesn't make requirements clearer

get anything done in a reasonable time, and IT believes they have to cover themselves to prove it wasn't their fault when changing business needs or desires cause requirements to change.

IMPROVING COMMUNICATION WITH THE BUSINESS

A common approach to addressing these problems is to work through a customer representative—someone in the customer organization

Customer representatives only truly represent themselves

who knows the business and has the job of communicating requirements to the designers in IT. Sometimes the representative is a "primary customer" who still devotes some percentage of his or her time to the real job; sometimes it's a manager who used to do the job but doesn't any longer; sometimes it's a "customer liaison" who used to do the job but is now working with IT full-time; and sometimes, as in many government contracts, requirements are communicated by an agency that prevents any direct contact with the end customer at all. Even in the best case, the representative only does personally one of the many jobs in the customer organization. And many IT systems impact work across several departments; customer representatives usually only represent one. Any "customer representative" has a serious challenge in truly representing all aspects of the customer organizations.

Many IT departments avoid these problems by stationing IT developers with the customer organization. This certainly succeeds in

Developers placed with clients can turn into the technical handyman

making IT more responsive to the customer, but brings a loss of control. The developers easily become focused on short-term problems and solutions—they tend to become the local fix-it man. The structure of the customer's work and long-term possibilities for improvement are no more visible to IT developers than to the customer, and without this perspective they, like the customer, focus on the immediate and most visible issues. And they are stationed in a particular department, so cross-departmental issues are as invisible to them as to their customers. They are rewarded for producing quick fixes to pressing problems. The usual result is dozens of small applications, each solving a single problem, that do not work together to support the work coherently.

In today's world, the systems that are needed are large and complex. They tie together all aspects of a department's work; they support business processes that cross departments; they integrate a company's systems with those of its suppliers and customers. To address these challenges, both IT and their customers need to step back, out of the day-to-day routine of doing business, to see the implications and possibilities. Design starts with who the designers talk to and where they are situated. When designers sit with the customer, with no time for reflection, the result is narrow, extremely focused designs. As process reengineering becomes more important, being able to envision and support large-scale process changes becomes critical to IT's mission. (Lubars et al. [1993] surveys the definition and use of requirements in different organizations for both IT and commercial systems.)

THE ROLE OF INTUITION IN DESIGN

The methods that IT organizations use to interact with their customers tend to capitalize on unarticulated knowledge or intuition. If the designer's intuition can't be trusted to produce a useful system because designers aren't the people doing the work, get the customers more involved in the design. They may not be able to say exactly what they do or why something is important, but they can say what they do or don't like about a design. Another way to bring intuition to bear is to seat developers with the customers so that their intuition gets trained by proximity. Commercial companies do the same thing when they hire accountants to develop accounting software, or send engineers to work with a customer organization for a long time, or run a focus group to allow potential customers to react to product ideas. They are making unarticulated knowledge available to the design team.

But can people reveal truths about their own work in such a situation? The underlying assumption is that people will say what's important given the opportunity, but people simply don't pay that much conscious attention to how they perform jobs that they do well. Think about how difficult driving was when you were first learning. Getting the steering coordinated with the accelerator and the clutch (if there was one) was awkward and

People don't think about jobs that have become second nature

jerky. With increasing skill came increased smoothness and less attention to each detail, until at last the whole process became unconscious.

Now, to teach someone else to drive, the teacher has to recover everything she worked so hard to forget. And driving is a simple, obvious task. How are you to know what aspects of everyday work are important? (Sommerville et al. [1993] describes the importance of understanding unarticulated procedures in the somewhat more important domain of air traffic control.)

Many of the important aspects of work are invisible, not because they are hidden, but just because it doesn't occur to anyone to pay attention to them. Intuition doesn't help make these aspects explicit:

> An entire project team hangs out in the hallway outside their offices every morning and chats over coffee and donuts. Does anyone on the team know this is a critical project coordination session?

> A worker in accounting calls a friend in order processing to gossip and mentions that a rush order is on its way. Does his manager know this informal communication is the only thing keeping the company's rush orders on time?

Intuition has other limitations in a design process. Intuition is entirely internal—it can't be shared with other team members. It can only be used as the basis for an opinion. But if my intuition and your intuition tell us two different things, then what? Either we have to argue, with no basis for making a rational decision, or we have to appoint someone else tiebreaker. Intuition comes from personal experience. It's not clear how to go from experience with one customer, or a small set of customers, and generalize it to a department or market. All these problems suggest that a design process needs to externalize the unarticulated knowledge behind intuition. Given an external representation of customer work, we can validate it, share it, and use it to justify design decisions.

The challenge is to make customer intuition external and sharable

CONTEXTUAL INQUIRY REVEALS HIDDEN WORK STRUCTURE

A commitment to making customer knowledge explicit and external isn't useful without a way to get at all the detail of work experience for all the different types of customers. But as we noted above, many common ways of working with customers remove them from their work. Consider trying to teach someone to drive not in a car, but in a conference room. With no pedals, turn signal, or steering wheel, explain what's involved in making a turn. Try to describe what the road might look like, when to slow down, when to put on the turn signal, when to turn the wheel and how fast. It would be tempting to borrow a pie plate for a wheel and blocks for pedals. But even then, it would be so much easier to take your student out on the road and demonstrate. Yet this is the situation that customers are in—trying to explain their work, in a conference room, to designers who don't do their work. This is the situation of anyone filling out a survey or participating in a focus group. To reveal all aspects of work practice, when so much of it cannot be articulated even by those who do it, you have to see the work. (Goguen and Linde [1993] evaluates different techniques for the ability to reveal unarticulated needs.)

We designed our field interviewing method, Contextual Inquiry, to address these issues: how to get data about the structure of work practice, rather than a market characterization; how to make unarticulated knowledge about work explicit, so designers who do not do the work can understand it; and how to get at the low-level details of work that have become habitual and invisible. We needed a technique that would allow marketing, engineering, analysts, and customer representatives to work together and share insights. These problems suggested an open-ended, qualitative approach that brings us in contact with the customer's real work. Contextual Inquiry is such a technique. (Goguen [1996] discusses how social techniques such as Contextual Inquiry fit into the requirements gathering process.)

Contextual techniques are designed to gather data from customers in the field, where people are working or living. Contextual Inquiry is a field data-gathering technique that studies a few carefully selected individuals in depth to arrive at a fuller understanding of the work practice across all customers. Through inquiry and interpretation, it reveals commonalities across a system's customer base.

Observe the work while it happens to gather detailed design data

Contextual Inquiry is based on a set of principles that allow it to be molded to each situation that a project encounters: *context,* go to the customers' workplace and watch them do their own work; *partnership,* talk to them about their work and engage them in uncovering unarticulated aspects of work; *interpretation,* develop a shared understanding with the customer about the aspects of work that matter; and *focus,* direct the inquiry from a clear understanding of your own purpose. These principles guide the creation of a data-gathering technique to collect the best data possible given the constraints of the situation. We've used these principles to apply Contextual Inquiry in many different ways. However, most of the time, the simplest form is sufficient: the contextual interview.

A typical contextual interview lasts two to three hours. A member of the design team meets the customer at his or her place of work and, after a brief introduction, watches the customer do work of the sort the team is interested in. From time to time, the interviewer interrupts, and the two discuss some aspect of the work just performed. Sometimes the discussion stimulates the customer to pull out a paper, form, or note, and they spend time analyzing the artifact in detail. Using these artifacts to support the conversation, the interviewer finds out about events that took place over a longer period of time.

Afterwards the whole design team works with the interviewer to interpret the results of the interview for the design problem. Any one of the design team, representing any business function (marketing, analysts, development, usability) may have run the interview; during the interpretation everyone shares their insight and perspective. Together, they develop work models to characterize the structure of the work of this customer. (Work models are described in Part 2 and the interpretation session itself in Chapter 7.)

Interpret the data as a team to create a shared perspective

Between 10 and 20 interviews like this, with people who perform widely different roles and work in very different ways, are usually sufficient to define an area of work. People only come up with a few different ways of approaching a task. The work models reveal this structure, showing the underlying commonalities across a wide variety of apparently dissimilar users. In every case we have studied, we discover that the underlying structure of work practice is consistent enough that by the time 10 to 20 interviews have been conducted, we are discovering little that is new.

By grounding the design process in detailed, trustworthy customer data, Contextual Inquiry addresses the major problems of both IT and commercial organizations. Commercial organizations find that

Contextual Inquiry provides a way for the design team to investigate specific work practice, once marketing has defined a potential product area. It gives marketing and engineering a common language for talking to the customer and sharing their knowledge. IT organizations find that Contextual Inquiry helps them build a new relationship with the customer. It brings them into contact with the customer's day-to-day work and allows them to

Let data become the basis for organizational cooperation

understand it in a way neither they nor their customer could before. The conversation between customer and interviewer about the customer's work (rather than about the system design) creates a shared understanding and commitment between the groups.

In the remainder of this part, we discuss the structure of the interview itself. We describe each principle in detail and show how the principles drive the form of the interview. We then discuss the practical questions of interviewing in the context of a real project: who to talk to, how to set up the interviews, and how different types of projects need different applications of the techniques. In Part 2, we describe the other side of the interpretation session—work models and how to construct them.

Principles of *Contextual Inquiry*

3

The core premise of Contextual Inquiry is very simple: go where the customer works, observe the customer as he or she works, and talk to the customer about the work. Do that, and you can't help but gain a better understanding of your customer.

That is the core of the technique, but we find people are generally happy to have a little more guidance. What do interviewers do at the customer's site? How do they behave? What kind of relationship allows customers to teach designers the depth of knowledge about their work necessary to design well?

In Contextual Design, we always try to build on natural human ways of interacting. It is easier to act, not out of a long list of rules, but out of a simple, familiar model of relationship. A list of rules says, "Do all these things"—you have to concentrate so much on following the rules you can't relate to the customer. It's too much to remember. A *relationship model* says, "Be like this"—stay in the appropriate relationship, and you will naturally act appropriately (Goffman 1959).

Design processes work when they build on natural human behavior

Many different models of relationship are available to us. A formal model might be scientist/subject: I am going to study you, so be helpful and answer my questions; it doesn't really matter whether you understand why I'm asking. A less formal model might be parent/child: I'll tell you what to do, and you'll do it because you want my approval (or else you'll rebel to show your independence). Each of these models brings with it a different set of attitudes and behaviors. Everyone knows what it is like

Use existing relationship models to interact with the customer

when someone treats us like a child, and the resentment it generates. Ironically, the natural reaction is to behave like a child and fight back. Relationship models have two sides, and playing one side tends to pull the other person into playing the other side. Find a relationship model that is useful for gathering data, and as long as you play your role, you will pull the customer into playing theirs.

THE MASTER/APPRENTICE MODEL

The relationship between master craftsman and apprentice is an effective model for collecting data. Just as an apprentice learns a skill from a master, a design team wants to learn about its customers' work from its customers. Though the model is no longer common, it is still sufficiently familiar that people know how to act out of it. When they do, it creates the right behaviors on both sides of the relationship for learning about the customers' work. We find that people with no special background in ethnography learn how to conduct effective interviews much more quickly by acting like an apprentice than by memorizing a list of effective interviewing techniques. Building on this relationship model creates a strong basis for learning about work.

Craftsmen, like customers, are not natural teachers, and teaching is not their primary job. But they do not need to be; the master craftsman teaches while doing. A master does not teach by designing a course for apprentices to take. Nor does a master teach by going into a conference room and discussing his skill in the abstract. A master teaches by doing the work and talking about it while working. This makes imparting knowledge simple.

Teaching in the context of doing the work obviates any need for the craftsman to think in advance about the structure of the work he does. As he works, the structure implicit in the work becomes apparent because both master and apprentice are paying attention to it. It is easy for the master to pause and make an observation or for the apprentice to ask a question about something the master did. Observation interspersed with discussion requires little extra effort on the part of either master or apprentice.

When you're watching the work happen, learning is easy

Similarly, in Contextual Inquiry, team members go to the customers' workplace and observe while they are immersed in doing their work. Like the driver of a car, customers don't think about how they are working. But they can talk about their work as it unfolds. They do not have to develop a way to present it or figure out what their motives are. All they have to do is explain what they are doing, as does this user of a desktop publishing product:

> I'm entering edits from my marked-up copy here . . . I'm working in 200% magnification so I can really see how things line up. It doesn't matter that I can't see all the text in this magnification because I'm not checking for continuity or natural flow of words; I'll do that in another pass later. . . .

Even if the master were a good teacher, apprenticeship in the context of ongoing work is the most effective way to learn. People aren't aware of everything they do. Each step of doing a task reminds them of the next step; each action taken reminds them of the last time they had to take such an action and what happened then. Some actions are the result of years of experience and have subtle motivations; other actions are habit, and there is no longer a good reason for them. The best time to unravel the vital from the irrelevant and explain the difference is while in the middle of doing the work.

Seeing the work reveals what matters

This holds true for customers as well. They are not aware of everything they do or why they do it; they become aware in the doing.[1]

> Once we observed someone sorting his paper mail. He was able to tell us exactly why he saved, opened, or threw out each piece because he was in the process of making that decision.

> Another time, a research scientist came to the end of a painstaking series of mechanical calculations, turned to us, and said, "I guess you're surprised that I'm doing this." *He* was surprised at how inefficient he was, once he stopped to think about it.

But it is not natural to stop your work to think about it; the apprentice relationship provides the opportunity to do so.

Talking about work while doing it allows a master craftsman to reveal all the details of a craft. As he works, he can describe exactly what he is doing and

Seeing the work reveals details

---

[1] Polanyi (1958) discusses what tacit knowledge people have available for discussion at different times.

why. When either master or apprentice observes a pattern or principle in action, he can point it out immediately.

Customers who describe what they are doing while doing it, or talk about a prior event while in their work, have the same kind of detail available to them. Every action they take and every object around them helps them talk about the details of their work.

> One customer said he would not use a manual's index to find the solution to a problem: "It's never in the index." He could not say what led him to this conclusion, what he had looked up and failed to find. All his bad experiences were rolled up into one simple abstraction: it's not there. But when we watched him looking things up, we could see that he was using terms from his work domain, but the index listed parts of the system. We learned what the problem was and what we could do to fix it.

People sometimes don't even remember how to do their jobs themselves; instead, they depend on the environment and things in it to tell them what to do:

> A customer was unable to describe how she made her monthly report. When asked to create it, she pulled out her last report and started filling in the parts. The old report was her reminder of how to produce the next one.

Talking about work while doing it protects the master craftsman and the customer from the human propensity to talk in generalizations that omit the detail designers need. When the work's right there, the details, even details people do not normally pay attention to, are available for study and inquiry.

The apprentice learns the strategies and techniques of a craft by observing multiple instances of a task and forming his own understanding of how to do it himself. This understanding

Seeing the work reveals structure

incorporates the variations needed to do the task well under a variety of circumstances. The master craftsman can communicate techniques and strategies without articulating them. By watching instance after instance, the apprentice builds up a big picture of how to do the work.

In the same way, interviewers observing multiple events and multiple customers learn to see the common strategies underlying the work. Once they understand the basic strategies, they can start to imagine a system that would support those strategies. For example, a basic pattern in coding is work on the code, test it, and see the results. Identifying bugs to fix leads back to working on the code. But this pattern holds true not only for code, but for creating analysis and design models and automated tests as well. We uncovered this pattern by observing multiple people working on multiple systems of varying complexity. We could then structure the CASE system we were designing to facilitate movement through this cycle. (Part 3 discusses making common patterns and strategies explicit.)

Every event serves as the starting point for discussing similar events in the past. In this way apprentices learn from experience gained by a master before their apprenticeship started. A particular occurrence or task reminds the master of other interesting times this event or task happened. If the event is reasonably close in time, the story is concrete and detailed. It is the retelling of a particular event,

Every current activity recalls past instances

told while the master is immersed in doing the same activity with all the triggers and reminders doing that activity provides.[2]

A design team typically has less time to spend with its customers than the years needed for an apprenticeship. But in the same way that an apprentice can learn from the master's experience, interviewers can learn about events that occurred in the past. Events that occur while the interviewer is present remind customers to talk about events that happened previously. The artifacts of work—papers, forms, notes, clipboards, and so forth—trigger conversations about how they were used, how they were created, and how their structure supported their use in a particular instance.

A customer describing how she learned a feature told us, "I looked it up in the documentation." But when we asked her to look it up again, she was able to show us: "I looked the function up in the index and scanned the section. I saw this icon in the margin that I recognized from the screen, so I read just this paragraph next to it. It told me all I needed to know." The documentation provided the context she needed to recover a detailed story, and the detail revealed aspects that had been overlooked—that the icon was her visual cue to the relevant part of the page.

---

[2] Orr (1986) describes such storytelling to transmit knowledge among modern-day system managers for similar reasons.

Contextual Inquiry seeks to provide rich detail about customers by taking team members into the field. Once there, apprenticeship

Contextual Inquiry is apprenticeship compressed in time

suggests an attitude of inquiry and learning. It recognizes that the customer is the expert in their work and the interviewer is not. An interviewer taking on the role of apprentice automatically adopts the humility, inquisitiveness, and attention to detail needed to collect good data. The apprentice role discourages the interviewer from asking questions in the abstract and focuses them on ongoing work. And customers can shape the interviewer's understanding of how to support their work from the beginning, without having to prepare a formal description of how they work or what they need.

THE FOUR PRINCIPLES OF CONTEXTUAL INQUIRY

Apprenticeship is a good starting point, but it is only a starting point. Unlike apprentices, interviewers are not learning about work in order

Contextual Inquiry tailors apprenticeship to the needs of design teams

to do it; they are learning about it in order to support it with technology. Interviewers cannot afford to spend the time an apprentice would take to learn the work. Unlike an apprentice, members of the design team contribute their own special knowledge about technology and what it can do. Apprentices

learn a single job, but different projects may require the team to study a widely varying work practice—from the surgeon in the operating theater, to the manager in a high-level meeting, to the secretary at a desk, to the family in front of the video game. Designers meet the needs of a whole market or department, so they must learn from many people—individuals doing the same kind of work and individuals doing very different tasks and taking on different roles in order to get the work done.

The basic apprenticeship model needs modifications to handle a design team's needs and situation. Four principles guide the adoption and adaptation of the technique: *context, partnership, interpretation,* and *focus.* Each principle defines an aspect of the interaction. Together, they allow the basic apprenticeship model to be molded to the particular needs of a design problem. We will describe each principle and how to use it in turn.

CONTEXT

The principle of *context* tells us to go to the customer's workplace and see the work as it unfolds (Whiteside and Wixon 1988). This is the first and most basic requirement of Contextual Inquiry. Apprenticeship is a fine example of doing this; the apprentice is right there to see the work. All the richness of real life is there, able to jog the customer's memory and available for study and inquiry.

> *Go where the work is to get the best data*

The customer made a phone call in the middle of doing a task. Is this relevant to the work? Was she calling on an informal network of experts to get help in the task? Someone stops by to get a signature on a form. What is the customer's role in this approval process? Do they talk about it before she signs? What are the issues?

Context tells us to get as close as possible to the ideal situation of being physically present. Staying in context enables us to gather *ongoing experience* rather than *summary experience,* and *concrete data* rather than *abstract data.* We'll describe each of these distinctions in turn.

SUMMARY VS. ONGOING EXPERIENCE. We are taught from an early age to summarize. If someone asks a friend about a movie she saw last week, she does not recount the entire plot. She gives overall impressions, one or two highlights, and the thing that most impressed or disgusted her. (Never ask a seven-year-old that question—they haven't yet learned to summarize and *will* tell you the entire plot of the movie in excruciating detail.) Ask people to tell you about their experience with a new system, and they will behave just the same way. They will give their overall impressions and mention one or two things that were especially good or bad. They will have a very hard time saying exactly why the good things were important, or why the bad things got in the way. That would require that they be able to talk about the details of their work, which is very hard to do.

> We once asked a secretary how she started her day. Her answer was, "I guess I just come in and check my messages and get started." She wasn't able to go beyond this brief

summary overview. It was the first thing in the morning and she had just arrived at the office, so we asked her to go ahead and do as she would any other morning. She unhesitatingly started her morning routine, telling us about it as she went: "First I hang up my coat, then I start my computer. Actually, even before that I'll see if my boss has left something on my chair. If he has, that's first priority. While the computer's coming up, I check the answering machine for urgent messages. There aren't any. Then I look to see if there's a fax that has to be handled right away. Nope, none today. If there were, I'd take it right in and put it on the desk of whoever was responsible. Then I go in the back room and start coffee. Now I'll check the counters on the copier and postage meter. I'm only doing that because today's the first of the month. . . ."

This person's morning routine has a definite structure: first she checks all her communication mechanisms to see if there is an immediate action that needs to be taken, then she starts the regular maintenance tasks of the office. But this structure is invisible to her. It would not even occur to most people as a topic of conversation.

Avoid summary data by watching the work unfold

The job of the interviewer is to recognize work structure. Discovery of work structure arises out of this level of detail about mundane work actions. Summary experience glosses over and hides this detail. Being present while the work is ongoing makes the detail available.

ABSTRACT VS. CONCRETE DATA.   Humans love to abstract. It's much easier to lump a dozen similar events together than to get all the details of one specific instance really right. Because an abstraction groups similar events, it glosses over all the detail that makes an event unique. And since a system is built for many users, it already needs to abstract across all their experience. If designers start from abstractions, not real experience, and then abstract again to go across all customers, there is little chance the system will actually be useful to real people. Even in the workplace, customers easily slide into talking about their work in the abstract. But there are signals that indicate the customer needs to be brought back to real life.

If the customer is leaning back and looking at the ceiling, he is almost always talking in the abstract. This is the position of someone who will not allow the reality all around him from disrupting the conception he is building in his brain. Someone talking about real experience leans forward, either working or pointing at some representation of what he is talking about. Words indicating the customer is generalizing are another signal. If the customer says, "generally," "we usually," "in our company," he is presenting an abstraction. Any statement in the present tense is usually an abstraction. "In our group we do . . ." introduces an abstraction; "that time we did . . ." introduces real experience.

The best cure is to pull the customer back to real experience constantly. Every time you do this, you reinforce that concrete data matters, and you make it easier to get concrete data next time. If the customer says, "We usually get reports by email," ask, "Do you have one? May I see it?" Use the real artifacts to ground the customer in specific instances. If the customer says, "I usually start the day by reading mail," ask, "What are you going to do this morning? Can you start?" Return the customer to the work in front of him whenever possible.

Avoid abstractions by returning to real artifacts and events

Sometimes the work that you are interested in happened in the past and you want to find out about it, so you need to elicit a *retrospective account.* Retelling a past event is hard because so much of the context has been lost. People are prone to giving a summary of a past event that omits necessary detail. Most people will start telling a story in the middle, skipping over what went before. They will skip whole steps as they tell the story. The interviewer's job is to listen for what the customer is leaving out and to ask questions that fill in the holes. Here is an example of walking a customer through a retrospective account. The customer is talking about how they dealt with a report. We've interpolated the dialog with the missing steps that the interviewer is hearing in the data.

Span time by replaying past events in detail

Customer: *When I got this problem report I gave it to Word Processing to enter online—*

(Why did she decide to give it to Word Processing? Did she do anything first?)

Interviewer: *So you just handed it on automatically as soon as you got it?*

C: *No, it was high priority, so I read it and decided to send a copy to the Claims department.*

>   (How did she decide it was high priority? Is it her decision?)

I: *How did you know it was high priority?*

C: *It has this green sticker on it.*

>   (Someone else made the decision before the report ever got here. Who and when?)

I: *Who put on the green sticker?*

C: *That's put on by the reporting agency. They make the decision about whether it's high priority and mark the report.*

>   (We can better pursue how the reporting agency makes the decision with them; we'll only get secondhand information from this user. Instead of trying to go further backward, look for the next missing step forward: doesn't Claims get a more personal communication than just the report?)

I: *Did you just send it on to Claims, or did you write them a note about why they needed to see it?*

C: *Oh, I always call Claims whenever I send them one of these reports.*

At each step, the interviewer listened for steps that probably happened but the customer skipped and then backed the customer up to find out. In this process, the customer walked through the steps in her mind, using any available artifacts to stimulate memory, and recalled more about the actual work than she would if allowed to simply tell the story in order. Using retrospective accounts, the interviewer can recover past events and can also learn more about events in progress. If the end of a story hasn't yet happened, the most reliable way to learn about that kind of situation is to go back to a previous occurrence that did complete and walk through it. Trying to go forward and find out what will happen next forces the customer to make something up; going to another past instance allows the customer to stay concrete.

The key to getting good data is to go where the work is happening and observe it while it happens. Observing ongoing work keeps the customer concrete and keeps them from summarizing. Keeping to the apprenticeship model helps with this; the apprentice wants to see and assist with real work. If the customer starts telling stories, the interviewer can (exerting a little more control than an actual apprentice would) either redirect him to ongoing work or delve into the story, using a retrospective account to get all the detail possible.

> *Keep the customer concrete by exploring ongoing work*

PARTNERSHIP

The goal of *partnership* is to make you and the customer collaborators in understanding his work. The only person who really knows everything about his work is the one doing it. The traditional interviewing relationship model tilts power too much toward the interviewer. The interviewer controls what is asked, what is discussed, and how long is spent on a topic. This won't get you design data—

> *Help customers articulate their work experience*

you don't know what's important to pay attention to, and you don't know what will turn out to matter. The apprenticeship model tilts power, if anything, too much toward the master-customer. It suggests that the customer is in full control, determining what to do and talk about throughout the interview. Traditional apprenticeship would reduce the interviewer to asking a few questions for clarification, at best.

This is too limiting for an interviewer understanding work practice. An interviewer's motive in observing work is not that of the apprentice. Apprentices want to know how to do the work; interviewers want data to feed invention of a system that supports the work. Apprentices are assumed to bring no useful skills to the relationship. Any skills they happen to have they subordinate to learning the way the master goes about working. Designers may not be experts in doing the work, but they must develop expertise in seeing work structure, in seeing patterns and distinctions in the way people organize work. An interviewer has to create something that looks more like a partnership than like an ordinary apprenticeship. This allows them to engage the customer in a conversation about the work, making the customer aware of aspects of the work that were formerly invisible and bringing the customer into a partnership of inquiry into the work practice.

In one interview with a user of page layout software, the user was positioning text on the page, entering the text and moving it around. Then he created a box around a line of text, moved it down until the top of the box butted the bottom of the line of text, and moved another line of text up until it butted the bottom of the box. Then he deleted the box.

Interviewer: *Could I see that again?*

Customer: *What?*

I: *What you just did with the box.*

C: *Oh, I'm just using it to position this text here. The box doesn't matter.*

I: *But why are you using a box?*

C: *See, I want the white space to be exactly the same height as a line of text. So I draw the box to get the height.* (He repeats the actions to illustrate, going more slowly.) *Then I drag it down, and it shows where the next line of text should go.*

I: *Why do you want to get the spacing exact?*

C: *It's to make the appearance of the page more even. You want all the lines to have some regular relationship to the other things on the page. It's always hard to know if it really makes any difference. You just hope the overall appearance will be cleaner if you get things like this right.*

I: *It's like everything you put on the page defines a whole web of appropriate places for the other things to go.*

C: *That's right. Everything affects everything else. You can't reposition just one thing.*

This is a common pattern of interaction during an interview. While work is progressing, the customer is engrossed in doing it, and the interviewer is busy watching the detail as it un-folds, looking for pattern and structure, and think-ing about the reasons behind the customer's actions. At some point the interviewer sees something that doesn't fit, or notices the structure underlying an aspect of the work, and interrupts to talk about it. This causes a break in the work, and both customer and interviewer *withdraw* from doing the work to discuss the structure that the interviewer found. It is as though they stepped into a separate conceptual room. The customer, interrupted in the moment of taking an action, can say what he is doing and why. The interviewer, looking at work from the outside, can point out aspects the customer might take for granted. By paying attention to the details and structure of work, the interviewer teaches the customer to attend to them also. When the conversation about structure is over, the customer *returns* to ongoing work, and the inter-viewer returns to watching. This *withdrawal and return* is a basic pat-tern of Contextual Inquiry: periods of watching work unfold, inter-spersed with discussions of how work is structured.

Alternate between watching and probing

Over the course of an interview, customers become sensitized to their own work and how it could be improved. Questions about work structure reveal that structure to them so they can start thinking about it themselves. "It's like every-thing you put on the page defines a whole web of ap-propriate places for the other things to go." This comment suggests a way of thinking about the work. It makes a previously implicit strategy explicit and invites a conversation about that strategy. Soon customers start inter-rupting themselves to reveal aspects of work that might otherwise have been missed. Over the course of the interview, a true partnership devel-ops, in which both customer and interviewer are watching work struc-ture, and in which both are thinking about design possibilities. (See Chin et al. [1997] on making customers participants in analyzing their own work.)

Teach the customer how to see work by probing work structure

Members of a design team also have special knowledge about how to use technology. They notice problems that they can solve and allow them to distract them from the work. They naturally figure out a solution to any problem or apparent problem that presents itself. But this is a distraction from the interview because, rather than listening to whatever the customer is saying, the interviewer is off thinking about the great thing she could make. She can't pay attention to the work while designing something in her mind.

It's not useful to tell designers not to design in the moment—they will anyway. One of the principles of Contextual Design is to work with people's propensities wherever possible. So rather than forbid designing in the moment, we manage it by allowing the interviewer to introduce her idea immediately. The customer is in the middle of doing the work that the idea is intended to support. There is no better time to get feedback on whether the idea works. If the idea works, the interviewer understands the work practice and has a potential solution. If the idea fails, the interviewer did not really understand what mattered in the work. By sharing the idea, the interviewer improves her understanding of the work and checks out her design idea at the same time. In addition, the idea suggests to the customer what technology could do. Customers start to see how technology might be applied to their problem.

Find the work issues behind design ideas

Articulating work structure and correcting design ideas during the interview gives the customer the power to shape the way designers think about the work. Any iterative technique (such as rapid prototyping or Participatory Design) enables customers to shape a proposed design. But iterating an existing design can only make small modifications to its structure. That initial structure—the first prototype—was driven by whatever way of thinking about the work that the designer had when she started. A process is truly customer-centered when customers can change designers' initial understanding of the work. Sharing interviewers' initial, unformed ideas with the customer and articulating work practice together allows customers to alter the team's initial thinking, opening the possibility of radical changes in system purpose and structure.

Let the customer shape your understanding of the work

AVOIDING OTHER RELATIONSHIP MODELS. The danger in all of this is that customer or interviewer will fall back into more familiar models of relationship. There are many other models available, each with its own set of problems. If you fall into one of these models during an interview, you will pull the customer into the other side of the relationship, prompting behavior that gets in the way of gathering data. If you are aware of what these other relationships are like, you can notice when you fall into them and take actions to shift back into the right relationship. Here are some common pitfalls:

Interviewer/interviewee: Interviewer and customer start to act as though there were a questionnaire to be filled out. You ask a question, which the customer answers and then falls silent. You, anxious that the interview go well, ask another question, which the customer answers and then falls silent again. The questions are not related to ongoing work because ongoing work has ceased. The best

> *You aren't there to get a list of questions answered*

solution for this is to suggest returning to ongoing work, which effectively prevents this question/answer interaction.

Expert/novice: As a representative of the design team, you go in with the aura of the expert. You are the one designing the system, with all the technical knowledge. You have to work to get the customer to treat you as an apprentice. The temptation of taking the expert role back is always present, especially when the customer is trying to use a system that you developed. Set the cus-

> *You aren't there to answer questions either*

tomer's expectations correctly at the beginning by explaining that you are there to hear about and see their work because only they know their own work practice. You aren't there to help them with problems or answer questions. Then, should the customer ask for help (or should you forget and volunteer help), step out of the expert role explicitly: "I'll never understand the problems with our system if I spend the whole time helping you. Why don't you go ahead and do what you would do if I weren't here, and at the end I'll answer any questions that remain." The only exception to this rule is if the customer is so stuck that he will not be able to do any more of the work you came to see. In that case, give enough information to help him find his way out of the problem. Then you'll have to say all over again that you came to see how he does things and he shouldn't depend on you for answers.

Guest/host: Because it is the customer's workplace and the customer is a stranger, it is easy to act like a guest. A guest is polite and not too nosy. A host is considerate and tries to make the guest comfortable by seeing to his needs. Unfortunately, none of this has much to do with doing real work. If you find yourself feeling like a guest, move quickly past the formal relationship to the role of partner in inquiry. This is where sensitivity to culture matters. If the customer won't be comfortable until you've had a cup of coffee, then have it and move into doing work. The relationship should feel like the kind of intimacy people strike up on airplanes, when they tell things that they would not ordinarily share with a stranger. Here, intimacy doesn't come from personal talk; it comes from a shared focus on the work. Move closer. Ask questions. Be nosy. Ask to see anything the customer touches, and get them to tell you about it. You will know you created the relationship you want when the customer says to you, "Come over here—you want to see this." The more you get them to tell you about themselves, the more you will move out of the formal role.

It's a goal to be nosy

Partnership transforms the apprenticeship relationship into a mutual relationship of shared inquiry and discovery of the customer's work. It retains the close working relationship from apprenticeship while equalizing the power imbalance. This results in an intimate relationship that allows for inquisitiveness about the details of the work. The relationship is maintained by honesty and openness on the part of the interviewer, who reveals insights and ideas as they occur, and guards against allowing inappropriate relationship models that take the conversation off topic and prevent getting good data.

Partnership creates a sense of a shared quest

INTERPRETATION

It is not enough only to observe and bring back observations. Interpretation is the assignment of meaning to the observation—what it implies about work structure and about possible supporting systems. The language our field uses to describe gathering data for design—data *gathering,* field *research,* requirements *elicitation*—

Determine what customer words and actions mean together

suggests that what matters is the facts about the work. Good products, by implication, are based on facts. Interpretation says that good facts are only the starting point. Designs are built on the interpretation of facts, on what the designers claim the facts mean. Here's an illustration:

> In working with one user of an accounting package, we learned that she kept a sheet of accounts and account numbers next to her screen. Here are some interpretations of what this fact might mean and what it might imply for our design:
>
> **1.** Perhaps account numbers are necessary but hard to remember, and all we need to do is make the cross-reference easier. We could put the cross-reference between numbers and names online.
>
> **2.** Perhaps numbers are unnecessary, a holdover from paper accounting systems, and all that is needed is a way to refer to an account uniquely. We could get rid of account numbers altogether and identify them only by name.
>
> **3.** Perhaps compatibility with paper systems is necessary, but referring to accounts by name is more convenient. We could keep the numbers but allow names to be used anywhere numbers are used.

Which of these designs is best? It depends on which interpretation is correct; the fact alone does not allow us to choose. The designer must choose which interpretation to lay on the fact. It's the interpretation that drives the design decision.

Interpretation is the chain of reasoning that turns a fact into an action relevant to the designer's intent. From the *fact,* the observable event, the designer makes a *hypothesis,* an initial interpretation about what the fact means or the intent behind the fact. This hypothesis has an *implication* for the design, which can be realized as a particular *design idea* for the system. For example, the second interpretation above starts with the fact (the chart of accounts is kept next to the screen) and makes the hypothesis that this is just a holdover from paper accounting systems. This interpretation, if true, has implications for the system: it doesn't matter whether the system provides numbers, but it must provide some way to refer to an account unambiguously. This implication can be acted on by requiring

Design ideas are the end product of a chain of reasoning

the system to identify accounts through unambiguous names only. This entire chain of reasoning happens implicitly any time anyone suggests a design idea. Usually it happens so fast, only the final idea is made explicit. But the whole chain must be valid for the design idea to work.

If the data that matters is the interpretation, we must have a way to ensure it is correct, and we can only do that by sharing it with the customer. We fail in the entire purpose of working with customers if we do not share and validate our interpretations of their work—the most important data we bring back would not be validated. Sharing interpretations ensures that the work is understood correctly. Sharing design ideas walks the chain backwards; if the idea doesn't fit, some link in the chain was wrong. When it's the customer coming to you with design ideas in the form of wish lists, treat them the same way: walk the chain backwards to understand the work context driving the wish. Understanding the underlying work practice yields much more flexibility in how to respond—many design ideas can spring from a single origin. Understanding and fixing the underlying problem in the work practice can address many design ideas with a single solution. The partnership we have built up with the customer provides a natural context for sharing observations of structure and interpretations of their meaning.

Design is built upon interpretation of facts— so the interpretation had better be right

Can you really check an interpretation just by sharing it with the customer, or will that bias the data? Will customers be prone to agree with whatever you say? In fact, it is quite hard to get people in the middle of doing work to agree with a wrong interpretation. It's not at all hypothetical for them because they are in the midst of the work. The statement that doesn't fit is like an itch, and they poke and fidget with it until they've rephrased it so it represents their thought well:

Sharing interpretations with customers won't bias the data

"It's like a traveling office," you say, looking at how a salesman has set up his car. "Well—like a traveling *desk*," he responds.

The difference between the two is small but real, and people will be uncomfortable until they get a phrasing that fits exactly.

Furthermore, remember that the data that matters is the interpretation of the facts, not the facts themselves. You can't form an interpretation without getting involved with the events, without trying to make sense of them *for you*. Where an event contradicts your assumptions, you have to inquire and probe, or you'll never be able to replace your current, flawed understanding with one that works. This probing is driven by your expectations and prejudices, yet it is the only way your prejudices can be overturned.

Finally, since customers are not generally experts in seeing the structure of their own work, the interpretation you suggest shows them what to pay attention to. Open-ended questions give the customer less guidance in thinking about their work than an interpretation and result in less insight.

Sharing interpretations teaches customers to see structure in the work

We might have asked a customer who was starting her workday, "Do you have a strategy for starting the day?" Even though the customer just went through the morning routine, she is not used to thinking about strategy driving ordinary work events. The most likely response would be "No, not particularly"—or a blank stare. But if asked, "You check for any urgent communication first, no matter what form it might have come in?" she can compare this statement of strategy to her own experience and validate it or refine it. She might respond, "Yes, lots of things here are time-critical and we have to deal with them right away"—simply validating the interpretation, adding detail but leaving it essentially unchanged. In fact, she responded, "Actually, things from my boss are most important because they are for me to do. Messages on the answering machine or faxes might be for anyone"—refining the interpretation, accepting the broad outline, but adding a new distinction.

Because customers respond to the interpretation in the moment of doing the work, they can fine-tune it quite precisely. Customers commonly make slight changes in emphasis such as those above to make the interpretation exact. They can do this because they are given a starting point that they can compare with the experience they are now having and adjust it, rather than having to start from scratch. In this way, we use the close relationship

Customers fine-tune interpretations

between interviewer and customer to get very reliable data. In fact, it's the only way to get reliable data; if we don't check it with the customer immediately, we take away an understanding that is at least partially made up.

However, interviewers do need to be committed to hearing what the customer is really saying. They may say "no" to an interpretation, but to be polite may not say "no" directly. Here are some indirect ways customers say "no."

> "Huh?"—This means the interpretation was so far off that it had no apparent connection to what the customer thought was going on.

> "Umm . . . could be"—This means "no." If the interpretation is close, the customer will nearly always respond immediately. A pause for thought means that they are trying to make it fit their experience and cannot.

> "Yes, but . . ." or "Yes, and . . ."—Listen carefully to what follows the "but" or "and." If it is a new thought, this is the right interpretation and yours was wrong. If it builds on yours, this is a confirmation with a twist or with additional information. Customers say "yes" by twinkling their eyes at you as they realize your words match their experience or by elaborating on what you said—or by saying "yes" flatly, as if the whole point was obvious.

We ensure the interpretation is true by creating and maintaining the right relationship with our customer. With apprenticeship as the starting point, we create a close, intimate partnership. Partnership is a natural consequence of a contextual interview. For the entire time, we pay close attention to this person, what he does and how he does it, what gets in his way, and everything that's important to him. We take an interest. Most people have never been the focus of so much positive attention or had such an extended opportunity to talk about what they do. They become invested in making sure we get it right—that we see everything that's relevant and that we take away the exact right shade of meaning. The closer our relationship and more invested the customer, the less willing they are to allow us to leave thinking the wrong thing. This is our safeguard that our understanding is true to their experience.

Nonverbal cues confirm interpretations

FOCUS

Focus defines the point of view an interviewer takes while studying work. Once the interviewer is in the customer's workplace and has created a collaborative relationship with her, what should he pay attention to? What aspects of work matter and what don't? If the customer has control over what matters, how can the interviewer steer the conversation at all? The apprentice learns whatever

Clear focus steers the conversation

the master knows, and the master decides what's important. But the interviewer needs data about a specific kind of work. The interviewer needs to guide the customer in talking about the part of her work relevant to the design. *Focus* gives the interviewer a way to keep the conversation on topics that are useful without taking control entirely back from the customer. Focus steers the interview the same way that friends steer conversations with each other. The topics the friends care about—the topics in their focus—are what they spend time on. Anything one friend raises that the other doesn't care about is allowed to drop without discussion.

Taking a focus is unavoidable. Everyone has an entering focus, a whole life history defining what they notice and what they don't. Consider three interviewers watching a scientist go about her work:

One interviewer, a software developer, notices the quantities of paperwork the scientist uses to define the procedure she follows, to record her actions, and to report her results.

Another interviewer is more familiar with the lab technology and sees the kind of instruments she has and the problems she has getting them set up and calibrated.

The third interviewer was once a scientist and sees how the scientist moves about her lab, getting out glassware and chemicals and putting them on the bench near the equipment she will use.

Each interviewer sees a different aspect of the work, all of which are "true," but which may be more or less relevant, depending on what is being designed.

Having a focus means that the interviewer sees more. The interviewer who knows that paperwork is important will learn to distinguish the different kinds of paperwork: the method that defines what the scientist will do, the notebook that records her actions for her experiment, the log books that record calibrations of equipment for the lab, and the formal report of her results. Each of these distinctions

Focus reveals detail

serves as the starting point for a new inquiry, pushing the interviewer's understanding of the lab work wider and wider. A focus gives the interviewer a framework for making sense of work.

To ensure the team sees aspects of work important to the problem at hand, we set focus deliberately to guide the interview toward relevant aspects of work. This *project focus* gives the team a shared starting point, which is augmented by each person's entering focus so they each bring their unique perspective to bear. (We discuss how to set focus for different types of problems in the next chapter.)

If focus reveals detail within the area it covers, it conceals aspects of work that it does not cover. Different people will naturally see different

Focus conceals the unexpected

things. Someone who notices paperwork cannot help but notice when papers are being dragged around the lab; someone who never thought about paperwork cannot help but overlook it until his attention is drawn to it. Meanwhile the first interviewer is ignor-

ing physical movement around the lab to get equipment, to the next lab to borrow supplies that have run short, and into another scientist's office to consult on the method used. These aspects of work may be equally important to the design problem. The first interviewer's focus has revealed rich detail in the use of paper, but how can she expand her focus and learn about the other aspects of work? First, we set focus deliberately to give the team a common starting point, an initial way to see the work, allowing them to build their own distinctions and interpretations on that base. Then, we use group interpretation in the cross-functional team to allow team members to learn and take on each other's focus over time and bring their own focus to bear on each other's interviews (we discuss these sessions in Chapter 7). Finally, during the interview, we use *intrapersonal triggers*—the interviewer's own feelings—to alert the interviewer when they are missing something.

HOW TO EXPAND FOCUS. Pay attention to intrapersonal triggers to create a deliberate paradigm shift, from the understanding of the work the interviewer started with to the understanding of work that is real for the customer interviewed and relevant to the design concern. The interviewer must be committed to seeing where an understanding does not fit and changing it, not to confirming existing expectations. Inner triggers are flags telling the interviewer when an opportunity for breaking a paradigm and expanding the entering focus exists. They work because your own feelings tell you what is happening in the interview and how to act to fix it. Here are some triggers to watch out for:

> *Internal feelings guide how to interview*

Surprises and contradictions: The customer says something, or you see them do something, that you know is "wrong." It's something no one else would do, something totally idiosyncratic. Or else it's just random; they had no particular reason for doing it. Any one of these reactions is a danger signal. It means that you are—right now—allowing your preexisting assumptions to override what the customer is telling or showing you. The tendency is to let it pass as irrelevant; the solution is to do the opposite. Take the attitude that nothing any person does is done for no reason; if you think it's for no reason, you don't yet understand the point of view from which it makes sense. Take the attitude that nothing any person does is unique to them; it always represents an important class of customers whose needs will not be met if you don't figure out what's going on. Act like the apprentice, who always assumes a seemingly pointless action hides a key secret of the trade. Probe the thing that is unexpected and see what you find.

Nods: The customer says something that fits exactly with your assumptions, and you nod. This is the reverse of the first trigger, and it is tricky. What you are doing when you nod is saying that you can hear the customer's words, match them with your own experience, and know as a result that everything that happened to you happened to them. Is this a safe assumption? Instead, take the attitude that everything is new, as if you had never seen it before. The apprentice never assumes the master has no more to teach. Do they *really* do that? Why would they do that? What's motivating them? Look for the paradigm shift. Look for ways that what they are doing differs from what you expect.

What you don't know: The customer says something technical that you just didn't understand or is explaining something and you just aren't getting it. Now what? Are you going to admit your ignorance? Wouldn't it be easier to research the subject a bit back at the office? No, admit your ignorance. Make the customer go back and take the explanation step-by-step. Treat this as a good opportunity to step away from the expert role. You are there to learn, and you might as well learn about the technology, too. No one else will be able to tell you better what this individual is talking about. Even if the customer doesn't really understand it either, the extent of their knowledge and misinformation can be valuable for design. Furthermore, if you don't ask, you'll get more and more lost as the conversation continues.

The easiest way to design a system is from your own assumptions and prejudices. Breaking out of your preconceived notions of what the system should be and how it should work is one of your hardest design tasks. Using the customer to break your paradigm intentionally counterbalances the natural propensity to design from assumptions. Triggers alert you to specific opportunities during the interview to widen your entering focus, and the open dialog encouraged by apprenticeship allows you to inquire when you need to.

> *Commit to challenging your assumptions, not validating them*

THE CONTEXTUAL INTERVIEW STRUCTURE

The principles of Contextual Inquiry guide the design of a data-gathering situation appropriate to the problem at hand. The principles say what needs to happen to get good data, but the design problem and the nature of the work being studied control the exact procedure to use. Studies of office work can be conducted much more simply than studies of surgical procedures. The most common structure for Contextual Inquiry is a contextual interview: a one-on-one interaction lasting two to three hours, in which the customer does her own work and discusses it with the interviewer. Each interview has its own rhythm, set by the work and the customer. But they all share a structure that helps interviewer and customer get through the time without losing track of what they are supposed to do. Every interview has four parts:

The conventional interview: You, as the interviewer, and the customer need to get used to each other as people. Running the first part of the interview as a conventional interaction helps with that. You introduce yourself and your focus, so the customer knows from the outset what you care about and can start with work relevant to the focus. You promise confidentiality, get permission to tape, and start the tape recorder. Explain that the customer and her work is primary and that you depend on the customer to teach you the work and correct your misunderstandings. You ask for any opinions about the tools the customer uses (if relevant) and get an overview of the job and the work to be done that day. This is summary data, not contextual data, so don't pursue any issues; instead, watch to see if they come up in the body of the interview and pursue them then, when they are in context. Unless the work domain is unfamiliar, this part should last no more than 15 minutes.

Get to know customers and their issues

The transition: The interviewer states the new rules for the contextual interview—the customer will do her work while you watch, you will interrupt whenever you see something interesting, and the customer can tell you to hold off if it's a bad time to be interrupted. Anytime you want to break social norms, it's best to define the new rules for social interaction so everyone knows how to behave appropriately. If you declare "lady's choice," ladies will ask men to dance and no one feels awkward. Here, you want to create the new rules for the contextual interview, so you state them explicitly. This should take all of 30 seconds, but it's a crucial 30 seconds; if you don't do it explicitly, you run the risk of spending the entire time in a conventional interview.

Explain the new rules of a contextual interview

The contextual interview proper: The customer starts doing her work task, and you observe and interpret. This is the bulk of the interview. You are the apprentice, observing, asking questions, suggesting interpretations of behavior. You are analyzing artifacts and eliciting retrospective accounts. You are keeping the customer concrete, getting back to real instances and drawing on paper when the customer draws in the air to describe something she doesn't have in front of her. You are taking copious notes by hand the whole time; don't depend on the tape to catch everything. You are nosy—after a phone conversation, you ask what it was about. Follow her around—if she goes to the files, you go along and peer over her shoulder. If she goes down the hall, you tag along. If someone comes to the door and looks diffident about interrupting, you tell him to come on in. And, of course, if the customer says she needs a break, you let her

Observe and probe ongoing work

have one. The principles of context, partnership, interpretation, and focus guide your interaction during the interview.

The wrap-up: At the end of the interview, you have a chance to wrap up your understanding of the work she does and her position in the organization. Skim back over your notes and summarize what you learned, trying not to repeat verbatim what happened, but saying what is important about the work, to her and to the organization. This is the customer's last chance to correct and elaborate on your understanding, and she usually will. Allow 15 minutes for the wrap-up.

Feed back a comprehensive interpretation

Running a good interview is less about following specific rules than it is about being a certain kind of person for the duration of the interview. The apprentice model is a good starting point for how to behave. Then the four principles of Contextual Inquiry modify the behavior to better get design data: *context,* go where the work is and watch it happen; *partnership,* talk about the work while it happens; *interpretation,* find the meaning behind the customer's words and actions; and *focus,* challenge your entering assumptions. If all these concepts start to become overwhelming, go back up to the higher-level idea of apprenticeship. You want the attitude of an apprentice; you want to create an intimate relationship in which you and the customer collaborate in understanding their work, using your focus to help determine what's relevant. That's enough to run a good interview.

Contextual Inquiry in Practice

4

What are we supposed to do?" an engineer asked us. "Knock on people's doors, asking them to let us watch them use our product?" The answer in this case was "Yes, do that." Not without setting up the visit ahead of time, of course, and there's some planning to do, but in the end it all comes down to showing up and watching. Sometimes the most difficult barrier to introducing a new way of working is people's assumptions about what is or is not "done."

But once people accept the idea that they are going to do something they never considered a possibility before, they need to know exactly what steps to follow. Otherwise no real action can take place. We're now ready to discuss the concrete actions that will enable a Contextual Design project to get started. We will deal with team formation in a later section; here, we will describe how to set the focus for a project, how to plan who to talk to, and variations on the data-gathering process that may be required by different problems.

SETTING PROJECT FOCUS

Before you can do useful work, you must define the problem you intend to solve in terms of the work you plan to support. Typically, a project's mission is defined in terms of the solution it will deliver: "an ordering system for all departments," "the next version of product X," "an electronic clipboard for doctor's offices." (As we discussed in Chapter 2, this is the kind of problem statement that is usually given to the project team by marketing or by the internal client.) To figure out what to do next—who to talk to and what to look for to decide what is important in this domain—the project team must transform this statement about the solution into a statement about the work.

Your initial project focus will usually be too narrow, too much restricted to exactly the work of the tool you expect to build. To see the whole work context and identify opportunities and potential problems, you want to expand the focus beyond tool use. Ask: What is the work we expect to support? How does this work fit into the customer's whole work life? What are the key work tasks? These are the aspects of work to find out about. Who is involved in making the work happen? Who are the informal helpers? Who provides the information needed to do the job, and who uses the results? These are the people to talk to. Where does the work happen physically? What is the cultural and social context in which the work happens? These constrain the interview situation you can set up. These questions will guide you in thinking about how your system fits into your customers' overall work. Use them to identify what kind of people you want to interview, what tasks you want to see performed, and what you want to watch for while you're there. Remember this is a focus, not a checklist. Use it to guide what you pay attention to during the interview.

Broaden your focus to include the whole work process

To expand your perspective on the work, look for metaphors for the work—unrelated kinds of work that have the same structure as the work you want to support. If you are studying online search and retrieval, you can study how people search for physical objects in libraries and grocery stores. This will help you understand the basic structure of finding, independent of technology and content. If you are studying PC maintenance groups, look at taxi dispatch services; the maintainers need to go out on calls without losing contact with a central organization in much the same way that a taxi is dispatched by the central office while maintaining contact with the office and with other taxis. Studying a taxi service would give insight into the problems of maintaining this kind of coordination and suggest different ways of organizing the PC maintenance group. Metaphors like this give you insight into the work you are supporting, suggesting hidden aspects that might be important. Use the metaphor to structure your thinking, and conduct

Study analogous work to stimulate insight into how work is structured

interviews in the metaphor's work domain if it would be useful to know how it really works.

With a clear statement of project focus, you are ready to apply it to the particular project situation, starting by defining how to gather data. Different kinds of projects will constrain the data-gathering process in different ways: If you are extending an existing system, that system defines the work you need to study. If you are addressing a new work domain, you need to be open in what you study. The kind of data you look for will be driven by the work you plan to support, but also by the goals of the project.

DESIGNING THE INQUIRY
FOR COMMERCIAL PRODUCTS

A project in commercial software may be generated in three principal ways. Each different starting point implies a different set of issues and a different way of collecting data.

Designing a known product: A "known product" is one of a class of products that is known and accepted in the marketplace, like a word processor or a spreadsheet. Competitive products are already established. The market has expectations for this kind of product—you must include certain capabilities to be taken seriously. This may be the next version of a product you are already shipping.

Gather data on people using competitive products. You must meet the market expectations they create. Gather data on the basic work practice of the market, whether the customers use competitors, your products, or no automated systems at all. Use your existing customer feedback channels to help set your focus. This will reveal what aspects of work are currently not well supported. Designing your product to support these unmet

Look for the new delighters: the unrecognized needs

needs will differentiate your product from the rest of the market. If they are important enough, you will define the new field of competition for the next generation of products, just as the formatting capabilities of early versions of Lotus 1-2-3 defined the new ground of competition for spreadsheets. At the same time, gather data on detailed tool use. You want to make sure that you do the expected function just a little better than anyone else. You also want to pay attention to what aspects of existing products get in the user's way, and design ways to streamline it.

Addressing a new work domain: A new work domain is totally new. It has been created by changing work or life practice (the fitness industry) or new technological possibilities (tele-commuting) and is not addressed well by any prod-uct. Any new product will change the way people work in the market, and there's no existing product to use as a guide. The danger lies in thinking that because the work will be changed, there's no way to study it. Before spreadsheets were invented, people did the work—they used paper ledgers to chart their accounts. Before word proces-sors were invented, people did the work—they used typewriters. Define the work your new systems will replace, and study it to learn what matters and how it is structured so the market can make the transition to your new products. (This will not stifle any innovation in your products. Both the first spreadsheets and the first word proces-sors were developed through detailed understanding of the people in their prospective markets.) Define the intent people are trying to achieve. Gather data on people achieving their intent with current tools. Look at how they use paper, informal contacts, and whatever else is available to do what they need to do. Look for problems and places where the lack of tools keeps them from trying to achieve their real intent. Use metaphors to think about what may be important in the new work domain.

> *All work is already being done some way; study it for clues*

The new market may be best addressed not by a single product, but by multiple products working together to support the work com-prehensively. When we discuss designing the system in Part 5, we'll show how to manage multiple coordinated products.

New technology: Sometimes a project seeks to take advantage of a technology that has just become available or affordable. Instead of being tied to a particular work domain, the project is looking for opportunities to use the technology. You may define specific products, you may design alterations to existing products to take advantage of the new technology, or you may discover that whole new markets open up once the technology is available.

Look for analogs of the technology and how they are used in the real world. If you are automating something that already exists, such as sound or text-to-speech, look for places in everyday life where sound or speech is already used effectively. Look at the context: What else happens when people talk, such as eye contact and nonverbal cues? When is silence important? Look at what the new technology replaces: for example, infrared links replace signal-carrying wires, so where are wires used? Network wires, control pad wires, speaker wires. Look for the underlying metaphor of the new technology and study that: a PDA (personal digital assistant) is like a Day-Timer with smarts, so look at Day-Timers and ask what you could do with them if they were smart. Look at the fundamental new characteristics introduced by the new technology: Wireless links allow moving around, so how is movement important? PDAs are small, so how does size matter? And use metaphors for the technology to get a different perspective of its use. Go to the places where the new technology can make a difference to stimulate your thinking about how it might be used.

Build on how analogs of the technology are used in the real world

DESIGNING THE INQUIRY FOR IT PROJECTS

IT projects tend to be driven by business needs. However, the statement of need tends to focus on the immediate problem as perceived by the customer. Responding only to the stated problem usually results in a patchwork of small systems, each addressing a small part of the work in isolation, and none working well with any of the others. It's often necessary to negotiate the project focus with the customer so that customer needs are met but the resulting system also ties work together. The proper role of IT is to work with the customer to step back, determine the underlying issues that resulted in this problem, and work out a solution that ties the work and the information systems that support it together. IT organizations always want to create and deliver coherent systems that work together to support a business seamlessly. Any new system should be defined to fit into the overall business strategy. Tying the work together means IT organizations always want to be in the business of process redesign. Rather than automating whatever idiosyncratic work practice exists, IT benefits from working with the customer to imagine changes to their process that take advantage

IT's role is to tie the work together through information systems

of technology. There are three kinds of requests IT usually has to deal with.

Upgrades: The request is to add or modify a feature of an existing system. Typically this is called "maintenance" by the IT department. We avoid this term because "maintenance" implies that no new, interesting work happens in this task. In fact, much of IT's workload is in this kind of "maintenance," and much of the improvement or degradation of the information systems taken together is the result of "maintenance" work. So we borrow a term from the commercial vendors and call these "upgrades." The upgrade request is often stated in terms of a design change: "Just make it so I can enter several orders at once." Your challenge is to understand the reasons behind the request and design a solution that fits the need, keeps work practice coherent, and preserves the integrity of the system design. Look at the whole of the work task and related tasks to understand how the change affects the work as a whole. Look at detailed tool use to see what UI mechanisms work and which get in the way. Look for other point requests that can be addressed with the same mechanism.

Look at tool use and its edges to extend the system

New systems: The problem as stated is to provide a system to support some aspect of the business (e.g., order processing). There is no explicit intention on the client's side to change the way they work in any major way. Introducing a new system to automate the inefficient ways that things are done currently is a waste. The challenge is to move the design team and the client together to invent ways to improve the work. The result will be to define new ways of working and the software systems that support them. Expand your statement of focus by looking at the whole work process that the original request is a part of. How does it support the real work of the department? If this is the primary intent of the process, look at how the intent is accomplished. If not, ask what the intent is and whether it can be accomplished in a more direct way. Is the process contained in one department, or does it span departments? Plan interviews with people at each point in the process.

Ask: how will the new system support the real work of the department?

Process redesign: The project is started to implement a business process reengineering directive. Typically the directive does not specify exactly what the new work practice will be or the exact requirements on supporting systems. Instead, it just gives broad outlines of the new process and hints of supporting systems. "In the new claims-handling process, one person will be responsible for the claim from the time it comes in until it is settled. All claim data will be available to all parts of the company through a central database." The directive leaves open how the claims process works on a daily basis, how people will interact with the new system, and exactly what kinds of interactions the new system must support. The focus for such a project needs to look at the customers of the new process: what do they need, and why? Look at how the work is accomplished now: What have people had to do to make the process work? What will get in the way of introducing a new process? Helping people accept and adapt to the new way of working is a part of the design problem. Plan how to include the customers in the design process. When they are a part of redesigning their own lives, they will more easily accept and adapt to changes.

CD develops the details of business process redesign

The project focus gives the team an initial cut of what they are working on, who their customers are, and what the key tasks are. It suggests things to look for in the field and suggests some of the places to go. This prepares you to determine the specific interviewing situations needed to get the right data and make the project work.

DESIGNING THE INTERVIEWING SITUATION

Your initial inquiry into the work gave you a focus for the project and also revealed some characteristics of the work domain and told you what work tasks you need to observe. Exactly how you will set up the interviews is driven by the nature of these tasks. The key questions for defining the interviewing situation are always: How do I get close to the work? How close can I get? How do I create a shared interpretation with the customer? Different kinds of tasks make different demands on the interview.

Normal: A normal task can be planned, is performed in a reasonably continuous session, and can be interrupted by the interviewer.

Writing a letter, delivering mail, installing software, and writing code are all normal tasks. The interviewer can plan to be present to observe

Use a standard contextual interview

a normal task and can interrupt at will to understand it. Normal tasks can be studied through a standard contextual interview. It may be useful to ask the customer to save work of the sort you want to study to do during the interview. This does alter the normal work flow, but very minimally, and the increase in relevant data makes it worth it. Audiotape these interviews, but videotape is rarely worth the extra trouble. Videotape them only if the work is so UI-intensive that you have to see the interaction to understand what's going on, or if it's especially important to communicate the customer experience to developers who can't go on interviews themselves.

Intermittent: An intermittent task happens at rare intervals over the course of a day. It cannot be scheduled and does not last long. It's

Create a trail to walk and talk with the user

so infrequent that the chances of observing it during a standard contextual interview are low—you'd spend hours to get five minutes of data. Looking something up in documentation and recovering from a system crash are intermittent tasks. The key to learning about them is to create a trail that will enable the user to re-create a retrospective account of the event. In documentation, you could ask the user to keep a paper log of every time they use the documentation, perhaps numbering the pages themselves so they can walk through the story later. You could design the documentation so the user can keep their log right in the documentation itself. You might instrument online help, so the software automatically records what the user did. Start with a face-to-face interview, then leave them to log what they do. Return later to perform an interview that follows the form of a retrospective account, walking through each artifact in turn to discover what the user did.

Uninterruptable: Some tasks simply cannot be interrupted to do the interpretation. A surgical operation, a high-level management meeting, and a sales call are all situations that cannot be stopped to

Plan discussion breaks between events

talk about what is going on. In these situations you want to capture the events clearly enough that you can recall all the details later. You might plan interruptions, such as providing for regular 15-minute breaks in a long meeting where participants can discuss what happened in the part of the meeting just concluded. You might videotape the event, then review the videotape with the customer, stopping to discuss events as they occur. If even videotape is too intrusive, you can at least keep good notes and review them with the customer. If you videotape, interpret the tape with the customer. You lose too much insight and cannot be sure of your interpretations if you review the tape alone later.

Extremely long: Some tasks take years to complete. Shipping a major software system, developing a new drug, and building a 747 are all tasks that take substantially longer than the two to three hours of a typical contextual interview. To understand tasks of this sort, pursue two strategies: first, interview a wide range of users at different points in the process and playing different roles in the process. Since work strategy repeats, common patterns will emerge even though the cases are different. Then, choose willing customers with the best examples and do a work walkthrough, which is like an in-depth retrospective account. Set up an event in which customers bring in project documentation from all parts of the process and walk through the history of the project, week by week, meeting by meeting. Use the project artifacts to ground the inquiry. Include project documents, such as plans, reports, and designs, and also process documents, such as the calendars and email of those most concerned. Use the artifacts to drive the conversation. Expect this re-creation to take a day or two.

Create interviewing situations that reveal a cross section of work

Extremely focused: Sometimes the problem is so focused on the minutia of a person's actions that it's too hard to run a standard interview. You might be polishing the detailed interaction of a computer user with an application's UI or studying the details of how a craftsman manipulates his tools. You would miss too much if you depended on unaided observation, and you would also get in the way of the work too much if you interrupted every moment. This is a case where videotape can be useful. It will capture the details you would miss, and you can run it repeatedly until you understand a particular interaction. But view it and interpret what you see with the user. You cannot understand all their motivations on your own.

Videotape and interpret with the user

Internal: Sometimes the inquiry needs to focus on internal mental processes, such as how decisions are made. In this case, the interviewer must be present when the mental process is happening because there's no way to recover enough in a retrospective account. You may need to create events that will cause the mental process to happen so that you can be present. Then interrupt a lot; make a lot of hypotheses about what the customer is taking into account in their thinking. Warn the customer this will be very disruptive, but as long as the customer has to make the decision, they will keep working through it and you will learn something about how they do it.

Use ongoing observation with lots of interruption

DECIDING WHO TO INTERVIEW

At this point you know what you are looking for and you know how to set up the interview for the tasks you need to observe. Now you must start putting names on the customers you will visit. In general, you want to interview two or three people in each role you identified as important to the focus. You want to collect data from 10 to 20 people in all, unless the focus is very narrow. Six to ten interviews is sufficient if there is only a single role or you are studying detailed UI interaction instead of overall work process. If you are making commercial software, you want to go to at least four to six businesses to see variety. In choosing sites and individuals, go for diversity in work practice. You are looking for the common underlying structure that cuts across your customer base. You will do this best by studying very different customers, rather than studying similar customers to confirm what you learned.

Diversity in work practice usually is not equivalent to diversity in market segment. Financial institutions, high tech, and retail may be different market segments, but office work is done very similarly in any modern corporation. These different types of companies will not give you substantially different perspectives. In fact, office work is so similar it is actually hard to get a different perspective. One design team studied the military and Japanese companies, in an attempt to find cultures that would be substantially different; they found little that was new. To get different work practice, look for different business strategies (doing the work as a business for hire vs. doing it as a department in a large company). Look for cultural differences (a trucking company vs. a high-tech

Interview customers whose work is as different as possible

company). Look for different physical situations (a company distributed across several states vs. a company located at a single site). Look for differences of scale (a small business vs. a large corporation). If your customer is internal, see if you can study similar work practice in other companies. Look for other places in your own company where similar work is done, and study it. Use metaphors to give you different ways of thinking about the work.

Given these parameters for numbers and diversity, choose the people you will interview. It's okay to be smart when choosing— include the important client who has to buy into an internal project. Focus on customers from the key markets you think are most likely to spend money.

Let focus changes drive customer selection

Expect setting up customer visits to take a couple of weeks, by the time you've found the right person to interview, talked to all the people who are affected, and have set everyone's expectations correctly. However, don't get too far ahead in lining up the visits. As you study the data, you will change your idea of what to find out about next. You don't want to be locked into studying ten documentation writers after you've studied three and discovered that, for your purposes, they all work in much the same way. Make sure you talk to the people you will interview individually in advance and that they understand what will happen.

Your inquiry into the work that the project supports will yield lots of detail about the work and what to look for. It will be too much for anyone to keep track of during an interview. So boil it down to a short statement of the key characteristics of the work. This statement can be written by interviewers in their notebook and will keep them on track during an interview. A focus for an ordering system might be "how people find out about,

A pithy focus statement keeps the interview on track

decide on, and make requests for the things they need to do their work." Such a focus implies things to look for during an interview: "how people learn about what is available, through catalogs, friends, and local experts, whether formal or informal; who is involved in the decision and how they come to agreement; what processes have to be used to make the request and who gets involved in filling it."

The initial focus will be revised and expanded through inquiry into the work. (In the above example, the team discovered that it matters to people to track the requests they have made and when they are expected to be filled.) Focus statements are best when they use simple language. People looking for "requests" will think more broadly about what a request might be and how it might be filled than people looking for a formal-sounding "order." The result will be greater insight into the work and consideration of a greater range of possible solutions.

MAKING IT WORK

For commercial software and internal systems alike, the crucial first step is to ground the design in relevant customer data. This part of the book has given you a solid grounding in the basics of setting up and running a successful interview. This way of collecting customer information is new, and most organizations do not have the procedures in place to make scheduling these interviews easy.

Customers feel heard and valued after an interview

The groups that have the easiest time are those who already create events with individual customers, such as usability tests or focus groups. There can be internal resistance, too. The sales force, marketing, or the internal customer representative can be suspicious of letting engineers talk directly to customers. (See Chapter 20 for strategies on dealing with resistance.) But reactions to the visits are nearly always enthusiastic. Customers feel like they are being listened to for the first time, and the sales force and marketing soon come to recognize the benefits. When the customers are internal, they feel like they have control over the new system. Teams developing custom software often do more interviews than strictly necessary to allow everyone to participate.

As with all skills, experience comes with practice, but you need neither experience nor practice to get started. Whether you are working on the initial requirements for a large system or are refining the UI of a small system, you can define a data-gathering strategy appropriate to your project. A few interviews run along these lines will return a wealth of data on the customers you serve and the work they do. Increased interviewing skill will come with experience.

But be warned: it's addictive. People who get used to having contextual data when they design often have a very hard time breaking the habit.

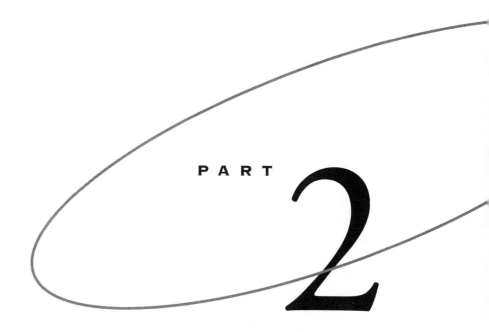

Seeing Work

A Language of Work 5

For customer-centered design, the first task of a design team is to shift focus from the system that the team is chartered to build and redirect it to the work of potential customers. Work, and understanding work, becomes the primary consideration. But "work" is a slippery concept. What is work? You could keep a log of each action I take throughout the day. Is this work? I talk to a colleague and agree on who will handle which parts of a writing task. Is this work? I worry about the latest merger and whether my job will be cut. Is this work? I get up, walk down a corridor, up a flight of stairs, and into a locked room to get a printout, only to discover that the print queue is hung and I will have to restart it from my office. Is this work? If you want to know about work, what do you pay attention to?

This question is particularly acute for a design team. Any system is the result of agreement between engineering, marketing, customers and customer representatives, documentation, and testing. If these disparate people are to use their different disciplines to contribute to the system, they must come to a shared perception of how customers work. Putting work experts—psychologists, anthropologists, or domain experts—on the team helps, but they need to learn how their unique insight contributes to system design. Other members of the team may not be experts in understanding work practice, how it is structured, and how it hangs together as an organizational and social whole. As we discussed in Part 1, what people see and talk about is constrained by their entering focus—by what they have concepts for. If they have no concepts for work, they will talk about things familiar to them: the technology they can use to build the system, its internal structure, and its user interface. To take best advantage of techniques such as Contextual Inquiry, people need to learn

A system design results from agreements between the responsible people

concepts that show them what to see when they are with the customer—and given the constraints of real engineering projects, they need to learn these new concepts quickly.

USING LANGUAGE TO FOCUS THOUGHT

A formal language for talking about work organizes concepts that help people learn to see work. It is natural for people to embody a new domain of knowledge in a language that expresses ideas in that domain. A language makes the key concepts of the domain concrete in symbols or words. This is what jargon is—specialized words and specialized uses of ordinary words that embody concepts useful to some domain of expertise. So knitters create "purl" to describe a stitch, use "knit" to describe another stitch (as well as the whole activity), and when they "cross stitches," they do something quite different from the "cross-stitch" in needlepoint. In the same way, mechanics use "ping" and "knock" to describe specific symptoms common to engines, confusing those of us who think those words just represent noises.

A specialized language of this sort creates a focus—a set of things to pay attention to. Expertise about the knowledge domain is captured in the language and becomes available to anyone who learns the language. Once you know that engines ping and knock, you can start to make sense of the noises your engine makes. The language gives you a way to see—a framework for interpreting the things you observe and a structure of understanding

A language creates a way for people to see and talk together

you can elaborate as you learn more. (Once you know about ping and knock, you can ask what other noises your engine makes. Do they provide more clues to potential problems?) The new language expands the team's entering focus to include work concepts, enabling team members to see more of the details of work when they interview. And just like the interviewing focus, team members can expand on their language of work, creating new concepts and distinctions unique to the work domain they are designing for.

Because a language creates a focus, it is not neutral. It directs your thought. Any language is designed to say certain things easily—the things for which it provides concepts. Artists have a language of color, shape, and shade to talk about the sky; meteorologists have a language for talking about the sky, too, but it is very different from the artist's language. Which language is better depends on whether your current concern is aesthetics or weather. A language of work for design will represent those aspects of work that matter *for design.* A design team building accounting systems for lawyers doesn't need to know everything about the law—just those aspects of legal practice affecting how lawyers run their businesses. Even a lawyer or anthropologist on the team will have to learn to focus on those aspects of work that matter to the design problem at hand.

> *A language directs thought*

GRAPHICAL LANGUAGES GIVE A WHOLE PICTURE

Languages don't have to be textual. Graphical languages—formalisms or diagramming techniques—share all the advantages of a textual language. Instead of words, graphical languages use symbols, each conveying a defined concept. Just as syntax rules restrict how words can be combined in a textual language, drawing rules restrict what can be drawn in a graphical language.

For design, a graphical language has definite advantages. Because the number of symbols in a graphical language is small—usually less than 100—a graphical language focuses thought even more intensely than a textual language with thousands of words. It is possible to learn all the symbols of a graphical language, and once learned they suggest how to use them. Just as when you learn a new word, you suddenly notice the word used everywhere, the symbols of a graphical language cause a design team to notice the distinction they represent. They become part of the design focus, revealing more detail about work.

> *Sparse graphical languages provide greater guidance for thought*

Unlike a textual language, graphical languages let you take in a whole picture at once. A textual language must be read and parsed; this is not only a difficult chore, but the information has to be taken in sequentially, one idea at a time. Given reasonable methods for handling complexity, a picture can be scanned and taken in as a whole. A picture is a better external representation than a page of text because it's easier

A picture reveals pattern and structure of work

to see what you are talking about. A picture reveals overall pattern and structure by showing each part in relationship to the whole. This is critical to creative work and to design (Suchman 1989). Once a team understands how work fits together, they can identify sets of problems and needs to address together. Without a coherent understanding of work, each need stands alone and can only be addressed as a point problem. It's impossible to see when a solution to one problem creates new problems elsewhere—just as automated phone systems solved the problem of giving quick answers to standard questions, but made it difficult to get to a live person to deal with non-standard situations. A diagram supports systemic thought and makes it possible to create a coherent design response that fits well with the work it supports. (Hutchins [1995] discusses how artifacts support and enhance thought.)

WORK MODELS PROVIDE A LANGUAGE FOR SEEING WORK

For these reasons, we use *work models* as a graphical language to capture knowledge about work. They provide a shared focus on work that gives

Writing things down is a central tool for creativity

the team an external, concrete form to record and communicate what they saw on customer visits. As long as work practice remains insubstantial and invisible, there's no good way to share what you learned, to validate your understanding with the customer, or to check that your design really accounts for the work practice you discovered. Models make concepts concrete, creating a physical artifact that the team can share, talk about, and touch. Teams can use them to understand what each team member is really saying about the work. If the team includes work experts, models give them a way to make their insight explicit and communicate it to the rest of the team. The team can share their understanding with customers to ensure that it is correct. And designers can check the models to ensure they are not forgetting some aspect of the work that will cause their design to fail. Creating concrete artifacts is critical to creativity—it's a cliché that great designs are first recorded on the back of a napkin. Models provide a way for people to record their thinking so it can be seen and manipulated.

By providing a coherent, synthetic view of work practice, work models give design teams effective ways to handle qualitative data. Any qualitative technique such as Contextual Inquiry produces huge amounts of detailed knowledge about the customer. This knowledge is critical to system design, but it isn't amenable to reductive statistical techniques: you can't take the average of 20 interviews to identify the "typical" customer.

Graphical models organize huge amounts of data

Work models provide a coherent way of structuring all this detailed data, revealing underlying structure without glossing over the detail.

Graphical languages do exist already in systems design. Process flows, state transition diagrams, object models, data flow diagrams— all use graphical languages to represent some aspect of system design. Each, by the concepts it presents, focuses the designer on a certain way of thinking about the problem. But few of these diagrams focus on people and how they work. A data flow diagram focuses on the flow of data, and the operations performed on it, independent of the people involved (Yourdon and Constantine 1979). A process map shows processes and tasks, but not how they map to a person's responsibilities or environment. An object model shows things—objects— and the operations that the objects perform or their responsibilities.

It is logically possible to use a technique like object modeling to represent other concepts, but in practice it can't be done. It's like saying that all programs could be written in machine code so any other programming language is unnecessary; it's logically true, but actually writing any of today's systems in machine code would be so overwhelming that they would never be written. In the

Good models substitute for seeing the work itself

same way, you might represent all the aspects of work in an object model, but the conceptual task of interpreting the model would be overwhelming. You would have to inquire into each object and interpret what it said about the work. The work of people is still invisible. Furthermore, the language of work needs to focus on the concepts of work that matter; generic object modeling cannot provide a focus. It cannot guide our thoughts. (Sumner [1995] provides further research into designers' use of multiple representation.)

Instead, design teams need a representation of work that makes the important aspects of work for design apparent. The models will stand in for seeing the work itself; once team members are familiar with them, the team should be able to look at a model and envision people doing the work it represents. A mental translation from the distinctions in the model to relevant work concepts gets in the way.

WORK MODELS REVEAL THE IMPORTANT DISTINCTIONS

Contextual Design provides five different types of work model to represent customer work practice: *flow,* representing the communication and coordination necessary to do the work; *sequence,* showing the detailed work steps necessary to achieve an intent; *artifact,* showing the physical things created to support the work, along with their structure, usage, and intent; *culture,* representing constraints on the work caused by policy, culture, or values; and *physical,* showing the physical structure of the work environment as it affects the work. (The next chapter describes each in detail.) Each type of model provides its own perspective on the work and synthesizes all aspects of work in its focus into a single, coherent diagram. Having multiple types of work model gives a team more ways to see issues and structure in the work, while allowing each model to focus cleanly on one aspect of work.

We find that these five models are usually sufficient to support all the design conversations a team needs to have—the combined focus they provide covers the main issues for most design problems. As we will see, they support the chain of reasoning from data to design. As with any focus, the work models both reveal detail in the areas they cover and conceal detail that falls outside. When it's necessary to expand a focus to explore issues that the work models do not cover, having work models suggests that new models might be created. For example, though the flow model shows the overall coordination between people, it does not show the continuous give-and-take between two people collaborating on a project. It also does not show what is going on interpersonally between people

Five different perspectives make the complexity of work comprehensible

over the course of a conversation. When a design problem requires understanding these or other aspects of work, we create new models to show them explicitly. (See "Readings and Resources" for other approaches to modeling work.)

After interviewing each customer, the team runs an interpretation session to recapitulate the interview and record what they learned (interpretation sessions are described in Chapter 7). During the session, they draw work models relevant to their project focus. Once a team has generated a set of work models for each customer interviewed, they can use the models to look across customers and identify common pattern and structure. This is the basis of our consolidation process, which takes a team from the work of individual customers to understanding the work of a whole market or department. Since any system will be used by multiple people, this is a critical step in design. Without an explicit way to build a representation of how potential customers of a system work, the design team must generalize in their heads from specific instances. The models make this an external step that can be communicated, shared, and validated. The final consolidated models are the basis of design—the single statement of the work practice that must be supported, improved, replaced, or obviated if a new system is to be successful.

Work models capture user activities observed during a contextual interview

We'll discuss the consolidation process in Part 3. In the following chapter we'll discuss each work model in turn and then describe the interpretation session in Chapter 7.

Work Models

6

Each of the five types of work models has its own concepts and symbols representing one aspect of work for design. The five models were developed over time to meet the needs of the design problems we encountered. They represent the key aspects of work that design teams need to account for in their designs. We have found these five to be necessary to almost every problem and sufficient for most.

Work models are first built to describe work from the point of view of the one person interviewed. They do not and are not intended to represent everything that a person or his organization does. Each interviewer learned about some part of the customer's work as it related to the project focus. They also learned something about the work of the organization, as understood by this one customer. The first models we build represent this *individual* perspective. We even use conventions to show which parts of a model are built from the customer's actual experience and which represent the customer telling us how his organization is supposed to work.

THE FLOW MODEL

To get work done, people divide up responsibilities among roles and coordinate with each other while doing it:

> A rush order comes in. The woman who receives it calls the person responsible for filling it and mentions, in passing, that a rush order is on the way. The rush order will be shipped on time only because of her informal advance warning. When a new order-processing system is introduced, it does not allow this advance warning and rush orders start shipping late.

> A purchasing department is responsible for paying invoices as they come in. But they don't know if the goods were

actually received; they have to figure out who received the goods, send the invoice to him for approval, and pay it only when he returns it signed. Making the purchase and paying for the goods have been separated from the actual work of the organization. Formal sign-off and review processes keep the system working. The purchasing department gets so involved in maintaining these formal processes that they cannot handle finding vendors and making purchases well.

A specialist in another organization gets ready to produce a report. In times past he would have had a secretary type in and format the report; these days he not only creates the content, but he also defines the formatting and layout, checks spelling, and proofs the document as well. He has more control over the document in his own hands, but it's not clear that it's cost-effective for a highly paid professional to do basic stenographic and editorial tasks.

In each of these cases, the key issue is how people's roles are defined and how they communicate to get the job done. The *order receiver* had to communicate with the *order processor* to get rush orders accomplished on time; the *invoice payer* had to communicate with the *goods user* to find out if the invoice should be paid; the *content provider* became the *page designer,* instead of

No real work happens in isolation

handing the content off to a secretary who could have played that role. All work in this world involves other people to some extent. Books are written for an audience, based on sources, submitted to reviewers, and passed to publishers. Code is written by developers for its users, from requirements, tested by a testing group, marketed by a product marketing group, and distributed to customers. Departments exist because a single person alone can't get the work done; the work must be broken into parts, which then must be coordinated. Different departments coordinate the different parts of the work, and people within a department coordinate to get its work done. The flow model represents this communication and coordination necessary to make work happen.

RECOGNIZING COMMUNICATION FLOW

Work flow (Figures 6.1 and 6.2) defines how work is broken up across people and how people coordinate to ensure the whole job gets done.

FLOW MODEL DISTINCTIONS

The *individuals* who do the work. In the consolidated models, the roles they play (see Part 3 for a discussion of consolidation). Each person or group is shown as a bubble. The interviewee's bubble is annotated with user number and job title. Everyone else's bubble just has job function.

The *responsibilities* of the individual or role. This is a list of what is expected of them—"coordinate schedules of all managers," "ensure samples are processed in the shortest possible time." Every bubble and place on the flow model is annotated with responsibilities.

Groups, sets of people who have common goals or take action together. Outside people may interact with the group as a unit, without knowing any individuals in the group. They say things like "I sent it to purchasing"; the particular person in purchasing doesn't matter. Groups are represented when a person has the same interaction with all its members. We may also show the interaction between a group member and the group as a whole.

The *flow,* the communication between people to get work done. Flow may consist of informal talk and coordination, or it may consist of passing artifacts. Flow is shown as arrows between individuals.

Artifacts, the "things" of the work, which are thought of and manipulated as if they were real. An artifact may be physical, such as a document or message. It may also be conceptual; for example, if a design conversation is thought about as though it has members, a history, attributes (public or private), and an existence separate from any one member or topic, it may warrant representation as an artifact. Where appropriate, the *mechanism* is shown—email vs. paper, for example. Artifacts are shown as small boxes on a flow.

The *communication topic* or *action* representing the detail of the talk or coordination represented by a flow. These are actions as opposed to artifacts, such as talk to set up meetings, arranging for review, asking for help. Examples might be "question about the system" or "request for help." Communication is written on a flow without a box.

Places that people go in and out of in order to get their work done, if it is central to the work of coordinating and collaborating. This is often a meeting room or communal space such as a coffee area. It is shown as a large box annotated with name of place and responsibilities.

Breakdowns or problems in communication or coordination, represented as a red lightning bolt (black in this book). ❏

How do job responsibilities get assigned to people? What are the different roles people take on to get work done? How do new tasks get passed to a person? Who do they get help from? Who do they have to work with to accomplish their tasks? How do they use physical places and artifacts to help them coordinate? Who do they give the results to and in what form? Work flow is the rich pattern of work as it shuttles between people, the interweaving of jobs and job responsibilities that gets the work done. Work flow represents every phone call between

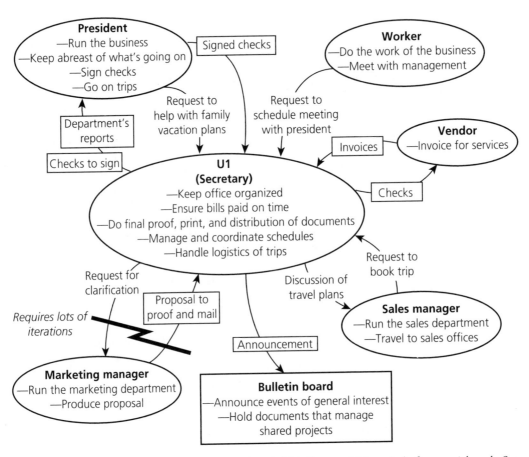

FIGURE 6.1 Secretarial work. This flow model is typical of secretarial work. Secretaries often act as the center, the hub, of a department. In this model, we see this graphically in the many lines that diverge from the central bubble. We can see the great diversity of the hub function in the many types of communication on the lines—everything from formal reports being passed up the management hierarchy to informal requests to smooth the personal lives of people in the department. The accretion of hub responsibilities in one person is natural; once a person is coordinating one aspect of an office, it is natural for them to coordinate other aspects as well. From this diagram we see the nature of hub work—lots of different activities, communication with lots of different people, lots of interruptions, and lots of tasks going on at the same time.

two people, every document passed for review, every email message, every conversation between people in the hall. These are all instances of passing an artifact, communicating information, or coordinating to

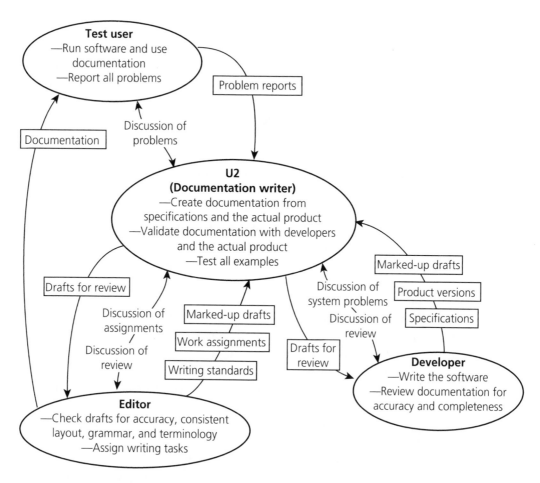

FIGURE 6.2 Creative work. This flow model is typical of creative work. We see communication with those who depend on the work and with those who assist in the creation. But most of the interactions are focused on the task of creation. Compared with the "hub" type of job, this work is much more continuous and coherent.

do a job, whether as part of a formal process or as an informal way to get the job done.

When people coordinate through email or paper, it's easy to see. It's harder to see how casual conversation and handwritten notes support work flow. Here's what to watch for in an interview.

COORDINATION. Any artifact received or handed on indicates coordination with someone else. Where did it come from? Who created it? Who will see it next? Find out the whole story to see how the work fits together. Any discussion with someone else, through a phone call, email, or by dropping in personally, also indicates coordination. Is this discussion critical to the work? Where are the problems in coordinating? Do people forget? Do they spend a lot of time on it? Look for opportunities to automate communication that is currently manual and haphazard. See if you can eliminate the need for coordination by providing information directly or by combining roles that are currently separated.

Represent every contact people make

STRATEGY.   What strategy is implicit in how the roles are organized? Listen to how the customers talk about their job. How do they see themselves in the organization? What do they consider to be their unique contribution to their department? What is the unique contribution of the department to the company? How does it further the business? Ask whether the role is really critical to the business. If not, why was it put in place? Could that intent be accomplished more directly, or is the intent irrelevant to the business? (One purchasing department has a role devoted to providing PO numbers. PO numbers support their process, but give no direct benefit to the business.)

ROLES.   What makes a coherent role? Watch the tasks people do. How do they hang together? Which tasks require similar knowledge, tools, procedures, or data? When does doing a task require knowledge of the progress made in doing another task? These tasks tend to be performed by the same role. Technicians, for example, need to know the history of a problem and of prior attempts to fix it in order to serve the customer well. If problem calls are handed out to the first available person, regardless of history, service will be poor.

Note what responsibilities people take on—even responsibilities that are not part of their jobs

INFORMAL STRUCTURES.   Look at the ways people go beyond the formal structure: A secretary becomes known as the expert on creating forms. Soon whenever anyone has a particularly difficult form to create, they pass it to her and she does it for them. A scientist has special instructions to communicate to her lab technician. She writes a note on a materials tracking tag, knowing he will see it. A manager has to assign resources to get things out on time. He invents a status meeting to get it all done. He consciously runs it like a combination bingo game and commando operations center to keep people involved and excited. Each of these people is inventing process and communication mechanisms to support the work they need to do. They show where the formal process definition

Look at the actions people take without thinking

of the organization is inadequate and reveal opportunities for supporting people's needs more directly. Could you give scientists a better channel to their technicians? Could you eliminate the need for the status meeting with a work assignment and coordination tool? Study the meeting to see what the tool needs to do—and don't overlook the way people ask for and get help around the edges.

CREATING A BIRD'S-EYE VIEW OF THE ORGANIZATION

The flow model offers a bird's-eye view of the organization, showing the people and their responsibilities, the communication paths between people independent of time, and the things communicated—either tangible artifacts or intangible coordination. People and organizations are bubbles on the model, annotated with their position and responsibilities (roles are not represented directly until we consolidate models across people). Flow is indicated as arrows between bubbles, with the kind of communication written on the line. Artifacts are shown in boxes on the line; informal communication and actions are written without a box.

Where places such as meeting rooms or virtual places such as shared areas support communication, the flow model shows them as well. When a place is important to coordination— meeting rooms, bulletin boards, and shared dropoff areas—they appear as large boxes at the end of a flow. Just as individuals are annotated with their responsibilities, places list their responsibilities in supporting communication and coordination. Automated systems and databases usually should not

Represent locations, things, and systems when they make a place to coordinate

go on the flow. The only exception is when they are acting like a physical place or like an automated person, and they are critical to coordination between people. Then they are shown as a large box with responsibilities.

When communication breaks down—people don't get something they should have received or don't respond when a response is needed—we show the problem with a lightning bolt.

Do not limit the model to the formal definition of how work is supposed to be done. The defined process of the organization is not a good guide to how work is actually accomplished. Every day, the people in the organization design how their jobs will really be done. As they encounter problems and obstacles, they create solutions, and the solutions become part of the real work. The flow model needs to capture how work is really done, including all the informal interactions that make it work. From this representation, you can find good work practice to incorporate into a system, identify problems to eliminate, and see the pattern of communication a system must allow for.

The real interactions between people reveal glitches in the work

THE SEQUENCE MODEL

Work tasks are ordered; they unfold over time. But the steps people take aren't random; they happen the way they do for a purpose:

A man reads a mail message and, after replying, saves it in a folder called "Phone book." He'll never need that message again. He's just saving it because it has the sender's telephone number on it, and it's a convenient way to look it up. So telephone numbers matter even when email is the primary form of communication, and telephone calls may be triggered by email. Anyone trying to build the complete personal organizer can build on this to tie phone contacts and email together.

A woman paying her bills first gets out her checkbook, bills, paper record of accounts, envelopes, and stamps; then records the amount of every bill and makes sure she can pay them all; then writes each check in turn; and then puts each in an envelope and addresses it. So the stages of paying bills are collect and organize; plan what to pay and how, making sure not to overdraw the account; actually pay the bills; and put them in envelopes to send out. A home accounting program can build these steps in directly.

A scientist is interpreting the results of an experiment. He puts the raw numbers in one column, then in each successive column shows the result of one transformation. He needs to see not just the final result, but the process by which those results are achieved. An analysis tool that hid the calculations, and only revealed the result, would not be acceptable.

The actions people take in doing their work reveal their strategy, their intent, and what matters to them. A system that builds on these can improve the work they do. Understanding the real intent is key to improving work practice; you can redesign, modify, and remove steps as long as the user can still achieve their underlying intent. An intent is stable—for example, people have had the intent of communicating over a distance for ages. The steps, the way that intent has been achieved, have changed over time—from handwritten messages to the telegraph, the telephone, and videoconferencing. Supporting the current work steps just automates the way things are done currently (and because paper is almost always faster than computers, if the system does nothing but automate existing steps, it almost always loses). The goal is to change the work steps to make work more efficient. But the system must support all the intents concealed in the work, not just the primary espoused intents. If users have an intent of planning how to pay bills before they start writing checks, and the system doesn't support planning, the system will not be accepted.

Understanding customers' intent is the key to design

All work, when it unfolds in time, becomes a sequence of actions—steps to achieve an intent. A sequence model (Figure 6.3) represents the steps by which work is done, the triggers that kick off a set of steps, and the intents that are being accomplished. They are your map to the work that your new system will change. Sequence models supply the low-level, step-by-step information on how work is actually done that designers need to make detailed design decisions. The sequence model is most similar to flow diagrams or task analysis (Carter 1991), but is unique in stating the intent and trigger for the sequence. A sequence model starts with the overall intent of the sequence and the trigger that initiates it. Then it lists each step in order, at whatever level of detail the interviewer collected. Any steps that cause problems are labeled with a lightning bolt. When modeling the work of an individual, the

From any one person's point of view, all work is a series of actions

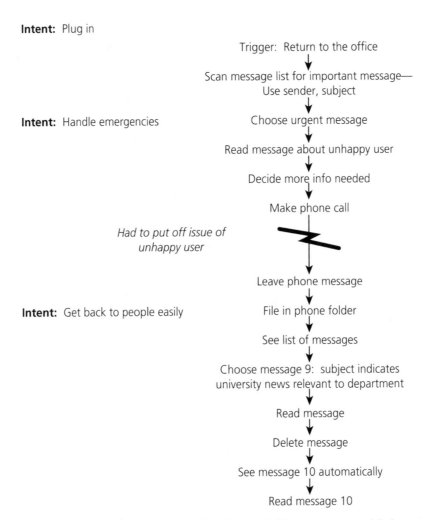

Intent: Plug in

Trigger: Return to the office

Scan message list for important message—
Use sender, subject

Intent: Handle emergencies

Choose urgent message

Read message about unhappy user

Decide more info needed

Make phone call

*Had to put off issue of
unhappy user*

Leave phone message

Intent: Get back to people easily

File in phone folder

See list of messages

Choose message 9: subject indicates
university news relevant to department

Read message

Delete message

See message 10 automatically

Read message 10

FIGURE 6.3 Sequence model for handling mail. This sequence model shows how one user handled mail on one specific day. The intent is stated at the top left: "Plug in." This conveys the nature of handling mail for this user: much of his communication is through email, and when he left his office, he separated himself from this communication. Returning and checking mail was a reconnection, a "plugging in." This is implied by the trigger for starting this sequence, which indicates he does it whenever he returns to the office. The arrows indicate the sequence of steps. When he completed handling an emergency, he saved the message in a folder he uses as a phone book. This action indicates an unrelated intent, keeping a contact list up-to-date, which he handles opportunistically.

sequence model does not attempt to show pattern or repetition; we identify those when we consolidate. Sequences may be studied at any level of detail, from the high-level work to accomplish an overall task to the detailed interaction steps with a particular user interface.

COLLECTING SEQUENCES DURING AN INTERVIEW

Collect sequences in an interview by watching people work or by getting a detailed retrospective account of their work. The hardest thing about seeing sequences is knowing what to pay attention to, and this changes depending on the project focus.

STEPS.   If you are studying the work across the department, or if you are learning about a new market, you'll collect sequences at a fairly high level of detail. You want the actions people take, but not necessarily broken down into each movement. So writing a letter might look like: Get project information from project manager. Extract deliverables and delivery dates important to the customer. Write

SEQUENCE MODEL DISTINCTIONS

The *intent* that the sequence is intended to achieve. Secondary intents will be embedded in this primary intent, and they are named as they are identified.

A *trigger* causing the sequence of actions. It is the notification to the user to take action. Triggers we have seen include the height of a stack of paper on a desk, the arrival of mail, receiving a request, and seeing a misplaced line of text in a document.

Steps, the action or thought preceding an action. In an actual sequence model, a step represents what actually happened. As we step back from the actual steps and look for purpose and strategy, the steps become more abstract. They move away from specific behaviors toward fundamental purpose.

Order, loops, and branches indicated by arrows connecting the steps. These reveal strategic and repetitive patterns of work. When the customer must make a decision about how to proceed, we show that as a branching path. The order gives us an access road map to ensure smooth transitions between tasks and allows us to see what steps could be combined or skipped without serious violation to the users' conception of what is going on in their work.

Breakdowns or problems in doing the steps shown with a red lightning bolt (black in this book). ❑

introductory paragraph describing current project state. Enter dates. . . . This level of detail shows the overall structure of the work and how it fits together without giving huge amounts of detail about each task.

If you are designing a system or tool, study the tasks the tool supports in more detail. Look at what people do and also *how* they do it.

Capture actions at the level that matters for your project

So writing a letter might look like: Scroll window to find last letter written. Open it. Delete all content. Save under new name. Enter name of recipient. Pull Rolodex closer. . . . At this level of detail, we see the structure of the task and the actions that make it happen.

If you are designing the user interface, look at eye movement, hand movement, hesitations, everything. So writing a letter might look like: Use vertical scroll bar until icon for last letter written comes in view. Double-click on item to open. Read recipient name and scan first paragraph to make sure this is the right letter. Choose "Select All" from Edit menu. . . . This level of detail shows how the user interacts with the UI and reveals the issues for the UI to address.

In practice, the levels of detail blur somewhat, and it's safer to get more detail rather than less. Each action has a purpose in the user's

Customers' actions are never purposeless

mind. If it looks random to you, that's only because you don't know what the purpose might be. In a word processor, we repeatedly saw the user, with the cursor at the end of the line, hit the right arrow, see it move to the next line, then hit the left arrow to move it back. Even this was not random; he was checking to see if he was really at the end of the line or if there was extra white space because, in that word processor, the white space would make the line wrap.

HESITATIONS AND ERRORS.   Notice when the customer hesitates or makes errors. These are your clues to his thoughts. Intervene and ask questions to find out what he is thinking about. Hesita-

Any glitch reveals a thought step

tions and errors indicate places where the customers' understanding of work is being contradicted by the tools they are using. This is an opportunity for your system to do better. If a task is largely a thinking task, hesitations reveal decision points in the process.

Stop the customer and ask him to explain what he is trying to decide at that moment. Try to get him to think aloud, to reveal more of the issues.

TRIGGERS. Every sequence has a trigger—the event that initiated it. Triggers may be discrete events, such as the ringing of a telephone, the arrival of an invoice, or a person arriving at the door. Triggers may be based on time, like the first of the month or the first thing in the morning. Triggers may be less tangible, such as the pile in the in-box getting too large. Whatever the trigger, if the work is automated, it must have an analog in the new sys-

Watch how automation removes effective prompts to action

tem. The system needs a way to tell the user there's something to be done. Otherwise, the user won't take action—for example, one mail product simply gets slower the larger the in-box gets. This doesn't act as a trigger for the user to clean it out; it just makes the product more and more frustrating to use.

INTENTS. The intent defines why the work represented by a sequence matters to the user at all. Every sequence has a primary intent, which applies to the whole sequence. Then there will be secondary intents, which drive the particular way the work is carried out. So our bill payer has a secondary intent of not overdrawing her account and of redefining who to pay and how

Find the intents implied by the actions

much to pay so that important bills are paid and the account is not overdrawn. Intents are usually identified after the sequence is written, when there is time to look it over and think about what lies behind the customer's actions.

Sequences capture the most basic information about work practice. Not only do they tell you how work is *really* done, they show how it is structured and the intents people care about. They present the detailed structure of work that designers will need when it comes time to structure the system. And they cut across the other models, tying them together. Because sequences are

Sequence models reveal the detailed structure of work

time-ordered, they show how different roles interact in different places, using artifacts to support communication and actions to get the work done.

THE ARTIFACT MODEL

People create, use, and modify things in the course of doing work. The things they use become *artifacts,* like archaeological findings. They each have their own story to tell about the work:

In one organization, a first-level supervisor prints the spreadsheet he uses to track projects weekly and gives it to his manager. His manager makes check marks against each project to indicate his approval and may make additional notes on the side. Then he signs at the bottom and gives it back. In this way the supervisor's personal tracking sheet becomes a sign-off mechanism and a way for the manager to communicate problems and issues. It suggests that sign-off and feedback are part of the job; an automated project-tracking system could build these features in.

Another woman builds a spreadsheet to calculate end-of-year results. The calculations take 15 minutes to do—then she spends the next 45 minutes making the spreadsheet look good so she can hand it out at the next management review. When a spreadsheet is given careful formatting, it's clear that the way information is presented is an important consideration and that spreadsheets are presentation tools as well as calculation tools. The original spreadsheet tools only displayed text; they were replaced with tools that could do fancy fonts and gave full control over the look.

Another organization has the goal of raising the level of cost consciousness among its people. They have a standard form for making a request for a purchase. The form has a place to describe the item and a place to justify why it's needed but no place to show the cost. When a purchasing form has no place to show cost, it suggests that cost is not a big concern in the organization. An automated purchase order request system could raise cost consciousness just by making cost prominent on the screen.

Artifacts are the tangible things people create or use to help them get their work done. When people use artifacts, they build their way of working right into them. The artifacts show what people think about when they work and how they think about it. An artifact reveals the assumptions, concepts, strategy, and structure that

Artifacts capture traces of people's work practice

guide the people who work with it. Artifacts might be to-do lists, forms, documents, spreadsheets, or physical objects under construction (circuit boards, cars, airplanes). Artifacts may be bought, designed intentionally, or created on the fly. They are manipulated in the sequence models and passed between people in the flow model.

In their structure—how they are arranged into parts and the relationship between the parts—artifacts show the conceptual distinctions of the work. When displays showing the status of a network are separated from displays of trouble alerts, this indicates that tracking ongoing status is different work from responding to alerts. When notes are written on a presentation handout, not where there is white space to write them on, but

Artifacts make customers' conceptual distinctions concrete

jammed in next to the text they refer to, this indicates that the close spatial relationship of text and note matters to the writer. When the list of things that a person would like to get is separated from the shopping list, this indicates that a clear distinction exists in the person's mind between the nice-to-have-someday items and the I-will-buy-this-today items. An automated shopper's planner had better provide a way to track long-term possible purchases separately from today's shopping list (Johnson et al. 1988).

An artifact model (Figure 6.4) is a drawing or photocopy of the artifact, complete with any handwritten notes. The model extends the information on the artifact to show structure, strategy, and intent. Highlight structure with lines and labels marking the different parts. Annotate the location of the parts showing how they are placed to give them prominence or support the artifact's usage. And write intents directly on the part of the artifact that supports the intent. Lightning bolts show where the artifact interferes with the work, whether because the defined structure does not match the work, because needed information is missing, or because it is too cumbersome to use.

COLLECTING ARTIFACTS DURING AN INTERVIEW

Artifact models always require interpretation to reveal their intent and usage. You can do this best with the customer during the interview. Look for and inquire into:

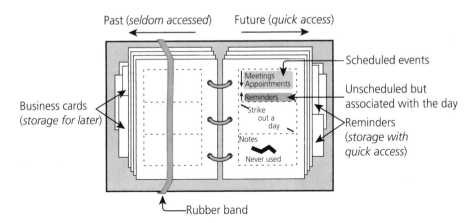

FIGURE 6.4   Artifact model. This physical model shows the structure of an artifact, in this case a personal calendar. The usage of this calendar reveals that it is not only about managing time; it is organizing an entire life. The rubber band makes the distinction between past and future. The calendar is acting as a storage place for reminders and to-do lists as well as a calendar. When the calendar gets too fat, this is a convenient trigger for dealing with the to-do lists. The usage of the day view shows additional distinctions: meetings are listed from the top of the day down, but reminders of a more general nature are written from the bottom going up. Reminders are attached to a day; they are not kept in the provided "notes" area, so it is not used.

STRUCTURE.   All artifacts have structure, even the most informal. People naturally create a structure to represent their thought, even when they start from a blank page. If they didn't create the artifact on the fly, they may start from a given structure, either because it came as part of an artifact they bought or because they designed it themselves before starting the actual work. In this case, the structure inherent in the work wars with the given structure, and the artifact will show every place there is a mismatch. So the notes space on a daily calendar may be used for notes, but it may be left blank or used as a rolling to-do list. If everyone uses it like a to-do list, then organizing the day and scheduling are intimately intertwined.

Structure reveals how the work is organized

Look to see how the artifact is structured. How does the presentation—layout, fonts, formatting, and white space—reveal structure? Assume every grouping of information corresponds to a conceptual distinction in the customer's work. Can you and the user figure out what it is? Can you make these distinctions real in your system?

ARTIFACT MODEL DISTINCTIONS

Information presented by the object, such as the content of a form (e.g., a doctor's name, nurse's name, patient's name, and diagnosis).

Parts of the object, which are distinct in usage, such as page, kind of page (table of content vs. title page), headline, or figure in a diagram.

Structure of the parts explicitly in the object as given and implicitly in its usage: the division of a form into a section for the doctor's use and a section for the nurse's, the grouping of cells in a spreadsheet to represent part of the data for a single purpose, or the way some people use the top of a day within a calendar for meetings and the bottom for reminders.

Annotations, which indicate the informal usage of the object beyond that allowed for by its explicit structure: Post-its stuck to a document, highlighting, and notes written on the side of a report.

Presentation of the object: color, shape, layout, font, white space, emphasis, and how they support usage.

Additional *conceptual distinctions* that are reflected in an artifact and that matter in its creation and use: past, current, and future in using a calendar; structure and content that repeats in a report from month to month; x-height and caps height in page layout.

Usage of the artifact—when created, how used, how people move through the parts of the artifact.

Breakdowns or problems in using the artifact, represented as a red lightning bolt (black in this book). ❑

INFORMATION CONTENT. The content of an artifact is the information, specific to the work, that the artifact carries. The content of an artifact tells the story of a part of the work—how the content was put in, how it was used, and who used it. The content fits into the structure of the artifact—or it doesn't, in which case customers modify the defined structure. Seeing how the content is manipulated reveals the artifact's usage—how it supports the work and also the detailed interaction with the artifact in the course of working. So each meeting on a personal calendar suggests the story of the work task that the meeting supports, but it also suggests the detailed story of how the user interacted with the calendar to put the meeting on it.

Content is the trail left by real events

Look for the information the artifact carries and how it is used. Use the artifact to drive a retrospective account, as we discussed when describing interview principles in Chapter 3. Why is this artifact an appropriate carrier for this information? Who will see it and when? What would happen if the artifact didn't exist? Can you make the needed information available more simply in your system?

INFORMAL ANNOTATIONS.   Informal notes and annotations are a gold mine of information. They tell you about the actual usage of the artifact. Did the defined structure get used? Was it

Annotations reveal usage and communication

extended? Was the artifact used to carry additional information by writing notes on it? Why was it used? What made the artifact the convenient carrier for the message? Can you put other channels in place to make this unnecessary? Can you see how the artifact didn't match the work, and can you see how to make your system fit the work better?

PRESENTATION.   Content and structure are revealed in the artifact's presentation. Look at formatting, the layout of parts on the

Presentation directs the eye and reveals importance

page, and the use of white space. How does the artifact attract attention to some parts of the content and downplay others? The presentation supports the intent of the work if well designed and gets in the way if not. If the artifact is redesigned or put online, how should your system present it for easy interpretation in the same kind of way?

INQUIRING INTO AN ARTIFACT

There are two levels of inquiry into artifacts. The first is to see how an artifact supports the customer's intent. The presentation, content, and

Walk through artifacts with the customer to see what they mean

structure are all clues to what matters in the work. So notes scribbled on a materials-tracking card telling the technician how to handle the material show that direct communication between user and handler is important. Any system that interrupted the communication (such as an automated tracking system) would cause problems in the work. To be successful, such a system would have to provide another way to accomplish the same intent. At this level of inquiry, we look at structure and usage to derive intent, to show why the artifact matters and what any automated system needs to account for. (See Muller et al. [1995] for an example of such an inquiry.)

If you think that the artifact might be supported or automated, then a detailed inquiry into the interaction with the artifact provides clues in how to structure the system. Things that cluster in the artifact are conceptual groups that should be kept together. The natural pattern of inter-action with the artifact is a good guide to appropriate interaction with the system. So the notes on the

Bring back copies of used artifacts

materials-tracking card indicate that, if we want to automate materials tracking, we have to support informal communication between user and handler. This communication may happen at any time after the materials are received, so a single note that can only be entered when the materials are received won't do. Since the handwritten note is its own record, and having the record matters, the automated system needs to keep instructions related to the material available over time.

Artifacts are the concrete trail left by doing work. They capture multiple stories of how work happened, making it possible to walk through a retrospective account of those events. As a physical object, an artifact makes the way customers think about their work tangible, so you can see and inquire into it. But artifacts do not speak on their own; collect examples that have been used and interpret them with the customer during the interview to reveal their meaning.

THE CULTURAL MODEL

Work takes place in a culture, which defines expectations, desires, policies, values, and the whole approach people take to their work:

> A vendor creates a product that helps development teams control their development process. The product is well designed and well made, but fails in its target market of UNIX shops. UNIX shops pride themselves in getting code out without needing a formal process.

> Another vendor makes an instrument so straightforward that unskilled operators can run it with ease. Their customer base won't buy it because they consider themselves highly skilled professionals who can run complicated systems.

> Another company gives their scientists software that sim-plifies the reporting of experimental lab results. The scientists

reject the system because they consider proper reporting of results to be part of the job of a scientist and don't want it simplified.

In each of these cases, there was nothing wrong with the system delivered. It was designed and built well and solved a real problem. There was no technical roadblock to its use at all. In each case, what prevented the system's success was the culture of its proposed users. If a system conflicts with its customers' self-image, or doesn't account for the constraints they are under, or undercuts the values important to them, it will not succeed.

Successful systems fit with their customers' culture

The *cultural context* is to us like water to a fish—pervasive and inescapable, yet invisible and intangible. Cultural context is the mindset that people operate within and that plays a part in everything they do. Issues of cultural context are hard to see because they are not concrete and they are not technical. They are generally not represented in an artifact, written on a wall, or observable in a single action. Instead they are revealed in the language people use to talk about their own job or their relationships with other groups. They are implied by recurring patterns of behavior, nonverbal communications, and attitudes. They are suggested by how people decorate and the posters they put on their walls.

Culture is as invisible as water to a fish

The cultural context includes the formal and informal policy of an organization, the business climate created by competitors and by the nature of the business, government requirements, the decor of the site, the self-image of the people doing the work, and the feelings and fears created by the people or groups in the organization. Culture influences work by altering the choices people make. Because they don't want to have to deal with a certain group, or because they consider themselves professionals, or because they are worried about what their competitors are doing, people change the way they do their work. Design teams that understand these constraints can build their systems to account for them.

The cultural model makes influences concrete

CULTURAL MODEL DISTINCTIONS

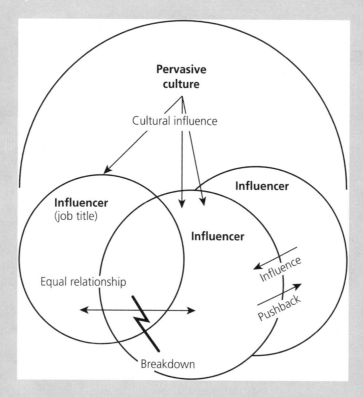

Influencers who affect or constrain work, shown as bubbles. These may be individuals or formal groups in the organization. They may be a collection of people who are not a formal group but are thought of together ("management"). They may be external influencers such as customers (and possibly multiple customer organizations), government regulatory bodies, standards groups, or competitors. They may represent the overall culture created by the organization or shared by the people doing the work.

The *extent* of the effect on the work shown by the amount the bubbles overlap. It suggests whether essentially everything about the work is affected by this influence or whether the influence is more partial. So the Food and Drug Administration influences the work of food and drug companies through its reporting and testing requirements, but this influence does not constrain everything about developing the food or drug product. On the other hand, everything an assembly line worker does is affected by the requirements of the assembly process.

Influence on the work. Arrows represent the direction of influence (who is primarily affecting whom) and how pervasive it is (whether this is an influence of one individual or ▷

group on another or whether it is more pervasive across an organization). We also represent pushback; in real situations it is rare that influence is all in one direction.

Breakdowns or problems interfering in the work, represented as a red lightning bolt (black in this book). Because all influences restrict work in some way, we only show breakdowns on the cultural model when they are especially harmful.

The following kinds of influence tend to be relevant to design:

Standards and **policy** that define and constrain how work is done or what can be used or bought, or the lack of such standards as a policy. So many companies define a standard PC configuration that they will support: "Use this configuration or you're on your own." Other companies live with standard procedures defined by themselves or imposed on them by the government or by customers: "Prove your process is compliant or we'll use another vendor."

Power, both formal in the organizational structure and informal through people's networks, expertise, and history. Power shows up in who has the right to decide who will do what in their work and the extent of autonomy a person can have. So one boss sets up his secretary's computer environment, limiting her ability to recover when anything breaks down: "I'll fix your machine in the way *I* think is important." In another organization, reimbursement for expenses is controlled by administration, which enforces the requirements for filling out paperwork and can choose to allow exceptions: "Jump through my hoops and I'll let you have your money."

The **values** of a company or team: what they stand for that produces a set of expectations about how people will interact and work. So one organization has the expectation that a project will be completed the same way as it was the last time, resulting in a feeling that innovation is unwelcome: "If it's a different plan, be prepared to justify it."

A group's own sense of **identity,** the way in which what they do is affected by how they think of themselves. So one UNIX shop held that they did not need to do formal up-front analysis and design because "we don't do process."

People's **emotions** about what they do, including fear about being laid off or getting in trouble for raising issues, or people's pride in what they do. So knowing that "email can be read by anyone, including management" led people in one organization to discontinue its use.

The idiosyncratic **style, values,** and **preferences** of an individual or team, creating a work environment that circumscribes others. So one boss will not use the computer, forcing his secretary to handle all his email communication: "Use the computer for me because I won't." Or a team can't work past 4:30 because everyone has outside activities that pull them away: "We are committed to home activities; schedule around them." ❏

RECOGNIZING THE INFLUENCE OF CULTURE

Culture is invisible, but can be deduced from things you see and hear.

TONE. When you walk in the door, what is the tone of the place? Industrial and sterile? Carefully designed and trendy? Formal and elegant? Messy and haphazard? When the customers design their workplace for elegance, they are unlikely to accept a system that looks haphazard. When they spend little time designing their workplace, just the bare minimum so that they can work, they are unlikely to accept a system that is overdesigned, which looks like time and money was wasted on elegance.

> *A valuable system helps people be who they want to be*

POLICIES. What are the policies people follow, and how are they recorded? Are there policy manuals, and are they used? Do people wanting guidance on doing their work routinely check them? Or is the operational policy—the policy that affects work on a day-to-day basis—really passed by word of mouth? If so, how much is based on real directives, and how much is folklore? Is policy generated by fear of a regulatory agency, of another organization, or of a manager? You can hear policy in the words people use: "We won't buy anything but UL-rated power supplies. They had a non-UL supply catch fire over in building 10 a while back." If UL rating matters, you can highlight UL-rated equipment in the catalog you develop. "Better get these procedures documented properly. One of our competitors was cited for out-of-date documentation, and their stock dropped three points." If written records are an important part of the work, you can implement systems that maintain them. The policies that people care about point to problems you can solve.

> *A valuable system makes conforming to policy easy*

ORGANIZATIONAL INFLUENCE. Are there organizations, individuals, or job functions that keep showing up, either as troublesome or helpful? What are the organizations or job functions that always seem to get in the way? Who are the people who constantly show up as the ones who can solve the problem? Listen to how people talk about others: "Don't call maintenance about this. They'll take it away to check it out and you won't see it again for a week." Can you change the design of your system so that maintenance doesn't have to take the machine away to run diagnostics? "Oh, I can't give this report to Mike looking like this. He runs this whole place—I'll put it in my word processor and make it look really good." If the reports that your product creates are given to management, you can make them high-quality presentations.

A valuable system reduces friction and irritation in the workplace

MAKING CULTURE TANGIBLE

The cultural model (Figures 6.5 and 6.6) provides a tangible representation for these intangible forces. In a cultural model we represent *influencers* (people, organizations, and groups) in the customer's culture, showing how they influence each other. Influencers are shown as large bubbles. Because culture is felt as a weight or pressure influencing actions, the bubbles sit on one another, showing how one organization forces another to take or not take actions. We represent *influences* as arrows piercing the bubbles and label the arrows to represent the type of influence. Influences are labeled with language representing the experience of the people doing the work, so the influence from an internal help organization might read, "We are unreliable and will wipe your hard drive on a whim." No one in that help organization would ever actually *say* those words, of course, but the people who use their services operate as though they were saying exactly that. Using direct language on the model makes the culture it represents stand out. Where an influence stands out as being particularly harmful and counterproductive, we mark it with a lightning bolt, our universal symbol for problems or breakdowns.

The cultural model speaks the words people think but don't say

Cultural models do not map to organization charts. They show how power is experienced by people, rather than the formal power of the organization. So it's unusual to see the whole management chain represented on a cultural model. Individual managers will appear when they are part of the work, as when a manager makes his secretary interact with the computer for him. There's often a bubble to represent the organization's culture, with

An organization's culture is not reflected in its organization chart

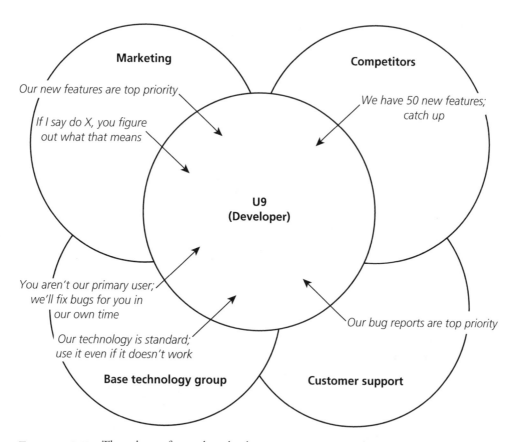

FIGURE 6.5 The culture of a product development organization. This is a typical cultural model in a product development organization. In the center we see the interviewee, U9. Since cultural models are initially built as the result of an interview with one person, they represent the point of view of that one person. U9 is in the development organization, and the model shows two major constraints on them. The marketing organization constrains them through ill-specified product requirements. Competitors constrain them by creating a climate in which keeping up with the number of features is the primary goal. The basic appearance of this model—the interviewee surrounded by influencers—is very typical.

influences like "We are totally customer-focused" or "Spending money is not a problem." In adversarial situations, "management" may appear to represent how "they" do things to "us"—"We think you salesmen are children who need to be watched every moment" might be an example. Individual managers appear as managers only when they are charismatic figures who define the organization's culture. In this case,

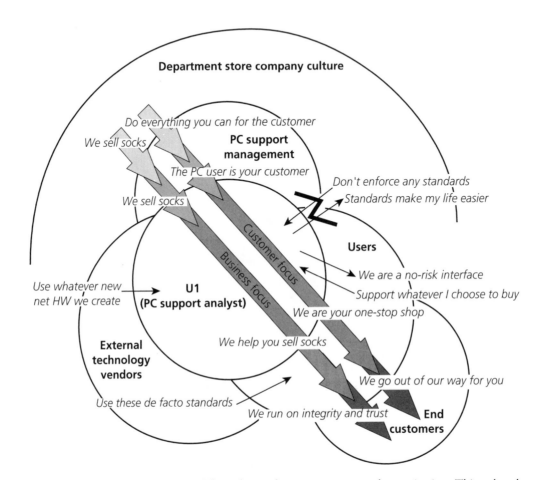

FIGURE 6.6   The culture of a customer-centered organization. This cultural model is typical when there is a definite corporate culture to account for. This cultural model represents a department store that has made customer satisfaction its first priority. Unlike many places that espouse that goal, this company has really done it—so much so that people throughout the organization are conditioned to think who their customer is and how to give them the best service. Paired with this focus on the customer is an equally pervasive understanding of the business—so much so that "We sell socks" is a watchword within the company. We show the pervasive company culture as an umbrella over everything, with individual influences going back and forth between the bubbles. The lightning bolt indicates a place where two values conflict: being customer-centered leads the store to avoid setting standards for computer configurations, but such standards would make the PC support analyst's life easier.

their power is experienced as direct and personal. McDonald's franchise owners used to tell about how Ray Kroc, then CEO of McDonald's and a fanatic about cleanliness, canceled a franchise because he found one fly in its kitchen (Boas and Chain 1977). Everyone lived in fear that he would show up in their kitchen next. Ray Kroc would appear on a cultural model.

THE PHYSICAL MODEL

Work happens in a physical environment that either supports and enables the work or gets in the way:

> One company creates a page design product in which the look on-screen doesn't quite match that of paper. They think it is close enough because they expect their users will print draft versions and use the paper output for the final draft. They don't know that most of their users don't have printers by their desks, or even close by. So users spend time running back and forth to the printer and copying good drawing elements from one document to the next.

> Another company gives their sales force portable computers to do presentations. They don't know that salespeople are only given a few minutes at a site. The salespeople don't have time to bring up a computer, and they depend on leaving materials behind with their customers. The portable computer doesn't fit either need.

> A utility company gives their electricians documentation in a three-ring binder. Only later do they discover the electricians are trying to balance this awkward binder on a cherry picker in all types of weather. They redesign the documentation as a small, spiral-bound flip book with laminated pages and a clip so it can be hung from a belt.

Any product or system must live with the constraints of the physical environment as it exists. If it ignores those constraints, it creates problems for its users. In each of the above examples, a system created problems for its users because it assumed things about the workplace that were not true. Studying the users' workplace ensures that the system accounts for the physical environment.

The physical model reveals design constraints

The physical environment constrains what people can do, but within those constraints people do have some control over their envi-

Model both site and workplace

ronment. Studying the workplace offers important clues to the way people structure and think about work. People restructure their workplace to support doing work in the way they prefer, to the extent they can. Because they structure their environment to be convenient, the structures they create mirror their thought. The structures show what people group together into conceptual units and coherent tasks. An office worker sets up places in her office to keep her work organized. The chair receives urgent messages from coworkers; the space next to the computer is kept clear so that when she starts a task, she has a place to lay it out; the in-box is the "guilt pile"—things she feels that she ought to deal with, when she has time. The places she creates mirror the way she thinks about her work: urgent, current, guilt pile. They make work distinctions concrete. A system that makes these distinctions real will fit with the work easily. The workplace shows us issues in doing work; from the elaborate system of piles that people create, we can deduce that tracking multiple little tasks is a problem, and people might benefit from better ways to track them.

The physical environment is the world people live in: the rooms, cars, buildings, and highways they move about and work in; how

People reorganize their environment to reflect the work they do

each of these spaces is laid out so that it supports work; and how they use these spaces in the process of working. It includes how they move about, how the space supports or hinders communication, and the location of the tools people use (hardware, software, networks, machines) to do work. The physical environment affects how work is done at every scale: the multiple sites and their relationships to each other, the structure of a single site, and an individual's workplace. The work site may be structured as an open "bull pen" with supervisors' offices around the outside. It may consist of many individual cubicles dividing up a large room. A person's workplace may be an entire building or buildings, if they are maintaining equipment. It may be a car or airplane if they work on the road. Within a work site there are places to do work, which may be offices, labs, workbenches, or workstations. Workstations may be dedicated to one person or shared.

PHYSICAL MODEL DISTINCTIONS

The *places* in which work occurs: rooms, workstations, offices, and coffee stations. The model shows whether the space is small or large, a primary or secondary workplace, private or open, cluttered, or empty space available for changing work activities.

The physical *structures* that limit and define the space: sites, walls, basements, desks, file cabinets, and other large objects.

The *usage* and *movement* within the space—how people move about in it and move things about in it in the course of accomplishing their work.

The *hardware, software, communication lines,* and other *tools* (calculator, Rolodex, in-basket, measuring tools, Post-its, printer, fax) that are present in the space and support the work or seem related. We show network connections, not to model the network itself, but to emphasize who is connected to whom and therefore what communication among people we can automate.

The *artifacts* that people create, modify, and pass around in support of the work—folders, spreadsheets, to-do lists, bills, ID cards, approvals, piles of stuff. The physical model shows the artifact and its location, not the detailed structure and usage of the artifact.

The *layout* of the tools, artifacts, movable furniture, and walls in relationship to each other to support specific work strategies.

Breakdowns or problems showing how the physical environment interferes in the work, represented as a red lightning bolt (black in this book). ❑

SEEING THE IMPACT OF THE PHYSICAL ENVIRONMENT

The physical environment is easy to see—it's all right there. It's harder to tell what matters. What will affect the design problem, and what will not? Here are some things to look for.

ORGANIZATION OF SPACE.   Are there stations, and how do they relate to the work? Are stations grouped to follow the flow of work to make work efficient, or are similar stations placed together to make management efficient? Are the people who made the decision conscious of the trade-off? This will indicate what they care most about and therefore what the most important problems for you to solve are.

Planned space reflects organizational assumptions

DIVISION OF SPACE.   Where are the walls, and how do they break up the work? Do they follow the structure of the work, or do they interfere with it? If they interfere, how do people overcome them? Do they run back and forth a lot? Do they shout? (During one inter-

Look at how people ignore walls or create walls that aren't there

view, the user directed a question at the wall, and the wall answered. It was so thin he could carry on a conversation with his colleague on the other side.) Every communication breakdown creates an opportunity for you to ameliorate it: Who needs to communicate? How and when? Can you obviate the need by providing information where it's required, or can you make it easier?

GROUPING OF PEOPLE.   How are people grouped into the spaces? By function or by project? Does each person have their own

Find barriers to community and communication

separate office area, or do they mix and share spaces? Often specialists sit with other specialists, not with the project they are assigned to. Creating a sense of belonging to the project team becomes difficult. Conversely, developers who are seated with their internal clients tend to identify with them. They

tend to adopt their perspective against that of the development organization. What can you do to make the whole interrelated set of information systems apparent to all developers, so they are continually reminded of the effect their short-term fixes will have on the whole?

ORGANIZATION OF WORKPLACES.   How are the individual stations, offices, or work areas organized? How do they support the

Placement of objects and piles makes the work efficient

work? What is kept out (immediately visible), ready to hand (accessible without moving), and available (in a drawer or across the office)? What does this say about what's most important to the work? Things kept together tend to be used together. What does this say about the structure of a task? Can you see what makes

up a whole task in what is kept together for easy access? Can you design your system so that the most important function is available where needed and so that whole tasks are coherent in the system?

MOVEMENT.   When do people move? Why do they leave one place and go to another? What triggers them to do so? Is this intrinsic to the work, as when a maintenance person goes to look at a machine? Does it provide an opportunity for informal discussion and problem solving? Do the customers see it as a problem, or are they like system support people, who generally enjoy getting out of their offices? Understanding why the movement happens will help you decide whether it makes more sense to support it better or eliminate it.

Movement reveals human preference and work needs

SHOWING WHAT MATTERS IN THE PHYSICAL ENVIRONMENT

A physical model (Figures 6.7 and 6.8) is a drawing of those aspects of the workplace that are related to the project focus. The physical model shows how the physical environment affects the work. It is annotated to show how the space is used and to show strategies, intents, and cultural values that are revealed by the way space is used. A good physical model evokes the experience of the workplace in the same way as a caricature. Aspects of the environment are only represented if they matter to the work; for

The physical model is a caricature of the workplace, not a floor plan

example, "basement" might mean "far away, uncomfortable, and inconvenient to get to." If the worker must nonetheless go there or worry about what happens there, we represent it in the model. Wherever the physical environment interferes with the customer's work—things are too far away, or too cramped, or the right tools aren't where they are needed—we show it with a lightning bolt.

The physical model shows how people respond to the environment by restructuring it. Do people accept the workplace as it is, or do they work around it? If the environment consists of doorless cubicles, do they put things in front of the door to gain a measure of privacy? How else does the work as it is experienced mismatch work as the environment wants it to be? What do people do about it?

A physical model is not a floor plan for the work site. Nor is it an inventory of the computer room. Either a floor plan or an inventory can be collected easily, without resorting to contextual techniques. A physical model does not show extraneous detail unrelated to the project focus—potted plants, kids' toys, and family pictures are usually not relevant and can be omitted when you're designing a system. If you were designing the work environment itself, you might have to take them into account.

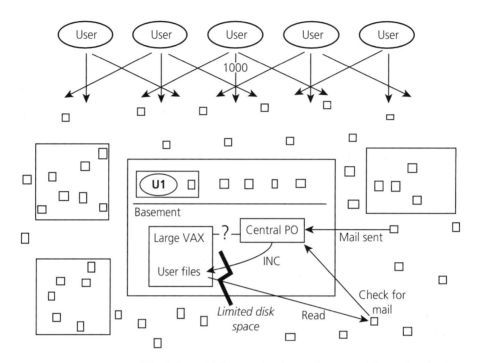

FIGURE 6.7 Physical model for a university environment. This university has set up its workstations so that anybody can use any workstation. The small boxes represent the workstations—over 1000 distributed all around the campus. To indicate their independent nature, we show them as standing alone and show the users separated from them, to indicate any user can access any workstation. "U1" means "user 1" and indicates the office of the user we talked to in a central building, with the central VAX machines in its basement. All user files are stored on the VAX. The "central PO" is a piece of software that routes mail between users. We have shown the routing of one message because we were designing a communications product. This work model shows the value of choosing a representation that is expressive of the data—in this case, that there are many workstations spread out over the campus according to no particular plan.

THE FIVE FACES OF WORK

Each of the above work models presents a different perspective on the work. These perspectives interlock: a person plays roles; a role has responsibilities, undertakes tasks, and exchanges artifacts with other people to discharge these responsibilities. The sequence models show how these tasks are accomplished in detail and how artifacts are used in accomplishing them. The responsibilities and manner of accomplishing

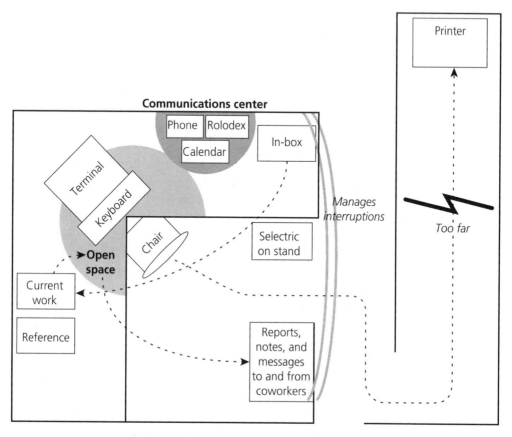

FIGURE 6.8 Physical model for an office. This physical model shows the work-place of one user. The model represents a cubicle and shows how she has structured her environment to help her get work done. The placement of her IBM Selectric in the doorway, the in-box next to the door, and the shelf used as a drop-off place all suggest a strategy to minimize interruptions caused by working in an open cubicle. The phone, Rolodex, and calendar are all grouped together, suggesting that these tools work together to support communicating and coordinating with others. And the open space around her workstation suggests an intent to keep this area clear so she can lay out her next task. The team has annotated the model to reveal these distinctions and to show breakdowns, such as the printer being too far.

them are driven by organizational context and culture as shown on the cultural model. The work represented by the sequences is done within the work environment described by the physical model. Stepping back and looking at the models together reveals all the different aspects of work and how they relate to each other. It reveals how the whole work of one person hangs together.

Seeing how customers work drives design. A design team needs to know what they should make—what work might be supported, what the big problems are, what the customers care about. They need to know what they must account for in their design: the roles and how they interact, physical and cultural influences and constraints. They need to know how to structure their design: the strategies people use to get their work done, the way they break up and think about their work conceptually. By organizing and presenting customer work clearly, work models make it possible to answer these design questions. They provide an integrated view of the customer's work practice and also show the details of work structure that guide the fine points of design.

Work models show designers what to account for

The individual work models as described above represent the work of each customer that a team interviewed independently. In Part 3, we'll see how to consolidate models so that instead of showing each customer independently, they show the common structure and pattern of work across all the customers a system needs to support: a whole market, a department, or multiple departments. With consolidated models the design team has a single statement of the work they need to address, rather than trying to support each individual separately. We do this by first observing, inquiring into, and representing the work of specific individuals. Then we consolidate the models of each type. We bring all individual flow models together into one consolidated flow model to reveal the common roles and their interaction. We consolidate all the cultural models, all the physical models of whole sites, and all the physical models of individual workplaces. We consolidate all the sequences representing similar tasks and all the artifacts achieving the same intent.

What you see in the work determines what you will think to build

These consolidated models make the underlying patterns of work across customers explicit. At the same time, they capture the variation between customers by showing any unique structure or details put into practice by each customer site. The design team can then decide what aspects of work they want to support. They can take a good idea for approaching the work implemented by one customer site and build it into the system to make it available to all. They can streamline the work, removing extra steps and taking advantage of technological possibilities. From this redesigned work practice, they can design a system that supports the new work practice and drives the design of the user interface and system implementation. The rest of this book discusses these steps.

The Interpretation   7
Session

"I just talked to a potential customer at COMDEX, and he said he wanted that feature we talked about—"

"But I just went along on a service call and that guy hated it. We should do this other thing—"

"No, I talked to one of our really big clients and they said—"

These are the voices of people who have talked to their customers. Each one learned something valid from one customer. Now they are faced with the difficulty of communicating what they learned, reconciling the different messages from different people, and coming to agreement on what the customers really need. They have feedback (of a sort) from customers; they do not have a shared understanding of what it means or what they should do about it.

It's not enough for the members of a design team to understand the customers they visited and talked to individually. If a team is to agree on what to deliver, all members of the team need to understand every customer as though they had been there. They need to build an understanding of all their customers and how they work that is shared by the whole team. A team develops this understanding through conversation and mutual inquiry into the

Interpretation sessions let every team member experience all interviews

meaning of the facts about their customers' work. In this way, the different members of the design team can learn each other's perspective, the unique focus each person brings to the problem. They can probe each other's understanding, learning from and teaching each other what to see. When one thinks another is wrong, they can look at concrete instances to see how their different perspectives reveal different issues in customer data.

BUILDING A SHARED UNDERSTANDING

We allow for this mutual discovery through the *interpretation session*. In an interpretation session, an interviewer walks through a single interview for the benefit of the team. The rest of the team listens, asks questions, draws work models, and records issues, interpretations, and design ideas based on this interview. In their discussions of what to model and what to record, the team wrestles with the data and what it means, learns how each team member views the data, and develops a shared understanding of that customer. The interpretation session is an efficient way to achieve several desirable benefits:

Better data: Because everyone asks questions of the interviewer, the interviewer remembers more than he would on his own. The questioning prompts him to recall details he didn't know he remembered.

Written record of customer insights: The interpretation session records the conversation while it occurs, in the appropriate form to drive design. By the end of the interpretation session, the work of this customer has been characterized in work models, and the team's insights, design ideas, and questions have been captured online. No one needs to take additional time to write up or analyze this customer interview. People who weren't present can read the models and the notes to catch up on what was learned.

Effective cross-functional cooperation: The interpretation session is a forum in which diverse job functions can cooperate, whether they be customers, marketing, engineering, documentation, UI, test, or any other group relevant to delivering the system. The interpretation session provides a clear task and a clear set of roles for everyone in the meeting to perform. It focuses the meeting not on the participants and their differences but on the data and on extracting meaning from the data. Instead of arguing with each other, participants argue over whether a model accurately reflects the customer's work. Instead of arguing about people's opinions, the only topic for discussion is whether an interpretation can be justified based on the data. This makes a safe environment for a new team to learn to work together. Each person and each job function makes a contribution to understanding the customer. Learning to recognize and value the unique contribution of each person as an individual and each group in the organization happens almost by accident.

Multiple perspectives on the problem: Each team member brings their own focus to the problem, which is derived from their personal history, their current job function, and their understanding of the project focus. A cross-functional design team will always see more in an interview than any one person would alone. For this reason, the interviewer does not filter the information at all; something she dismissed as irrelevant will be picked up by someone else to reveal an insight of great importance. Any kind of predigested presentation of the interview—a report or presentation, for example—would limit the information that would be extracted from an interview to the point of view of one person.

Development of a shared perspective: The open discussion between team members enables them to learn and take on each other's perspective. By hearing everyone's questions and insights on the data, every team member expands their own focus to include the concerns of others. The questions that people raise suggest new lines of inquiry and new directions to take the inquiry. The team moves toward a common focus on the problem, which accounts for the aspects of work that matter for the problem and all the particular issues of the team. Team members learn the new focus by participating in the session; there is no need for an elaborate process to redefine the focus.

True involvement in the data: It is hard to process data—to think through what it means and might imply for design—when it is just presented. A report or a talk delivers information to a passive reader or listener. It's easy for attention to wander; even dedicated listeners must do something to make the information their own, whether by taking notes, writing ideas, or asking questions. The interpretation session reveals the data interactively, through questioning and discussion. Team members immediately represent it in work models, so they must internalize it to write the models, and everyone else must internalize it to check them. And since everyone has a job, it's hard for attention to wander.

Better use of time: Without an interpretation session, all the team members would still have to talk to the interviewer to ask questions about the interview and understand the implications. They would still have to talk to each other to learn what others on the team saw in the data. The insights into the work would still have to be written down. Without the interpretation session, all this would happen in informal, one-on-one discussions in hallways and offices. With the interpretation session, it can happen once, with the whole team together.

Interpretation sessions enable sharing that has to happen anyway

THE STRUCTURE OF AN INTERPRETATION SESSION

Doing creative work in ongoing, face-to-face sessions as a team is hard. As we've discussed, the industry does not generally provide good models for face-to-face cooperation on the same project; it's easier and more common to split projects up into parts small enough for individuals to do independently. But there's no way to leverage multiple perspectives if everyone works independently. It's hard to get the same sense of common direction. And there's no good way to build on different people's skills; everyone has to understand the work practice, the technology, the market, the user interface, and all the other influencers on system design in order to produce their part. Doing the design together provides multiple perspectives and leverages people's different skills, but then the team really has to learn to work together. The interpretation session provides an easy way for a team to get started.

TEAM MAKEUP

It's best for diverse job functions to share points of view and learn to work together during an interpretation session. For the widest amount of buy-in and cross-fertilization, the first sessions often include everyone on the design team. However, when the team is large, a single meeting is hard to manage just because there are so many people trying to be heard. (Never go above 12 under any circumstances.) After the initial sessions, it's more effective for large teams to interpret interviews in subteams of four to six

Plan meetings and participants to make the process work

people and share the results with the larger team afterwards. Each subteam should itself contain a mix of job functions, so that diverse perspectives are brought to bear on every interview. Four people on a subteam is comfortable. If necessary, on small projects where there simply aren't very many people involved, you can do subteams of two. Everyone on the subteam should think that this is their job; if they think they are on the team to help someone else out, it will not seem like real work to them. At least half of a team should have a design background (e.g., engineering, UI design). And it is important that the subteams be formed of different people each time, so that people are continually challenged with new points of view, so that small cliques do not form within the team, and so that the entire team stays a cohesive unit. (See Chapter 6 for more on forming a team.)

ROLES

Any effective meeting needs clear roles to drive it forward. The interpretation session is supported by defined roles, which give the meeting structure so everyone knows what to do and what is appropriate. The roles also give everyone in the meeting something concrete to do, which forces everyone to interact with and process the data. Everyone should have a defined role, and it's okay for people to have more than one role.

> *Give everyone a job to keep them involved*

THE INTERVIEWER.   The *interviewer* is the one who interviewed the customer. They are the team's informant, describing everything just as it happened, in the order that it happened. Just as we try to keep customers from giving summary information, the interviewer does not summarize. Just as interviewers extract retrospective accounts from customers, the team backs the interviewer up every time they think she skipped a step or missed a detail. In many ways, it's as though the team interviews the interviewer, to find out what she learned in her interaction with the customer. The interviewer draws the physical model, since it tends to be easiest for the one who was there to draw it. Being the interviewer takes patience because the interviewer is interrupted at every moment by team members sharing insights and demanding clarification.

> *Do a retrospective account with the interviewer*

WORK MODELERS.   *Work modelers* draw work models on flip charts as they hear them. It works well to have two work modelers—one person models flow and culture and another models sequences. Artifacts are put up, analyzed, and annotated as they come up in the interview. Modelers draw the work models at the same time as everything else is happening. They do not stop the meeting to get agreement at each point; it's up to the rest of the team to raise an issue if they think the modeler got it wrong. Work modelers have to be comfortable putting up one or two elements of a model as they hear them without waiting for the whole story to be complete. They can't get the whole story, then stop the meeting and repeat it so they can draw the model. They have to draw it as it comes out. Work modelers do ask questions driven by their models. If the flow modeler can't show where a communication flows to because the interviewer never said, he won't be able to draw the model and will ask.

Write while you listen— don't slow down the meeting to capture data

The work models keep the team from filtering too early—from deciding that aspects of work aren't relevant before the design has been decided. The interviewer already filtered what they saw based on their focus. Work models capture in coherent form everything the interviewer discovered. The team can decide how much to use later. It's faster to represent everything than to stop and ask whether each point is relevant. Drawing the models during the meeting not only keeps everyone involved, it ensures quality. The entire group watches and checks them as they are drawn. If they had been drawn by one person ahead of time, that person would miss more, reviewers of the models would not catch everything, and they would spend as much time reviewing the models independently as the whole group spends together. Some teams have drawn models in advance of the meeting; those models have been the least detailed of any we have dealt with.

The work models are kept true to the data that the interviewer saw. Because it is so easy for people to create abstractions that are not well grounded in real events, we do not record the customer's general statements of "how we do things" on the models. Only if the interviewer actually saw it, or found out about it through a retrospective account of a specific event, does the data go on the model. Sometimes a customer is on the design team,

Work models keep the team true to what really happened

```
U4 18   Copies of sample cards kept in shoeboxes; has to keep
        them two years (regulation)
U4 19   Home office lost sample cards she had sent in; she had
        to make photocopies of her copies and send them again
U4 20   Keeps last 6 months of sample cards in her home
        office; then puts them in shoebox and moves them to
        garage
U4 21   Q: Is there any defined procedure for storing and
        disposing of sample cards?
U4 22   Has a video screen to do presentations that she has
        never used; was given it automatically
U4 23   Has to rent a slide projector; wasn't given that
U4 24   DI: give sales reps a budget they can use to buy the
        things they really need
U4 25   Insight: Home office thinks they know the equipment
        the sales reps need, but it doesn't match their needs
```

FIGURE 7.1   Extract from the online notes typed during an interpretation meeting. Each note is preceded by the user code and a sequence number. This section of the notes shows the development of an idea from a problem identified in the work to a design idea (DI) and an insight about the work situation. These notes are displayed during the meeting so all can see and correct them. They are a permanent record of the design conversation, capturing the discussion, and used to build the affinity diagram later.

and they may be insistent on what the formal process is. In this case, we do record the formal process but in green, a color we use to mean that this is the formal policy, or that we heard about this part of the work but didn't actually see it.

THE RECORDER.   The *recorder* keeps notes of the meeting online, displayed so everyone can see them using a monitor or LCD projection panel. Every key observation, insight, influence from the cultural model, question, design idea, and breakdown in the work is captured as a separate note (Figure 7.1). These notes provide a sequential record of the conversation and are used later to build the affinity. We usually keep the notes in a word processing document, one line per note, preceded by a sequence number and the user code. More elaborate tools are possible,

Write the thoughts of the meeting before they are expressed

```
U4:      Field sales rep; works near home office; been with
sales for three years; in home office doing market research
before that. Very large territory.
```

FIGURE 7.2   Customer profile.

but this simple approach works well. This is the only technology we use in the room in this session. Except for breakdowns and influences, elements of work captured by the work models—steps of a sequence, communication between people, a description of the physical environment—do *not* go into the notes. Demographic information (the customer's age, length of time on the job, skill level) does not go into the notes either, because these are not aspects of work practice. Demographics goes in a separate profile for that customer (Figure 7.2).

The recorder will often have to rephrase an idea that has only been expressed indirectly to capture it in clear, succinct language. A team will get stuck at a particular point in the interview, talking around it. A good recorder states clearly what the insight or issue is and moves the meeting on. Anyone else who hears what the underlying issue is can do the same: they state the issue; someone says, "Capture that!"; the recorder writes it; and the meeting moves on.

PARTICIPANTS.   The rest of the team are *participants*. They listen to the story of the interview, ask questions to understand, and develop their own insight into the work. They propose interpretations for the team, make observations, and suggest design ideas. The design ideas are not for discussion, but so that they can be captured in the context of the data they respond to. Recording them

Capture design ideas to avoid discussing them now

unloads the participant's mind so it can get back to thinking about the customer's work. This is a generally useful technique for keeping a meeting moving forward: any time someone gets stuck on a point, write it down in a form that won't be forgotten and will be used at the appropriate point in the process. Then the person can go on. Participants watch the models to make sure they are complete and watch the online notes to make sure they agree with the way they are written.

THE MODERATOR.   The *moderator* is the stage manager for the whole meeting. Any meeting has a *mainline conversation*—the discussion that is the primary purpose of the meeting. The job of the moderator is to keep the meeting on this conversation. In the interpretation session, the mainline conversation is: What happened on this interview and what do we need to capture from it? The moderator keeps the pace of the meeting brisk. The moderator keeps track of where the interviewer is in her story and reorients her when she has been interrupted and lost her place. The

No meeting works without someone taking the role of moderator

moderator ensures that all the data from the interview is recorded in an online note or in a work model. The moderator makes sure everyone is involved and participating by encouraging the quiet people who don't know how to be heard to jump in, toning down the people who dominate the conversation, and ensuring that people can share insights and design ideas without being ridiculed.

Keep everyone busy and on topic

The moderator has to stand outside the process enough so that they can see what is going on. Moderators who get too involved have to hand moderation over to someone else.

THE RAT HOLE WATCHER. The *rat hole watcher* keeps the meeting on track. A rat hole is any distraction from the mainline conversation. A rat hole is an innocent-looking hole in the ground that, if you dive down it, branches and turns until you are totally lost in the dark. In a meeting, a rat hole entices the entire meeting into a long discussion that is not relevant to the purpose of the meeting. In the interpretation session, when all the engineers get caught up in talking about whether a

Neutralize people problems by making them legitimate topics of conversation

design idea is technically feasible, they are in a rat hole. Later, this will be the mainline conversation, but not now. Evaluation of any idea, sharing your own personal experience with a product, or introducing data from another user ("My guy did that too!") are all rat holes. It is the responsibility of the rat hole watcher to call "Rat hole!" and get the meeting back on track.

In practice, everyone acts as a rat hole watcher. Identifying the role isn't so much to give it to one person, but to give the concept to the whole team. By naming the role, the team accepts that rat holes exist and waste time. Without realizing it, each person on the team has given everyone else permission to point out when he or she is off topic. Then, instead of getting defensive and angry when someone calls "Rat hole," everyone laughs sheepishly and gets back to the subject of the meeting.

RUNNING THE SESSION

Interpretation sessions fit into an ongoing cycle of interviewing and interpretation. The team interviews a few people representing a cross section of customers. Then there are choices for how the interviewer prepares for the interpretation session: If the session will happen the same day as the interview, they run the meeting from their handwritten notes. If it will happen the next day, they annotate their notes from the audiotape of their interview. If they delay longer than 48 hours, they transcribe their notes from the tape. This trades amount of detail off against the time it takes to prepare. If the interpretation meeting is held close enough to the interview, the interviewer can remember enough that the extra time for transcription isn't worth it.

Interpret interviews within 48 hours

Every user is assigned a user code. This code protects the user's anonymity and is used in the notes, on all models, and in all discussions. It's recorded in a list of interviewees that the team keeps private. The interviewer starts by giving a brief profile of the customer—their job function, the type of organization, and any demographic information. This profile is recorded in a separate file, so that later when someone asks, "Was U10 a secretary or a scientist?" the answer is easy to get. Then the interviewer draws a physical model of the customer's workplace and walks through the interview step-by-step. Everyone listens and probes to develop new insights into the work, calling "Capture that!" whenever there is a succinct insight, question, or design idea to capture.

Capture demographics in a profile

The tone of the meeting is active and involved, tending to slightly chaotic; the interviewer is trying to tell the story, everyone is asking him questions, two or three people are drawing models, the recorder is typing away, and the moderator is advising people all at the same time. The tone of the meeting is also open and trusting: everyone is expected to share insights and design ideas without stopping to think whether they are going to look stupid or whether the

Be nonjudgmental and keep a brisk pace

design idea is any good. No evaluation happens at this point; everyone is thinking out loud. The interpretation session usually lasts two hours, but the first in a new work domain will be longer, and later interviews on very focused tasks may be shorter.

At the end of the interview, everyone stops and looks back over what has been discovered. Then they list their top insights from this interview, capturing them online and also writing them on a flip chart to post on the wall. This reflection acts like the wrap-up phase of an interview, where the whole work practice can be brought together and implications for design drawn out. People see more, and see how work hangs together

Models, insights, and design ideas are the first deliverables

better, when they have a chance to reflect. The other reason for doing this is so that the team has an answer when a manager or skeptical peer walks in the room and says, "So what did you learn?" This is quite a serious concern. Many projects fail because they do not communicate what they were doing effectively to the rest of the organization. Making an insights list crystallizes what the team learned from each interview, helping them to talk about their new understanding. It starts the process of *communication out,* which is the topic of Chapter 10. And it makes it possible to take advantage of what was learned immediately, if related work is going on in parallel to the interpretation sessions.

THE SHARING SESSION

When a team has broken into subteams for the interpretation session, they need a sharing session to learn what the other subteams have done. A sharing session has its own roles: a *speaker* for the subteam presents the models for a particular user, starting with the physical model, then the flow, then the cultural model, then sequences and artifacts. The speaker walks through the flow by first

Sharing is active—it's not a presentation

describing the interviewee's role and responsibilities, then walking to each outlying bubble, describing the nature of their interaction with the interviewee. When presenting the sequences, rather than read every step, the speaker summarizes the key strategies or breakdowns that the sequences reveal. As the speaker presents each model, a *helper* stands behind and updates the model because we find that the spokesman always describes more than actually got written down. Everyone else on the large team listens, questions, and adds interpretations and insights. The *recorder* adds any new points to the online notes, and the *moderator* keeps the meeting moving and makes sure everyone is heard. When all the models for an interview are presented, the whole team reviews and adds to the insights. This brings the whole team back into one understanding and does a quality check on the models. It also allows people outside the team to learn what the team has done. A sharing session should take no more than half an hour.

There's a culture in our industry that says real work doesn't happen in meetings. "Another time-wasting meeting!" we say to each other. Yet it's through the stimulus of bouncing ideas off each other that people work most creatively. It's through the cross-check of several people looking at the same work that people work with the highest quality. The interpretation session is a working meeting that allows for creativity and quality. It brings together activities that might otherwise happen individually and sequentially and allows them to happen simultaneously in a team process. It's an efficient way of turning an interview into data useful to a project, recorded in a form that can be saved, communicated, and used to drive design. You'll know your interpretation sessions are working when people start clamoring to get in because they know that's where the creative design work starts.

> *Interpretation sessions foster cross-functional creativity and understanding*

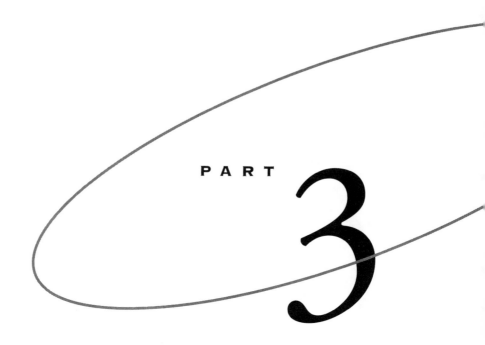

Seeing across Customers

Considolation

8

It's remarkable that systems can be built to support large numbers of people at all. People don't coordinate across industries to make sure they work in consistent ways. Even in a single department, people develop idiosyncratic ways of doing their job. But as we've discussed, any system imposes work practice on its users. It structures work and interacts with work in many complex ways. Since a system always structures the work of its users, and since they don't coordinate to work consistently, why should a single system work for them all? Yet we take it for granted that products and systems can be built and will be successful with all their disparate users.

Systems are not designed, for the most part, for individuals; they are designed for whole *customer populations*—intended users of a system in the market to which a product is sold, or in the departments of an organization. If a system can address the needs of a whole customer population, it's because aspects of work hold across all customers: common structure, strategy, and intent. A design responds to this common work structure while allowing for individual variation among customers.

The challenge is to design for a population, but meet the needs of individuals

But how can we discover these common aspects? How do we recognize them among all the surface differences in how people work? And how do we represent the common aspects of work so a whole design team can respond to them? As discussed in the last part, a design team needs to make the work of their individual customers concrete, tangible, and available for sharing with others. Without an external representation, the team has only their opinions and unarticulated knowledge of customers to base their decisions on. They have no concrete way to communicate what they know and to justify their designs. But the work models introduced in the last part represent individual customers. What models will show the work of a population?

Without the ability to *see* the work of the people they support, design teams are limited in what they can do. They are less able to act strategically to address the needs of their customers, taking short-term actions to advance long-term goals. Strategic action is as important to IT departments as to commercial product developers, but the motivations differ. We will discuss the issues for the two groups separately, then show how a single set of design tools meets the needs of both.

CREATING ONE REPRESENTATION OF A MARKET

A commercial vendor supports a market—the people who are interested, or who the vendor wishes were interested, in their product. The challenge for a vendor is to address the market with a coherent set of products, supporting the customer's primary work within the vendor's area of expertise.

Providing complete support for the work is important—any gap is an opportunity for a competitor to start selling to the vendor's customers and perhaps win their loyalty. (Or, for niche vendors of products that fill gaps in others' product lines, understanding the whole work practice is important to recognize and take advantage of the gaps.) A gap in a product line can happen because the vendor's line is incomplete, because they do not have the skills to address everything about the customers' work, or because they do not recognize how the work hangs together. For example, Microsoft dominates the office market largely because they recognized that providing a bundled suite of products would give them an advantage. Office work hangs together, so packaging a well-priced set of products that support the whole office is better than selling word processing, calculations, and presentations separately —even if the products in the package aren't particularly well integrated.

Incomplete support for the work creates an opportunity for competitors

Without a clear picture of the work of their customers, a vendor's grip on their market is limited. It is common, for example, to hear vendors of generic office tools say, "We have millions of users, and they all use our product differently. There is no one office user." Those who say this put themselves at a standstill. There's no way to go on to understand those aspects of work that are common. There's no way to find the common tasks that, if they were better supported, would give a single product a market advantage. There's no way to see the common flow of work that a suite of products could support directly and that would give that suite a market advantage.

It isn't just the vendors who say that their customers all work differently. People are invested in being unique, and the first thing that customers often say is how different they are from everyone else in the industry. But much of the detail that makes people different is not relevant to the common pattern and structure of work practice, and it is this common pattern and structure that make generic software possible.

When we studied configuration management, we found that some companies make it a very formal process: there are people who have the job title "Configuration Manager," who decide what goes into a configuration and make sure it gets built and tested. We found that UNIX shops generally don't work this way—they value minimal process and a "just do it" mind-set. But, in a UNIX shop on the afternoon a base level was supposed to be finished, we found someone walking the hallways saying: "Okay everybody, the build starts in an hour! Get your code checked in! Bob, get your testing done. We need that feature in this build. Sue, hold off on your stuff. We don't need it and we don't want to destabilize the build with too much new code. . . ."

Don't let individual differences blind you to common patterns of work

The first organization recognized the role and formalized it as a job; the second didn't recognize the role formally, but made sure someone was responsible for performing it informally. The role is part of the common work structure of the market; the different ways of assigning the role as a job are differences of detail. A product could be structured to support both types of organizations, though it might have to be packaged and marketed differently to deal with the customers' different attitudes.

A SINGLE REPRESENTATION IS A MARKETING AND PLANNING TOOL

When companies can't see the work of the whole market, they have no way of saying who their market is. They fall back on segmenting markets in ways they do understand—by demographics and market characterization of the sort we discussed in Chapter 2. People say things like, "This accounting tool is useful to small businesses; this other product is for home-based businesses." But do "home offices" work differently from "small businesses" in any real way? Don't they have essentially the same tax, payroll, and cash flow issues? And what happens when a "home business" grows up and becomes a "small business"? Do they suddenly acquire a new set of issues? Or another division might say, "This is a query and report tool for flat files. It doesn't substitute for a database." But don't users of flat files care about data integrity? What happens when their small, flat file application is used by two people? What happens when they want to access their database with the same flexibility as their flat files? Or a company will say, "This product is for home and school use." But do people at home have the same needs as schools? Is there any reason to think that an environment of school-age kids, adult teachers, and administrators, sharing computers in the regimented time structure of a school, has the same needs as a family in the flexible environment of a home? In each case, people are segmenting the market using the only tools they have available—demographics. Without a clear understanding of work practice and work practice differences, there's no other way to segment the market.

Segment markets by differences in work practice, not industry types

Without a way to recognize work practice, vendors also find it difficult to address a market over a series of releases with a coordinated set of products. "This is a data manipulation tool; that is a charting tool." Which is responsible for reducing the data into a form the charting tool can use? "This is an operating system work environment; that is an office work environment." Which is responsible for finding a file, or switching between applications, or maintaining reminders? Without a clear understanding of work practice, there's no good way to look at the whole range of customer activities and carve them up so that each product supports a distinct set of tasks and every handoff between tasks and products works. There's no good way to grow a product over a series of releases, recognizing the whole work problem and expanding support for it over time. Instead, vendors tend to drive products from customer wish lists: "Which features can we get

Plan products to address coherent work practice

into this version? Which one is most important? Who is yelling the loudest?" They respond to the immediate demands of individual customers, not to the coherent needs of the work practice.

Contextual Design gives vendors of commercial products the tools they need to address a market strategically. As we will see, consolidation creates a coherent understanding of the work in the affinity diagram and consolidated work models. With these tools, a vendor can grow a point product into complete support for a market. If a product supports one task, natural progressions (either with the next product version or with related products) might be to support the work tasks that precede or follow the first task, to support other tasks performed by the same people, or to support others who interact with these people. The vendor can see all the issues that matter to the market and prioritize them, planning an attack that delivers coherent product versions over time. Vendors can see who the customer is and what they care about most.

Grow product offerings to support related work

Work models give vendors rational ways to segment a market. If the work practice is common, it can be represented in a single set of consolidated models that define a market. A single product or suite can address the needs of this whole customer population. Where the models identify differences—such as different cultures—they show how the product must be packaged or sold differently to different groups of people. But when one set of models cannot represent all customers, it shows that there is not one market. It shows that the work is too different for a single product to address.

With the consolidated work models of a customer population displayed on the wall, a vendor can use them like a map to show what aspects of work they support, what aspects are the prime targets to support next, and what related work they might support in the future. A vendor could show their competitors on the same chart to reveal relative strengths and weaknesses and where the competition is vulnerable to a well-positioned product. Such a map drives a company's product strategy, just as the detailed work practice knowledge drives the structure of the company's products. Without it, marketing, like designers, operates off intuition and misses opportunities for a strategic advantage.

A map of customer practice supports rational decisions

Facilitate the partnership between IT and customers

IT departments exist to help the business take advantage of technology—to implement and maintain the systems that make the business run. Because IT's job is to deliver systems that support the work of the business, they may well become more aware of the processes that run the business than the departments are themselves. A department in the business is nearly always focused on getting their part of the job done most effectively, spending less energy on understanding how that part affects other departments. Even within departments, groups and individuals focus on their own job rather than worrying about how others do their jobs.

IT can be the voice for coherent business processes

More and more, IT departments are being asked to support larger business processes. It's the IT department that notices when they have to waste time delivering systems that duplicate work because the departments themselves are duplicating work. The IT department has the problem of recognizing and rationalizing the work practice of the business, so they can develop a coherent set of systems to support it with minimum effort and redundancy.

As a result, the IT department is often at odds with its clients. If a client wants something to simplify their work, but their work is part of a larger process, does IT optimize that one part of the process at the expense of the whole, or do they antagonize a client to make the overall process work better? IT is often the player stuck with the job of thinking about process and systems across the business. They need a way to talk to the business about how they work and how to build information systems that not only support current processes, but provide opportunities to simplify and automate them.

A systems perspective reveals overlap in business processes

IT departments have the opportunity to drive process improvements themselves. They also must respond to organizational change driven from above—from management and business process reengineering (BPR) initiatives. These efforts tend to focus on the large organizational structures: departments and their responsibilities, flow of materials between departments, and large process steps. Individuals trying to figure out how to do their jobs in the new organization are often lost and confused. They need a way to bridge the gap from the policies and directives of management to define daily actions and expectations. It's a good idea to include the people who do the job in redefining it—only they know what's really required—but their own work practice is not conscious to them. They need techniques to make work practice visible so they can design procedures that meet management's directives and work on a day-to-day basis for the people and for the job.

From this perspective, a job description for the business analyst (or the cross-functional team doing analysis) might be, "We are responsible for understanding our client's business and helping them to do it better." To do this, a business analyst needs knowledge in the work domain of the client, skill in seeing process issues that elude even those who do the work on a daily basis, and understanding of the technological possibilities, as well as

Fill the gap between high-level directives and redesign of daily work

ability to design the infrastructure, or work with the technical people who can do so. It should be clear from the book so far that this is not an impossible task. Interviewing and work modeling enable the analyst to learn the business and see process issues; consolidation represents the work of the department in a stable way. By including customers on the team, and creating events for including customers, the analyst can partner with the business in process design and specification of the infrastructure, maintaining the coherence of the supporting systems.

Consolidated work models help drive consistent process design. Departments, like customers in a market, tend to be invested in thinking their work is unique. The highly advanced, fast-moving, innovative part of the company doesn't want to think that their work is really structured just like that of the stodgy, old-fashioned part of the company. Engineers don't want to think that ordering their complex supplies has the same structure as ordering refrigerators. So they resist using the same

Reveal common work patterns to support cross-department system consistency

system as another department uses, insisting on one tailored to them.

But if these people see the structure of their work in an external model, they can see how similar it is to the work done by others and can come to accept that the same system might actually work for both. Similarly, if people see how the work they do fits into the larger process, they can make rational decisions about what makes sense. For example, if they see how all the work they put into formatting their report is thrown out and redone by the people who roll results up into a final report, they might accept a system that applied standard formatting automatically.

The overall work structure is a backbone, showing how small systems and individual customizations are variations within the larger framework. A consolidated view of the work allows IT to be strategic about the systems they deliver, building systems with the most impact first and extending initial versions to build up complete support for the work.

"Enterprise models" are another approach to seeing consistency across departments. But enterprise models focus on shared data—important, but not the only aspect of work practice that matters. Object models showing the information infrastructure are an important part of the representation of the business, but are built up as part of systems design, later in the process. Neither of these address the common structure in the work, which, if recognized, could lead to reusable systems across the organization.

Extend models over time to reveal the full business process

Consolidated models become a strategic resource to the business. They show what is going on in the day-to-day doing of the work and how the work hangs together so the business and IT can have conversations about the work people do. The IT organization can maintain models that show the work of the business they support, extending them over time as new projects bring them into contact with more and more of the business.

REPRESENTATIONS OF WORK STABILIZE REQUIREMENTS

Participation in redesign fosters buy-in to change

Whether it's new systems or new processes, IT departments face the huge problem of introducing changes to a skeptical and change-resistant customer population. People know these changes will affect the way they work on a daily basis—unless they buy in, they will find ways to subvert the new systems. People can accept change when they are part of the process of looking at the work and designing new systems that make work more efficient. Since IT is the department chartered to provide systems, it is a natural part of IT's job to raise process awareness in the departments they work with. Then the business department and IT can work together, combining technical knowledge and knowledge of the business domain to identify process problems and define process and system solutions.

Contextual Design generates representations of the work of a business that make process management and collaboration with the customer possible. It shares with Participatory Design a concern for including customers in the design of how their work will change. Consolidated models and affinity diagrams show where the breakdowns and bottlenecks are and drive design conversations about removing them. For example, the consolidated flow model might reveal that most of the purchasing department's job has turned into mechanical, clerical work, leaving no time for the knowledge work of creating relationships with suppliers. Knowing this is an issue, a team can design systems that automate the clerical work and provide the information needed to support purchasing's real job—and customers on the team can communicate the new ideas back to their organization and prepare them for redesigning their roles.

Consolidated models elevate what would otherwise be a bunch of anecdotes to reveal systemic problems: from "He's complaining about the PC support group. It doesn't mean anything—everyone complains about the PC support group," to "Look at this! Everyone is getting held up by the PC support group! We have to fix this!" Making elements of work practice explicit makes their impact apparent and helps set priorities.

Move from process anecdotes to known data to drive decisions

Consolidated models give the IT department a way to talk back to the business about prioritization decisions: "I know this system is important to you. But look, it will be more powerful if we put it off until we implement this other system here. That system will tie this whole process together and can drive your system with the data you need instead of requiring you to enter it manually." It's easier for people to be flexible when presented with a rational—and externalized—plan than when they are just told they can't have what they want. A shared

Make the big picture concrete to help departments prioritize their parts

representation of work can foster a partnership between business and IT, in which both focus on the work of the business and how it can be improved and supported.

Making work practice visible stabilizes shifting requirements. Client organizations don't change requirements on a whim—they are trying to respond to real work issues. But without a way to see the underlying structure of work, everyone responds to the immediate current pain without looking for the underlying problem causing the pain. One-shot solutions to point problems always run the risk of becoming obsolete quickly. Stability depends on seeing how work hangs together and responding with a system that supports it coherently. An old story has it that one company employed an army of mops to clean up spots of water appearing on the floor before someone noticed that the janitor's bucket had a hole in it.

Models reveal work issues, so customers can choose what to redesign

Requirements change because they are trying to patch surface details, and tomorrow a new detail may seem more important. Understanding the structure of work leads to supporting work at the level of structure, which rarely changes, and suggests structural changes that radically improve the work.

SEEING THE WHOLE

Customer data informs a team what kind of system is needed and reveals the detailed structure of the work the users do. Both commercial and IT organizations can use the data to learn what kind of system to deliver. But customer data also reveals the pattern and structure of work. It guides a team in designing the detailed structure of the system they develop.

The work practice of a customer population has its own coherence. It is a web of interrelated parts. Change any part of it, and everything else has to shift to adjust. To respond with a coherent system, designers need to see the interwoven pattern of work as a single whole. Whether designers support internal customers or an external market, they need a guide for what we will call *systemic thinking:* seeing the pattern of customer work practice as a unified whole and responding to

See the work as a whole to invent systems that support the work coherently

it with a coherent system. Systemic thinking views both work and system as coherent wholes that respond to each other, not as a collection of features, each meeting a specific need.

With a coherent understanding of work, designers can recognize people's different work styles and strategies and account for them in the system. They can check that the work still hangs together and anticipate what may break as a result of the new system. They can balance needs against each other, recognizing which have the most impact on the work as a whole. No list of needs or requirements will give designers this synthetic view; treating each "need" or "requirement" as an independent entity makes it too hard to see how they interrelate.

The first step in systemic thinking is to develop a coherent understanding of work, based on actual customer data. That's what consolidation does.

Creating One View
of the Customer

9

The challenge of consolidation is to do explicitly, on purpose, and externally what is usually tacit, haphazard, and internal: develop a sense for a whole customer population from particular instances and events. At this point in Contextual Design, particular instances of customer experience have been captured through interviews and interpretation sessions. Affinity diagrams and consolidated work models show how individual examples of work practice are instances of overarching patterns that define the whole population, and they provide concrete representations of those patterns.

Affinity diagrams and consolidated work models have different forms and reveal different issues, but a similar thought process underlies them all. They are all built by *induction,* reasoning "from the particular to the general, from the known to the unknown" (Fowler 1876). The goal of consolidation is to generate new insights about customers and how they structure their work. You can't develop new insight by applying existing rules and concepts to the data; all you'll ever discover is more detail about the things you already know. The consolidations we build in Contextual Design use induction to bring together many instances from individual interviews, building up structure from detail to reveal new concepts and patterns. These form the understanding of the customer and provide the challenge for design.

Reveal the customers' story by seeing the pattern behind the instance

We don't create consolidations from rational arguments of what must be true. It is easy to make decisions about the work that are based not on what you saw, but on logic. For example, it's only logical to suppose that, faced with a system problem, a system manager would try to figure out what's wrong. In fact, observing system managers at work suggests otherwise. Often system managers start by applying a few techniques that fix most problems (of which rebooting the machine is the most notorious). Only if these fail, do they do any real diagnosis. And it often doesn't matter if they never discover the actual cause of the problem—making it go away is good enough. So designing for logically deduced behavior would not be as effective as designing to support trying a few standard actions quickly. Stepping out of the work to think about it increases the probability of making work more rational than it is. So never depend on theoretical arguments to decide what's true. Decide what's true by induction from the data.

Because the structure is built up out of the detail, consolidations naturally accommodate variation among customers. Where designers might previously have seen only random differences between customers, bringing these instances together with induction reveals that differences are variations on a theme. If one person prefers key commands and another prefers the mouse, we can see these as alternative strategies for controlling the system appropriate to different cognitive styles. If one person prefers to write an outline before starting a paper and another just talks out her ideas, we can see these as different ways of clarifying thought and structure before starting the writing. New variants can be recognized and positioned within the structure—so someone who wrote lots of different rough paragraphs and then went back to rewrite them could be recognized as achieving the same intent of clarifying his thoughts in a new way. Variations exist within a structure.

Variation across customers exists within a structure —it isn't random

We support induction by creating external representations of work practice. Without such representations, people base their design on their unarticulated sense for the common patterns of work derived from individual experiences or customer interviews. When the designer is good, the work practice is simple, and the system is small, this works well enough. The designer can hold all the different aspects of work in her head, can maintain all the implications of a small system, and can keep control of a project with few people on it. But once a problem gets complex and the team gets large, an explicit representation of the work to respond to becomes critical, for several reasons.

First, the sheer complexity of the problem requires a representation. Just as anyone can multiply single-digit numbers in their head but needs physical props to multiply six-digit numbers, as soon as the problem starts to grow designers need to write their understanding down. In fact, nearly all design thinking demands props. A sketch of your thinking provides something to interact with, something to push your ideas against. By representing the work practice of a customer population externally, Contextual Design takes part of the design conversation out of the designer's brain and puts it on the wall as a model. The designers then respond to it as an external entity. It holds the memory of the customer and forces designers to be accountable to the customer data. It becomes not just a prop, but a partner in design. (In fact, one team convinced their management to give them an extra office to act as a team room on the grounds that the customer voice lived and breathed and deserved its own room.)

Work models become a partner in design by holding work complexity

Second, the design is owned not just by one person, but by the cross-functional design team. They have to get the design out of their brains and on the wall just so they can act as a team—so they can share their thinking, take advantage of each other's points of view, and all contribute to the one design. Any one person is stuck in his own point of view; externalize that point of view and everyone on the team can see and modify it. If the extended team is too large for one design meeting, the models hold the thinking so different groups can interact with it. Contextual Design provides both external representations and team processes to use them to encourage the team working together and building on each other's ideas.

Finally, building up a sense of the market instance by instance works against a real shift in perspective. It works against the creative leap that might produce a next-generation product or radical business process improvement. When faced with one new piece of customer data, people assimilate it; they modify their entering conceptions just enough to account for the new piece of data. They say, "Look—we can handle that with just a small fix over here." A creative leap comes not from such small adjustments, but from seeing the large cumulative effect of lots of little pieces, which forces designers to abandon existing assumptions and come to the data from a fresh perspective. In Contextual Design, we encourage this by making consolidation a separate step. Instead of

Consolidating all models at once challenges entering assumptions

looking at each piece of data individually and assimilating it, we combine all the data together so it has the maximum impact. (And along the way we use tricks, such as forbidding old terminology, to prevent our entering assumptions from showing through, which we will talk about in the next chapter.) We do it fast—a day for each model and a day for the affinity. Doing it slowly would encourage assimilation; doing it fast swamps our old paradigm with new data. Doing it slowly would encourage point solutions to each problem in turn; doing it fast encourages broad, systemic responses to the whole work practice of the whole customer population. The consolidated models and affinity become the statement of the customer that forces us out of our rut. They drive the designer to make a creative leap.

Consolidation is the inductive process of bringing all the individual data together and building one affinity diagram and one set of models that represent the whole customer population. It's a process of inquiry—looking at details from specific customers and asking how each detail informs the team's focus. Then the parts can be brought together based on meaning to reveal structure across customers. Though it's applied differently for each kind of model, this same thinking process is used in all consolidation. We'll start with the affinity to see how to do the thinking and then look at the other models to see how it is applied to each type of consolidation. We will unpack the thought process in detail to reveal how this kind of inquiry works.

Inductive reasoning is the key to seeing pattern

THE AFFINITY DIAGRAM

The affinity diagram organizes the individual notes captured during interpretation sessions into a hierarchy revealing common issues and themes (Figure 9.1). The affinity shows the scope of the customer problem: it reveals in one place all the issues, worries, and key elements of work practice relevant to the team's focus. It also defines the key quality requirements on the system: reliability, performance, hardware support, and so forth. The hierarchical structure groups similar issues so that all the data relevant to a theme is shown together, creating stories about the customer relevant to the design problem. By reading the affinity, a designer not only

Create a bottom-up hierarchy of key points to see issues

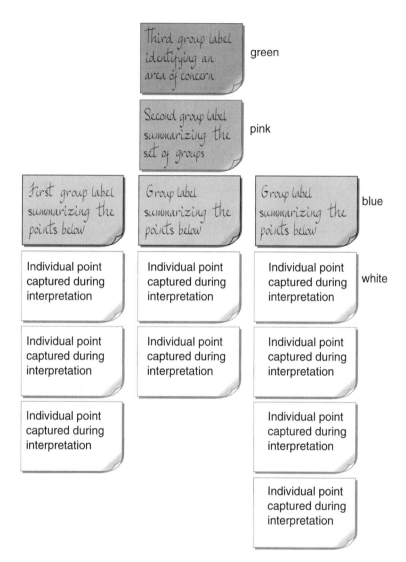

FIGURE 9.1   Structure of an affinity diagram.

learns the key issues, but can see the exact data that contributed to identifying each issue in the work.

The affinity process was introduced as one of the "seven quality processes" from Japan (Brassard 1989; also known as the K-J method in Kawakita [1982]). In the quality community, affinities on the order of 200 notes are usual. We have optimized the process to handle much larger affinities, typically about 1500 notes. We build the affinity after a good cross section of users has been interviewed—usually 15–20 customers at four to six work sites, with 50–100 notes from each customer. We always prefer to finish the affinity in a single day because it's simply too exhausting to allow it to drag on. This is possible if we have one person per 100 notes to build it. If our team is smaller than that, we invite others who are interested in or affected by the design to participate.

The affinity is built bottom up, by raising common structure and common themes out of the individual notes captured during the interpretation sessions. We do not start from a predefined structure or set of categories such as "UI issues" or "Quality." Starting from such a set of categories reduces building an affinity to a sorting task; each note goes in its own bucket, and at the end you know no more than you did before. Instead, we allow the individual notes to suggest categories they might belong to. We intentionally resist using categories that might be familiar to the team, suggested by their experience instead of by the customer data. We even ban words the team is too familiar with; for example, a configuration management group was not allowed to use the word "version." Banning the term forces the team to say how the concept is relevant to the problem and helps them to come at the problem with a fresh perspective.

Ban words to force rethinking old concepts

The affinity is the first consolidation step, and it teaches the thinking for all the rest. Building an affinity is inductive reasoning at its purest. The basic process is to put up one note, then for everyone to look for other notes that seem to go with it. There's no need to justify *why* they go together—just as you can feel an affinity for a friend without justifying why. But we do push for a certain kind of affinity: two notes have an affinity if they are saying similar things about the work as it relates to the design focus of the team—they are expressing a similar intent, problem, or issue in the user's work. So deciding if notes go together is the result of an inquiry into the meaning of the words on the note to understand the work issue they represent. When it's not clear how to interpret the words, the team can appeal to the interviewer to check whether an interpretation is valid. The team is responsible for ensuring that the data will support the claim they wish to make.

Here are some examples of using the data captured on a note to infer meaning for the work. Each example gives some of the context

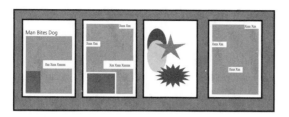

```
12.                                                    U6
Searches for desired text by turning pages in full page
view—big headline was the distinguishing feature
```

FIGURE 9.2 Capturing a search strategy.

(which the team would be aware of) and shows how to look at the data from a particular focus and see implications for work practice and design. If these insights occurred to team members during the interpretation session, they would be captured in separate notes; otherwise the affinity process gives the opportunity to consider the data again. These notes are all taken from an interview with a user of a page layout tool.

Inquire into the design significance of each note

The note in Figure 9.2 describes how page designers identify their pages. Even though full page view makes the page too small to see any detail, it's still possible to identify the desired page by its overall pattern and by large elements that show up even at reduced size. The work implication is that page designers, concentrating on the layout and look of pages, find it more natural to search by look rather than by text on the page.

The note in Figure 9.3 describes a UI issue, but inquiry provides deeper insights about how these users conceptualize their work. The product provides a box to contain text, but the characters in that box don't stay strictly within its bounds—risers stick up past the top, and descenders can stick out the bottom. The "snap to" guides snap the box boundary to the guide, which isn't what the page designer wants. Page designers want to align the tops of the risers, the tops of the small letters, the center of the small letters, the bottoms of the small letters, or the bottoms of the descenders. Those are the distinctions that matter to the page designer—the box is a construct that has no

Guide

Text box

```
┌────────────────────────────────────────────────────────────┐
│ 124.                                                    U8   │
│ "Snap to guide" snaps to the top of the text box, not to the │
│ tops of the letters that stick up past the top of the box   │
└────────────────────────────────────────────────────────────┘
```

FIGURE 9.3   Capturing a UI issue.

meaning in their work. Even product ideas such as fixing the top of the box so it coincides with the tops of the risers misses the point. A more general solution would build knowledge of the alignment points for text into the product.

The meaning a designer reads in a note and the way he groups them together is driven by the project focus. A single note will often suggest different aspects of customer work. The designer wants the meaning that will give the affinity the most insight, allow it to tell the best story about the customer for the focus. For example, consider the notes shown in Figure 9.4, collected from people in grocery stores and legal offices during an inquiry into search strategies.

Group Post-its to reveal new insights into the work

Note 110 could be paired with either 214 or 360. The thinking behind pairing 110 and 214 would be that both notes are about legal cases and how they are found, so they should go together. The thinking behind 110 and 360 would be that the two notes are about using a similar search strategy to find things: the more recent the thing, the better. Given the focus on how people find things, pairing 110 and 214 doesn't lead to new insight—it's no surprise that legal cases are searched in law offices. The only aspect of work that the group reveals is details about the job of the paralegal staff, which is better represented on work models. Pairing 110 and 360 raises up a common search strategy. It's the more interesting pairing because it shows how this strategy pertains across work domains (searching for cases and searching for groceries). It might be combined with other data to make the strategy explicit, as in Figure 9.5.

```
┌─────────────────────────────────────────────────────────────┐
│ 110.                                              U2          │
│ The more recent a legal case, the more persuasive it is      │
└─────────────────────────────────────────────────────────────┘

┌─────────────────────────────────────────────────────────────┐
│ 214.                                              U2          │
│ Legal case precedents are searched by paralegal staff        │
└─────────────────────────────────────────────────────────────┘

┌─────────────────────────────────────────────────────────────┐
│ 360.                                              U4          │
│ At milk case, buys 1 gallon or 2 quarts depending on         │
│ expiration date                                              │
└─────────────────────────────────────────────────────────────┘
```

FIGURE 9.4   Grouping notes to reveal design significance.

Recent stuff is best

```
┌─────────────────────────────────────────────────────────────┐
│ 110.                                              U2          │
│ The more recent a legal case, the more persuasive it is      │
└─────────────────────────────────────────────────────────────┘

┌─────────────────────────────────────────────────────────────┐
│ 360.                                              U4          │
│ At milk case, buys 1 gallon or 2 quarts depending on         │
│ expiration date                                              │
└─────────────────────────────────────────────────────────────┘

┌─────────────────────────────────────────────────────────────┐
│ 720.                                              U8          │
│ The most recent house listings are the most desirable; good  │
│ houses sell quickly                                          │
└─────────────────────────────────────────────────────────────┘
```

FIGURE 9.5   Revealing a common theme.

When notes are collected together, they are given a name to represent the group. A good group name states the work issue that holds all the individual notes together. It is a succinct phrase that summarizes the content of the group. "Different ways of searching" would not summarize the content in the above example; it would just say what you could learn by reading the content. "Recent stuff is best" states the issue; then the individual notes give examples of this

Labels are the customer's voice speaking from the wall

general statement. A good group name is written as though the user was talking to the designer; direct, immediate language has more impact than third-person language. When the notes use the user's language, the whole wall speaks the user's issues to the design team—they become a central communication device.

First-level groupings like the above are themselves collected into a group of groups, which are grouped into higher-order groups. The

Labels become the meaning we design from

result is a hierarchical structure that breaks the data about the user into manageable chunks. We use green Post-its at the highest level, which describe a whole area of concern within the work practice. Under this, pink labels describe the specific issues that define that area of concern. Blue labels describe each aspect of the issue. And the individual notes under the blue labels describe the instances illustrating the blue label. When well written, the labels tell a story about the user, structuring the problem, identifying specific issues, and organizing everything known about that issue. The labels represent the new information in an affinity. We limit each first-level group to four notes to force the team to look deeply and make more distinctions than they would otherwise be inclined to. It pushes more of the knowledge up into the group labels.

For example, Figure 9.6 is a section of an affinity describing delegation. It's part of a larger story about why people communicate in doing their job—one reason is to delegate (individual notes have been skipped for brevity).

This section of the affinity brings together data from many customers and many work situations to tell the story of delegating work.

The affinity tells a story of the customer that matters for design

When sharing the data or reviewing the wall yourself, you might read it like a story: "People delegate work either because they don't have time to do the work themselves or because they choose not to deal with it. They pick someone else to do it either by who has time, who reports to them, or is otherwise appropriate given the organization. Different ways of delegating have different styles: people can delegate doing the work but remain responsible for it, they can delegate a task by assigning it during a meeting, or they may pass it on informally." Each pink label names an issue that is described by the blue labels underneath it so that each section of the affinity tells a coherent story about part of the work,

We delegate our work	(green)
Why we delegate	(pink)
I don't want to deal with it	(blue)
I have too much work.	(blue)
How I choose who to delegate to	(pink)
Whoever is available does it	(blue)
The person with the job does it	(blue)
How I go about delegating	(pink)
I gave it away, but I'm still responsible	(blue)
I gave it away at a meeting	(blue)
I pass it on informally	(blue)

FIGURE 9.6   A section of an affinity diagram.

and the whole wall brings together all issues and observations to tell a single story about the customer population.

STEPS

- Print the notes captured during interpretation sessions in a 3 × 5-inch grid and cut apart so each is on its own label-sized slip of paper.
- Put notes up on the wall one at a time. After each note goes up, add notes that go with it.
- When there are too many groups to keep track of, start labeling them with blue Post-its.
- As groups accumulate individual notes, break them down so there are no more than four notes in a group.
- Add pink- and green-level notes to collect groups.

Others who use the affinity process forbid talking while building the affinity; we encourage it. We view this process as an opportunity to gain team consensus, which is best supported by discussion. All work is done in pairs so people can discuss their insights with each other and get someone else to check their thinking. Writing the labels reveals what you're thinking; if anyone disagrees they can object. All the data instances are there to

The affinity captures the insight of all the brains on the team

support one interpretation or another. Each person's different perspective is shared, and a common perspective built through discussion. Discussion also helps move people from thinking in buckets (all notes with "legal case" on them get tossed in one group) to thinking in work practice—people police each other's notes. When people can't agree on where a note should go, they talk about what underlying work issues they see. When people don't understand a note, they go back to the list of notes from that interpretation session or to the interviewer to ask what happened in the interview. We've seen no problems resulting from letting people talk, and doing the inquiry together requires talk. It lets all the brains work together.

Building the affinity in a day creates a team event that binds the team together and encourages creating new perspectives. Building smaller affinities more quickly, or building up one affinity over time, would allow team members to incorporate each piece of data before having to deal with the next; as we discussed above, this leads to assimilation instead of promoting a paradigm shift. Instead, in a single day the team has to face a whole new way of looking at things. As a team process, the affinity forces the team to learn each other's points of view and discuss their differences. But like the interpretation session, it puts strict bounds on disagreement; team members talk about the different meaning they draw from one note at a time. When they are done they have a single structure representing all their customer data, which organizes their knowledge and insight and gives them a basis for design.

Building a 1500-note affinity is exhausting. It's an entire day of reading and conceptualizing hundreds of little bits of data and matching them with other little bits of data. It's like a combination of "Concentration" and translating Shakespeare into Latin: the words on a note have to be interpreted to translate them into the underlying work practice issue; then the note has to be matched with the note you saw five minutes ago and you know is on the wall somewhere. Everyone's working at once, moving back and forth along the wall, discussing notes with each other, yelling general questions to the group at large ("Who interviewed U4?"). Some team members will be more comfortable with the apparent disorganization than others. But the result is exciting for everyone: a single, sweeping reorganization of the customer data arranged like a

The affinity organizes hundreds of Post-its into a story in a single day

story. You can read a good affinity from beginning to end to see every issue in the work and everything about it the team has learned so far, all tied to real instances. There's no better way to see the broad scope of the problem quickly.

Consolidating flow models

Consolidating the flow models reveals the communication patterns that underlie the way the customers do business. It's a basic marketing tool—it shows who the customers are, what they do, and how they interact with each other. It shows what part of the work practice of a customer population you currently address and how you might expand existing systems to support more of the job, more of the whole business process, or more people in the

The flow model reveals the common roles in different job definitions

workplace. The flow model shows the scope of the work domain a project intends to address and shows how the work the project is focused on fits into the customers' larger work practice. Flow model consolidation reveals the common structure that underlies all the different ways organizations define jobs. It does this by using roles as the essential element of work practice on which to base consolidation.

Roles are collections of responsibilities that accomplish a coherent part of the work (Wirfs-Brock [1993] uses roles in a similar way). Roles have a primary intent, the reason why the role was created in the first place. When people organize themselves to get a job done, they naturally break the job up into roles: "You write the paper," they say. "I'll review it." The roles people create are not random or idiosyncratic; they are driven by the needs of the work (Fisher 1980; Wirfs-Brock [1993] applies these ideas to software). Writers are too familiar with their own work to review it well, so splitting the reviewer and writer roles makes sense. Reviewing for technical accuracy and reviewing for grammar and spelling could go together, but they use very different skill sets, so technical review and editorial review are often separated into different roles. But checking for appropriate references and checking that the content is technically valid both depend on knowledge of the field, so it doesn't make sense to break these responsibilities into different roles.

Because they are driven by the needs of the work, roles tend to be consistent across organizations. The mapping from roles to individuals—the selection of particular roles an individual takes on—is much more idiosyncratic. A person will take on roles they find congenial or have skills for; organizations will create jobs that combine different sets of roles. The roles don't change; the mapping to people does. We do care to track whether a particular set of roles commonly is assigned together and who tends to take them on in a segment of the market—that a particular role tends to be taken by women or that banks tend to merge these two roles. This will affect how a system helps people switch roles and may influence how we package or sell the system.

Roles are very consistent across any work domain

The primary job of consolidating the flow model is to identify the roles played by individuals and combine similar roles across individuals. The roles that a person plays are suggested by their responsibilities and tasks and by their interaction with other people. But we aren't just grouping similar responsibilities. The responsibilities of a role hang together in the work practice, and responsibilities may be repeated in different roles. It should be possible to conceive of hiring a person to play a role—if that doesn't make sense, the role is probably not real.

Individuals play multiple roles

The first step in consolidating flow models is to generate a complete list of responsibilities for each individual.

ANALYTICAL SCIENTIST

—run experimental tests on substances
—interpret test results
—document and report results of tests
—schedule test requests from multiple people and departments
—clean glassware
—research appropriate test equipment for group
—report results and trade-offs to group
—order basic supplies
—**help other scientists run tests**

It is common, when flow models are created by real teams, to discover overlooked responsibilities by examining the interaction between

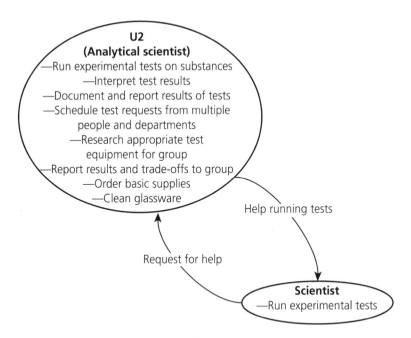

FIGURE 9.7 Identifying responsibilities.

people. In Figure 9.7, the flow to "Scientist" indicates an additional responsibility: to give other scientists help on running tests. Informal responsibilities such as this are as important to how work really gets done as the formal responsibilities assigned by the organization. So we add it to the list before considering roles.

A role is a collection of responsibilities, organized to accomplish one primary intent. For a role to be coherent, it must include all the responsibilities that are critical to that intent. These responsibilities cannot be separated into different roles. So the first responsibility we identify is "Experimenter"—the person who runs an experiment. It's a good starting point because it's the primary job function of this individual. Then we look at the rest of the

A role collects responsibilities, which accomplish an intent

responsibilities and ask if they go with this role (much as we asked whether two notes should go with each other in the affinity): "Interpret test results" is critical to the Experimenter. An experiment is run by the strict rules of experimental science; scientists need to know that the results are reported by the same strict rules or their hard work is wasted and their reputation jeopardized. It belongs with the Experimenter role.

"Document and report results of tests" is more of a judgment call. It's possible to conceive of a head scientist who oversaw the experiment but left it to others to report results. But we aren't building logical structures here; we are deriving structure from the data. If every scientist interviewed in this work domain reports his own results, then it's not real *for this work domain* to separate documenting and reporting into a distinct role. It's just another responsibility of the Experimenter. We keep "help other scientists run tests" with the role for the same reason—all scientists advise and assist each other. This is a claim about what it means to be a scientist in today's laboratories. It can be supported with the data, by checking with the interviewers, and by checking back with the customers if necessary.

EXPERIMENTER

—run experimental tests on substances

—interpret test results

—document and report results of tests

—help other scientists run tests

We then go on to the next responsibility, "schedule test requests from multiple people and departments," and ask the same questions: What's the primary contribution of the responsibility to the work? What other responsibilities go with it? It doesn't seem that scheduling test results has to be part of the Experimenter. It would be reasonable, in a high-throughput lab, to hire someone to schedule experiments for maximum efficiency. So we define a new role. The result of looking at the rest of the responsibilities is a tentative list of roles and their responsibilities for this individual:

LAB SCHEDULER

—schedule test requests from multiple people and departments

LAB MAINTAINER

—clean glassware

—order basic supplies

EQUIPMENT RESEARCHER

—research appropriate test equipment for group
—report results and trade-offs to group

In each case, these roles can reasonably be separated out into a different job function from the Experimenter. The group's manager might act
as Scheduler, tracking requests and handing them out so that equipment
and people are busy but not overbooked. Lab assistants might play the
Maintainer role, keeping the lab running smoothly. And an outside
agent might be assigned to research equipment and provide options.

The assignment of roles to individuals or job functions varies
from one organization to the next and from one individual to the
next. Roles that are separate in one case may be combined in another.
In our example, the team identified a different set of roles for another
analytical scientist:

TESTER

—run a test on samples
—convert raw data into meaning
—report results of tests to requester
—describe what's needed of new equipment

METHOD DEVELOPER

—develop a new test procedure through experimentation
—document the new test procedure in standard form
—assist other scientists in using the new procedure

Consolidation in a flow model happens by recognizing when different people are playing the same roles. Here, Method Developer is a
new role, but Tester is clearly the Experimenter role
with a different name. (If the same people analyze
both individuals and recognize the similarity they
would use the same name. But when the team breaks
into subteams, different people may do the analysis.)

*Multiple people play the
same role*

Even when it's the same people they don't always recognize the role
until they have a chance to step back and compare.) Experimenter and
Tester each have a responsibility the other doesn't have—"help other

scientists run tests" and "describe what's needed of new equipment," respectively. But both responsibilities fit right into the role, so we can combine the two roles into a single consolidated role definition. Here again we use affinity-style thinking to look at the meaning of two different items and combine them when they go together.

We choose the name "Experimenter" as a better description of the primary intent of the role. Just as we use plain language on the affinity, we try to keep role names plain and everyday. This makes the real work of the role more immediate. However, we try to capture the essential work of the role in the name. Even though some experiments are tests, "Experimenter" better captures the flavor of the work and mind-set of the people.

EXPERIMENTER

—run experimental tests on substances

—interpret test results

—document and report results of tests

—help other scientists run tests

—describe what's needed of new equipment

It is normal to build up responsibilities of the consolidated role this way. We expect that not every responsibility will be discovered in every interview, and in fact, our second scientist may never have had the occasion to help another. But the consolidation shows what's natural to the role. It tells us to expect that the first scientist may be called to give opinions on equipment and the second may be asked for help. It tells us that any new design for the system or organization must allow for these events. For example, if the organization were to measure scientists strictly on the number of experiments they perform, they would lose the synergy of interaction between scientists. This is how we build up an understanding of a whole job out of multiple interviews. This is how consolidation reduces requirements skew—it identifies needs that the customers haven't stumbled over yet. And this is how to deliver systems based on actual customer data without sacrificing flexibility; the flexibility built into the system accounts for the actual variation in work practice, not hypothetical situations that never actually occur.

Design the system for the role variation that actually occurs

In consolidation, we keep track of how roles map to individuals. It will matter for design to know that one person played a dozen roles, or that a single role was played both by low-level technicians and Ph.D. scientists. (Why is a Ph.D. doing work a technician could do? Couldn't we sell them a system or change the process to make better use of their time?) So we assign a color to each job function, department, or demographic group we wish to track, and color the role to show where it came from. If scientists are yellow, the Tester role will be yellow. If lab technicians (who also run tests) are pink, the Tester role will be yellow and pink. With this coding, designers can scan the model and see immediately how it maps to people's job functions.

The final step of consolidating a flow model is to consolidate the artifacts and communications between people. Each artifact and each communication represent an interaction not just between people, but between roles. When the second scientist tells the first what she needs from a new spectrometer, she is the Experimenter talking to the Equipment Researcher. When the first gives help to another, he is an Experimenter helping another Experimenter. The consolidated flow model carries these individual flows over, showing them between roles rather than between individuals. The artifacts or communications themselves may be consolidated and given a single abstract name: "help on device use," "assistance reading a method," and "suggestions on getting around device limitations" might all be represented on the consolidated flow as "help with devices and procedures." The flow can be simplified by showing only the flows relevant to the project focus.

Link the roles with real communications

STEPS

- Select six to nine individual flow models that are complex, interesting, and cover the key variants of the work domain.
- List responsibilities and identify roles of each person, group, and place on the individual flows. Name the roles.
- Collect similar roles from all models and lay them out on a consolidated model.
- Rewrite responsibilities and name each role.
- Collect artifacts and communications from the actual models. Draw them between roles on the consolidated model.
- Transfer any breakdowns from the actual models onto the consolidated model.
- Compare the remaining individual models against the consolidated flow. Add any roles, responsibilities, or important flows that are not represented by the consolidated model.

Flow model consolidation leads a team from knowledge of individual users to understanding the structure of work across a customer population. It's a fairly efficient method for doing this; after consolidating about nine good and diverse models in a work domain, additional models will offer few surprises (teams that have gathered much more data—from up to 40 customers—quickly discovered that they were duplicating what they already knew). Between 15 and 20 customers from a typical work domain is enough to see the pattern of the flow of work between people as they do their jobs.

Between 15 and 20 customers is enough to see the pattern of role and communication

The flow model is nearly always a useful model to build and consolidate. Nearly any job requires working with others, receiving information and handing results to others, or cooperating with others in some way. Only when the project focus is narrowed to the interaction with the tool only—usability of an interface or interaction with a device—can the flow be omitted. Even then, there's a potential for overlooking important interactions. It's better to build it anyway.

The consolidated flow model is the designer's tool for seeing the roles that underlie idiosyncratic organizational structures and interpersonal communication patterns. It shows the central roles and key responsibilities of the work practice being studied and how they coordinate and pass artifacts around to make work happen. The consolidated flow model is the best map to how work is done, showing the breadth of work and the details of how people interact. The flow model shows what roles people play, so that if you have systems already in place, you can see what roles you support. It can show how the systems taken together support the whole of the work (or don't). It shows what other roles the same people are likely to play, which are natural roles to support next—the potential customers would already be sold on your system or your company. It shows who else a role has to interact with to get a job done; supporting these other roles or the interaction between them is also a natural growth path. The consolidated flow model is your map to your customer population. It shows you where you are and where you are going.

The consolidated flow maps the players in the customer population

Consolidating sequence models

A consolidated sequence model reveals the structure of a task, showing the strategies common across a customer population. Individual sequence models describe one real instance of work, showing how a person accomplished a task in that case. Consolidated sequence models bring together many instances of many individuals accomplishing the same task, revealing what is important to doing the work: what needs to be done, the order and strategy for doing it, and all the different motivations driving specific actions. A consolidated sequence model shows a designer the detailed structure of the work they need to support or replace. It shows all the different intents that must continue to be accomplished in the presence of the new system or rendered unnecessary. It shows the overall structure of the task, which may be mirrored in the system to make it more useful and intuitive. And it shows where the task is needlessly complex and could be simplified by a new system.

Consolidated sequences show task structure and work strategies

Tasks to be supported by a new system may be performed by a customer population that spans organizations and industries. Even within a single company, different departments will implement different procedures, and people with different cognitive styles will approach the work differently. Nonetheless, over and over again, we find common structure within any domain of work. People only develop a few different strategies for accomplishing similar tasks. The key is to learn to see the common structure in the detailed actions people take: the common activities, intent, and strategies for accomplishing a task.

People use only a few strategies to do a task

The sequences in Figure 9.8 show how two system managers diagnosed problems. Skimming U5's sequence, we see that he is notified by an automated process that something is wrong; he pokes around looking for problems; then he calls for help. These immediately become potential activities: notify, diagnose, get help. Shifting our attention to U4, she is notified by a person, pokes around on the hardware until she recognizes that the problem is something AT&T has to fix, and she puts in a call to them. Again we see the

Identify the activities across all sequences

U5	U4
Fix All-In-1	**Fix router problem**

• Trigger: Watcher sends mail that the All-In-1 (A1) mail system isn't working	• Trigger: Person walks into office to report problem—can't access files on another machine
• Log onto failing system to search for problem	• Go into lab to look at equipment
• Discover the A1 mail process has crashed (ACCVIO)	• Flick switches to do loop-back tests, isolating wire, MUX, router
• Look at the time of the crash: only this morning	• Determine problem—bad router
• Try to restart the process by hand	• Call AT&T people in second organization
• Process won't restart	• Do something else while waiting for AT&T to show up
• Look at the process log; can't tell why it won't start	• AT&T comes to look at problem
• Call expert backup group for help	• Look in book to tell which wire is which; show which nodes are on which wires and which wire goes to which router; paper for easy access
• Ask them to log into the system and look at problem	• Tell AT&T people which router is at fault and which wire it's on
• Keep looking for problem in parallel	• AT&T people fix problem
• Search for problem	• Log problem and fix
• Discover that process can't create a needed directory	• Done
• Try to create needed directory by hand	
• [Look to see if directory created]	
• Can't create directory; disk is too fragmented	
• Call expert backup to explain problem; type and talk on speaker phone at the same time	
• Discuss problem; agree on the exact procedure to follow	
• Implement fix	
• Write mail to users describing changes that affect them	
• Done	

FIGURE 9.8   Two ways to diagnose a problem.

U5	U4
Notify	
• Trigger: Watcher sends mail that the All-In-1 (A1) mail system isn't working	• Trigger: Person walks into office to report problem; can't access files on another machine
Diagnose	
• Log onto failing system to search for problem	• Go into lab to look at equipment
• Discover the A1 mail process has crashed (ACCVIO)	• Flick switches to do loop-back tests, isolating wire, MUX, router
• Look at the time of the crash: only this morning	• Determine problem—bad router
• Try to restart the process by hand	
• Process won't restart	
• Look at the process log; can't tell why it won't start	
Get help	
• Call expert backup group for help	• Call AT&T people in second organization

FIGURE 9.9   Identifying activities.

basic structure of activities: notify, diagnose, get help. (We'll save the rest of the sequences for later.) For now, we'll match up the steps in the sequence that initiate a new activity in Figure 9.9.

The first step of a sequence is the trigger that initiates it. Triggers may consolidate, as when several individual sequences start with someone reporting a problem in person. More often, as in this case, the trigger steps identify alternatives. Either way, we define an *abstract step* to represent both triggers. An abstract step states the work done in each of the instances independently of the specifics of that instance. In this case, we just list the two different triggers we have discovered (Figure 9.10). In other cases, triggers might introduce different strategies—a system manager who is notified of a problem by a help desk may go right into hypothesis testing, but a problem report that comes from an automated process may always start by researching the problem. When this happens we keep the triggers separate, to show how they initiate different branches of the sequence. It also happens that triggers are not at the same point

Identify and name abstract steps across all sequences

ABSTRACT STEP	U5	U4
• Trigger: Find out about problem —Automated procedure —Someone reports problem	• Trigger: Watcher sends mail that the All-In-1 (A1) mail system isn't working	• Trigger: Person walks into office to report problem; can't access files on another machine

FIGURE 9.10   Alternative triggers.

in the sequence at all. Email from a user may in fact not be the first report of a problem, but the response to a query as part of the research activity. Such a trigger needs to be moved down in the sequence.

The next steps all contribute to diagnosing the problem. Our task is to match up steps accomplishing the same thing in each instance and define abstract steps for them. We don't yet know exactly how the steps match up; we only know that they all have to be sorted out before getting to the steps in which U4 and U5 call for help.

Match up steps doing the same thing

The first step in each case positions the user logically (in the case of logging in) or physically (in the case of going to the computer lab) to start diagnosing the problem. Logging in or going to the lab are details unique to the instance; the work being done is for the users to go where they can deal with the problem: our next abstract step (Figure 9.11).

Both U4 and U5 next try different things on the system until the problem is identified. "Discover the A1 mail process has crashed" and "Determine problem—bad router" both seem to mark the point at which the user identifies the problem. U4's sequence has a step in which U4 flicks switches and runs tests to determine the problem. The team who wrote U5's sequence didn't write down such a step, but it's implied by "Discover the A1 mail process has crashed"—U5 must have done something (looked at running processes or looked at process logs) to discover the process is down. But as U5's sequence indicates, all that's happened so far is to discover why the symptom is happening; the underlying problem (a full disk in U5's case) may not have been determined yet. So the consolidation looks like Figure 9.12.

At this point, we're consolidating the different kinds of problems that the system managers discover to see the common structure of diagnosis across all problems. If we wanted to design for each kind of

ABSTRACT STEP	U5	U4
• Go to the place where the problem can be solved (physically or logically)	• Log onto failing system to search for problem	• Go into lab to look at equipment

FIGURE 9.11   Going to deal with a problem.

ABSTRACT STEP	U5	U4
• Execute commands and tests on suspect system to identify anomalous behavior	• (Do something to discover the A1 process isn't running)	• Flick switches to do loop-back tests, isolating wire, MUX, router
• Determine cause of symptoms	• Discover the A1 mail process has crashed (ACCVIO)	• Determine problem—bad router

FIGURE 9.12   Identifying a problem.

problem uniquely, we wouldn't do this; we would keep the kinds of problems separate in the consolidated sequence. But for this problem, seeing diagnosis is a fine enough level of detail.

Next, the two users diverge in their strategies. U5 goes on to try to fix the problem. But U4 decides that she can't fix this problem and that she has to call on AT&T to do the fix. Neither U5's decision to go forward nor U4's decision that AT&T has authority to fix the problem are written explicitly, but both are implied by the user's actions. So the abstract steps branch to account for the two cases. Consolidating them, we get Figure 9.13.

Watch for different strategies to do the same thing

This process repeats until the whole sequence is consolidated. We identify the sections of the sequences that match, match up individual steps, and name abstract steps for them. Either after a whole activity or at the end of the sequence, we step back and ask the intent of each step. Why is the user doing this at this point? What are the obvious and the nonobvious reasons for doing the step?

Identify intents of the steps

There may be more than one intent to any step, and there may be high-level intents that cover a whole set of steps. It's easy to identify and support the main intent of the sequence. It's harder to see all the additional, secondary intents that are also important to the customer.

ACTIVITY	ABSTRACT STEP	U5	U4
Diagnose problem	• Estimate impact of problem	• Look at the time of the crash: only this morning	
	• Decide whether I can fix the problem	• (Decide to fix)	• (Decide AT&T has to fix)
	• If I decide I can fix it:		
	• Attempt fix	• Try to restart the process by hand	
	• See if fix worked	• Process won't restart	
	• Try to figure out why it didn't work	• Look at the process log; can't tell why it won't start	
Get help	• Decide I can't fix it, call on help	• Call expert backup group for help	• Call AT&T people in second organization

FIGURE 9.13   Diagnosing a problem.

We decide what they are and write them down. We talk to the interviewer if we aren't sure of an interpretation or check back with the user. The result, for the sequences we've been doing, looks like Figure 9.14.

Of course, a team would consolidate three or four actual sequences at once, not just two. The first cut at abstract steps would be correspondingly more robust. Once the initial set of sequences has been consolidated, the rest of the sequences are compared with the consolidated sequence and used to extend it. Incorporating more sequences will add additional steps, show new strategies, and provide more alternatives for steps that are already represented.

STEPS

• Select three or four sequences addressing the same task. Look for detailed sequences that, at a quick scan, seem like they will consolidate reasonably well.

• Scan the sequences to identify activities. Mark the point where the first activity ends in each sequence.

• Match the triggers across sequences. Be aware that the instances may start at different points in the story.

• Match steps of the sequence within the first activity. Write in omitted steps if necessary to make matching steps easier.

• Write abstract steps as you go. Write any breakdowns on the abstract steps as you come to them.

• At a convenient stopping point—the end of the activity or the end of the sequence—go back and write intents for each step.

ACTIVITY	INTENT	ABSTRACT STEP
Find out about problem	• Learn about problems quickly • Discover problems before users do • Provide quick response	• Trigger: Find out about problem —Automated procedure —Someone reports problem
Go to problem location	• Make it possible to do diagnosis and take action	• Go to the place where the problem can be solved
Diagnose problem	• Find cause of problem • Decide who's been affected • Decide if any additional action should be taken to notify people of status • Make sure I don't do things I'm not supposed to	• Execute commands and tests on suspect system to identify anomalous behavior • Determine cause of symptoms • Estimate impact of problem • Decide whether I can fix the problem
Fix problem	• Fix the problem at once	• If I decide I can fix it: • Attempt fix • See if fix worked • Try to figure out why it didn't work
Call on help	• Get the people involved who have the authority or the knowledge to fix the problem • Ensure problem gets fixed, even if not my job	• Decide I can't fix it; call on help

FIGURE 9.14 A consolidated sequence model.

Consolidated sequence models show the common structure of a task across a customer population. Developing a consolidated sequence of a task shows strategies used to achieve it, the structure of the task in activities, and the intents achieved in doing the task. These define a backbone into which new variations can be incorporated and accounted for. In our example above, it's not hard to see how a new trigger or new step in diagnosing a problem could be accounted for within the structure we developed. Armed with this knowledge, designers can structure their systems to reflect the structure of the task. Where the structure is inherent to the task, it can be built into the system; where it is driven by constraints of the environment, the system can remove steps and streamline the work.

Only consolidate tasks that the system will support, that you will redesign, or that you need to understand in detail. Use the flow model to identify the important tasks—the ones that help the user accomplish their central responsibilities. If the task will not be supported by the system, there's no need for a consolidated sequence model for that task. It's sufficient to scan the individual models for intents or breakdowns that might need to be addressed or that might inform another model. If a task is to be obviated, the consolidated sequence may still be useful because it identifies the intents that the current work practice addresses. Getting rid of the task will cause problems unless all these intents are supported in other ways or rendered irrelevant.

Make sure your system accounts for all intents before automating a task

Consolidating artifact models

Consolidated artifact models show how people organize and structure their work from day to day. Individual models show the structure and usage of the things people create and use while doing their jobs. Consolidating artifact models shows common organizing themes and concepts that people use to pattern their work. They complement sequence models by describing the things manipulated while doing the task described by a sequence. They provide clues to the appropriate structure for a system in the concepts they represent. They reveal work intents that must be supported and that might otherwise be overlooked. And an inquiry into the details of their structure shows how to support specific tasks.

Consolidated artifacts make conceptual distinctions concrete

Just as people only use a few strategies to plan their work, and define consistent roles to break it up among people, they use a consistent set of conceptual distinctions to organize how they think about work. These conceptual distinctions become concrete in the structure that people impose on artifacts they create and use—either by building the artifact in a particular way or by making annotations on an artifact given to them. Because the tasks that people do have similar structure, the intent and usage of artifacts are also similar. An inquiry into the individual artifacts that support similar types of work reveals this common structure.

The first step when consolidating artifact models is to group artifacts of a similar type—all artifacts that have the same intent or usage in the work. Deciding what is similar enough to consolidate together is modulated by project focus. A project to develop a personal organizer tool might want to study different kinds of calendars: personal organizers, shared wall calendars, online calendar tools. Which of these should be consolidated together? Consolidating all types would highlight common aspects of scheduling and organization, but would tend to bury the unique usage and intent of the different tools. For example, the primary characteristic of a wall calendar is that it is shared and can coordinate multiple people; a personal organizer is private but easy to carry anywhere. Consolidating the different kinds of calendars separately would spotlight each kind, but would tend to hide common issues across all types. Since our project is to create a new organizer product, we decide to try consolidating all the tools together so we can identify and transcend common issues. If we were creating generic PC software, we might have chosen to consolidate online calendars separately to better understand the strengths and limitations of the competition.

Let project focus determine which artifact types to consolidate

Once similar artifacts are collected, we identify the common parts of the artifacts (Figure 9.15). These parts and their relationships are the first and primary distinctions created by the artifact. These initial distinctions are driven by physical and cultural limitations as well as by the nature of the work. So a personal calendar has a cover to protect it from spills and scuffs. The need for a cover is driven by the environment, not by the nature of scheduling. The cover creates pockets that are useful places to store things, but they are not inherent to scheduling either. The to-do lists and kids' pictures one finds in these pockets suggest how, when a personal organizer becomes part of daily life, it can play a larger role in keeping things organized than just scheduling. On the other hand, the rubber band and tape both identify the current day and seal off the past—this suggests a recurring intent that *is* inherent to scheduling. Both these

Identify common parts of the artifacts

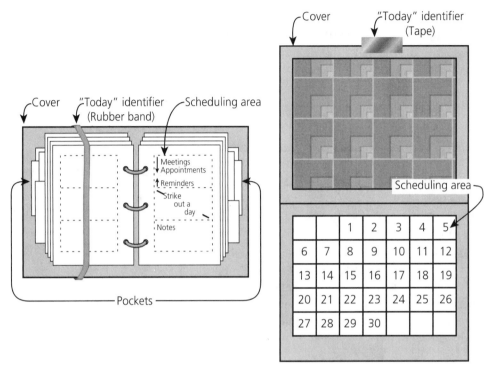

FIGURE 9.15   Two kinds of calendars.

mechanisms suggest that you schedule into the future and use the past only for reference.

Having identified common parts, we can look within similar parts to identify structure, intent, and usage. While the primary parts of a calendar are pretty much determined by the manu-

Identify the usage and intent of each part

facturer, the user has more scope for structuring the contents of a part in the way that makes sense to them. So a common part of a calendar is the scheduling area—the week or month view that everyone uses. Within that area we look for the different ways people organize time. So a multiday meeting is usually represented with a symbol that crosses days—people clearly think about one event spanning several days, not about a series of days, each of which is individually booked. Our tool had best provide for events that span days. So the inquiry into a part starts by observing one characteristic of one model, inquiring into its meaning for the work or the concept it embodies, and identifying that concept in the other models.

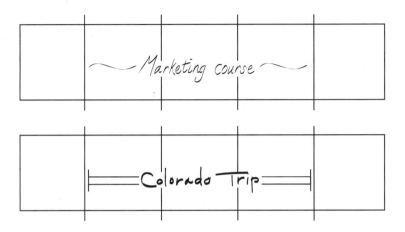

The contents of a part identify concepts and also presentations of those concepts. Looking at how events are written, we see that some are highlighted so they stand out from the rest. Clearly "important event" is a distinct concept. We also see a variety of ways that the event is highlighted. Depending on our focus, we may care to capture these different presentations. If we are developing an online calendar and if most people use double underlines to highlight important events, it makes sense to use double underlining in our calendar tool.

Look at how the parts are presented to grab your eye

The artifact will keep us honest if we let it. The artifact suggests that some events should be marked as important. It is natural for engineers, trained to worry about future extensibility and to hate special cases, to argue from this to something like a numerical priority scheme. Events could be given a priority from 1 to 10, views could be defined to show only events above a certain priority, functions could be defined to search for the next

Keep online artifacts simple by letting real data guide design

priority 1 event, and so on. But we do not have the data to support any of this. Saying some events are important is a very much simpler concept. Not only would these extensions make the implementation more complicated, they would also make the tool harder to understand and deal with. The result is a loss for the user, not a gain at all. Or to take another example, people sometimes tell us they write in different pens for different reasons. But the artifact tells us that in reality people write in the pen that is handy at the time. Being true to the message that the artifact gives us will help keep us from overcomplicating the system.

When an artifact like a calendar is predefined for later use, the structure people use may not match the structure they are given. They may go beyond the given structure, as when they separate reminders from meetings on a day. Or they may simply ignore the given structure, as when they draw the line for a multiday meeting right across the lines separating the days. Whenever the users depart from the given structure of the artifact, it reveals concepts and strategies that are real in the work. They represent opportunities for you to support the work better.

Having identified the parts and their usage and looked at their structure, we are ready to draw the consolidated model (Figure 9.16).

Make the consolidated artifact a good communication tool

In this case, we decided to look at calendars of different types knowing they might not consolidate well. In the event, we've identified many common intents and structures, yet because personal calendars are so different from wall calendars, the usage and mechanisms differ. It often works well to put the common or typical case in the center of a consolidated artifact, with variants around the sides. So we choose to put personal calendars down one side and wall calendars down the other, highlighting common intents and showing how each kind of calendar achieves that intent in its own way. The actual schedule part, where we saw little difference in intent or usage, we put in the center. Finally we step back and scan the whole model, looking for additional intents revealed by putting all the information together. By putting everything about this kind of artifact together, the diagram helps designers consider all aspects of the artifact coherently: common intents and the different ways they are achieved, the structures people create to help them, and the concepts they use to organize their work.

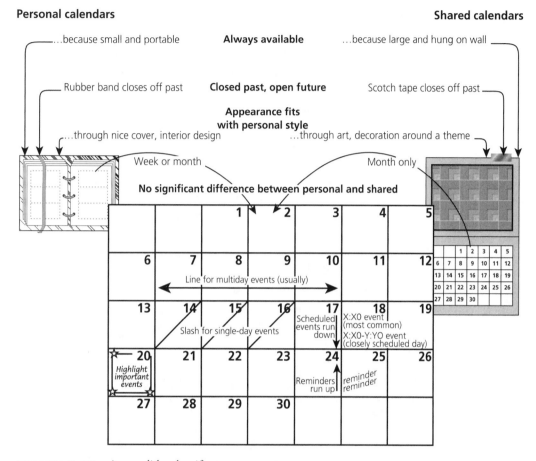

Personal calendars   Shared calendars

...because small and portable   **Always available**   ...because large and hung on wall

Rubber band closes off past   **Closed past, open future**   Scotch tape closes off past

**Appearance fits
with personal style**
...through nice cover, interior design   ...through art, decoration around a theme

Week or month   Month only

No significant difference between personal and shared

Line for multiday events (usually)

Slash for single-day events

Scheduled events run down

X:X0 event (most common)
X:X0-Y:Y0 event (closely scheduled day)

Highlight important events

Reminders run up   reminder reminder

FIGURE 9.16   A consolidated artifact.

STEPS

- Group the artifact models by the role they play in the work.
- Identify the common parts of each artifact. Identify the intent and usage of each part.
- Identify common structure and usage within each part. Identify breakdowns.
- Build a typical artifact, showing all the common parts, usage, and intent, and showing how they are presented where relevant. Show breakdowns.

Consolidated artifact models open a window into the mind of the users, showing how they think about the work they do. They are the most direct way to see how your users think. In addition, they help identify hidden intents that might otherwise go undetected and be unsupported in the system you build. They record the footprints left by

Consolidated artifacts show the footprints left by tasks

multiple sequences, often more than you could ever observe in person. One team examined scores of tracking tickets, collecting from each one the different intents and events that it recorded. In this way they quickly learned about different issues in the work represented by many hours of actual experience.

The level of detail to follow in consolidating an artifact depends on your project focus. If you expect the artifact to be rendered obsolete by the new system, do a quick consolidation emphasizing usage and intent. Look for secondary intents that imply potential problems should the artifact be removed. If you expect to support the work that the artifact supports, do a full consolidation, looking at concepts and structure as well. This will inform the organization of your system. And if you expect to put the artifact or its equivalent online, or if your system will create instances of the artifact (e.g., if you print calendars), capture details of presentation as well.

CONSOLIDATING PHYSICAL MODELS

The physical model shows the structure of the physical environment as it affects the work. Individual physical models show the workplace

Physical models reveal how space and layout affect work

and site for each user interviewed. Individual models show how the place is structured, how it is organized to support work, and how people and things move through the space in the course of getting work done. The consolidated physical models show the common physical structure across the customer

population and the key variants that a system will have to deal with. It keeps the design team aware of the limitations and constraints imposed by the physical environment.

Just as with the other aspects of work practice, physical structure repeats over and over. At first glance, office buildings present many different shapes, materials, and architectural styles. Yet inside the door, there is invariably a lobby area, with a receptionist or security

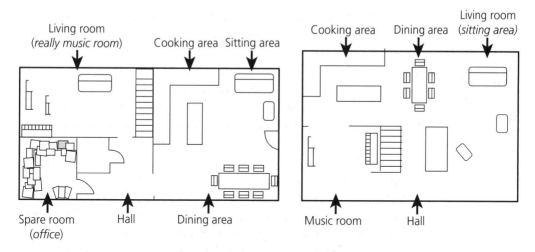

FIGURE 9.17 Determining the usage of space.

guard behind a desk who helps locate people. Beyond them are people's offices, labs, and shared work areas. Looking beyond a single
building, as soon as a company grows, recurring issues crop up around
travel between sites, communication between sites, support for meetings attended by people at several sites, and so forth. Consolidation
identifies and highlights these common structures and issues.

Consolidation of the physical model begins by separating the models into types of spaces. Usually one set of models represents a whole
site or multiple sites. It focuses on whole buildings
and relationships between them. Then there's another set that represents individual work spaces. Individual work spaces may be separate rooms, cubicles in a
large open room with partitions, or separate desks in
a larger room. And sometimes there are specialized spaces that are useful to consolidate—labs, loading docks, meeting rooms, and so forth.
Individual models belonging to each of these groups are collected
together (Figure 9.17). Always depend on the usage of a space to determine where to sort it, not its formal name—an unassigned office with
a round table where staff meetings are held is a meeting room, not an
office. A salesman's car may be his workplace.

*Identify unique usages of
individual space*

Within each set of models, we catalog the common large structures and organization. Buildings, rooms, walls, where people sit in

relationship to each other and the hardware they use—these are all distinctions that can be identified on site models if relevant to the project focus. Within an office, the location of desks, chairs, the in-box, and the telephone relative to each other and the occupant all reveal the organization of the space to support the work. Identify types of hardware, software, and network connections. At this point, the relative position of spaces, objects, and people is what matters. Whether an object is on the left or right is irrelevant; whether the user can reach it without getting up is what matters. When deciding how to interpret placement always consider the actual usage of objects, not their formal role. An in-box with gum wrappers and empty soda cans in it is a trash can.

Look at how objects cluster and their proximity to people

Once the large structures have been identified and cataloged, the model is open to another layer of inquiry (Figure 9.18). Sites are large and hard for individual users to change much, so they suggest constraints a system must live with and problems it might overcome. Identify these and write them on the model. But workplaces are much more malleable and reveal how people think about their work. The way people lay things out represents their attempt to build a physical environment that mirrors the way they do their jobs. When people do similar work, in a similar culture, to accomplish similar jobs, they re-create the same structures to support it. When telephones, calendars, and address books are repeatedly collected in one corner of the desk, it suggests a place for communications and coordination as a common theme. It suggests that a tool supporting coordination had better include finding people, talking to people, and scheduling work with people, since the physical model revealed that these are all part of the same task. Write these insights directly on the model as well.

Identify the constraints that the environment imposes on work

Movement through a space is also driven by the needs of the work, and we identify movement on the physical models when it is relevant to the project focus (Figure 9.19). Movement of people through space and movement of documents around an office are both useful to represent. The movement of people through space shows what the system must allow for and suggests opportunities to reduce the need to walk around. Movement of things in the course of

Show movement patterns and breakdowns

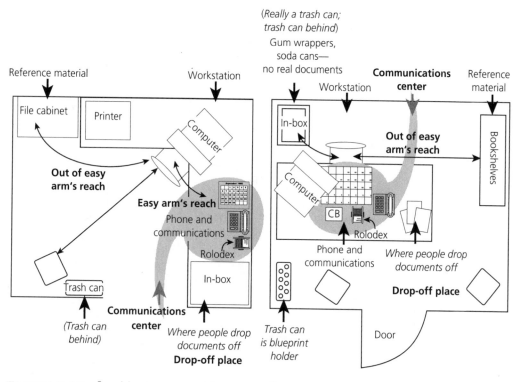

FIGURE 9.18 Inquiring into usage and structure of space.

doing work makes the sequence of work physical, highlighting transition points in the sequence when an artifact moves from one place to the next. Draw the movement on the models.

When all the spaces and artifacts are identified and examined, you are ready to create a consolidated model (Figure 9.20). Draw a single model, showing one instance of each common space. Where possible, use a single picture to show the structure of that space and things within it. For a system design focus, ignore aspects of the environment that do not matter to the work. Absolute distance from the worker doesn't matter; whether things are ready to hand does. Whether things are to the left or right doesn't matter. Potted plants don't matter. Where artifacts and tools really are in different places, we show them in all the places they might be—so we show a printer in the office and down the hall. The

Draw the model to reveal the issues the team should talk about

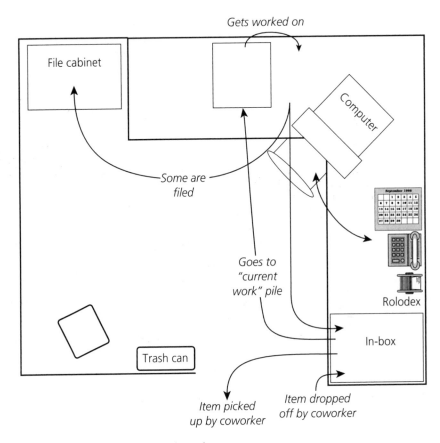

FIGURE 9.19   Movement through a space.

consolidated physical model shows the common structure and all the variations in that structure across users.

STEPS

- Group the physical models by type of place.
- Then walk each model in turn, identifying the different places in the model. Label each place with name and intent.
- For each type of place, identify common structure. Show where the artifacts and tools appear in the place.
- Look at movement on each of the individual models.
- Build a consolidated model showing all the parts and their structure. Carry over intents, usage, and breakdowns from the individual models. Write any insights on the model.

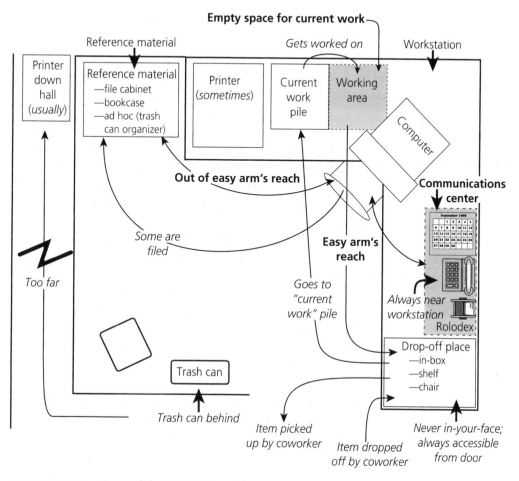

FIGURE 9.20 A consolidated physical model.

The consolidated physical model is a single model that shows the common issues imposed by the physical environment. It shows the hardware and software used by people in its context of use, the kind of access and movement allowed by the physical environment, and the constraints that affect people across the customer population. If a system does not live within these constraints or provide ways to overcome them, it will not be successful. Businesses studying their own work practice can make good use of the consolidated physical model not only to work around constraints of the current physical plant, but also to assist in designing new buildings and building layouts.

For these projects, system design can include redesign of the walls around people.

The consolidated physical models also show the common strategies in how people structure their environment to support work. This structuring provides clues to how people think about and organize their work. A system that incorporates this organization has a better chance of being acceptable to users and supporting the work well. And the consolidated physical model shows how people and things move through the workplace, indicating the stages of work process that a system may support or eliminate.

> *The physical model shows how the physical environment supports and constrains work*

A physical model is particularly important whenever the work to be supported involves multiple places or movement between places. This is a broad set of problems: even writing is printed on a printer (usually in another room), using materials that had to be collected (usually from another place), for review by one or more other people (who usually sit somewhere else). So even if the primary job is stationary, the whole job taken together may interact with the physical environment in interesting ways. Anytime the job includes handing work off between groups, or coordinating between multiple people, the physical model will be interesting for seeing how the groups transcend or manage physical separation. It will force the design team to be real about the impact a design direction will have. When the job is stationary and doesn't interact with others in other places, how things are clustered and used in the workplace reveals thought patterns and distinctions relevant to the system. Building physical models of each space important to the work reveals this structure and gives important clues to how people think.

CONSOLIDATING CULTURAL MODELS

The consolidated cultural model shows the common aspects of culture that pertain across the customer population. It is an index of issues that matter to the people doing the work—what they care about, how they think about themselves and the jobs they do, and what constraints and policy they operate under. The consolidated cultural model can be crucial to choosing the direction a design should take. Do system managers like running around to do their job? Then don't try to tie them to their desks. Either make them a portable system, or make their application quick to get in and out of. Are salespeople closely monitored? Then either make it easier for them to report their actions so they spend less time on it, or redesign their organization so they have more independence. Are customers closely regulated by the government? Then make producing the required documentation simple. These are the kinds of issues addressed by the cultural model. It indicates a direction for the design, and it shows within that direction what constraints have to be accounted for.

The cultural model reveals common values, friction, and policy

Every organization has its own culture—its own ways of doing things and its own attitudes about the world and the work it does. Yet these differences exist within severely restricted limits. Any environmental testing lab will be strongly influenced by the Environmental Protection Agency in the United States. Any computer hardware maker is affected by the competitive and fast-paced nature of the business. Any service industry has to worry about reducing turnaround time on their service because turnaround time is money in such a business. The nature of the business itself creates many of the pressures on an organization.

Culture is not unique within populations doing common work practice

Within the organization, the same kind of repetitive patterns emerge. Any organization that combines watchdog and service responsibilities creates a web of influences and attitudes around them. Purchasing, for example, both helps you get what you need and makes sure you follow approved procedures. Internal PC support both keeps your machine running and tries to make you run standard configurations and standard tools. Whether the service or watchdog aspects of the organization predominate, a pattern of interpersonal friction, influence, and pushback appears.

Even between people and work groups, we find repeating patterns of influence. Networks in companies are typically global these days, which means it is the working day for some part of the network all the time. Often 24-hour maintenance is provided by handing off responsibility rather than working three shifts. This shows up

Even patterns of friction repeat across businesses

as an interdependency on the cultural model. Asking a secretary to handle ongoing coordination of all aspects of an office is a common strategy for getting work done, but it creates a relationship of nagging and helping out in one direction, and requests and dependency in the other.

The first step of consolidating cultural models is to walk through each individual model, cataloging and grouping influencers (bubbles).

First, find all the influencers

We group influencers when they have the same kind of cultural influence, guided by our focus. So, for most purposes, regulatory agencies can be grouped together—but in the United States, a pharmaceutical company is so intertwined with the Food and Drug Administration that we might keep them separate from other regulatory agencies. If we are supporting system management, we might group all clients together—but if we notice that there's a special relationship to client management, we might keep them separate. If we are modeling an internal client, we generally keep the departments separate and use their real names so we can see the real interaction between them. We keep an eye on the influences—if we'd be prone to group an influencer with others, but notice that the actual influences are very different, we may choose to keep it separate so we can see the difference. After identifying and grouping the influencers across all models, we lay them out on the consolidated model, adjusting them to show relationships and overall direction of influence cleanly (Figure 9.21).

Next we consolidate influences. We walk through the instances again, collecting all the influences between each pair of influencers.

Then, add unique influences between influencers

When we've collected them all, we do a quick sort to get rid of duplicates and near-duplicates. The remaining influences are written on the consolidated model (Figure 9.22). As we go, we settle on wording that reveals the emotional tone of the influence and get rid of information about communication flow that wandered onto this model (a common error).

Every organization has its own culture and attitude about the "right way" to do business. This culture may be promoted directly by management or may be pervasive, with no clear source. We sometimes find it useful to represent both cultures on the consolidated model (Figure 9.23). The model will show both where the culture is

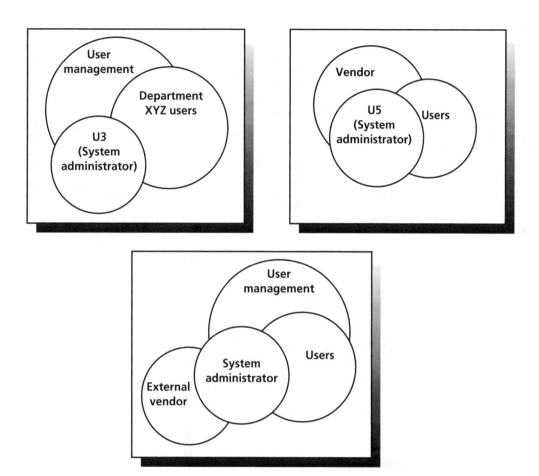

FIGURE 9.21   Identifying common influencers.

common across instances and where it differs. For example, some companies are totally customer-driven, while others appear not to know customers exist. The consolidated cultural model represents the issue and either shows the common attitude across the population or the variety of differing positions. Figure 9.24 shows a complete consolidated cultural model.

Keep variation across business or national cultures

The cultural model is one of the easiest to consolidate—it's usually fairly clear what goes together on the model. But the impact of the model is very great. The consolidated cultural model takes a bunch of

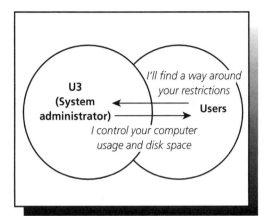

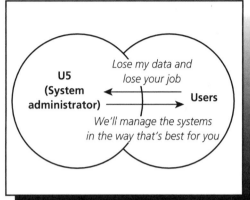

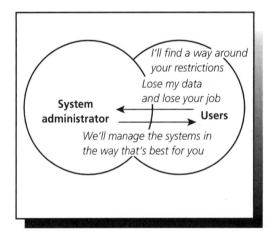

FIGURE 9.22   Consolidating influences.

STEPS

- Catalog influencers from the individual models.
- Group influencers who constrain the work in the same way.
- Collect influences from the individual models. Group by the pair of influencers they go between.
- Sort each group of influences, eliminating duplicates.
- Draw the final model, showing all unique influencers and influences. Copy over any breakdowns.

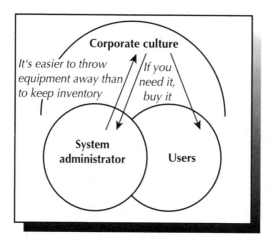
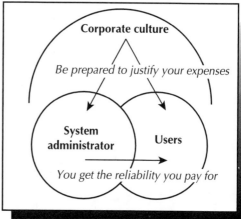

FIGURE 9.23 Two cultural attitudes toward money.

disconnected anecdotes and reveals the common themes and issues that a whole customer population cares about. By addressing these primary values, a system can distinguish itself from its competitors. The design team can address the issues, and the marketing team can use them to highlight benefits people really care about. Then the rest of the cultural model shows how to keep the system from trespassing on the customers' way of doing business either by violating a value or by failing to fit into the user's work style or environment.

The cultural model is always important when a system is designed for an internal organization or group. It's critical when characterizing a market—it shows what the market cares about and what pervasive influences they have to respond to. It's also important when the work being supported involves multiple groups of people interacting—the way people push back on each other shows up in the cultural model. The model is less important when the project is narrowly focused on the work of an individual; in this case, the few cultural issues of the user's values and self-image can be collected on the affinity.

The cultural model reveals the important values to address

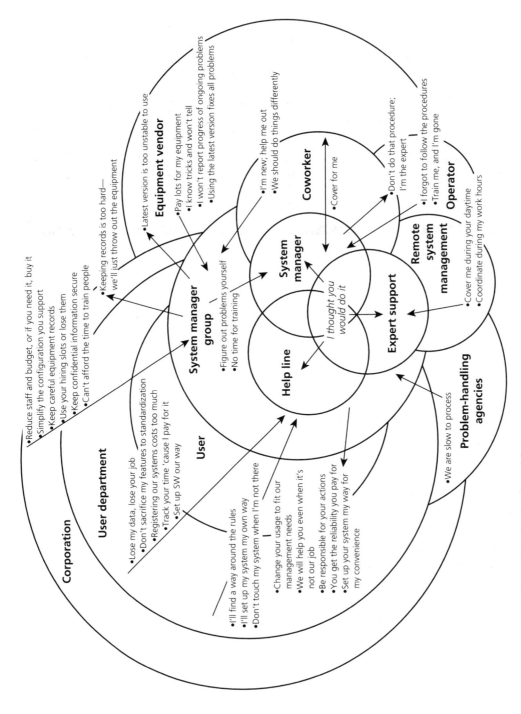

FIGURE 9.24   Consolidated cultural model.

THE THOUGHT PROCESS
OF CONSOLIDATION

Looking back over the different kinds of consolidation, it's apparent that the same kind of thinking process drives them all. We collect the data points of an affinity across users and build them up into groups. We organize responsibilities from different users into roles on the flow. We collect work steps and group them into abstract steps and intents. We collect and group parts of artifacts and places in the physical environment. And we collect influencers and influences in the cultural model. The detailed items say what to pay attention to; inquiry into each item reveals meaning for the project focus and how to group it with others. Out of that comes common structure and meaning.

Induction reveals the pattern and meaning hidden in work instances

Taken together, the consolidated models provide the detail about work needed to inform system design. Out of these models a design team can draw implications that guide design.

The customer's *intent* is the first and most critical implication to draw from the models. Sequence models show what the customer is trying to do and how they go about doing it. Artifact and physical models identify additional intents from the structures people create. The affinity shows intents directly. And the cultural model shows why people care—the constraints and values that are the reasons why an intent is important to customers. If designers can invent ways people can achieve their intent more directly, they streamline the work and reduce unnecessary steps.

People achieve their intents by putting *strategies* in place. The flow model reveals strategies for breaking up the work into organized units across people. The affinity collects strategies and shows how they relate to other work issues. The sequences reveal alternate strategies used to achieve the same intent. Designers can build these strategies into their systems or choose to improve on them.

Some strategies are made concrete in *structure*. Grouping tools into a cluster, separating work into piles, and organizing notes on a page are all different structures that make work strategies possible. These structures can be re-created in an online system when they are useful; when not, the system can provide better alternatives.

Structures also represent *concepts*. Concepts are created by people to help them manage and think about their work. When they create arti-facts in the course of doing work, they naturally repre-sent the concepts in the artifact. The affinity names and highlights additional concepts. With an under-standing of the concepts that organize work, designers can structure systems to implement and communicate in terms of those concepts. Building the user's con-cepts into the system makes it easier to learn and use.

> *Useful design data reveals the intent, strategy, structure, concepts, and mind-set of the user*

Finally, all these implications are affected by the customer's *mind-set*. The cultural model shows mind-set explicitly, but it can also be inferred from the physical environment and the detailed steps that people take in accomplishing a task. Understanding the customer's mind-set points designers at the important issues to solve and ensures that the final system will fit with the customer's work and culture.

Understanding intent, strategy, structure, concepts, and mind-set are key to effective process and system design. The work models make these aspects of work visible to designers. Each model captures a unique perspective, and each shows the common pattern of work and the variation across a customer population. They make the customer real to the engineer—so real that when, at two in the morning, he or she must make a design decision one way or another, the consolidated customer work has sufficient weight that there's a chance that the decision will be made in favor of the customer.

Communicating to the Organization

10

There's no point in gathering customer data if you don't use it for design. We've talked about how to bring a design team to a shared understanding of the customer, but teams are embedded in larger organizations. The design team cannot include everyone who cares about the result. There are the rest of the engineers on the project who have to believe in the system enough to code it. There are the three project teams working on systems that have to interface to yours. There's your manager, and his manager, and the very scary CEO who seems to read all your email. There's the marketing and product-planning department, who tend to be skeptical of ideas coming out of engineering. There's the sales force (of a commercial product), which needs to understand what makes the new product worth selling. And there are the customers (of an internal system), who need to be convinced that the new system will improve their lives. All these groups need to know what's going on, and many of them have important contributions to make to the design of the system. Projects often fail because their organizations don't understand or believe in what they are doing and don't support them.

Communicating to people who have a stake in the project is part of the job

A cross-functional design team might naturally include members from many of these organizational functions. But we've learned that while having a person from a group on a team is useful to incorporate that group's perspective in the design, it doesn't communicate what the team is doing back to the group effectively, and it doesn't give the group the sense that it can influence the design. It is just too hard for individuals

A cross-functional team doesn't guarantee communication back to the functions

to carry the whole burden of communication by themselves. So communication back to each group remains the responsibility of the whole project. Projects that do not assume this responsibility—that expect the other groups to find out what they are doing and comment if they care to—do not do well.

The communication that a project creates must be designed to inform each external group what the project is doing, to provide details that allow the group to understand the project's design direction, and to provide meaningful ways for the group to comment and contribute ideas with knowledge of the customer data. Each organization has its own perspective, expertise, and interests. This suggests multiple strategies to communicate to each group in a different way. The message needs to be tailored to the audience—what works for marketing may not be effective with programmers. There are many forms of communication open to the team, who must incorporate each group into the design process in the appropriate way.

COMMUNICATION TECHNIQUES

A good communication mechanism includes a hook, an activity that forces people to interact with the data. People don't incorporate new information well if all they do is hear it or read it. To get customer data in properly, people need to manipulate it, use it, or in some way engage with it. They need to make it their own. Then they will be able to offer suggestions and criticism based on the

People need to manipulate data to make it their own

data, not just their own preferences. A good communication mechanism also provides for immediate feedback. Contributing ideas and finding holes helps people stay engaged. People find it easier to buy into the design when they have contributed to it, and the contributions themselves improve the design. Finally, a good communication mechanism will reveal the customer work practice (or, later, the system design) as a coherent whole, not as individual, unrelated points. It encourages systemic thought, understanding and responding to the whole work practice together. The artifacts of Contextual Design support these goals naturally, and there are a few techniques that are generally useful.

WALKING THE AFFINITY

The affinity diagram was structured to tell the story of the customer—to arrange all the customer data to present the issues and concerns coherently. "Walking" the affinity gives the team a chance to review and think about this story. It can be done immediately after building it or right before doing the visioning. It's the team's first chance to see the whole scope of data together and to consider how to respond with a coherent design solution.

Anyone can walk the affinity: the whole team together, individual members on their own, or outsiders, interested parties, and other teams building related products. Each person reads the affinity silently. Often the team will designate an appropriate starting point, a place in the affinity that introduces the major issues well. To make the affinity easier to digest, teams do well to spend a little time cleaning it up. Some decorate the large divisions of the affinity with pictures, clip art, or artifacts illustrating the issue that part addresses. Groups can be directed to those parts of the affinity most immediately relevant to them, and they can work from there to the rest of the wall. Seeing the part they care about gets them interested; from there, they can see how it hooks into the larger work context.

Walk the wall to balance individual thinking with team discussion

Participants read starting from the green, then the pinks, then the blues, so they start with the high-level statement of an issue and work down to the specifics. They read the individual notes as necessary to get examples and details summarized in the blues. If several people are reading at once, they read quietly, like people in a museum; each person is following their own thread, building their own understanding of the data, and loud discussion would be disruptive.

As they read, each reader writes two kinds of notes: holes and design ideas. One records additional information and questions the reader would like answered. These are holes the team might fill in future interviews. The other records ideas for responding to the data. Initially, these ideas will be vague and respond to specific points, but as the readers see more and more of the scope of the data, their ideas will get more detailed and cover more of the work. The readers try to build up their ideas so that rather than responding only to a single blue or pink, they end up

The challenge: address the whole wall of issues with a single design idea

with ideas for how to address entire greens—or the whole wall. These notes are posted on the affinity next to the part of the affinity that they respond to. On a second pass, people can read each other's notes and see how others are responding to the data.

Writing design ideas on the wall is a way of interacting with the data. It provides a way to capture design ideas so that the design team can act on them, and everyone can feel they contributed something to the design. Posting ideas clears people's heads to go on to something new or to build an idea up into something larger. The nature of the affinity pushes people toward systemic thought. The first ideas may tend to respond to single notes with point fixes to small problems. But as people see more and more of the whole work practice revealed by the affinity, they naturally start to weave together themes and develop ideas that address larger aspects of the work expressed in the pink and green labels.

WALKING THE CONSOLIDATED MODELS

Similar to walking the affinity, walking the consolidated models is a way for people to engage with the work models. In pairs, people read through and talk about each work model in turn. They write issues on Post-its: key problems a design might address, constraints a design might account for, or a role the design should support (we will go into more detail about how to identify design issues using models in Chapter 18). When everyone has walked all models, the team shares all the issues collected for each model in turn. Some groups benefit from games of various sorts; for example, if participants work in the organization that the models represent, they may be challenged to find themselves in the models. Participants may be asked to answer three questions by finding the answers in the models. The models might be posted in the customers' own workplace, so they can annotate and correct them as they do the work the models describe. This is entertaining, and it gives participants more reasons for engaging with the data.

Models promote systemic thought about work and the system response

The models promote systemic thought by their very nature. By showing how the work hangs together, they suggest thinking about coherent solutions. Each model does take its own perspective on the work, but each perspective is a slice of the whole of work practice: the cultural model shows everything about culture; the flow model shows everything about communication and coordination. Looking across them quickly, the brain synthesizes an understanding of how the whole work practice fits together. Participants can see, respond to, and capture their ideas and issues using the model to drive their thinking about the work and about the systems that might support work better.

TOURING THE DESIGN ROOM

Using the models and affinity as communication tools is much more powerful if the team has a design room. Any team that does real, face-to-face, creative work needs a space of their own. Creative work requires props—the sketches and drawings capturing people's thought and discussion, of which work models are just one example. Trying to meet in conference rooms is unsatisfactory because all this paraphernalia must be cleaned out of the way of the people who have the room booked next. Individual offices are usually too small for a team and its data. A design room dedicated to a team means they can interrupt a conversation when they need to and come back to it with the context of their conversation still intact. It means they can keep the customer data on the wall and in front of their face. Some teams have even chosen to stay in their rooms during the coding phase of their projects—they had the data and use cases on the wall and could coordinate with each other whenever they needed to.

A team room lets you keep your customer in your face

A team room acts as a mechanism for communicating to the rest of the organization. Because the team's data is on the walls, walking the affinity or consolidated models is easy. Anyone walking into the room is immediately surrounded by the customer. Teams can and do design the room to communicate, using clip art and graphics to highlight portions of the wall, leaving Post-its with good ideas up, and so forth (Figure 10.1).

Not only does the data on the wall help communicate, it becomes the team's public memory and conscience. It's too hard to keep every aspect of work practice in your head at once—you will inevitably forget something. The models and affinity keep all the parts cataloged and available for quick reference. Though it's worthwhile to create online versions of the affinity

A team room is your public memory and conscience

FIGURE 10.1   A design room. The affinity diagram and work models on the walls keep the customer data instantly available for reference and sharing with others.

and consolidated models because online versions are harder to lose and easier to share with remote sites, the paper models are always the primary design tool. Keeping them on the wall in paper means each model can be much bigger than a screen, incorporating more data and allowing more people to gather around them at once. What's more, people have a spatial sense that helps keep the data organized. It's common for someone referring to customer data to back up a claim by pointing at part of an affinity that covers all four walls. They nearly always point to the right place.

TAILORING THE LANGUAGE TO THE AUDIENCE

Each group that a project might need to deal with has its own issues and concerns, its own way of speaking, and a different direction it can take the team's knowledge. In each case, the team needs ways to communicate that are tailored to the concerns and work style of the group. To understand those needs, we'll discuss some of the primary groups we've dealt with. Use this discussion to think about different groups' needs and how best to talk to them.

MARKETING

Marketing is responsible for ensuring a product meets a need for which people will pay money and for seeing that money actually is made on that product. When thinking about the customer, marketers tend to focus on demographics rather than work practice—what kind of customers make up the market, who has money to spend, and so forth. Marketing departments are responsible for defining what a product will do, but not for defining its structure in detail. Marketers are not designers—it's not their job—and they do not need to understand a product as a coherent system in the way designers do. Marketers are used to communications such as feature/benefit lists, lists of customer needs, requirements lists, wish lists, and so on. These lists emphasize individual points over seeing how things hang together.

Yet marketing is a major primary beneficiary of work models. As we discussed in Chapter 8, work models can be their map to the market they wish to dominate. For marketing, the affinity, flow model, and cultural model are the primary tools. The affinity elevates key issues that cross the market, acting almost like a checklist of issues to address. The cultural model reveals the attitudes and pressures central to developing a market message—it's easiest to

Help marketing see the real people they are selling to and their story

sell to someone when you know what they care about. The flow model is the primary map of the market, allowing marketing to see what roles they currently cover and how they might grow their product offering.

The primary issue with marketing is to see the real customers they need to sell to in the abstract representations of the work models. The roles on a flow don't reveal who the flesh-and-blood people playing the role are. It's important when talking to marketing to show how roles map to individuals in terms of the demographics they care about: young or old, man or woman, type of industry, and so forth. Marketing needs to see this to know how to build market messages that speak to the different kinds of customers.

A helpful way to communicate to marketing is through scenarios. A scenario is like the story of a single customer, but the "customer" is carefully designed to typify the market. A story is written about this customer, describing who they are, what they do, and how they work. The details of their lives and their work are chosen to include all the major findings from the consolidated models. (When it would be nonsensical to throw all these details into one story, or when it's important to show that the market comprises different types of users, several scenarios can be written.) The story should be no more than a page. Building a scenario is a useful exercise—it forces you to be concrete about what you understand and to prioritize. You can't put every detail from the models in the scenario, so you have to include only the most critical and relevant aspects of work.

CUSTOMERS

Communicating to external customers is marketing's job. But when the customer is internal, it becomes the design team's job. They have to make the customer organization—not just those customers on the design team—partners in redesigning the work and designing the system because it's the customers' lives they are changing. Redesigning work practice is much more direct, and potentially more extensive, because the design team can work directly with the customers. Including customers in the design team is important, but only a few can actually be on the team. The whole rest of the organization needs to be included in the design somehow.

It's difficult to include the rest of the organization because it's not their job to design systems. In fact, it's not even their job to design

Help customers see their own work practice so they can redesign it

their job. It's their job to *do* their job—anything else is a distraction. So absconding with large amounts of customers' time is usually not possible. Working through customer representatives—who have given up doing the job in order to be a representative—is also not ideal, since someone who isn't doing the job has a hard time speaking for the whole organization.

Because people do not generally reflect on the work they do, consolidated models can be invaluable in speaking back to the customer organization about how they work. If work practice is as invisible to those who do it as water is to a fish, consolidations lift the customers out of the fishbowl so they can see the water. Then, they can use their unarticulated knowledge to spot errors and holes and to add more information to the models. They can decide whether they like what they see or whether there are breakdowns that ought to be fixed. This is the basis for discussions, not just about what system to design, but about what new work practice to put in place in the organization for systems to enable.

Customers benefit from walking the affinity and models, but other kinds of participation are important as well. Interviews with a broad cross section of the customer organization are important, not just for the data, but so everyone knows they have been heard. Groups within the customer organization can walk the affinity and models. The models can be hung in the customer's work environment for people to extend and correct as they work. The models can act as a focus for process discussions among people in the customer organization and with the management of the customer organization. Contextual Design puts internal customers on the design team and includes customer contact at every phase. This involvement can and should be used to drive the design, to generate feedback, and to build excitement and involvement in the new system.

Use multiple techniques to involve customers

ENGINEERING

Engineers are designers. They understand the importance of seeing how things hook together. However, there are two problems with engineers: they have a long history of working with marketing, who worry more about point features than about system design, and they are overfocused on code, technology, and "clean" design. We'll take these in turn.

Because engineers traditionally get direction from marketing, they are used to directions of the form "build a system that does *this*"— specifying what the overall system is to do, but leaving open its structure and specific features. They prefer this, viewing the structural design of the system as their domain. Engineers are used to being the final sanity check. They view it as their job to ensure that all the individual mandated features can be combined into something that hangs together for the customer.

On the other hand, engineers have their own focus on technology and what makes a clean design. Just as marketing tends to define products from demographics because those are the tools available to them, engineering tends to design for clean implementation. Without a clear, explicit representation of work practice to act as a counterweight, they inevitably push for clean design in the implementation. This doesn't necessarily translate into simplicity; it may mean building in more flexi-

Customer data counterbalances the urge for technical elegance

bility than needed because each feature might possibly be needed by someone.

The affinity and work models give engineering exactly the information they need to structure a product. They not only learn who the customer is and what their issues are from affinity, flow, and cultural models, they also learn exactly how their customers think and work from the sequence and artifact models. This gives them a ground on which to design a system, basing design decisions on concrete data. (How to do this is the subject of the remainder of this book.) The engineers on a Contextual Design team are generally happy with the data and know how to build on it.

However, it's not possible to put the whole engineering organization on the design team, and those engineers who are not on the core design team discover that their role is more limited than it used to be. It's in the design of the system structure that the customer's work practice is redesigned, so this design must be based on consolidated models, not done by individual engineers. No longer are engineers given function lists that they are responsible for weaving into a coherent system. The new rules of the game are that all decisions are based on customer data. The design team produces a systemic design based at every point on customer data represented in consolidated models. (And, as we'll see in Chapter 17 on prototyping, the design is checked with customers all along the way.) The engineer's new role is to design and code the best implementation of the system design that they can, using the data, rather than their own preferences, to fill any design holes. Engineers who embrace this role are ecstatic—they hand off the job of understanding the user and structuring the design and focus all their efforts on the technology they love. Others have a harder time adjusting.

Walk data to give implementers structural information to guide design

Engineers benefit most from exercises that force them to interact with the data. Engineers are prone to inventing immediately from the data. They move so quickly from fact to design that they need ways to capture their ideas as they go. They also need to be moved from responding immediately to an individual piece of customer data with a single feature, to understanding the whole work practice and designing whole system structures in

Walk data to help engineers avoid one-shot solutions

response. Walking the affinity and work models are good ways for them to engage the data and push to a systemic response.

MANAGEMENT

Managers' first and primary responsibility is to ensure that the system gets out the door. Their focus is therefore less on exactly what features are shipped and more on whether the promised features are being completed on time, with acceptable quality. But managers have little direct control over a project—they depend on others to do the design and write the code. They have little visibility into the insides of a project and often do not discover that the whole project is in disarray until the day before a milestone is to be met, when they are told that the team is three months behind. The prime concern for management is milestones and deliverables because these are the only handles they have on the project. If a deliverable is completed at the planned date, the project is okay; otherwise, there's cause for concern.

Management is under intense pressure to ship fast. Most IT departments are running under the perception that they have up to a two-year backlog. For a commercial product, every week that a product slips is a week of sales irretrievably lost. But management typically discovers that a project is in trouble only when it fails to deliver something expected of it. For these reasons, design groups in the computer industry are under intense pressure to deliver, and code is the most visible deliverable. Any process that threatens to stretch out the time before code is delivered has to fight this pressure.

Help management see progress by using models as deliverables

Everyone recognizes that determining what to build before you start building saves time during coding. But it's hard to take that time when there's such pressure to ship and when understanding the customer doesn't produce anything concrete. Introducing a new deliverable—the consolidations—demonstrates the team's progress to the organization. Furthermore, these deliverables are of real value in themselves. They provide the map of the market that drives product strategies, or the map of the organization that makes redesigning the organization possible.

The favorite way of communicating the customer knowledge to management is through a slide show. A slide show is information packaged for immediate comprehension and action. For most purposes, management doesn't need to work with the data in detail. They need to understand overall themes and primary insights. The main use for the detailed structure of work practice is to design the system, which isn't management's job. Scenarios are also useful ways to communicate with management, since they present information in brief, concrete ways.

Talk to managers in their language: slide shows and UI mock-ups

Management has the right to demand clear, complete consolidations as one milestone in a project. This defines a deliverable that can indicate whether a team is making progress during the amorphous phase of initial design. It promotes quality, by ensuring that the team has developed a reasonably complete understanding of their customer and has it represented in a form that they can keep going back to in order to check their designs. And it ensures that the team captures their knowledge in a form other teams can learn from.

USABILITY

Usability groups are not directly responsible for the design, but they perceive themselves to be left holding the bag if the design is flawed. In this they are like test, human factors, or quality control groups. All these groups are used to holding the voice of the customer for the design process. They have direct, firsthand experience of the problems caused by a flawed system, but no good way to feed that experience into the design process early enough for it to be useful. They are typically brought in at the tail end of the cycle, after the design is finished and much of the product coded. At this point they are asked to identify easy fixes to a system that may be fundamentally flawed. The process sets them up to be in opposition to the engineers who built the product.

These are good people to include in the design team from the beginning. Including them makes their point of view available even in the initial stages of understanding the customer. They have experience understanding issues from the customer's point of view.

Put usability people on the team—they can be experts in customer data

They will see different things in the customer data and teach other designers this perspective. They can ensure that the usability problems they've seen don't get designed into the product. And incorporating them into the team short-circuits the organizational conflict between the groups, giving them a common goal to work toward. If putting them on the team is impossible, include them in certain working sessions—interpreting an interview or building the affinity.

There's another reason to include usability people on the team. They have usually been the primary focus for working with the customer on design problems, and they have developed techniques and expertise in working with customers. A new process that appears to cut them out of the loop can appear threatening. Making them part of the process from the beginning ensures they have a place in the new way of doing things and takes advantage of the skill they have in working directly with customers.

Once the overall design of the system is decided, there's still work in getting the details right and in defining a test plan for the system. The consolidated models define appropriate test cases; the roles indicate what customers should be part of the test. Up-front work on the system design complements usability testing; it doesn't replace it. As we'll see in the next sections, these tasks build on the design work of the team, and that work starts with the consolidated models. When usability and test people are on the team, they have a head start on their tasks.

MODELS MANAGE THE CONVERSATION

These are some of the main people a design team needs to communicate with. Each group has their own perspective and their own set of issues, and each group will use the models in a different way. Some groups, like management, really do best with an abstraction from the consolidations showing the key points. Other groups need to understand the consolidations at a very detailed level. We suggest different mechanisms for learning the data, allowing each group to interact with the data in a congenial way and to get from it exactly what they need.

An affinity diagram and coherent set of consolidated models don't just collect knowledge, they organize that knowledge in a way that reveals how work hangs together. They push design teams to think, not about a single task or problem in isolation, but in its context of interrelationships with all the other parts of the customer's work. Partly because of the intense time pressure and partly just because thinking about a whole customer population is hard to do, designers are often more comfortable designing one-shot solutions to single customer

Don't live in an ivory tower—keep your process open

problems. See a need, design a fix, code it in—it's simple, fast, and manageable conceptually. But systems designed this way get more and more unwieldy over time. Each fix is a single feature, added to the system without being fully integrated. Soon there are several ways to do every major function, dozens of windows and panes to handle every special case, and hundreds of customization options. The system becomes hard to use and impossible to learn. Not all complexity can be blamed on one-shot thinking—sometimes the work is complex—but the more complex the work, the more critical it is to maintain a coherent representation. It's inevitable that designers will design point fixes as soon as they hear a problem. By capturing individual ideas as they occur, Contextual Design allows for these one-shot fixes (and they can be useful in short-term work), but they are not coherent solutions. We capture the ideas and provide a place in the process where they can be collected and used as fodder for inventing a system solution. But that isn't until after consolidation has brought the whole work problem into a single focus.

Consolidation is the culmination of all the hard work of understanding the customer. The individual interviews brought designers

The goal is to design a whole system, not fix a point problem

face-to-face with the reality of customers' work. Interpretation sessions opened their eyes to all the different insights and interpretations a single event allows. Consolidation reveals the common pattern and structure underlying the variations across people. By doing so, it pushes people from one-shot, feature thinking to systemic design. Seeing how the work is a coherent whole enables a team to respond with a whole system that supports that work. Equally important, consolidation teaches how to see pattern and structure in masses of detail. This inductive thinking will prove to be a skill we draw on again and again as we move from understanding the customer into systems design.

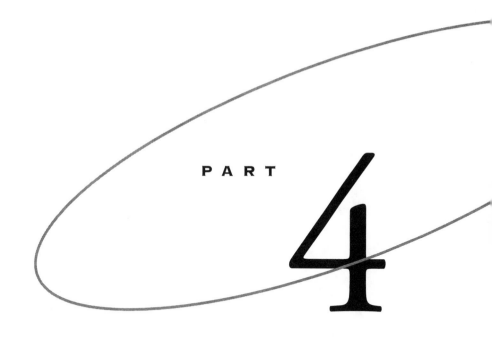

PART

4

Innovation from Data

Work Redesign 11

When a design team invents a system, they aren't just putting bits of software and hardware together to make a neat gadget. The real invention of a design team is a new way for people to work. If you're building a commercial product, you want to make a splash in the market by offering a new, attractive, and desirable way to work. If you're building an internal system, you're looking to transform the business through the appropriate use of technology. Even the smallest tool with the most limited effect on the work must fit into the larger work practice. In every case, what makes a system interesting to its users is the new work process it makes possible.

Though we introduced this perspective at the beginning of this book, it's a startling change for most teams we work with. We've seen how corporations split up the job of delivering a system across multiple roles, each role focusing on its own part of the problem. Engineers care about the hardware and software technology; marketing cares about how to sell to a market and build a product business. Of course, these are important components of delivering a system, but it's the work practice they enable that the customer cares about. IT departments have an advantage here; having a closer relationship to their customers, they are more likely to be thinking about how to support the whole business—and the recent focus on business process reengineering pushes them more than ever into the domain of thinking about the whole business.

> *Teams invent new work practice, not tools*

Teams deliver work practice, but the way they deliver it is through a system solution. That includes the system itself—the hardware and software that constitute the tangible deliverable—but also includes documentation and training. An IT system may include changes to procedures, policies, and organizational structure that enable the organization to take advantage of the new system. A commercial system will include additional services, support, delivery mechanisms, and the marketing approach that communicates the benefits of the new work practice. All these things together are the *corporate response* we introduced in Chapter 1. Though a different function is responsible for each part of the corporate response a corporation delivers, they are experienced by the customer as different aspects of a single system. Poor customer support affects the experience of quality as much as poor code.

This is the challenge for a design team: to come to an understanding of customers' work and needs; to invent a new work practice that

Teams deliver the corporate response: software, services, processes, and delivery methods

customers will want and that will improve their work; and to design a solution that brings together the different functions to deliver a unified corporate response. But just any response won't do. Today's business puts a premium on thinking "out of the box"—coming up with the creative solution to a work practice problem that no one else has thought of. For a commercial product, this can be the competitive edge that makes it possible to dominate a market. Internal systems are looking for the innovative work practice that will transform the work of the business. In both cases, customer data is the key to innovation. Customer data is also key to discovering the needs that no one knows how to articulate, but that if you addressed, everyone would say, "Wow! Someone finally got it right!"

Customer data drives innovation

The current cultural myth about how innovation happens is that some brilliant person goes up a mountain, or into a garage, and invents

Innovators are immersed in customers' work practice

something new out of whole cloth. We've even heard that one company kept their engineers away from customers intentionally because they didn't want to stifle innovation. But an examination of where brilliant ideas have actually come from suggests the opposite is true: not only does working with customers not stifle innovation, it is the most basic prerequisite.

Dan Bricklin designed VisiCalc, the first spreadsheet, while he was taking accounting classes in business school (Beyer 1994). He saw the tedious and mechanical work required to manage a paper spreadsheet and realized that with his knowledge of computer systems, he could automate the calculations while maintaining the spreadsheet metaphor in the user interface. WordPerfect, one of the first of the modern word processors, was invented when Alan Ashton and Bruce Bastian were working downstairs from the secretaries who were their customers. They would bring new ideas and new base levels upstairs on a daily basis for the secretaries to try and comment on.

These people did not innovate by doing what their customers asked them—no one was asking for an electronic spreadsheet. As we discussed in Part 1, customers don't have a good, articulated understanding of their own work. They are focused on the day-to-day issues of doing their jobs. What's more, they have only a limited understanding of what technology might do for them. Rather than responding to explicit requests, we find

Innovators design for needs that customers can't articulate

innovators immersed in the work culture of their prospective customers. Innovators observe problems firsthand and use their technical knowledge to recognize opportunities for using technology in ways the customers themselves may not see. By talking with people immersed in the work, building prototypes, and testing them out in the workplace, innovators turn these ideas into working systems. (We'll talk more about the role of prototyping in Part 6.)

The spreadsheet and WordPerfect examples also provide some insight into what an innovation actually is. No innovation is ever totally disconnected from what went before. Paper spreadsheets already existed for VisiCalc to model; editors and word processors existed before WordPerfect. Many people are tempted to say, "Well then, that's not *real* innovation"—as if these examples of successes in the marketplace are somehow not real. This kind

Work transformation comes from continuous evolution

of innovation, which builds on what went before to create a new class of product and capture (for a time) a new market, is good enough for most people. And it's absolutely dependent on using an understanding of the current work situation to invent new ways of working.

But that doesn't mean that it's impossible for technology to transform work; over time, the introduction of technology may completely transform a work task. Spreadsheets have grown beyond anything accountants envisioned 15 years ago. Word processing has very little in common with the creation of documents with typewriters. Work was transformed gradually, as people adopted the new invention and began to explore its possibilities. They invented new ways of using the invention, unforeseen by the inventors. Through their use and transformation of the invention, people became partners in creating wholly new ways of working. (It's through this process that products take over markets. The early adopters show how the product might be used; then as the product matures, it becomes easier for the larger market to adopt it. Through continuing innovation that fits the product to the market, the product becomes more likely to succeed [Moore 1991].)

Good inventors naturally follow the chain of reasoning outlined in our discussion of interpretation in Chapter 3: see a fact about the

Design is invention created by a team in response to data

work; see why the fact matters for people in the world; recognize the implications for bringing technology to bear on the work problem; and turn the opportunity into a concrete design idea. The design isn't explicit in the data. This is often a stumbling block for those new to customer-centered design. They expect that, with all this data, every aspect of the resulting design will be found in the data they collected. In fact, specific design ideas are rarely in the data; they are inventions created by the team in response to the data. So the critical design skill at this point is to see how the data guides, constrains, and suggests directions an invention can respond to.

CREATIVE DESIGN INCORPORATES DIVERSITY

Work is complex, multifaceted, and intricate with detail. How is a design team to immerse itself in this detail so they can see and respond to the work issues together? Each different consolidated model puts a specific dimension of work into focus for the design team; each model reveals problems and issues related to that dimension of work. Probing into one model after another in quick succession leads naturally to a synthesis of the issues across models. The team can absorb one coherent aspect of work at a time, making this complexity manageable. Discussing each model in turn begins a dialog about the data and what it means to the team and develops a shared understanding of the data and sense of direction for the design. In this way, work models give the team a handle on the complexity of work, encouraging them to respond to the work practice as a whole, not only to isolated issues and problems.

> *Creative and coherent design accounts for the complexity of real work*

The work models introduce one kind of diversity. The different perspectives on a cross-functional team introduce another. The skills and perspective of the people on the team determine what kind of a design they develop; everyone has a unique perspective and a unique pool of technology to draw on. As we saw in the examples of invention above, it's the application and recombination of existing pieces of technology to the work problem that make invention possible (see Grandin [1996] for an excellent description of this process). So the more different perspectives available to the team, the more design options the team can consider. This is the thinking behind the Total Quality Management movement: get the right skills in the room, and you'll address the problems of all the parts of the organization.

The "technology" that's important to the team means more than the hardware and software possibilities. Marketing has its technology of packaging, product structure, and how to talk to a market. Manufacturing has its technology of how to build and deliver the physical product. Business analysts have their technology of work process thinking. What marketing sees isn't the same as what development sees, and customer service has a perspective different from either. Yet each of these perspectives is important to delivering a coherent corporate response.

> *The diverse perspectives of a cross-functional team ensure creativity*

Creative design comes from a blending of these perspectives, the different views on work provided by the models and the different ways of seeing and bringing technology to bear provided by the people. The challenge to the design process is in supporting the human task of engaging with the models and other people, discussing what the models reveal and all the ways the team might respond, and developing a unified response that the whole team can support. Through the discussions, team members learn each other's perspectives and the skills and technical knowledge they bring to the table. As designers, they reassemble the whole work practice in their minds and respond to it systematically to keep the work and the corporate response coherent.

CONTEXTUAL DESIGN INTRODUCES A PROCESS FOR INVENTION

But doing this discussion and synthesis, in a group, without arguing, and in a reasonable amount of time depends on a clear process—a set of concrete actions to take. That's what Contextual Design provides. The team needs to immerse themselves in the data first, so inquiry into the consolidated work models is the first step. Then Contextual Design provides a visioning step, in which the team brainstorms new work practice that addresses the issues they saw. But creative design is hampered by agreeing too quickly. It's important that the design team think widely, consider several alternatives including radical solutions, before converging on a single approach. So the team develops multiple solutions, pulling out different aspects of the work situation to address. These different solutions are consolidated into one response that incorporates the best ideas into a single unified corporate response. And to be successful, this corporate response has to be tied back down to reality. It has to fit with the customer's work in detail, it has to be feasible, and the corporation has to have the skills and technology to deliver it. The different functions of the corporation can each work out their part of the vision in parallel.

It's important that the process make these steps explicit. Much of the argument within a team at this point typically looks like arguments about features: "Sue wants to implement a weekly coordination meeting among a district's sales force. Can't she see that giving them all laptops would be better?" But this isn't just an argument about a feature; it's actually embedding a whole chain of reasoning: What data would support one idea over the other? How would each idea affect the work on a day-to-day basis? What are the implications for the design? What goals or values should the design achieve? And only then, which specific idea

Reduce interpersonal friction through an explicit invention process

would work for this set of users? Giving the team time to think about the different aspects of work and the implications for design both makes it easier for the team to have the design conversation together and makes the team more creative.

This is the goal of work redesign: to look across the different models and see a unified picture of work practice, to use the different team perspectives to reveal the issues, and to use a wide exploration of multiple possibilities to drive the invention of a creative design solution. A good design process will define explicit steps for these activities.

WORK REDESIGN AS A DISTINCT DESIGN STEP

We've described a step in the design process in which to do work redesign, but how does it fit into the overall development process? Where does the development of a corporate response tying together all the parts of a complete customer solution fit in? The corporate response drives requirements for software and hardware, but it also drives requirements on the associated business processes, infrastructure, the marketing message, packaging, delivery, and associated services. It's a much broader design than just saying what the software will do. What's its relationship to the steps currently expected of engineering teams?

Figure 11.1 shows the software life cycle typical in the industry (Davis 1993). This life cycle starts with requirements gathering and analysis and goes on with design of the software implementation, followed by the implementation itself. But analyzing classic requirements (see "Unraveling the Software Process," below) shows that software requirements embody the implications

Traditional requirements assume changes to the work

of a new work redesign for the supporting software system. Because requirements say what the system will do, they assume changes to the work. Work redesign had to happen even in the traditional life cycle; otherwise requirements could not be written. But if it's an implicit step, with no process support, it's hard to see the work coherently, hard to ensure that the design offers a coherent work practice, hard to tie all parts of the corporate response together, and hard for the whole

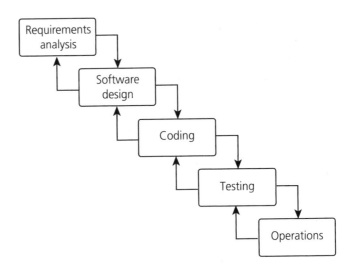

FIGURE 11.1   The traditional software life cycle.

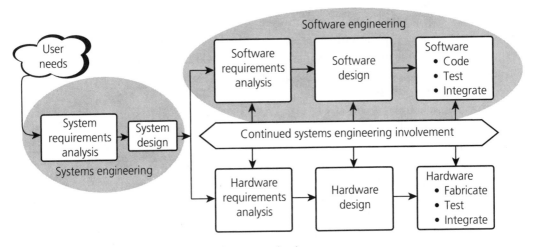

FIGURE 11.2   The systems development process.

team to understand and contribute. So Contextual Design makes the work redesign step explicit—and systems development processes, such as Figure 11.2, suggest how to do that (Keller and Shumate 1992).

Figure 11.2 shows the *systems* development process, which covers the entire deliverable system, of which software is one component. (It doesn't explicitly recognize the other parts of a corporate response.) In

UNRAVELING THE SOFTWARE PROCESS

We've claimed that requirements embody work practice design, but let's look to see if that's really true. "Design," when it refers to the software process step, is a technical term referring to the design of how the software will be put together. It's more restrictive than the normal English language usage, meaning the invention and organization of any structure. "Analysis" is defined in different places as a model of the real world (Martin and Odell 1992), a description of what the system should do without saying how it should do it (Rumbaugh et al. 1991), or a description of the solution assuming perfect technology (McMenamin and Palmer 1984). Leaving aside the question of how to reconcile these conflicting definitions (how can the same activity model the real world and describe the new system?), none maps to the work redesign step as we described it.

To illustrate, here's a specific example: the requirements specification for a CAD tool states that the tool must allow drawings to be locked while they are being worked on, so that two engineers don't try to update the same drawing at the same time.[1] This is a requirement in the classically correct form: it states what the system is to do, without saying how it should do it. Using the alternate definition, it assumes no technological limitations in saying what a perfect system would do.

But it is not a model of the real world. You cannot walk out into the real world and find locks. Instead, the requirement specifies one technical design element that implements a work practice solution to the real-world problem. Locks make it possible to ensure that only one person at a time can change a drawing; this is the underlying work practice to be implemented by the system. It's possible to state the user need in a way that does not imply a design solution: "Multiple people must be able to use the system simultaneously without getting in each other's way." But this would not be an adequate requirement—it would not tell the engineering team what to build.

Requirements go beyond a description of the real world to invent and choose one specific solution to a need. Other designs might meet this need equally well: The system might allow simultaneous update of the same diagram, but support easy comparison and merging of diagrams. Or, if two people started changing the same drawing, the system might show them both what the other person was doing in real time. Both these alternatives meet the underlying need. Because requirements embody a design choice, we do not view analysis as a process of successive refinement (Loucopoulos and Karakostas 1995). Instead, we see it as an act of invention (Potts 1995).

The three design options—locks, merging, and simultaneous update—differ in the work practice they support. Other considerations being equal, which option to prefer depends on which work practice is better for this population of users. If engineers work on a drawing for a while, but conflicts between them are rare, it might be reasonable to keep two people from working on the same drawing, and locks might be the best choice. If people make small quick ▷

---

[1] This example is taken from Rumbaugh et al. (1991). Because we are focusing on the underlying thinking process, we find that a textbook example reveals the issues most clearly. It was constructed, after all, to be a good example of a clean requirement.

changes but often work on the same drawings, merging might be better. If changes are rapid and no one is the primary owner of any drawing, but collaboration in changes is necessary to keep the drawing consistent, simultaneous update might be best. The specification of the first design option as the system requirement implicitly defines the work practice to be preferred over all others. And it does so without making the design choice or the underlying issues explicit.

So the choice of requirement embodies a work practice design choice. And this design choice can be informed by the work models—the manual work patterns that preexist the automated system are usually a good indication of what's really needed in the work. Work models of the organization in the example above might show that engineers commonly print out diagrams and hang over them together, discussing changes and marking up the diagram as they go. This is a good argument for simultaneous update (though the system had better account for that informal discussion that happens at the same time). But if models show that diagrams are handed from person to person, each person reviewing and modifying the predecessor's work, then locks (which implement a similar work practice) are probably the way to go. Unless there's concrete evidence of breakdowns in the work practice that should be overcome—such as errors introduced because people aren't coordinating their changes enough—you want to design for the work you see. ❑

this model, the entire software engineering life cycle follows after the initial "systems engineering" design process. Only once the needs of the overall system have been identified and the overall system designed, can the requirements on the software be analyzed and software engineering start. Working out the details of the software and hardware design will reveal issues and problems for the whole system, which are worked out by keeping systems engineering involved throughout the process. Software requirements analysis is a response to the systems design, not an initial activity responding to the real world directly.

Contrasting the typical software life cycle of Figure 11.1 with the systems life cycle in Figure 11.2 gives the impression that software

The standard software life cycle is missing a work redesign step

engineering as a formalized discipline started by splitting off from the engineering process for embedded systems. It's as if the industry adopted only the "software engineering" part of the process, without recognizing that the initial design of the overall system was still necessary. There is still a broader system to be designed, including the work practice of the user into which the software fits. When that's done, the software analysis step can reveal what the software has to do to make it possible.

In the organization, the transition between organizational roles tends to support this traditional split. Business analysis decides what the business needs and what the system should do. Software development figures out what the analysts want (requirements analysis) and how to build it. Marketing (in theory) decides what the customer would buy, what features it has to have, and how to design a whole corporate response around it. They pass requirements to engineering, who then analyzes those requirements and builds the system. In fact, as we discussed in Chapter 2, it's never so clean—marketing can't determine the right response without the detailed technical knowledge held by engineering. Business analysts can't specify the system in isolation from the business processes and support structure. Designing the corporate response is its own integrated activity.

Calling out work redesign as a distinct step gives a straightforward way to fit the design of a corporate response into the software development life cycle (Figure 11.3). Designing the corporate response is an initial activity that includes deciding how people will work and what software has to do to support that work. Software requirements analysis produces a model of the design solution as it affects the software, not a model of the real

Giving time and place to work redesign makes coherent creativity possible

world. The design decisions currently embodied in requirements are made during the redesign of work practice. This is indeed a design step, which provides a place in the life cycle to make the design choice between alternative models of work. As a design activity, it responds to the understanding of the customer needs and drives the subsequent development activities. (See Catledge and Potts [1996], Hefley et al. [1994], and Kelley and Hartfield [1996] for other perspectives on this distinct design step.)

In the rest of this part, we'll discuss how to design the corporate response. We'll show how to use work models with the multiple perspectives of a cross-functional team to see issues in the work and create a vision that responds to them. We'll show how that vision can drive an integrated corporate response, including the definition of the system component.

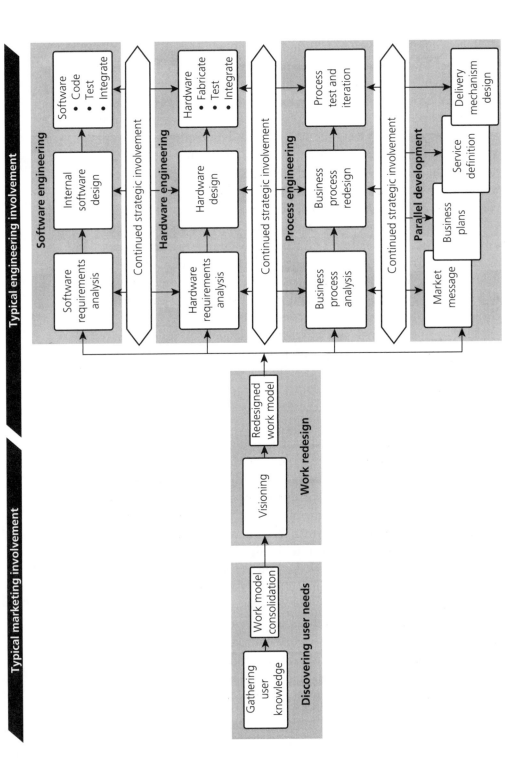

FIGURE 11.3 Contextual Design in the software life cycle. With a vision in place, developed by redesigning customers' work practice, it's possible for each function of the organization to work on their part of the corporate response in parallel. Continued coordination ensures that the teams keep working to the vision, that their parts work together, and that changes are reflected throughout the system.

Using Data to Drive Design

12

We've defined a new process step, work redesign, and we've located it in the systems engineering process. It's the job of the work redesign step to invent the new work practice that a corporation will deliver by building systems, offering services, and redesigning procedures. Invention of work practice is based on a foundation of customer data, driven by knowledge of the different available technology and how to apply it to the design problem.

There are all kinds of technology a team might take advantage of—hardware, software, delivery mechanisms, service possibilities, and process design, to name just a few. But there's one critical kind of technology that a team must have yet is not commonly available. The team's primary task is to design work practice—which means that knowing how to manipulate work practice is a central skill for the team. The "technology" of work practice—how to see issues in the data, how to think about redesigning work to address the issues, different process options for redesigning work and their benefits and drawbacks—these are necessary skills for a design team. Yet they are skills most teams don't have.

The critical team skill: how to see and design work practice

There are two ways to learn how to see work structure. One is inquiry into the consolidated models. Inside each work model are hidden issues and insights that will inform the design process, but it takes knowledge and inquiry into the models to pull the issues out. The second way to see work structure is to look at work that has the same structure or pattern as the work you're studying, but that is more familiar or transparent. By using this

See work structure in consolidated models and metaphors

work like a metaphor, drawing parallels between it and the work you care about, you see issues and structure you might not think about otherwise.

What follows suggests some ways to look at consolidated models and see the issues they suggest. Then we'll discuss metaphors and how to use them. These ideas will get you started thinking about how the work models might suggest design possibilities.

THE CONSOLIDATED FLOW MODEL

The consolidated flow model ties together much of the critical information about the customer. It's your best starting point for understanding work practice and driving design. The flow model shows the roles people play and how they map to individuals; looking at the roles, and the flows that support them, reveals communication patterns and problems in the work.

Every mapping of roles to individuals raises unique problems. When too many roles are assigned to one person, that person is overwhelmed and unable to focus on one thing. When they are split up among many people, then those people have to coordinate to get the job done. Departments often oscillate between these extremes: overcentralization causes a bottleneck so they diversify, then when they realize that diversification caused communication problems, they recentralize. But any arrangement of roles creates its attendant problems. It's our goal to build the solution to the problems into the work process rather than search for the perfect role structure that solves all problems.

Look at how roles map to people and organizations

With that introduction, let's look at some of the issues associated with roles and mapping them to individuals. To facilitate discussion, we'll give each issue a snappy tag and then discuss its implications.

ROLE SWITCHING

Everyone plays more than one role. Each role is a coherent set of tasks and responsibilities that hang together organically. Switching roles is like switching hats; it means putting aside an entire way of thinking and set of concerns, and taking up another. Sometimes the new role

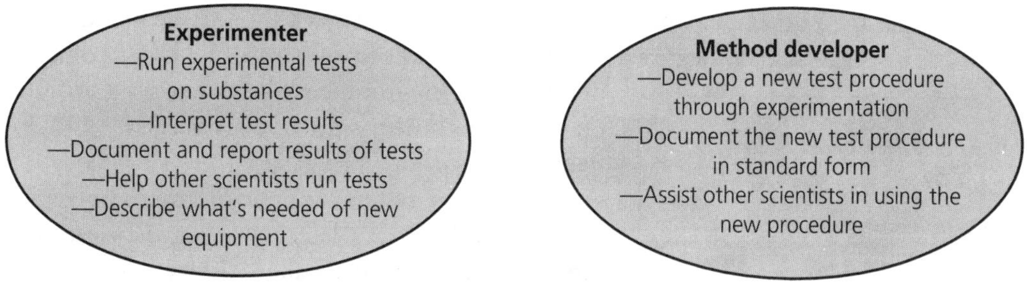

FIGURE 12.1 Two roles played by a scientist (the two roles are shaded alike, indicating that the same person plays both). Switching between roles is part of the scientist's life, but do the tools support putting down one role and taking up another?

just continues the work, as when a developer who does her own testing starts testing a module. But sometimes the new role is an interruption, in which case the whole context of the interrupted task has to be stashed away to be recovered later, and a new context brought out to worry about. Every transition between roles is an opportunity to forget something, to allow an issue to fall through the cracks.

Consider the scientist who also develops methods: formal procedures for doing an experiment (Figure 12.1). He's in the middle of defining a method when a test run completes. This forces a switch from the Method Developer role to the Experimenter role. He may choose to analyze the results immediately or save them for later, but he must at least clean up after the test. He has to save everything about the method to one side in such a way that he can resume the work later.

Role switching creates opportunity for something to fall through the cracks

Role switching suggests issues a system could overcome. Do people have to reenter the same information in each of their different roles? If the roles are played by more than one person, redundant data entry is wasteful, but if the same person reenters the same data, it's exasperating. A scientist who creates a method shouldn't have to reenter information about the method in order to use it. Can systems share data to eliminate reentry?

Do the systems in place support the movement from role to role? Are they completely disjoint systems, so switching roles means starting up an entirely new interface? Are some roles not supported at all, so users are cast back on their own resources for part of the job? The developer who finds herself having to switch back to the command line and homegrown scripts to run tests won't think she has a complete development environment. Look for ways to integrate systems so they provide seamless support for the work.

The system's job is to hold work context for people switching roles

And do the systems support putting a role aside and coming back to it later by saving the context of the task? Do the systems allow the task to be interrupted? What context does the user need saved? Saving context doesn't have to be complicated—Microsoft Word saves your last position in a document so you can pick up right where you left off.

HINTS

- Eliminate redundant data entry
- Support movement from role to role
- Support consistent interfaces for the different roles
- Save state to support interruptions

ROLE STRAIN

When people play too many roles, they get overwhelmed. They are trying to wear too many hats, each of which has its own imperatives, its own concerns, and its own demands. There are just too many roles to switch between. Any small business person is plagued with this problem, as are secretaries. Dual-income families have it in spades. The constant switching increases the demand on the person and increases the chances that they'll lose track of things. Furthermore, the roles themselves may call for different skills or meeting different goals.

Look for people who drop the ball because they wear too many hats

The person who has the primary responsibility for running a household provides the classic example of role strain (Figure 12.2). Each different role has its own needs and tasks, its own demands on time and concentration. But when there are so many, the people are always juggling them, trying to give enough time to each that nothing important falls through the cracks.

When you see people under role strain, look for ways to alleviate it. Are there roles that could be totally automated, or substantially supported? Online shopping eliminates the Shopper role, reducing

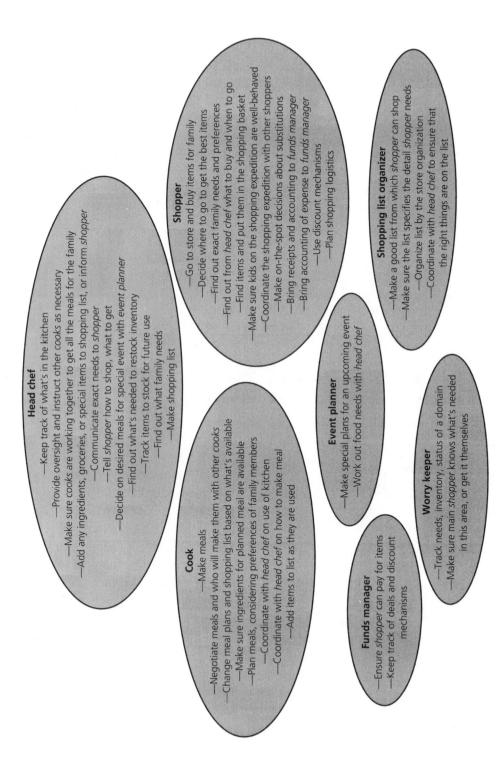

Head chef
—Keep track of what's in the kitchen
—Provide oversight and instruct other cooks as necessary
—Make sure cooks are working together to get all the meals for the family
—Add any ingredients, groceries, or special items to shopping list, or inform *shopper*
—Communicate exact needs to *shopper*
—Tell *shopper* how to shop, what to get
—Decide on desired meals for special event with *event planner*
—Find out what's needed to restock inventory
—Track items to stock for future use
—Find out what family needs
—Make shopping list

Shopper
—Go to store and buy items for family
—Decide where to go to get the best items
—Find out exact family needs and preferences
—Find out from *head chef* what to buy and when to go
—Find items and put them in the shopping basket
—Make sure kids on the shopping expedition are well-behaved
—Coordinate the shopping expedition with other shoppers
—Make on-the-spot decisions about substitutions
—Bring receipts and accounting to *funds manager*
—Bring accounting of expense to *funds manager*
—Use discount mechanisms
—Plan shopping logistics

Shopping list organizer
—Make a good list from which *shopper* can shop
—Make sure the list specifies the detail *shopper* needs
—Organize list by the store organization
—Coordinate with *head chef* to ensure that the right things are on the list

Cook
—Make meals
—Negotiate meals and who will make them with other *cooks*
—Change meal plans and shopping list based on what's available
—Make sure ingredients for planned meal are available
—Plan meals, considering preferences of family members
—Coordinate with *head chef* on use of kitchen
—Coordinate with *head chef* on how to make meal
—Add items to list as they are used

Event planner
—Make special plans for an upcoming event
—Work out food needs with *head chef*

Worry keeper
—Track needs, inventory, status of a domain
—Make sure main *shopper* knows what's needed in this area, or get it themselves

Funds manager
—Ensure *shopper* can pay for items
—Keep track of deals and discount mechanisms

FIGURE 12.2 Some of the roles played by a head of a household. When one person plays so many different roles, just tracking the work of the different roles becomes a problem.

the number of roles people have to juggle. Failing that, can you keep much of the information needed by a role in the system, so people don't have to rely on their own organization? If you capture the issues a Worry Keeper tracks, and remind him of things he might forget, it will be easier to play that role. Or it may be possible to move a responsibility or a whole role to another person. In this way, the advent of word processing moved most of the document production role from secretaries to professionals, giving the professionals more control and reducing the cycles of passing the document back for correction.

The system's job is to off-load people by automating work

HINTS

- Automate or eliminate roles
- Support and organize roles
- Move responsibilities or roles to other people

ROLE SHARING

When multiple people with different job responsibilities all play a role, they are role sharing. Doctors, nurses, and technicians may all take samples from a patient (Figure 12.3), but they'll do it differently. Doctors draw samples in the context of a patient consultation; lab technicians don't have any other contact with the patient. The different people have very different skills and expectations: doctors assume their time is at a premium and have no patience for dealing with computers, but it's the lab technician's job to make sure all data is entered and is correct. And the context of use is different: doctors will do the work in a consulting room, while lab technicians often have stations set up especially for taking samples.

People with different jobs, skills, and tolerances play the same role

So how should the system respond? Recognize the different needs and characteristics of the different users. Even though it's one role and one task, don't assume one interface will fit all users. Design for the most demanding user, and create a system that is cleaner for everyone. Doctors may not be willing to put up with a complicated interface, but an interface that works for them may be an

The system's job is to work for all the people who share a role

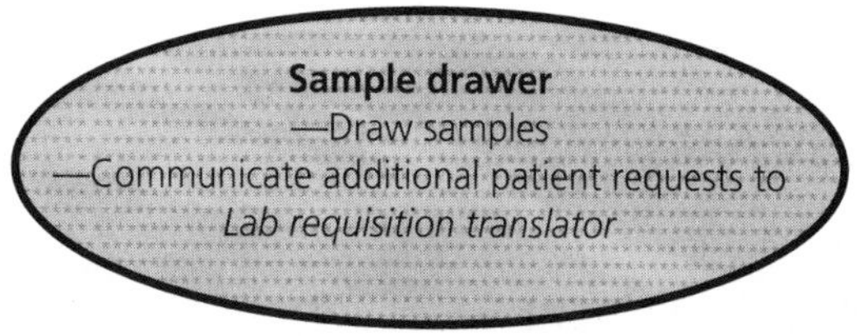

Sample drawer
—Draw samples
—Communicate additional patient requests to
Lab requisition translator

FIGURE 12.3   A role annotated to show how individuals play the role. The shade shows that nurses play the role, the pattern shows that technicians do, and the dark outline shows that doctors play the role.

improvement for other types of users as well. Doctors may need a portable system with pen input that they can take with them on their rounds. Technicians may be able to use a desktop interface and may be willing to do keyboard entry. But they'll need the system to integrate with the rest of their work, including sending the sample to the lab for test. Also, look to see whether all users need the same information. The doctors may need less detail than the tech, even though they may share data in the underlying system.

HINTS

- Tailor the interface style to the user
- Tailor the data presented to the user
- Share data internally across the types of user
- Fit with the rest of the roles each type of user plays

ROLE ISOLATION

Any of the above problems may be resolved by separating roles cleanly among individuals. But that just raises a new set of issues. Each role has a coherent job to focus on, but it needs to hand off work to other roles and communicate the context of the work—the roles depend on each other to get the job done. When people don't do a job, they don't know what's involved in doing it or why it's hard, and they often end up blaming the people responsible for it for not doing it well. It's like a manufacturing line—everyone understands their own part of the job and blames the other parts for not producing the materials or using the results properly.

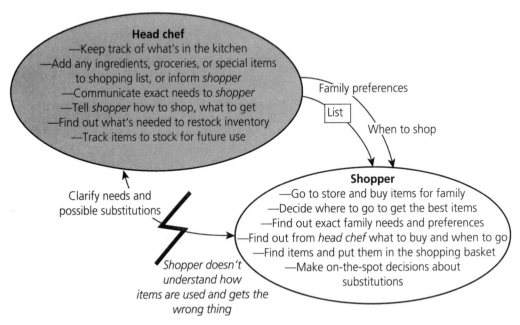

FIGURE 12.4 Shopping as a role isolated from the Head Chef. The Head Chef or Cook knows what the meal is and what ingredients will work. The Shopper only knows what they've been asked to buy. So if the list doesn't specify the exact brand and size, or if the Shopper can't get the exact item and has to substitute, they don't get the right thing.

Sending someone else to do your shopping invariably creates role isolation (Figure 12.4). If the store didn't have something on your list, your shopper has to choose whether to substitute something else or come back with nothing. How can they decide which to do? They'll only know which to do if they know what you want the items for and how they fit together. Otherwise, they'll come back with half a meal. So each role has to have enough of the whole work context so they can really do their tasks on their own.

Division of labor doesn't eliminate the need to coordinate

When roles get too isolated, and it becomes clear that communication is a major problem, organizations sometimes create liaison roles whose sole job is to maintain communication. A typical situation for IT departments is to have the business customer communicate requirements through a customer representative, the person on the customer side chartered to say what they need (Figure 12.5).

The system's job is to carry context between roles

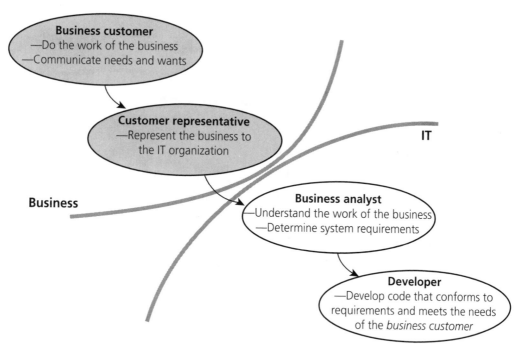

FIGURE 12.5 Role isolation at work. Two new roles have been created to manage the communication between the business and the developer.

These requirements are communicated to an analyst, the person on the IT side chartered to find out what customers need, so the developers can build it. These intermediary roles exist only as an attempt to overcome role isolation.

Deal with role isolation by addressing the communication problem. Can you capture and communicate state by introducing a new artifact, or by automating and improving an existing one? Can you show each of the different roles exactly what they need to do their part of the job—so the Head Chef sees "cream cheese," but the Shopper sees "1 Philadelphia Cream Cheese, 8 oz. block"? Can you coordinate the handoff process so that the communication from one role to another doesn't look like passing an artifact only, but allows for a conversation around it? Can you show the context of a communication, so the Shopper finds out which ingredients all go together? Where intermediary roles have been created, can you facilitate their communication, or should their responsibilities be folded back into the primary roles on either side?

HINTS

- Communicate the whole context between roles
- Support communication between roles
- Present only the information each role needs
- Automate or eliminate unnecessary liaison roles

PROCESS FIXES

When you're an IT department working with internal users, there's a wider range of fixes available to you. In partnership with the business, you can redefine job responsibilities, reassign roles to different people, put new procedures in place. If you decide to eliminate a role, you can do so by automating everything it does, but you can also simply reassign its responsibilities to other roles or introduce new procedures to make it unnecessary.

Redesign the work by changing role structure directly

One company completely rethought the purpose of its purchasing department. The department's primary role was the Shopper, placing orders for people and paying bills—and making it more difficult and slower to buy things. In fact, much of their work was clerical and added no value. They decided they wanted to give up the Shopper role entirely, returning it to each individual department. They would restrict themselves to the Finder role, helping people locate and set up relationships with vendors for the things they needed. Integrate process fixes such as these into your system response—your system won't just support the work as it is, it will support the system as you and your business partner redesign it. Include the people responsible for looking at your business process on the design team so they are included in the discussions and you have the benefit of their expertise.

HINTS

- Design the organization as part of designing the work
- Consider process and procedure changes
- Consider defining new roles and job responsibilities
- Include business process designers on the team

Target the customer

Once you've looked at the flow in detail in all these different ways, step back and scan across the whole model. Ask: Where is the center of the work? All aspects of work are there for a purpose. What's core to that purpose? An analytical lab's sole purpose is to get its clients the answers to specific questions about the materials being tested. Everything else an analytical lab does is in support of that. So the Experimenter role is central—but if there was a way to run experiments automatically, even that role could be dispensed with. Every role is a means to an end. Look for the fundamental intent and seek ways to address it more directly.

If you're a commercial product developer, this central role is the key leverage point for your market message. Even if you're actually selling a product to support another role, you'll want to show the benefit of the product for the Experimenter. If the lab can't get the procedures done fast enough because it takes too long to wash the glassware, emphasize how your glassware washer will improve the Experimenter's life. Even if they don't make the buy decision, they will make recommendations, and their problems become the lab's problems.

Find the key roles to leverage the market

Look across the model to see what roles you address in your current product set. What other roles do they touch? What other roles are played by the same people? Those roles are natural to address in future products. Use the flow model to plan how you'll address the whole market.

Pitfalls

Your last inquiry is a sanity check. What will you mess up if you do the things you plan? By automating a role, have you broken a communication path that the role maintained? By shifting a role to another person, did you create role strain for them? Is there a natural separation of roles that you should maintain, such as the separation between writer and editor? By separating roles, did you create role isolation that you will have to overcome with additional tools? Remember that every division of roles creates its own set of problems. Make sure you cover the mapping of roles to people that

Caution: don't create new problems with your fixes

occur in the market, and make sure your redesign addresses the new problems it will create.

THE CONSOLIDATED CULTURAL MODEL

The cultural model reveals values, standards, constraints, the emotional and power relationships between people and groups, and how they all intermix, conflicting and supporting each other (Figure 12.6). Because it concentrates on feelings, the cultural model contributes very little structural information to the design. What it does is give lots of guidance on what matters to address and what constraints to respect. It reveals the hot points, the interpersonal and process problems that people really care about fixing.

The information provided by the cultural model suggests a couple of different design options. Some influences are constraints you cannot change. These will affect how any product is accepted; a good design should conform to the constraint. Some influences reveal problems in the cultural climate that a system might overcome or ameliorate. Or, if the influence is a good thing, the design can actively encourage and support it. Finally, when an important value seems to be missing from the workplace, the design can seek to introduce a new value as part of the new work practice.

Choose the culture to build into your system

INTERPERSONAL GIVE-AND-TAKE

If the flow shows the communication between people, the cultural model shows the emotional aspect of the relationship. The different ways that people attempt to impose their will on others and get resistance are captured on this model. Relationships in which the power is unequal reveal this power imbalance in the language and type of influences (Figure 12.7). Look for irritation or subversion in the influences; these will indicate where people are rubbing each other the wrong way. "I'll find a way around the rules" indicates people aren't happy with the way the rules have been set. Look for people fighting over turf: "I manage databases. Don't touch them." "I only work on hardware problems."

Positive influences show where people join forces to get things done, or where a group value shows up in the way the work is done. Look for the positive values: "It's my job to fix your problem no matter who's at fault." "We cover for each other." Look for ways to support these positive values.

Redesign to reduce interpersonal friction

Look at what's creating friction to see how to alleviate it. Is it caused by role isolation, such as the isolation between system management and users? Then increasing communication between the groups may be the answer. Or maybe it would be better to design systems that meet everyone's requirements. If you can ship a system that does what users want and is still easy to manage, part of the friction will go away. Look also for pervasive influences coming from the company or professional culture. These influences will be the hardest to work around—find a way to live with or support them.

HINTS

- Alleviate role isolation
- Increase communication
- Address the immediate complaint

PERVASIVE VALUES

Formal policy set by the organization and the organization's implicit values constrain what people do, how they act, and even how they think. The values that an organization makes real in its culture determine what people care about and what motivates them. Some values are driven by the organization. They constrain people in the organization, defining what they care about and think they are up to as a group. Other values are driven by groups and individuals, and either reinforce the organization's values or push back against them.

Pervasive values may show up as a single influence that runs into multiple bubbles, but they may also appear as multiple influences that together point to larger attitudes and mind-sets. When the organization pushes the value "keep careful equipment records" on the system managers, this is part of a constellation of values having to do with being a careful, managed organization that is in control

Choose whether to support or alter customer values

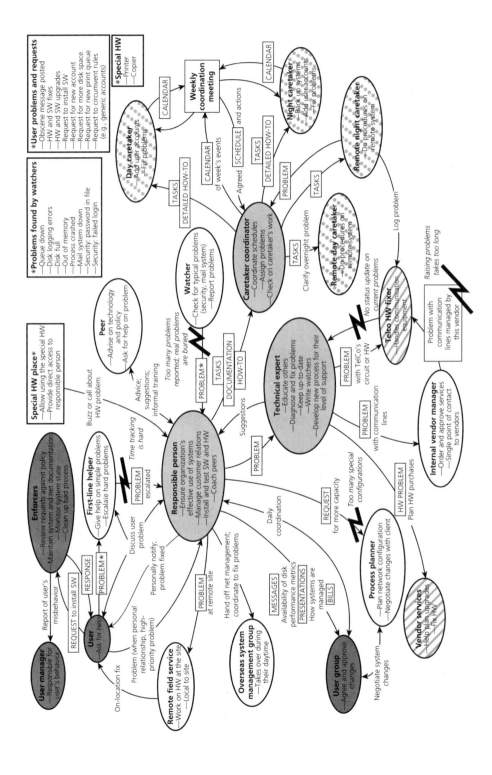

munication between isolated roles. The First-Line Helper can handle simple problems, provide quick help, and escalate the real problems that need fixing. But the Responsible Person loses some of the context of the problem, as indicated by the three-way discussion that sometimes follows. And the escalation process takes time. Users will send urgent problems to Responsible Persons directly if they can.

Looking over the whole model, it's no surprise that the system administrator's roles are in the center of the work—but the model shows exactly *how* they are in the center. Administrators work with users to keep the systems working for them and to communicate policy. They work with operators to do the day-to-day chores. They have automated alarm systems (Watchers) informing them when things go wrong. They work with planners on expanding the system and with vendors on problems and on fixing the systems. The administrators are in the center of a web of relationships that work together to keep the system running. That's what system management work is about and what a product has to maintain if it's to be successful.

FIGURE 12.6 This consolidated flow represents part of the work of system management. This model uses shading and pattern to show how the roles map to job functions—light gray for the roles that system administrators typically take on, dark gray for users, dots for operators, and stripes for outside vendors. (The roles with white backgrounds don't map to specific job functions.) An inquiry into this model pulls out of all this detail the key issues a team might focus on in a design supporting system management.

The relationship between the Caretaker Coordinator and the Caretaker roles reveals role isolation—especially in the number and type of flows between the roles. Caretakers are the administrator's hands for routine jobs, but communication with them needs to be clear and detailed or they won't perform the administrator's intent. Caretakers also contribute to role strain on the administrator—they off-load routine tasks, but the administrator has to manage them. There's so much management that it effectively creates a new role for the administrator.

The First-Line Helper is an intermediary between User and Responsible Person. Such a role is often put in place to manage com-

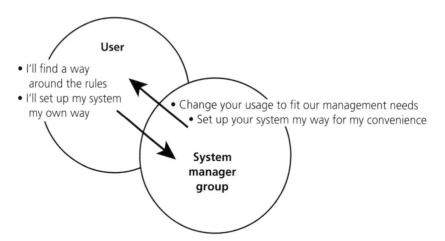

FIGURE 12.7   Showing the nature of a relationship: the use and subversion of power between system managers and users.

of how it does things and documents actions thoroughly (Figure 12.8). But individuals or groups may push back. "It's easier to throw equipment away than keep careful records" indicates both a willingness to counter the corporate direction and a willingness to spend money. These attitudes will show up in other values and in concrete behavior.

Dealing with pervasive values usually means deciding whether to work with them or against them. To work with a value, introduce systems that make it easier to achieve—perhaps an automated tracking system will make it easy to keep records without requiring major overhead. Look at the flow model to see what roles the value touches and where systems might make a difference. Work against a value when you decide it's counterproductive. So you might decide that your organization is *too* willing to spend money. Then introduce systems that expose how much people are spending and when; make the budget visible and show how much is left against each budget item. Be aware when you're bucking the culture that this may make your system less attractive—you'll need a good story for why it's better to use the system anyway or else it will have to be so subtle that no one minds.

Values and policies you decide to accept join another category: the absolute constraints you can't or won't do anything about. If the FDA (Food and Drug Administration) regulates your industry and failing an FDA inspection will cause your stock price to drop, there's no way to get rid of the value "We document our procedures every way we can

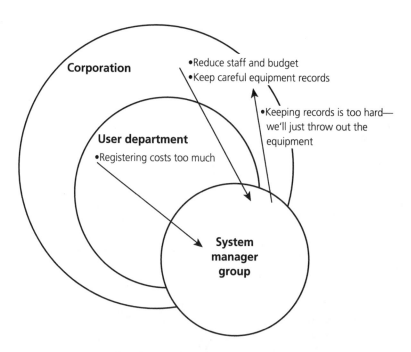

FIGURE 12.8 Identifying policy and values. They will show up on the cultural model, but watch what happens to them. Do they get picked up and carried through into all parts of the organization, or are they subverted?

for the FDA." If the whole corporation is organized around "Shipping hardware is how we make money," trying to focus on software will always be hard. Make sure your system promotes, or at least won't interfere with, these absolute constraints.

HINTS

- Make positive values and absolute constraints easier to achieve
- Make negative values harder to achieve
- Oppose negative values by introducing counterbalancing positive values

---

PUBLIC RELATIONS

The cultural model, more than any other, tells a team what their customers care about (Figure 12.9). It reveals the key issues that should be the focus of the team's efforts. So the cultural model can be a focus

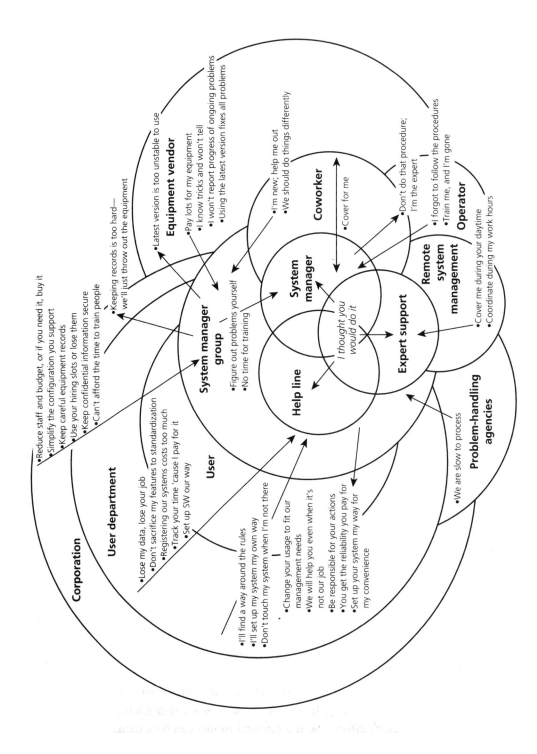

FIGURE 12.9 This consolidated cultural model for system management shows the relationships inside the system management group, the relationship to clients, and the relationship to external vendors. Within the group, it's apparent that communication and organization is a problem. Problems can be lost in handing them off between the different parts of the group, and coordinating with the operators is difficult.

With respect to the larger organization, the system management group is subject to some heavy constraints. They have to keep the users happy ("Lose my data and lose your job"). There's some evidence of role isolation causing friction between system managers and users in the influences going back and forth. The corporation also imposes constraints—both in demanding such things as equipment tracking and in limiting such things as funds for training. We see how the training problem filters down into additional problems running the group ("Figure out problems yourself"; "Train me and I'm gone").

Finally the model shows the relationship between the system management group and external vendors. (This can be particularly interesting when the team building the model is one of those external vendors—they are mapping their relationship to their customers on their model.) The model shows how external vendors aren't responding to system managers' needs. The refusal to share technical tricks and to provide status information is infuriating to people who prize knowledge as much as system managers do. And the assumption that everyone is eager to upgrade their systems at any moment is just unrealistic.

Because this model reveals the vendor's customer relationship, as well as the rest of the system manager's relationships, it's particularly conducive to developing a slogan. Perhaps the team might choose "We're on your side"—unlike all those other vendors we'll take your side in helping you do the work of managing systems. This might lead to specific product components that make it easier to handle tracking and handoff, but it might also lead to services designed to share knowledge with system managers.

for discussing how your team wants to appear to the customer—what message you want to give. You can write yourselves onto the cultural model (if you're not there already) and draw an influence to the customer population. What do you want that influence to say? Do you want to be the "We are your reliable protection against FDA audits" people? Or do you want to be the "We let you get your work done despite all those bothersome requirements" people? What's the message that will sell to the population?

A convenient way to capture this direction is a team slogan—a single, simple statement of the team's mission they can use to keep themselves focused. In one case, the marketing manager

Plan your impact; write your organization into the cultural model

looked at a cultural model and said: "Look there— what all these influences are saying is that our customers need flexibility in expanding their systems. They aren't going to plan ahead and they can't. What they really need is fast response. If we could turn around their order in 48 hours, they'd buy from us without thinking." "Turn around an order in 48 hours" became a slogan for the team—it emphasized a simple, achievable system characteristic, important to their customers, that they could focus on. The slogan becomes a rallying point, a way of choosing between options to advance the team's primary goal. Use the cultural model to define a slogan that fits your customer's desires and who your team wants to be.

PROCESS FIXES

It's easier to affect corporate culture when you can change management structure and process. Management can deal with interpersonal friction by introducing better communication channels of all sorts, from new systems to brown-bag lunches. They can introduce new values not only by ensuring that the systems enforce values, but also by changing management tone and procedures. Defining new cultural influences can be a task for the whole organization, of which the automated systems are just one part.

When you're building a system for an internal client, the customer

Change processes of internal organizations directly

can be on the design team, and they'll see possibilities in the data beyond system delivery. In one team, a manager in the client organization sat in front of the cultural model for a good five minutes, then jumped up and said: "But this is wrong! We want everyone in our organization to be conscious that the day-to-day decisions they make directly affect how long it takes to ship product. That's not here at all!"

It wasn't there, of course, because that value wasn't real in the organization—no one was acting out of it. The manager drew a new influence in to represent the new value he wanted to instill. It's part of a manager's job to monitor and manage the values of an organization, so it was natural for him to see the omission and to think he could do something about it.

PITFALLS

The primary danger with the cultural model is that you'll try to lead the customers where they don't want to go. Are you really supporting the issues they care about? If you're introducing a new value, do you have evidence that anyone cares about that value? The success of the first notes products were limited because they were pushing open, flat access to information on organizations that were, at the time, hierarchical and closed. Only

Don't try to take customers where they don't want to go

when the notes products started to include controls over the access to information did they become successful. Make sure the changes you introduce will cause someone in the customer population to sit up and take notice—otherwise, you aren't giving customers a reason to adopt your system.

THE CONSOLIDATED PHYSICAL MODEL

The physical model's primary message is about how physical space constrains what you can do. The world of walls and buildings is hard to change. Within the walls, however, there is room for adapting the physical environment to the needs of the work. People lay things out to meet their needs, define spaces to support the work they do, and otherwise make the physical environment work for them. The physical model shows both the constraints imposed by the environment and the structure people create within those constraints to get their work done (Figure 12.10).

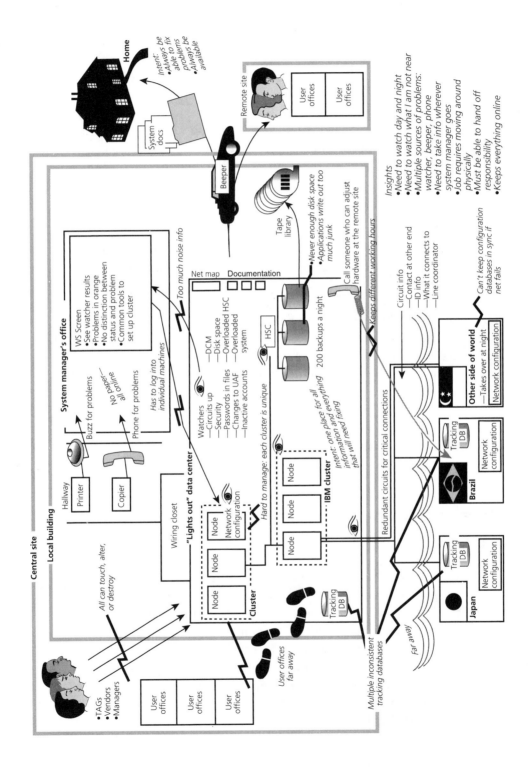

FIGURE 12.10 A consolidated physical model showing a system manager's environment. This model shows the nature of the large-scale physical environment and populates it with important work elements.

The first aspect of the reality check is just to look at the spaces: system management isn't just about the machine room. This is a global network, managed by people on several continents. They all have to coordinate, and they have to hand off problems and control of the network. Even within one site, the spaces aren't close. System managers have to walk between the users' offices, their own office, and the machine room.

Looking at the physical model like an archeologist, the aspect that jumps out immediately is all the different ways system managers create to stay hooked into the systems. Online watchers that send an alert when conditions change, telephones and buzzers by devices that may fail, telephones in the computer room to call other sites monitoring the network—clearly it's critical that system managers feel like they know what state all parts of the network are in at all times.

The message of this model might be summed up in two design implications: First, communicating and coordinating with all the other system managers that keep things going is critical. If a product can help system managers organize and manage their response to system problems and user trouble reports, it will be well received. Second, helping system managers keep tabs on their system is critical—and that means facilitating the communication of problems from users as well as from automated watchers.

THE REALITY CHECK

The first message of the model is to make it inescapable what the customers' physical world is like. If the work is spread out over several buildings, then expect communication to be a problem. Look for existing communication mechanisms: Are people networked? Is *everyone* networked? What other communication mechanisms exist? Maybe people communicate primarily by yelling to each other. At one site the user talked to the wall and the wall answered back—the partitions were so thin that workers could collaborate even though they couldn't see each other. Is the space noisy or quiet? How many people will be disrupted if the system starts beeping?

The physical model may reveal intents that augment those on other models and may reveal issues that are reflected in other models.

Know what you can and cannot change

The physical model may reveal that your customers walk around a lot; check the cultural model to see if this is a positive value you should encourage ("We know everyone and are always on the spot to help") or an annoyance you should alleviate ("Every phone call means another interruption and another hike"). The physical model may reveal that supplies from different vendors are kept entirely separately; this will explain why the sequence model for working with vendors shows that people work with only one vendor at a time. In this way, the physical model contributes to your understanding of what's important to the work, as well as helping you get real about the constraints your system must live under.

Design your system to deal with the constraints the physical environment imposes. Allow for the way people move around in doing the work—we've seen people call from a field site back to their main office in another town, asking their coworkers to log them out so they can log in remotely and get their work done. Let mechanisms that work be. If people communicate effectively by yelling to each other, they probably don't need email very much. And don't forget the other side: take advantage of the hardware that is in place. If most of your users already have two monitors, why not use them?

HINTS

- Don't depend on what's not there
- Account for movement and multiple locations
- Overcome communication problems
- Take advantage of what is there

WORK STRUCTURE MADE REAL

Where people can change the physical world to match their work, they build into the physical structures concrete representations of the work structure. Designers can learn the structure of work by analyzing the physical structures people create, just as archeologists learn about cultures by analyzing garbage dumps. When the consolidated model shows a "current work" pile, this is a concrete representation

Fit with the way people organize their work

of how people organize their days. A room dedicated to disposing of hazardous materials indicates that how disposal happens is an important concern. Each place—whether a pile, a corner, or a whole room—is a clustering that supports one particular work intent. That intent is real to the users and could be real in the system you deliver.

Then the relationship of artifacts and clusters to the user shows what matters in the detailed doing of the work. What's in front of the user, within arm's reach? These are the artifacts that the user chose to have "in their face"—they are the critical things to have handy. What's behind the user, pushed out of the way? These need to be accessible, but they don't need to be immediately to hand. If the user is technical and much of their work is online, look at the screen and how it's laid out—it will capture much of the organization of work.

Look at the structure built into the physical world for clues into how to build the system. When the structure exists because users made it that way (the physical environment didn't force it to be that way), it's a structure that matters to users in organizing their work. Build that structure into the system and you'll support the work better. When people create a "current work" pile, it says that the primary organization is "what I am working on now"—not by project. If you design a system that organizes work only by project folder, it will fight the way people think about their work. Look at placement to determine the detailed structure of the system. An artifact that is pushed out of the user's way probably shouldn't be the most prominent thing in the system, but things kept at hand can be easily accessible in the system.

HINTS

- Build conceptual structures into the system
- Match the intent of the place, not the detailed appearance
- Make the things in the user's face easily accessible
- Put things placed behind the user out of the user's way

MOVEMENT AND ACCESS

The pattern of movement of people and artifacts through the physical environment provides another layer of insight. The flow of an artifact through a person's office shows the important stages of working on it and indicates what stages an automated system should support. The movement of people through space shows important relationships in the physical environment—so frequent movement between the different system consoles in a lab indicates that the work is on all the systems together, not on each system individually.

Finally, the relationship between spaces reveals distinctions and intents. When home offices are repeatedly located up or down a flight of stairs from the rest of the house, it indicates that separating home office activities from household activities matters. When conference rooms are located around the entrance to the site, and none are found near offices, it indicates that meetings are thought to be how you work with clients, not how you work with each other. The arrangement of space indicates its usage, and its usage suggests attitudes, values, or intents that matter for your design. If it's a problem that workplaces are far away, look for ways to bring that work closer through automation.

Separate spaces reflect work distinctions: don't violate them

Movement in the physical world indicates how to structure a system. The steps people take to work on an artifact reveal stages of work. Look at the sequence model to see the work structure, and build a system that matches that structure or redesigns it. If two kinds of work are kept separate in the real world, maintain that separation in the virtual world—people won't want to mix them. Use the arrangement of the real world to find out what matters. But make sure you match the intent, not only the actual arrangement. Putting the office up or down a flight of stairs indicates this is separate work that wants to be physically separate, whereas the separation between phone and Rolodex is only a reflection of physical limitations.

HINTS

- Match or improve the flow of artifacts
- Maintain conceptual separation between parts of the work
- Support the intents implicit in the arrangement of space

PARTIAL AUTOMATION

It's hardly ever possible to put everything online. People increasingly use email, but paper mail still exists. So even if email is easier to file and track, it hasn't gotten rid of paper filing—what it's done is to introduce a new layer in addition to paper filing.

In the system you build, consider whether you've automated everything about a job or whether customers still need paper. When you build an automated ordering system, will people still print and file a paper version so they can track what they've ordered? When you automate scientific methods, will scientists still have to print them to meet FDA requirements? When you make lab orders electronic, do requesters still have to print the order and attach it to the sample? Make sure you've either covered the whole job or that you dovetail with the paper documentation that is still necessary.

Work with paper—it's not going away

HINTS

- Address all intents of the paper system
- Provide complete coverage in the online system
- Help keep online and paper in sync if paper is still needed

PROCESS FIXES

If you own the physical environment, you have the option of changing it. You can move people and equipment around to make places that

IT: consider moving walls and restructuring space

support a single intent in the work. You can hook all the people who need to communicate into the same network. You can reorganize offices to better support movement through them. You can give everyone PDAs and install wireless networks. These changes in the physical environment can be part of the overall response, supporting and supported by the systems you put in place. Planning the rollout so that changes to the physical environment are synchronized with process changes is part of designing the corporate response.

PITFALLS

The easiest way to mess up the physical environment is to not take it seriously. If people don't have printers by their desks, don't build a

Don't ignore the reality of the environment

system that requires frequent trips to the printer. If your users walk around all the time and like it, don't try to tie them to a desk by giving them a product that only runs on a desktop. Check the cultural model to see if they like walking around. Check the flow to see what communication is enabled. The physical model is your guide to what's real—let it drive what you can do in your system. But don't get too literal either. Try to achieve the users' intent, rather than matching the current environment's limitations.

CONSOLIDATED SEQUENCE MODELS

Sequence models make the detailed structure of a work task explicit. They show how the task is broken into activities, the intents that people are trying to accomplish in doing the task, the different strategies people use, and the individual steps that make up the task. Sequences are your best guide to structuring a system to match and extend the way people approach a task (Figure 12.11).

FIXING A PROBLEM		
Set up to tackle problem	• Set up place and context to tackle problem	Go to the place where problem can be solved
	• Orient self to problem situation	Get more information on problem
		Look at system to see problem in context
	• Anticipate need for help	Think about who is expert in this domain
Search for cause	• Identify cause of problem	Search for problem cause by hand
	• Eliminate repetitive tasks	Create and run specialized procedure to search for cause of problem
		Identify cause of problem
Fix problem		If a disk problem:
	• Minimize disruption of users' work	See who will be affected by work on disk
		Warn users of work to be done
		Wait for users to get off disk
		Dismount disk
	• Move substitute HW into place so users can keep working	Find scratch disk or new disk
		Mount new disk for use in fix

⇨

FIGURE 12.11 A consolidated sequence model showing how system managers solve problems. This is a partial model, but shows some of the major activities and intents in the problem-solving task. The sequence suggests both what issues a design might address as well as how it should be structured to support the user well.

Looking down the set of activities reveals an initial set of concerns a design might address. The very first activity is "Set up to tackle problem." How could a design support getting set up? Currently, system managers have to go to the place where the problem is. Looking at the intents reveals that "setting up" means both going to the right place and getting information and context about the problem. A system that could both provide remote manipulation and reveal what's going on at the failing system might address the whole activity.

In a later activity, "Escalate problem," the system manager coordinates with backup expert help. There are two strategies: one to work on the problem together and the other to hand over responsibility for the problem. Each strategy needs to be allowed for in a system. The system could focus on supporting collaboration between the system manager and the backup help with groupware-style tools so the two can see what each other is doing. Or, the system could support handing off problems, simplifying the process by passing context and history to the new owner automatically. Or the system could do both. The flow and cultural models will offer additional insight as to which solution would be most valued by the customer population.

FIXING A PROBLEM		
Fix problem *continued*	• Move substitute HW into place so users can keep working *continued*	Create directories if necessary
		Copy files to their right places
		Mount new disk publicly if it is permanent
		If other problem: process crashes, fix inappropriate message on VTX, create print queue, install SW
	• Apply and check fix	Attempt fix
	• Get answers to questions	Use documentation to help do task
	• Ensure hypothesis about problem is correct and problem is fixed	Determine if fix worked; if worked, go to "Document solution"
		Didn't work, try to figure out why
Escalate problem	• Get help, either keeping responsibility or passing it on	Can't figure out problem or not my job to fix problem; call on experts
		If trying to fix on phone:
	• Apply advice from expert to solve problem	Decide on fix on phone (go to "Attempt fix")
		If expert needs to see actual system:
	• Make it possible for expert to solve problem	Give information for expert to look at problem
		Check site documentation of setup to determine how to identify failing HW
		Give experts information necessary to locate HW
		Wait strategy 1: partner in fix
	• Save time and boredom, and maintain responsibility for the solution	Look for problem in parallel to experts (go to "Search for cause")
		Wait strategy 2: give responsibility to expert
	• Save time by passing responsibility and doing something else	Do something else while they handle it
Document actions		Document solution
	• Track work done and changes made	Document solution and actions taken

⇨

FIGURE 12.11 *continued*

FIXING A PROBLEM		
Document actions *continued*	• Make sure affected people hear directly	Notify important people directly
	• Make self a person to clients	
	• Make sure problem doesn't happen again	
	• Keep from creating future problems	Clean up—get rid of temporary files
	• Make sure full process works	Notify owners of other parts of the process to do their part
		Done with documenting
		Done

FIGURE 12.11 *continued*

WHAT THE USER IS UP TO

Every consolidated sequence has a primary intent—the reason why the task was worth doing in the first place. In the end, no individual sequence step matters. You can change, eliminate, or automate steps at will as long as you continue to support the user's intent. There are multiple levels of intent: a system manager's intent in responding to a call is to resolve whatever problem the user is having. But behind that, he intends to demonstrate that his organization has the systems under control. And behind that, he wants to show that he delivers real value to the corporation and should continue to be funded. Each level is broader and addresses more wide-reaching issues than the one before.

Every consolidated sequence has numerous subintents that are accomplished along the way. A subintent allows the user to achieve the primary intent—if you redesign the sequence, you may make some subintents irrelevant. That's okay because they are only a way to achieve a more fundamental intent. One team discovered that part of keeping records of lab procedures was to reduce graphs produced by lab equipment by 50% on the copier so scientists could paste them into lab notebooks. Through the development of an electronic lab notebook, the team eliminated the intent of pasting a paper graph into a paper notebook. They simplified the work to the point that the intent was no longer relevant.

A system has to allow for all the users' intents

Secondary intents are achieved in the process of performing a sequence. Unlike subintents, they are important in their own right— if you get rid of the whole sequence, you'll still have to find users a way to achieve these secondary intents. So system managers may depend on users asking them for an IP address to find out what new systems are being added and what's on those systems. No matter what happens to IP address assignment, system managers will always want to know about new systems.

The first design question to ask of a sequence is whether the primary intent needs to be met at all. If the intent of the whole sequence is to assign an IP address and you can automate the whole process (or introduce a network that doesn't require unique address assignment), then you've rendered the sequence unnecessary—you've simplified the job. But before you can eliminate the whole sequence, check all the individual intents that the user accomplishes along the way. Don't worry about the subintents—if you eliminate the need for the task, they become unnecessary. But if you eliminate the sequence, you must find another way for the customers to accomplish secondary intents or your system will fail. If you eliminate IP address assignment as a task, system managers will need another way to find out about new systems.

If you choose to keep the sequence, every intent is an opportunity for redesign. Each intent indicates something that matters to the

The system's job is to achieve intents more directly

work. If you can provide a way to achieve it more directly, you can simplify the work. When changing the steps for accomplishing an intent, treat it just as you treat the overall intent of the sequence: look at the part of the sequence you are designing away, and make sure your customers can still accomplish all the intents that matter to them.

Get behind the specific actions to understand what the user cares about. One design team was looking at the low-level interaction of users with a word processor. Analyzing the sequences of interaction revealed constant repositioning of the cursor. Users would click one character off their intended target, or lose track of where the cursor was, or be unsure where it would end up if they clicked on different places in their document. One user kept hitting the right and left arrows in quick succession. "He's just twiddling his fingers," said one engineer, and that's a natural reaction if you're not used to looking at pattern.

But other engineers on the team were used to looking at pattern, and what they saw was a recurring theme—positioning the cursor was a low-level but constant irritation and an impediment to getting work done. And this itself was part of an overarching theme of glitches and problems in the low-level interaction with the system. The team adopted a design direction of cleaning out all these glitches to make the interface disappear as a problem, including better ways to provide feedback on where the cursor was.

HINTS

- Render the primary intent irrelevant
- Support the primary intent a new way
- Account for all secondary intents
- Redesign to support achieving subintents

HOW USERS APPROACH A TASK

Where customers use different strategies to accomplish work tasks, the consolidated sequence models show what those strategies are. Each strategy indicates a different approach to the work, driven by different circumstances or values. The different strategies may be adopted by different roles, driven by different work styles, and may reflect different intents.

Your system needs to recognize the strategies and support them, or introduce a new way of working that supplants one or more of the strategies in use. If you choose the latter option, account for the underlying characteristics driving customers to choose the strategy you are eliminating. You might decide that system managers who continue to work on a problem after turning it over to their backup experts are wasting their time. But they may do this to save face—to prove that even though they had to ask for help, they are still experts and have just as good a chance of finding the problem as the people they called in. They may do this because they really want to have someone to talk to about the problem while they work on it. Or they may just be bothered by the problem and want to find out what the answer is. In these cases you won't be able to keep people

Support the strategies you know people use

from hunting for the solution on their own. You'd do better to recognize and allow for it.

UNNECESSARY STEPS

After you've decided that your system must support the sequence, it is your guide to the structure of the task. Look at the steps of the sequence to reveal the issues for your design. Are there wasted steps? Are there steps you could eliminate? What role could automation have in simplifying the work?

The major activities in the consolidated sequence show the coherent units of work the system must support. Use them to guide the dif-

Eliminate and simplify steps

ferent things your system must do and how they must be arranged to support the work. Look at the transition between activities. Is there a transition between roles as well? How will your system manage the handoff? Does the new activity imply moving to a new physical place? What needs to be taken to this place, and how does the customer make the transition? What, in general, disrupts the transition between activities, and how will you manage it?

Look at the steps themselves. Can you simplify them? Where the customer currently takes several steps, can you automate them down to one? Where a step is currently difficult, can you make it easy? Where is the pain, and where is the tedium? Look for ways in which technology can streamline the work, but make sure you don't have to add steps elsewhere (in setup, or loading information to use later) to eliminate them here.

HINTS

- Eliminate steps
- Automate steps
- Eliminate breakdowns
- Facilitate the transition between roles
- Don't create work no one wants to do
- Achieve intents directly

WHAT GETS THEM STARTED

The triggers show how to alert the user that something needs to be done. Pay attention to the style of the trigger. Is it noisy or quiet? Is it appropriate to the work being triggered? Does it work, or is it a nuisance? Choose whether to dupli- cate the trigger in your system, if it works, or to replace it with a trigger that works better. Look at the difference between users—the designer who

Create alerts in ways that fit people's needs

can't stand to have the mail icon blink in the menu bar versus the writer who has a dialog box come up to announce each new mail mes- sage. Look at how too many triggers defeats the purpose, as when sys- tem managers learn to ignore alarms because there are so many and so many are irrelevant. Choose a way to trigger users that works given who they are.

HINTS

- Provide triggers for work tasks
- Match style of trigger to appropriate kind of interruption and the user

PROCESS FIXES

When the work is internal, the sequence model captures the work procedure to redesign. Designing a new way of working means, among other things, redesigning the sequence model so it represents the new procedures. The organization can put these procedures in place directly. It's a typical failing of business process reengineering projects to overlook the secondary intents that are accomplished by the current process—failing to recognize them, the reengineered process doesn't cover everything that needs to be done, causing people extra work. By analyzing the existing process in this way, you increase the likelihood that you'll recognize and support all the intents that a work process must support. (We'll discuss prototyping new systems and process fixes in Part 6.)

Introduce new procedures to improve the work

PITFALLS

Certain problems are typical when automating and eliminating steps. We've mentioned failing to account for secondary intents—make sure all intents are accounted for when you redesign. But when you automate a set of steps, be aware that users won't trust that you did it right—at least not right away. They're going to want to see what you did until they are confident you won't mess up. Developers used to insist on seeing the machine code produced by their compilers—but as compilers have become standard and dependable, the need to see the machine code went away.

Reveal the workings of automation to gain user trust

Also watch out for the amount of extra work your automation introduces. Have you simplified many steps at the cost of vast amounts of setup and customization? Will the user have to set up the system like it is a separate task? If so, will any real users do this? And look at the amount of work it takes to interface with and maintain the system. Have you introduced a new role, that of the system baby-sitter, or feeder? If so, will your users be willing to adopt those roles?

CONSOLIDATED ARTIFACT MODELS

Artifact models show the common structure and intents of the different artifacts used in the work. They are important for showing both the detailed conceptual structure underlying a task and how that plays out when it's made real in the artifact.

WHY IT MATTERS

Just as sequences exist for a reason, artifacts exist for a reason: they enable customers to accomplish something they care about. There will be one or more intents for the whole artifact, and then each of the parts may suggest additional intents.

Look for ways to achieve the intents more directly in the system you design. When you see a report passed back with notes and questions scribbled in the margins, you know it supports discussion, not just reporting. Consider supporting the communication directly through email and bulletin boards. But make sure you support all the intents—you have to support them all before you can get rid of the artifact. If you put an existing

> *Beware: an online artifact can render informal usages impossible*

artifact online, pay special attention to the informal uses of the existing artifact—if you make it impossible to dog-ear corners, scribble notes in margins, or tear off bits to pin to the wall, you won't support the work.

HINTS

- Support the intent more directly
- Support intents indicated by informal usage
- Account for all intents

WHAT IT SAYS

An artifact presents information. Look at the data on an artifact for insight about the work. Does a purchase request form provide a field for justifying a purchase, but not for the cost of the item to be bought? That suggests that cost consciousness is not part of the environment. Who uses the information? Does the artifact pass information between people? Does it present the same information to every person, regardless of their role or what they care about, cluttering up the interface with irrelevant information? Is the artifact acting as the communication mechanism between two roles, to pass the context of a work task?

Consolidated artifacts collapse the history of use across all the actual events captured by individual artifacts. As a result, the artifact shows the scope of all the different usages, collecting data, intents, and concepts into one place. In this way the artifact shows the range of variation your design must account for and collects all the intents that matter to the work. It makes sure your design covers all the bases (Figure 12.12).

Company Name

Done; date fulfilled; order number

Department sent to;   **To:** _____

person assigned;   **From:** _____ *Filled in*

date   **Date:** _____

Notes, questions, answers, and dates about how replacement or change will impact system

Notes on approval (dated) and budget   **Subject:**   Type of request
High-level description

Remarks: _____

Uses
- Make SW request
- Make HW request
- Motivate quick and specified action
- Facilitate communication between departments
- Record information about exactly what to order
- Track status
- Track and trace assignees
- Record what was purchased
- Remind what to purchase

Rationale for purchase
to motivate ("dire need")
or justify based on impact on work

Description of what is needed
not vendor or model numbers
assumes knowledge of what already
exists and standard configurations

Exact specification of model # ordered

If hardware:
Location of where to put new
equipment

Rationale for location

Supplier to buy it from

Estimated costs:

Item	Cost	_____
Item	Cost	_____
Total	_____

RECEIVED DATE DEPARTMENT

Insights
- Can take up to one year to complete
- Structure is common even when not required
- Dates provide a history of when ordered, approved, and filled

FIGURE 12.12   A consolidated artifact. This model shows the parts of a purchase request as they might matter to the developers of an ordering system. It shows the parts, but also their intent and how they are used. An automated ordering system would have to support the intents implied by each part.

The model reveals that there are two primary intents to the purchase request artifact: first to justify the need for the item so the requester might actually get it, and second to communicate exactly what to get and where to put it. Automating purchase requests depends on understanding and responding to both intents. However, the description of what to buy is often informal. People assume knowledge of standard configurations and what has been bought before.

The model shows the parts that a purchase request should have, including where to put the item, where to buy it, and sometimes the exact model number to buy. A purchase request that matched a company's formal organization—where the purchasing department decides where to buy things—would not fit the need people feel to say exactly what they want and who should supply it.

Look for opportunities to put artifacts online. If the artifact helps two roles communicate (like a form), can you automate them entirely? Forms tend to capture all the data that anyone might ever need, which means that everyone sees all the data. When the form is used by different people for different parts of a job, the result can be overwhelmingly complex. When you automate the artifact, can

Artifacts should provide only the data people need

you collect all the data in one place, but provide to the different roles only the data they need, so that no one is distracted by irrelevant information? Can you provide information automatically (such as cost center on a purchase request) that is needed by some people but is not important to the requester? And what's the communication the artifact supports? If that communication is discussion, not just data or context, can you support it with communication tools?

HINTS

- Provide data automatically
- Share context between roles directly
- Support communication implied by the artifact

HOW IT CHUNKS

A consolidated artifact holds distinctions that are indicated by the structure of the artifact. Unlike the distinctions represented by a sequence or physical model, these are extremely particular to the work the artifact supports. An artifact model won't tell you what you should build; but once you have decided that this artifact is important to your proposed solution, it will give you the detailed structure you need to guide the design.

Each grouping of information on the artifact represents a chunk for your system to consider. A form might include routing information that an online version might automate away— but you must make sure that the automated form supports the same kind of routing that the paper form supports (unless you're redesigning that, too). Conversely, our calendar model showed the distinction between meetings and reminders. It showed

The structure of the artifact reveals distinctions for the system

that notes are associated with specific days. Distinctions like these must be carried over into the new design if it is to work well.

HINTS

- Use the structure of the artifact to guide the structure of the system
- Maintain the distinctions that matter to users

WHAT IT LOOKS LIKE

Artifacts don't consist only of structure and content. They also have a representation, an appearance, which is designed to support the work

Presentation matters: it leads the eye and makes parts salient

the artifact is used in. Look at how presentation is used to further the intent of the artifact—or how it gets in the way. When a part is made to stand out, it's intended to catch the eye—how will the analogous artifact in your new system catch the eye? Look at the different ways of making a part stand out. Do they represent different intents, or are they different ways of achieving the same intent? Is standing out the only intent, or are there secondary intents to consider, just as a newspaper headline both stands out and reflects the overall look and tone of the newspaper?

Take presentation seriously. It's often treated as secondary, but people work hard to make the things they use look right for the work.

HINTS

- Determine the intent of the presentation details
- Mimic the intent of presentation details, not the details themselves

PITFALLS

Artifacts, because they are real, suggest that every part is needed and every part is relevant. Look beyond the artifact itself to see what's use-

Don't just duplicate an artifact online

ful. Are all parts of a form used? Is any part of the form used, or is the real communication written in longhand over the top? Even if the data is used, does everyone need it, or would it be better to give different roles their unique views? And make sure that an online version of the artifact doesn't break it up too much. If every part of the artifact maps to a different dialog box, it will be hard to see all the information together.

USING METAPHORS

We discussed metaphors briefly in Chapter 4 as a way to think about work structure while setting focus for a project. As you study the work, you may find that these or other metaphors continue to be useful and enlightening. If so, consider redesigning the work explicitly by following the structure of the metaphorical work domain (Kensing and Madsen 1991).

For example, anytime the work you are supporting involves making things—software development is a prime example—housing construction is an interesting metaphor. As a team, draw a flow model of the roles in building a house. Look at the architect's relationship to the homeowner on one side and the primary contractor on the other. How does he or she mediate between the two? How does the architect communicate with the homeowner, and what representations show the homeowners

Explore parallel work domains to discover problems and opportunities in yours

what they will get? Where does the architect's responsibility leave off and the contractor's take over? Look at the emotional tone of the relationships. Architects and contractors frequently argue over what to build and how to build it—contractors have to work out the details of the architect's specifications in lumber and concrete.

Then use these questions to drive how you restructure the actual work you are supporting. Where is the architect role in software development? Do "software architects" play the same role as building architects? Do they create the same sense of partnership with the customer? How would you redefine the software architect role to incorporate more of the user focus of a housing architect? What tools do architects use in working out designs and in

Metaphors break you out of the weeds of your own focus

managing their relationships with client and builder? Could the intent of these tools be carried over into a system for software architects? Architects use a wide variety of props to help communicate with clients—floor plans, elevations or front views, perspective views, and complete three-dimensional models of the proposed house on its site. Do software architects have the same range of representations available to them? Could you create similar representations to improve the communication between software designers and users? Should software architects record their agreement with customers in a contract similar to that used by architects?

This inquiry just scratches the surface of the home building metaphor—you'd also want to look at the relationship between architect and contractor, and between contractor and subcontractors, to begin with—but it gives some sense of how to use the metaphor to drive your thinking. You may find that you need to understand the metaphorical work practice better to use it well. (How do architects and contractors really work together on a day-to-day basis?) If it's worth it, do some interviews in the metaphorical work domain; otherwise, find a more familiar metaphor.

Look for work domains that parallel the domain you're designing for. One team supporting home finances decided the roles were like the pilot and navigator on a plane: one person did the day-to-day work of keeping the finances on course, while the other got involved when deciding how, over the longer term, to get where they wanted to go. Another team decided that the order process in their company was like asking someone else to shop for you in a household. All the problems they saw in the interactions with the purchasing department mirrored the problems of getting someone else to understand what you want. Recognizing such a metaphor gives you a handle on how to support the work in new ways.

Steal and transform ideas found in a metaphor

Using models for design

These discussions of work models and parallel work practice should give you a guide in thinking about the implications of existing work practice for design. The models lay out different aspects of work in front of you so you don't have to hold it all in your head; doing the inquiry into one model after another helps you synthesize across the models, see overarching issues and pattern, and begin to put common solutions together. Discussing the models and possible metaphors in the team leads to shared understanding and perspectives. Through these discussions, teams start thinking about the design response, not just by responding to specific work problems with specific features, but by responding to the whole

Prepare the team brain: inquire into models and metaphors

work situation with a coherent system. By the time they get to actually designing, the team is so steeped in the data that they can't help but respond to it.

Through these activities and discussions, the team together works down the chain of reasoning from the facts in the work models, through interpretations, implications for the design, and finally specific design ideas. We'll present an orderly process for doing this in the next chapter.

Design from Data 13

Going from customer data to a design requires a creative leap, a leap from what matters to what to do about it. Customer data never dictates exactly what to design. Any set of facts can be taken multiple ways, used to inform different kinds of decisions. A product designer looking at a salesman's role might see how to provide information and tracking tools appropriate to life on the road. The division manager might see the frustrations and constraints of the job and how to alleviate them through training and communication sessions with individual salespeople. Upper management might see the constraints imposed by the organizational structure and how the sales role and relationship of sales to the rest of the organization might be redefined to make them more successful. Each different point of view reveals a different set of issues and different solutions.

The range of solutions a design team considers depends on who is on the team and the perspectives they take—the skills and knowledge they have available to them, the charter they think they have from management, and their shared assumptions about what they are up to as a design team (Gomaa 1983). Teams can't invent solutions that they don't have the knowledge to create, don't feel they have permission to carry out, or don't see as being their job. Shrink-wrap software developers won't think of restructuring the organization as part of their design— but even a team chartered to reengineer a business process won't think of restructuring the organization if they don't have the skill to see and design process and if they don't have the backing of management. A cross-functional team makes the widest possible set of skills and perspectives available, and increases the range of solutions they can consider. But that solution creates its own problem: team members tend

> *Teams can't invent solutions that they don't have the knowledge to create*

to pull in different directions, with individual members emphasizing the issues and ideas they see. It's up to the design process to unite the team behind a single corporate response. (See Kelley and Hartfield [1996] for further discussion of using multiple points of view to drive invention.)

Getting the team to be creative is tricky. We want the team to think widely, "out of the box." Yet it's in an engineer's nature to im-

Evaluation stifles creativity

mediately do a feasibility estimate of any idea they hear of or invent. That's why they respond so frequently, "We can't do that." Until the entire design for doing it is worked out, the idea does not seem

doable. Then the same engineer who said it was impossible Friday will come in Monday morning and announce that it's done. It's not possible to be creative when every idea gets immediately put to the test—and a truly creative idea may well require a substantial time to investigate whether it can be done or not. We often find that the idea we thought was a pipe dream when it was first mentioned turns out to be easy when the implementation is designed. So there's no advantage to filtering ideas early.

On the other hand, part of being free to think widely is to feel secure that you won't be committed to implementing the things you

Knowing that evaluation will happen later sets creativity free

think up. We encourage people to think broad, wide, and radical first, without worrying about how to implement their ideas or fit them with existing products. Once you've had the radical idea, you can reduce it to its core intent, decide what's important about it in supporting customers, and scale it back to

what's practical in limited time. Following invention, the process provides many evaluation steps within the team and with customers to ensure that the design works for the customer and can be implemented by the people in your organization. Knowing these steps are coming frees the team to step outside the bounds of what they know to be safe.

In Contextual Design, a team walks through a series of activities intended to get them over the hump of having a broad understanding of their customers' work practice but no agreed solution, to a clear sense of what problems to address and an innovative design to address them. Contextual Design provides a set of steps, linked together into a process, that move the team to a concrete representation of their shared direction, or vision:

Walking the data: to see the different aspects of work and synthesize them mentally

Visioning: to invent multiple possible responses to the data

Evaluation and integration: to develop a single corporate response

Concurrent action: to move all parts of the organization forward in parallel

WALKING THE DATA

The first activities are designed to explore the data and its implications for the design. At this point we aren't looking for specific design solutions; we just want to enable team members to think about the data in detail and explore all the different ways they might respond to it. Just as we set focus before going on an interview so people know what to look at, we use these activities to set the team's focus for design so they know what to build. When the customer data is understood and internalized, team members will find it natural to design solutions that respond to the primary issues it raises.

The first activity for immersing yourself in the data is to read the affinity from end to end—what we call "walking the wall." Walking the affinity right before visioning ensures that the customer issues are fresh in the designers' minds— that the solutions they invent will be grounded in the customers' work practice. Then when they review each other's ideas and see how other people are reacting to the data, they start to build a shared sense of how to respond. We discussed the detailed process of walking an affinity in Chapter 10—everyone who will be involved in the visioning session walks the affinity this way before visioning.

Anyone who visions must be steeped in the customer data

After walking the affinity, the team uses the consolidated work models to do the same kind of thinking as the affinity on the different perspectives on work. Each model represents a different point of view, a different dimension of work practice. When people walk one after another, they naturally synthesize all the different dimensions into a single three-dimensional picture of the customer. The previous chapter discussed in detail the kind of issues the team might consider for each type of model; designers do this individually or in small groups, discussing the model and how they should respond as a team. Each model will generate a set of goals: values to encourage; negative feelings to eliminate; roles and activities to support, combine, or eliminate; and so forth.

Once individuals or small groups have discussed each model, they share their discussions with the rest of the design team, and the team marks parts of the model that they want to support or eliminate. At this initial stage when the team is still deciding on a design direction, they are more interested in the "what matters" type of issue than the structural issues. So they look at flow and cultural models in detail; they look at constraints and primary intents on the physical; and they look at intents, activities, and strategies of high-level structure in the sequence and artifact models. As they read and discuss each model, issues from the other models and from the affinity are naturally incorporated into their discussion. What started as point solutions to individual problems weave together into a synthetic response to the whole work problem.

Walking the affinity diagram and work models focuses the team on specific aspects of work they want to respond to. The team can have an explicit and public conversation, recording the issues

Walking the data creates a team focus for the vision

right on the affinity and models. You can include others in the discussions by allowing them to participate in reading and responding to the models. And they ground your vision for redesign in real work issues.

After walking the affinity and each model, crystallize your thinking by making a list of the most important issues from that model. This gives you a single, crisp statement of the issues that you can return to as a reminder of your focus for the vision. When the lists are made, the team is primed to start the vision.

PRIMING THE BRAIN

Before starting with the visioning, the team brainstorms two lists, with no evaluation or filtering, that will be fodder for the vision itself:

Technology: Any design response uses technology to solve work problems. To bring the technology they have available to mind,

Lists bring possibilities to mind

teams list all the technology they might draw on. This list incorporates the mundane (networks, World Wide Web), specialized technology unique to the company (artificial agents, CAD diagramming), and implementation approaches that the team might otherwise not think of (process design, business partnerships). Anyone on the team who doesn't know about any of these possibilities can learn about them at this point.

Starting points: Discussing the work inevitably involves discussing how the team might respond to it. These initial discussions are starting points for the vision. In this list, we capture some of the most important starting points that people don't want to forget: design ideas that have captured the imagination of team members, a slogan that the team wants to commit to, or a metaphor for what the work could be like. "Put the system manager's whole job on a PDA." "Ordering should be one-stop shopping." "The lab should be like Federal Express tracking packages—you always know the state of every experiment." "Do shopping like bumper cars." Each of these ideas is a seed, a starting point for the team to elaborate into a whole approach to a design problem.

CREATING A VISION

We call our visioning process a grounded brainstorm—"brainstorm" because ideas are not evaluated as they are generated and "grounded" because ideas are driven by the customer's work practice. A visioning session gives a team the chance to choose a starting point and spin it out into a story about the new work practice transformed by technology. The story describes the brave new world the team envisions—without committing them to actually building it. (Greenbaum and Kyng [1991] describes a variety of approaches to inventing new work practices.)

Choose a seed to start the vision

In the visioning session, one person (the "pen") stands at a flip chart, drawing the ideas as participants throw them out. The pen has two roles: encourage people to talk, but also fit their ideas into the vision as it is developing. Unlike a normal brainstorm, where each idea is independent, a vision session starts with one of the ideas from the list of starting points and incorporates each idea into a coherent story about the redesigned work. The vision is a drawing showing what the new work practice would

The "pen" weaves the team's ideas into a story of new work practice

be like if the vision were in place (Figure 13.1). It shows people in the roles they play, the systems they use, how they communicate with each other and the systems, and how the systems are structured when that's necessary to thinking about the vision. Vision pictures are very informal—they are drawn quickly, without a lot of structure. They tend to have lots of arrows showing communication, lots of faces showing people, and lots of boxes indicating screens, systems, or other technology components. They aren't restricted to the system being designed but may include the delivery mechanism, third-party relationships, and additional services that work together to make the vision possible.

Any vision has a thread, which starts with the initial starting point and then is played out as participants expand on it. A facilitator helps participants pursue a thread by tying together ideas into a story of work practice and suggesting additional issues from the work models or affinity, additional roles from the flow model, or values the team agreed to from the cultural model:

The facilitator triggers inclusion of issues the team identified

Pen: *So we're starting with the idea that shopping is like bumper cars.* (Draws a bumper car.) *What happens?*

Designer (D1):   *Well, the whole idea is to get the kids involved. So the kids have to be able to drive.* (Pen draws a kid at the wheel.)

Another designer (D2):   *Yeah, put the adults in the passenger seat. Then organize the store so you can drive through it in order.* (Pen starts sketching the store.)

D3:   *And make the aisles narrow enough so you can pick things off both sides as you drive by.* (Pen draws aisles on either side of the car.)

D1:   *You'll have to make all the aisles one-way.*

Facilitator: *But what about backtracking? We saw people have to go back for things they forgot.*

D2:   *We'll give them a way to backtrack at the end of the aisles.*

The facilitator and the pen should listen for ideas that are on the thread, postponing ideas that are too far off the main line to be starting points for another vision. When an idea conflicts with the thread the team is working on, the pen adds it to the list of starting points.

This keeps the thread coherent while assuring the team member that his idea has been heard and will be dealt with. Eventually the thread will play out—people won't have more ideas for extending it without taking a new starting point. At this point the vision is put aside and the next one started. Don't duplicate ideas from vision to vision— good ideas will be recovered in the next step, so you don't need to go through them again.

Practicality is not a major consideration for a vision. If the team lets go of worrying about whether they can build their ideas immediately, they will be more creative and produce a vision that will account for more of the work practice, more coherently. Our team above is unlikely to ship a product that installs bumper cars in grocery stores, but working out the vision gives them a chance to explore issues of child control and participation that are very likely to be part of their final design. Balance creativity against practicality. After visioning bumper cars and some other fanciful ideas, the team might want to evaluate and consolidate them into a more conservative vision capturing the key benefits but using technology they think they can implement.

Any vision will specify more than the team wants to attempt in a single version, but that's all right—it means the team will have a plan, a strategy, that they can use to drive delivery over several versions. (We'll talk much more about strategic development over several versions when we introduce the User Environment Design in Part 5.) Even if you know you are focused on a short-term deliverable—say, your next update due to ship in six months—you're better off thinking and visioning widely first. Then you can either synthesize and pick and choose the best parts for the deadline, or you can vision widely and then vision explicitly for a six-month deliverable. You'll find you automatically pull in ideas from the wider visions to put together a coherent plan that you can do in the time you have (once you do the inevitable trimming).

A vision encompasses more than the team can ship in one version

A good visioning session is a lot of fun. Everyone is tossing in ideas for what to do based on what matters in the work. Everyone is talking at once and building on each other's ideas. The major gating factor for a visioning session is the ability of the pen to draw what he or she hears without a lot of filtering or explanation. If people feel like it's too hard to get their ideas on the paper, the

In a good visioning session, everyone feels their ideas have been heard

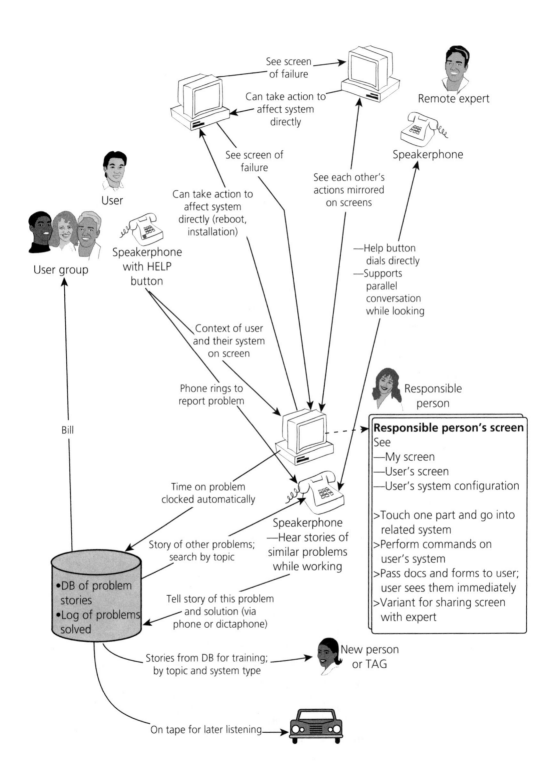

See screen of failure

Can take action to affect system directly

Remote expert

Speakerphone

See screen of failure

See each other's actions mirrored on screens

User

Can take action to affect system directly (reboot, installation)

User group

Speakerphone with HELP button

—Help button dials directly
—Supports parallel conversation while looking

Context of user and their system on screen

Responsible person

Phone rings to report problem

Bill

Responsible person's screen
See
—My screen
—User's screen
—User's system configuration

>Touch one part and go into related system
>Perform commands on user's system
>Pass docs and forms to user; user sees them immediately
>Variant for sharing screen with expert

Time on problem clocked automatically

Speakerphone
—Hear stories of similar problems while working

Story of other problems; search by topic

•DB of problem stories
•Log of problems solved

Tell story of this problem and solution (via phone or dictaphone)

Stories from DB for training; by topic and system type

New person or TAG

On tape for later listening

FIGURE 13.1 A vision for system management.[1] In this vision, the team has elected to focus on improving the communication between user and system administrator and on improving the diagnostic process. The vision started with the idea that the system administrators wanted to bring the problem to them, to make everything necessary to solve the problem available locally. In following the story, the team integrated a number of other issues—how to make it easy for users to get help, how the system administrator can get backup help, and how to use stories in diagnosing problems.

In the vision, when a user wants help with a system, they just push a big red "HELP" button on their phone. That automatically connects them with the right person for their system and organization and brings up their system information on the administrator's screen. The team wanted to make asking for help through the "approved" mechanism so simple that no one would be tempted to use personal or informal contacts to go around it. They found that having enough context about the user and system was a major impediment to administrators in providing support—researching the system was always the first step toward doing any real work—so they had the system provide as much context as possible. When the time comes to implement, the "HELP" button will probably not survive as visioned—it's not reasonable to make changing every phone a prerequisite to using this system administration software. But the idea will prod the team to think about simpler ways to achieve the same intent—perhaps stickers to put on the phone with the right number, or autodial in the software for computers that support it. The vision is a stake in the ground saying, "This is the goal." The team can scale back and decide on reasonable ways to achieve the goal later.

To support diagnosis, the team noticed that system administrators depend on story and anecdote a lot when troubleshooting. Stories capture knowledge about what might work in different situations, but capturing the stories and making them available is hard. Typically this is done through tale swapping in the informal system administrators' community. Even when people capture a log of what they did, it doesn't have the same flavor as a story—it doesn't include the different alternatives tried and the frustrations of trying to work things out. This vision attempts to capture stories and make them available when needed, while diagnosing another problem, through a database of stories. When done with a call, an administrator can tell the story of what happened into the phone—they are used to dealing with the phone. Later, they can search the database for stories relevant to the problem they are working on—perhaps from the same system or showing the same symptoms. Then they can listen to the stories while working on the problem. The challenge of the "story database" is not so much technical—it just depends on recording and playing back speech—as it is being able to capture enough information about each story so that the subsequent search picks out relevant stories.

This vision shows how even radical solutions to problems can be based directly on understanding the structure and nature of the work.

---

[1] This vision was generated by us for inclusion in this book. It's a disadvantage of working in a highly competitive industry that most of the data used to develop actual products and internal systems is considered too proprietary to release.

session will be frustrating for everyone. For the same reason, limit sessions to about 10 people—more makes it hard to get air time.

Expect to elaborate on each idea for about half an hour, then move on to the next. Keep going until you have at least three or four alternative visions, each on its own flip chart paper.

CREATING A COMMON DIRECTION

Doing multiple visions lets the team consider alternatives and work out some of their implications. Each vision is built by the whole team and incorporates everyone's different perspective. But at the end of a visioning session, you have multiple visions, each suggesting a different design direction or addressing a different part of the work. How do you choose among them?

In Contextual Design, you don't have to. Instead, you synthesize a new solution incorporating the best of the individual visions. Committees have the reputation of producing mediocre designs because people compromise; instead of doing either of two reasonable designs, they settle for something halfway in between, or they incorporate a few features to make everyone happy. Synthesizing a common vision is a way to avoid this. Rather than compromising on features, producing a design with a little something for everyone, the goal should be a design that is coherent and clean and that supports the work issues everyone identified.

Creating a common vision is not a compromise

The key to such a design is to treat each vision, not as a monolithic block that must be accepted or rejected as a whole, but as a collection of options that can be reconfigured and redesigned into a single solution. If the team had to choose one option over another, they would argue—each person would have their own preference as to how to trade off different issues. But it's a false choice. Every vision will have impractical or undesirable elements; most visions will have some elements you don't want to lose. Create a better solution by identifying elements that work, recombining them to preserve the best parts, and extending them to address more of the work and overcome any defects. The individual

Identify the positive and negative parts of each vision

visions become databases of design ideas that you can draw on and recombine to come up with a better solution.[2]

We do this through a structured evaluation of each vision. Look at each one in turn and first list the positive points of that vision—the reason why it's good, fits the customer work situation, solves real problems, is easy to build, or fits the skills of the organization. Even people who dislike the vision overall can find points about it that work; people who are particularly against it are on the spot to identify some points they like. List each positive point on a sheet and attach it to the vision. Then list the negative points—all the reasons why it would be hard to build or would break the customer's work practice. People who love the vision can find a few points to dislike—it will help them to let go of an idea they might be overly attached to. List these negatives and attach them to the vision as well. List positives and negatives for each vision in turn (see Figure 13.2 for an example of the system management vision). While you're listing negative points, people will tend to start solving them—to suggest ways that the potential problem can be overcome. These ideas become important in the next step of the process, but don't let them derail you now. Write them on Post-its and stick them to the vision to save them for later.

As soon as you list negatives, people start fixing them

Then look across the visions and at the positive points. Use them to identify the core parts of each vision you don't want to lose. Then look at how to combine these points into a single coherent vision. The team will be primed to do this as a result of the discussion of positive and negative points. They'll already have ideas for how to recombine the vision. Usually, most of the elements of the visions don't conflict directly—because each vision took a different approach, it will be possible to bring the best parts together without conflict. Where parts you like do conflict—two different

Invention is driven by recombining existing good ideas

---

[2] This process is based on the ideas underlying Pugh matrices (Pugh 1991). But where Pugh depends on individual creativity, we use the dynamics of the group to produce a single vision that incorporates everyone's perspective. This helps keep people from getting overinvested in one solution. People who feel they can't be creative in a group situation still have the option of working out a design and feeding it into the evaluation process.

Positives	Negatives
+Tracks time automatically +Provides access to similar stories +It's easy to document actions taken +Fast access to help +System manager is given what's needed to solve the problem +Database of stories addresses the training issue	—It's hard to search through verbal text —What if the user's not in their office? —What if not all phones are hooked in? —Need a realistic way of mimicking the HELP button —What if the responsible person isn't there? —Will people really tell stories of what they've done into the phone?

FIGURE 13.2   Positives and negatives for the system management vision.

ways of addressing the same problem, for example, when it doesn't make sense to do both—you'll have to choose. But now it's a very focused choice on specific aspects of each vision. If they both support the work well, choose the simpler or the easier to implement. If you aren't sure which is better for the work, use the ideas to identify what data will help make the choice and set up customer interviews to collect it. (We'll discuss working out the ideas with customers in detail in Part 6.) The final step of visioning is to draw the new consolidated vision reasonably neatly.

This whole process is designed to bring a disparate, cross-functional team of people to consensus. If some team member is hooked on an idea, be sure to include that idea in the list of starting points. In one team, one member was hooked on the idea of a large monitor displaying test states in a scientific lab—it had gotten to be a joke in the team that this was his solution for everything. Making the large monitor the core of a vision and then doing positive and negative points (he had to come up with three negatives) made it clear what real advantages the large monitor offered. But comparison with other visions revealed that those same advantages could be achieved more simply. In the end, he didn't have a hard time letting go of the idea.

The group process builds consensus and reduces overinvestment

MAKING THE VISION REAL

The code is only one component of a product. A commercial product also includes the documentation and services that help people use it, the marketing plan that publicizes it, and the testing plan that ensures its reliability. Internal systems downplay marketing and services, but they still have to help users take advantage of the product, tell them about it, and get buy-in. Internal systems also have

The vision directs concurrent activity

to roll out the infrastructure, new procedures, and new organizational structures that will take advantage of the new system. With the vision in place, all functions can start working on their parts in parallel. They can first look to see if they can do what the vision requires at all reasonably; this may require technical investigation or may require going for management buy-in. Once the team knows what's involved in doing a piece of the vision, they can choose to attempt it, leave it out, or scale it back so they get the underlying benefit of the piece in a simpler way. Then, once they've decided what part of the vision to work toward for this project, people can work out in detail what's required for their part. All through, the vision acts as a map that keeps the groups coordinated even while they work independently.

PROCESS AND ORGANIZATION DESIGN

Particularly when the system is for internal use, the vision may imply changes to business processes or business organization. The vision offers a new way of working, and the business structure may have to change to adopt that way of working. Salespeople may have a different reporting relationship to the home office. The purchasing department may no longer be an intermediary in making a purchase. Walls between offices might be knocked down to provide team rooms. Planning for these changes can proceed in parallel to the software and infrastructure development activities that will support them (though, of course, the implementation of any changes must be synchronized).

The vision can help a commercial vendor redefine how they do business as well as what products they deliver. Commercial vendors can mine their visions for implications on new delivery mechanisms, how customer service is viewed and how to improve it, and how to improve the sales channel to address issues that get in the customer's way. If one customer's issue is how long delivery takes, the delivery service might be changed. If salespeople are used as information resources by their customers, formalizing the information provision as a service might be part of the vision. If technology or products developed by a third party are important to the vision, the organization can start to create relationships with these other companies.

The vision directs organizational restructuring

MARKETING PLANS

Marketing builds the market message around the vision and consolidated models (and later the User Environment Design, described in the next part). The consolidated models show what customers care about and what message will interest them. Marketing can build scenarios from sequences and base the story of the new world on the vision. The vision captures the key innovations that constitute the substance of the market message. And the User Environment Design, especially when organized into components, gives marketing a way to communicate the design as providing coherent support for particular aspects of the work. This message communicates directly to people's experience; talking about features and benefits presents the system more abstractly.

The vision shows what customer characteristics make the difference in whether they will be interested in the product or not. The models capture qualitative data about customers—now marketing needs quantitative data to decide whether the product is viable. The vision drives surveys to size the market and make the business case: test how many customers have those characteristics and how much they are likely to spend. As engineering finishes more of the designing and prototyping, these can be incorporated into the marketing events and used as the basis for focus groups, test drives with customers, and so forth. Marketing can also use the vision for prioritization—they can split it into components and decide which components to ship together for a coherent product, and in what order.

The vision drives marketing techniques to develop the business case

SYSTEM DESIGN

The vision defines what is expected of any software and hardware components of the system. Engineers can get an advance look at what demands on technology the system will make. They can start investigating technological possibilities immediately, including possible platforms, whether specific technology is sufficiently reliable and whether it can meet the requirements of the vision, and UI possibilities. Then, when the decision is made to proceed, the rest of system design is based on the vision and consolidated models, as we shall see.

> *The vision drives technical investigation and hardware requirements*

STORYBOARDS

A vision drawing captures the new vision as a single picture, showing all parts of the vision together. It says *what* the new work practice will be without showing *how* it will happen over time. But to design well, we want to work out the system design in the context of doing work. We want to see how it fits into the overall work task to ensure that the transition into and out of the system works and that the task stays coherent. We do this by working out the vision in storyboards. (This approach to deriving system requirements from usage is becoming popular in the industry; see, for example, Carlshamre and Karlsson [1996]; Jacobson et al. [1992].)

Storyboards show how specific tasks will be accomplished in the new world. The technique was originally borrowed from movie making and has been used by others to work out system designs.[3] A storyboard captures the new procedure for doing a task pictorially, like a storyboard for a film. Each frame in the storyboard captures a single scene—an interaction between two people, a person and the system, a person and an artifact, or a system step. The storyboard frame might show the people interacting and the content of their interaction. It might sketch a system screen with annotations showing how it's used at this point. It might sketch the artifact and how it's used. Or it might just list the actions the system takes on the user's behalf.

Storyboards are based on the vision, follow the structure of a consolidated sequence model, and pull implications from other models as necessary. The vision defines what the new work is like; the consolidated sequences define the structure that underlies doing a task and

---

[3] Contextual Design is often useful as a framework giving structure to the front-end life cycle, which other techniques can plug into. In this spirit, we've adopted storyboards as a useful technique for working out a design (Rheinfrank and Evenson 1996).

the intents people achieve in doing it. To build a storyboard, choose a task to redesign that is represented by a consolidated sequence. Then

Storyboards tie the vision to the structure of the consolidated sequence

review the models and affinity, gathering issues relevant to this task. Collecting the issues resets your focus, allowing your mind to design from all the issues at once.

Then sketch out how you want to redesign the task. This is a more detailed vision, focused on the work of this task and constrained by the larger vision. In this step, you work out the exact approach you'll take to dealing with the different issues. Sketch out two or three options, do positives and negatives, and consolidate one approach. Do this quickly—it's more focused and can be fast.

With the detailed vision drawn out, walk through the consolidated sequence step by step. Look at the intents, different strategies, and steps.

Draw all steps: manual, system, and UI

Account for the intents—if the first step of diagnosis is to find out more about the system and its history, any new system should account for this need. You could support it, by displaying system context automatically when a call comes in; you could eliminate diagnosis by implementing an expert system that can always figure out what's wrong; or you could decide that they have ways to get context already and you don't need to give them more, and leave this step manual. Look for ways to overcome problems and achieve intents more directly, within the context of your detailed vision.

Capture the work practice as you've redesigned it in the storyboard, including interactions with the system, interactions with other people, and manual steps. The goal of the storyboard is to represent the whole work task coherently, so don't limit the storyboard to only those steps that interact with the system. Sketch storyboard frames to represent each step of the new work practice.

Because each frame of a storyboard is a sketch, it limits the amount of detail the designer can squeeze into that frame. This is

A UI sketch shows how people will use a system during a work step

intentional, just as the sketchiness of the vision is intentional. By its nature, a storyboard inhibits the designer's natural tendency to dive down into the low-level detail of each part of the system before the whole system has been roughed out. A screen sketch in a storyboard isn't a specification for the UI of that screen—it's a thinking tool enabling the designer to work out what has to happen in the user's interaction with the system at that point in the task. The UI sketches in the storyboard communicate ideas to the UI designer, who will create a consistent and comprehensible UI for the whole system later.

We usually build storyboards in pairs. After finishing the whole task, the pair brings the storyboard back to the whole team for review. They walk through the storyboard, and everyone posts issues on the storyboard: mismatch with the customer's work practice, mismatch with the vision, alternative design ideas, or implementation worries. The pair then reworks the storyboard to account for the issues.

A set of storyboards for the key tasks to be supported in a new system defines how the system will work in supporting those tasks. By telling the whole story of the task, including manual steps, automated steps, and interactions with the system, the storyboard keeps the work task coherent. Storyboards work out elements of the vision by unraveling them, laying them out step by step. They provide the next level of detail for the design. In working out the storyboard, all aspects of work come together: roles interact, people move around and pass artifacts, and culture influences everything. The storyboard synthesizes all these issues into a coherent redesign of a work task within the context of the overall vision (Figure 13.3).

Storyboards capture all the steps needed to do the redesigned work

REDESIGNING WORK

This is what it means to redesign the work: First, understand the structure of work as it exists and the issues implicit in the work. That will tell you what to address. Become knowledgeable about possibilities for redesign, either by learning about different possible technologies or bringing experts into the room and steeping them in the data. Then vision a new world, using the knowledge of the team and building on your understanding of the issues. Once that's done, you can work out the implications of that vision in storyboards that show individual instances of doing the work.

The vision and storyboards guide the corporate response

The vision holds your corporate response. It shows how all the different actions you might take as an organization work together to

FIGURE 13.3   A storyboard for the system management vision. This storyboard follows the structure of the consolidated sequence for dealing with a call for help. At each step, the storyboard reinvents how that step would be accomplished given that the user can take advantage of the new system.

address the user's work problem. With a vision in place, the different functions of your organization can work together toward a common goal. Each function then will follow its own process to work out the implications for its part. In the rest of this book, we'll discuss the process for engineering to develop the system itself.

KELLY'S STORY

Everybody talks about spending a day in the life of the customer, but it's very hard to do and get meaningful data. I've tried a lot of different processes and have found that the people who participate get insight, but there's no way to capture it, communicate what you learned, or use it again on the next project for the same market. Contextual Design is unique in that it gives a framework and models to capture the data in ways that are more meaningful than any other process I've used. It supports sharing and communicating the insight and lets others participate in a way they cannot otherwise.

I'm a product manager in a group building large computer systems. We wanted to address a new market segment with our product line, but we had not spent much time understanding what was important to these customers. We used the whole Contextual Design process, with a cross-functional team drawn from marketing, R&D, and manufacturing, and external facilitators to guide us.

We interviewed about 15 customers; consolidated the models and affinity; visioned new product, service, and delivery ideas for the market; built a User Environment Design for some parts; and used prototypes to test the ideas. We found the cultural model particularly useful for defining our marketing objectives, including defining the value proposition for the market. The other models were more useful to R&D in building the actual products.

The vision we produced drove marketing requirements for several different organizations. Producing a computer system for this market requires the combined effort of several software organizations, two hardware organizations, manufacturing, and service organizations. For example, we discovered how critical it is in this market to be able to add capacity easily—this recognition drove hardware requirements for ease of installation, software requirements for dynamic reconfiguration, and a manufacturing requirement for 48-hour turnaround of a new order. That will require process changes in the manufacturing organization, but they've put together a task force to figure out how to do it.

For us in marketing, the strongest part of the process was through visioning. This project wasn't driven by the engineering organizations, so we didn't have enough commitment to the results. No one organization felt their business depended on the success of the project. We could get individuals to buy in, but it was harder to affect the plans of the whole organization. So we found it easier to communicate the results of the vision using our traditional methods. We are getting the changes we designed into products to be delivered over the next 12 to 18 months.

I have to say that none of us had a clue how much time and energy this project would take, particularly since we had no data to start with. The results were well worth it, though. If we hadn't done this work up front, we would have had to do it later, when plans are harder to change. We're planning to use Contextual Design on our next project, but augmented with other marketing techniques and contextual interviews with people who make the buy decision. ❑

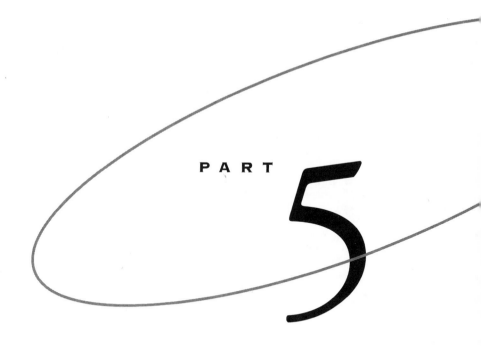

System Design

System Design

14

W e've understood the user's model of work, we've captured it in work models, we've envisioned new ways for people to work— but so what? How does this help us with software design? Way back in Chapter 1, we discussed the idea of a *system work model,* the approach to doing work that's built into every system. The vision of Chapter 13 defines a new way of working, with many delivery mechanisms. IT shops can define new roles and procedures in concert with the business partner; commercial product developers can define services and training. But in this book we're focused on software and hardware systems, which embody the desired system work model. How do you make the transition from the vision and storyboards to a system design that delivers on their promise? In Contextual Design, we introduce a new modeling technique to reveal the system work model and show how all the parts of the system relate to each other in the user's experience.

KEEPING THE USER'S WORK COHERENT

The challenge is to keep the system work model *coherent,* so that it supports the users and fits with their expectations while extending and transforming their work practice as prescribed by the vision. Coherence isn't just about consistency of the user interface—a coherent system keeps the user's work orderly and natural. When a presentation tool won't let its users change slide notes and slide contents at the same time, making them jump

> *Design challenge: to keep work coherent by keeping the system coherent*

back and forth between views, it breaks up the work. When a word processor provides three successive cascading dialog boxes to choose a bullet, it turns a minor function into a whole task, complicating the work. When an email system lets users search the address book by providing a simple text entry field that filters the address book names but uses a separate query window to search the "sent mail" folder (Figure 14.1), it provides inconsistent structures for doing similar work. When the system work model is coherent, it keeps the user's work coherent; when it fragments, it's the user's work that is disrupted.

Keeping the system model coherent is hard enough when it's one user doing a single task. It's even worse in real systems, which support multiple people playing multiple roles, across departments or the whole business, while using several systems. One user we talked to was verifying information given to her by another department. The information on the form was accessed by several different applications. By the time she was done, she had used 11 screens in four applications to check a single form. Another user wanted to see what drugs a person was taking while recording a clinical event. His information was online, but he had to leave the application he was using and get into an entirely separate one to get at drug records. In both cases, the users had multiple systems, each designed to solve a single problem. These systems didn't address the user's whole job and didn't attempt to make the work fit together across the different departments or tools. When work practice is too large and complex to see, or it's too hard to address all at once, it's easier to write simple systems that address single problems. But then the systems chop up the work and leave it up to the user to put it back together by taking extra steps or doing additional work on the side.

Users have to be the glue between incoherent systems

In the face of work complexity, designers create simple solutions

From the developer's side, the picture is no easier. Software development organizations start projects to address specific problems, and only later do they realize that the systems don't hang together and don't build up into a coherent solution. This leads to conflicts down the road:

> You've put a personal organizer in your product? But we're chartered to build the company's solution for personal organizers! And why does the operating system have a to-do list?

> We started 10 years ago with a basic system. But we've added on so much that now we have over 50 applications and

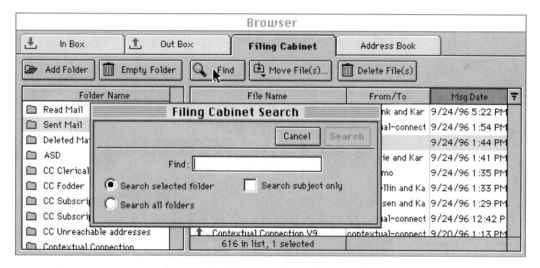

FIGURE 14.1 Claris Emailer: Two ways of finding: one with a query dialog box, one with a filter.

no clear idea how they fit together. I'm not even sure we know where all the duplications are.

We do charting. We don't do data reduction—that's the database's job. I know you can't currently do the data reduction you need to do to use our charts, but that's the database's problem.

How can an organization figure out where the boundaries between applications should be, so that every work task is addressed once and once only, and no part of the work falls through the cracks? In the end, the system work model that matters is the one supported by all the applications together—how can an organization see it, design it, and deliver it?

BREAKING UP THE PROBLEM BREAKS UP THE WORK

One solution to handling the complexity of work is to choose to address only a small part of the problem. As we've seen, that tends to break up the work for the customer. Addressing the whole of the work coherently means building a bigger system or tying together multiple small systems seamlessly (an even harder problem). As the size of the system or systems goes up, keeping the systems themselves and the work practice they support coherent gets harder and harder. A small system can be designed and built by one person—keeping it coherent isn't so difficult. But it takes multiple people working in parallel just to get all the details of a larger system worked out.

A common solution is to anoint an "architect" or architect team with the responsibility of tracking the whole system and catching any discrepancies. The work itself is done by carving the

No one person can keep all parts of a complex system in her head

system up into pieces, assigning pieces to individuals, and letting them work out the details. But as we discussed when introducing work models in Chapter 5, as soon as any system grows beyond the very simple, it's just too hard to balance all the factors without some external representation to manipulate. Furthermore, in a large system, too many different people and groups are building too many parts—it's too hard to keep track of all the relationships. As soon as several people get involved in the design, they need an external representation to focus their discussion and capture their agreements. It's no longer enough for the whole design to stay in one person's head.

Passing out pieces for people to develop independently throws the whole design out of balance unless everyone really knows the whole design and how their part fits. Give one person a single part to design and build, and what should be a minor feature can turn into a whole miniapplication (Figure 14.2). Designers find it hard not to treat their assigned part of the system as the most important—not only is their ego involved, but it *is* the most important part for them. It's no wonder so many small features turn into a larger and more complicated design than necessary.

Developing a piece in isolation leads to overdevelopment

It's no wonder that designers create a dialog box that is *almost* like the one their neighbor designed, but with the one or two extra features they can't do without. It's no wonder that what started as a simple dialog starts to feel like a small application. Dividing the system up among team members tends to pull the design apart—it's up to the design process to provide mechanisms that keep it whole.

A SYSTEM HAS ITS OWN COHERENCE

While storyboards capture a coherent story of a single task, each storyboard can only follow that one thread. A full system supports many different tasks and roles. Storyboards work out system implications sequentially, by considering what happens in order to perform a task. But the system needs to hang together with its own organization and structure. That organization and structure has to be designed as a whole if the system is to be coherent.

It's as if the stories of use are paths across a university quad, each one wearing out the grass a little along that path. Then the grounds-keepers look at the paths all together and decide that here, where two paths run almost together, they can be merged and paved; and there, where four cross, there might be a little courtyard with benches. The people making the paths are following their every-day life activities without thinking particularly

Good design for individual work tasks is not enough

about where they walk but following the best path for them; the groundskeepers are withdrawing from day-to-day events to see the implications on the whole "system."[1] And once the groundskeepers put new physical structures in place, people discover new possibilities and build on them—perhaps the courtyard becomes a favorite spot for

---

[1] This is the same alternation between *withdrawal* to see the structure of what's going on and *return* to the ongoing work that we first encountered in discussing partnership, in Chapter 3.

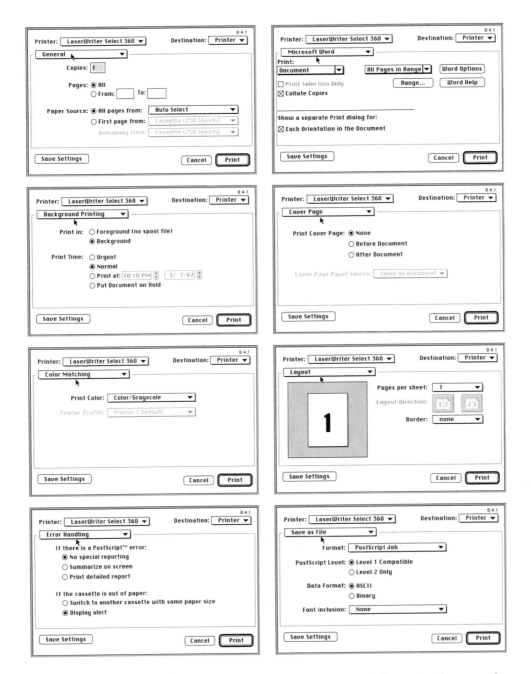

FIGURE 14.2 Apple's LaserWriter 8.4.1 print dialog—what happens when printing becomes an application. How many different dialogs are really needed to print a file?

street musicians. When structure is well designed, it's flexible enough to support additional uses, unforeseen by the designers.

In the same way, designing a system based solely on storyboards—or use cases—would optimize each sequence of use at the expense of the system as a whole. Tell the story of nine different users, each with different printing needs, and each dialog in Figure 14.2 might make sense on its own. It's only when they are seen together that it's clear the interface is overcomplicated. Walk two separate cases for filtering address books and filtering sent mail, and each interface in Figure 14.1 makes sense. It's only when put together in the context of a system that they become inconsistent.

Good design tends to alternate between sequential and structural thinking. The initial quad design was a structure, designed as a consistent whole and put in place to be used by many people many ways. The actual use by any person is sequential: they came in here, crossed to there, sat on the grass after that, and left over there. Each individual sequence of use hangs together for that person. The next step of design switches back to structure. The groundskeepers looked at all the patterns of use

Good design process alternates between sequential cases and structural models

together (as recorded by worn grass) and redesigned the structure to better fit its use. This step of seeing all the parts of a system as they relate to each other is an intrinsic part of systems design. Seeing and balancing the parts of a system against each other goes beyond a pure task-oriented approach by introducing a focus on the structure of the system itself.

THE STRUCTURE OF A SYSTEM

A courtyard's easy enough to see and design. How can the design process make it equally easy to see the structure of a complex system? What *is* the structure of a system that designers need to see and manipulate, and how does it relate to the structure of work?

Consider a user reading mail: First she scans her new messages looking for something important. She doesn't care to see the whole content of every message—that would be a distraction. She just wants to know who it's from and the subject line to decide what to read first. Then she decides on one to read, and suddenly

The structure of a system determines how well it supports work

she needs a new context for doing this new activity. She no longer needs to see all her messages, but she does need to see the whole content of this one. Her intent changes—she's not wondering what important messages she might have been sent anymore, she's reading to find out what this one message says. Accordingly, her tools change—instead of seeing and scrolling over message headers, she's reading through message content.

Our user situated herself in a place in the product that suited the needs of the activity she was engaged in and stayed there a while,

Systems provide places where related tasks are done

scanning messages with the tools provided. Then, when her activity and needs changed, she moved to a different part of the product where she could do the different kind of work associated with the new activity. The structure of the system consists of the *places* in the product where she can work, the *functions* that support work in each place, and the *links* that allow her to move from one place to another. The places do not impose any one sequence of use. Like the areas within a quad, they all exist together, offering the possibility of any number of different uses. But the structure they offer may make work convenient and easy to do or make it difficult. Customer-centered design seeks to build a structure into the system that supports the user's natural movement through her work and is flexible enough to enable the invention of new ways of working. Seeing this structure and reworking it to fit the user better is equivalent to the gardener restructuring a quad to better fit its usage. That's what designing the system work model is all about.

Designing the system work model as a whole runs counter to the engineering principle that every part should be self-contained so that

Any design change potentially affects the whole system work model

changes to any part are isolated to that part. That's one reason for thinking of the implementation in terms of opaque modules or objects. But some approaches to design that work well for engineering the implementation get in the way when designing the system work model. Suppose Joe invents a way for users to scan and search without entering a query and uses it in the piece he was assigned. There's no way to keep users from expecting this approach throughout the system because the parts aren't isolated in the users' experience. Having encountered the mechanism in one part, users expect to find it in every similar situation. So keeping the design coherent means that after a part changes, the designers must step back, look across the whole system, and see what impact that change has on the rest of the system. The system work model is a single whole—every part exists in relationship to every other part, and a change to one may ripple throughout the system.

DESIGNING STRUCTURE PRECEDES UI DESIGN

Designing the system work model to fit the user is a problem of structuring the system well, not of designing the user interface or implementation. User interface and implementation are the next layers of detail in the design process. When the makers of PowerPoint decided to make one view, and only one, that edits the contents and layout of a slide, they made a decision about the structure of their product. By implication, they made an assumption about the structure of users' work—that it is reasonable to concentrate all slide changes in this one view. In the same way, when they decided not to give control over flying bullets for on-screen presentations from this view, they decided that was a function that did not need to be part of this work. These are structural decisions—they decide what the system should do and how it should be organized, but say nothing about how it should look or be implemented (Constantine 1994a).

Structural decisions of this sort precede decisions about the user interface. It doesn't make sense to design screen layouts until you've decided what function the screen should implement. It would be as though an architect started design by choosing rugs and materials for the countertops. They don't; they start with rough sketches that they work up into a floor plan. The floor plan captures the right level of detail for talking about the structure of a house—it shows the parts and their relationships without showing how the house is decorated. The user interface of a system is equivalent to the decoration of a house. It matters, but if the structure is wrong, no user interface can fix the problems.

Use a language of structure to maintain a focus on structure

In our initial design teams, we found that team members tended to slide into conversations about the UI before they were ready—before they had agreed on base structure. They were like architects who could only communicate by drawing pictures of the proposed house. "We want this function in this window," one would say, sketching a row of buttons. "The style guide says those should go on a pull-down menu," another would reply. "Do you really want to use that word?" a third would ask. When the very language suggests that the user interface is the topic of conversation, it's hard not to be distracted by it. But how could we represent the system work model directly, free of any UI implications?

The pattern of working we found in software—working in a place, moving to a new location, and doing a new kind of work in that

Living in a house is parallel to working in software

place—is not unique to working in a system. In fact, it's very like living in a house (Winograd 1996). To start dinner, a person goes to the kitchen, where the tools for cooking are located (knives, bowls, stove). A drawer sticks, and he decides to take it to the workshop and plane it down while the water boils. He

moves with the drawer to another place, which has the different set of tools useful for minor carpentry, and works on the drawer there. Then he goes back to finish dinner. A house consists of places to do things, functions or tools that help do things, and access allowing people to move between places. The parallels between living and working in software and in houses suggest that studying the role of a floor plan might shed light on the appropriate representation of a system work model.

A floor plan occupies a unique role in the design of a house (Figure 14.3). It's less physical than an elevation, which shows a view of the

A floor plan supports the structure of life in the house

house as though you were looking at it (an elevation is more like a UI picture). It doesn't show wall color or how the house is finished (which would also be more like a UI). Yet it's not at the nuts-and-bolts level of a construction diagram, which might show how to put a wall together but doesn't show anything

the homeowner can relate to. The floor plan selects a few of the most salient aspects of a house as it supports living and represents them: the spaces in the house, their sizes and relationships to each other, the things in each space that support the kind of living done there (stoves, refrigerators), and the access between spaces.

As a diagram, a floor plan supports a conversation about how well a design supports a particular style of life, and allows the architect to compare that with the life the house's prospective owners want to have. Architects can walk stories of living through the floor plan to see how well it fits

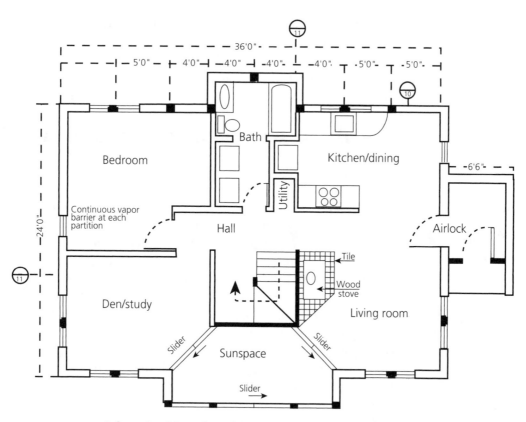

FIGURE 14.3 A floor plan. Notice how the important distinctions are immediately apparent—the relative size of the spaces and the access between them. Details that are unimportant for understanding the structure of the house—rugs, wall surfaces—are absent or inconspicuous. (Even the tile around the woodstove affects access because people will walk around it.) But the drawing does tie to the users' experience of moving through a house. It also puts construction details in context—the dark squares in the walls indicate supporting posts, and the numbers in circles key this diagram to cross sections showing wall construction. This is what we are missing in software design—a single representation that shows how all the parts of the system relate in the users' experience and how they relate to the implementation.

the homeowners. Is a room too small for the way the owners want to use it? Is it too hard to get from one room to another? Is there a lot of dead space devoted to halls or intermediate areas? The floor plan lays out all the parts of a house, letting the architect walk different cases and scenarios through it. Rules of thumb, such as constraints on minimum clearances, layouts that work well, and the limitations of construction materials, ensure that the resulting design is usable and implementable. Of course, once the house is built, meals may be eaten in the kitchen, and the dining room may become a music room. A good structure will permit different uses, which the architect never designed explicitly.

THE USER ENVIRONMENT DESIGN

A UED supports the structure of work in the system

Contextual Design represents the system work model in a new modeling technique, the *User Environment Design* (UED). The User Environment Design plays the same role in Contextual Design that the floor plan plays in house design. Just as a floor plan represents the key distinctions for supporting living, the User Environment Design represents the key distinctions for supporting work practice with software systems. Like the floor plan, the representation shows all the parts of a system that the user knows or cares about, what aspects of work each part supports, and how the parts of the system relate to each other (see Figure 14.4 for an example). Like the floor plan, it ignores UI details to reveal the underlying structure, uncluttered by surface appearance or by implementation details. In fact, the User Environment Design has no representation for these details, so it's hard for a conversation focused on a User Environment Design to go into details too soon. (In this way, it fills the need for a blueprint for software design identified by Denning and Dargan [1996].)

The User Environment formalism highlights the key concepts for designing a system work model. *Focus areas* show the coherent places in the system that support doing an activity in the work. They're the "rooms" of the system. Like rooms in the real world, they should support the activities that happen in them well. They should provide the function that's needed to do that work, and only the function that's needed. They should contain, organize, and present the objects that users need to work on. And like rooms in the real world, they are connected—the arrows between focus areas show how the user can move from place to place as their work requires it. Like paths traversing a quad, a new User Environment Design is built from storyboards, collecting the different stories of use into one structure supporting them all. User Environment Designs can also be built to represent existing systems, revealing their structure and highlighting problems (Figure 14.5).

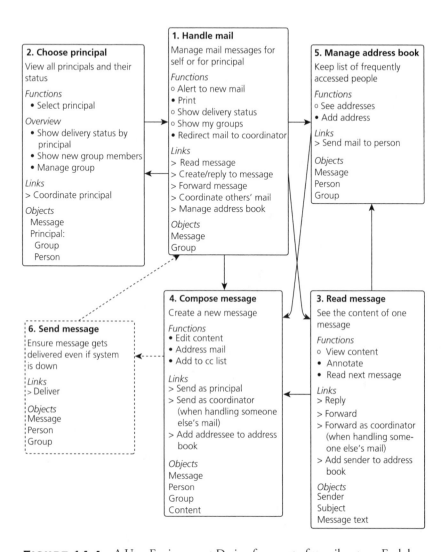

FIGURE 14.4   A User Environment Design for a part of a mail system. Each box represents a "focus area," a place in the system. These are like rooms in a house, which permit the user to focus on one particular activity. The purpose statement describes the work the focus area supports. Functions, which enable the user to do work, are listed in the focus area, as are the work objects that the user works on there. The arrows between focus areas are links and show how the user can move through the system.

This form of User Environment diagram is on its way to becoming a specification for the system. Each focus area collects and describes the functions provided the user in that focus area. The focus areas act like checklists, allowing designers to review the function in each place and verify that all the function is needed there and that all needed function is available.

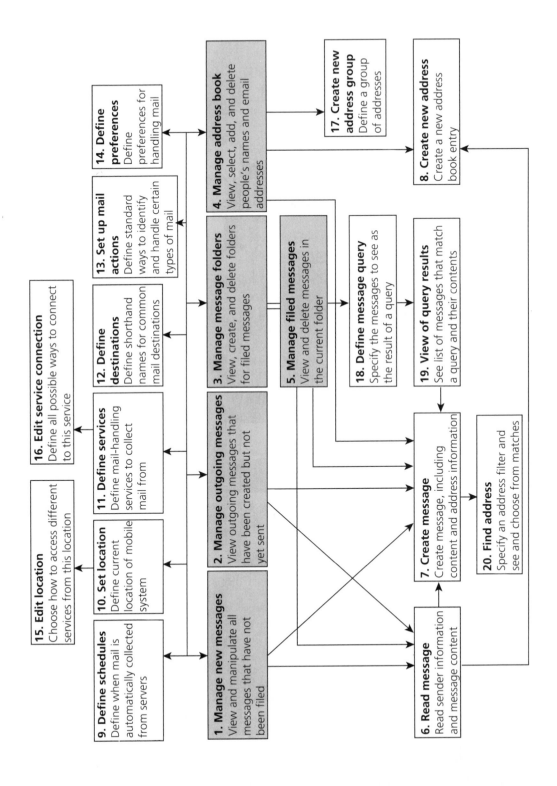

FIGURE 14.5 A full User Environment model of Claris Emailer UI. This more graphic form of User Environment diagram reveals the overall structure of a system, rather than the exact function in each place. Here, the core focus areas of Emailer are shaded for emphasis; in the product, each is a tab within the main window. The User Environment model immediately reveals that focus area 3, "Manage message folders," has a different user interaction style from the others—it's split into two interacting focus areas, 3 and 5. Beyond this core, the model shows two distinct parts of the product. One set (above) manages setup and preferences. Scanning the model reveals that setting one's location, a common function for those who travel, is treated as part of setup rather than an ordinary part of the core product. This contrasts with CompuServe's Information Manager interface, which more conveniently allows location to be viewed and changed right from the status window.

The second set of focus areas (below the core) support the actual work of creating and sending messages. Here, the model shows in

18 and 19 that users can only query on filed messages; that the results of a query appear in a special interface that shows both results and message content (not 6, the normal window for reading messages); and that though users can create a message from this results window, they cannot add the sender to their address book (8) as they could from the normal "Read message" interface. The model shows that the "Query/View results" pair (18 and 19) for messages provides a different structure for queries than the single "Find address" focus area (20) for searching the address book.

These are all structural issues, not user interface issues. They have to do with what the product does and how it is organized to do it. Whether this is a good organization or not depends on the actual structure of work in reading and handling mail—but the User Environment Design provides physical support for the conversation.

Because focus areas are the most visible concept captured by a User Environment model, the model helps designers organize the system so it fits the work. Do users spend time scanning their mail messages, choosing which ones to look at? Then it makes sense to create a distinct part of the system that helps them do that. After choosing a message, do they then concentrate just on that message and what it's about? Then seeing other messages is a distraction, so it makes sense to provide a separate area to focus on a single message. What's involved in reading a message? If users often want the sender in their address book, adding the name to the address book should be a function available in that place. If users never scanned messages, but simply worked through them one by one, there would be no need for a separate place to see all messages. If they needed to see what messages preceded and followed the message they were reading, the place to read should be integrated with the place to scan messages. (In a bulletin board, where messages are captured in threads of connected conversations, readers do want to see the context of messages, and products often do connect the two places.) The structure of the system must be designed to fit the structure of the work, and the User Environment model makes the system structure explicit.

A focus area is a place where users focus on one kind of work task

The UED reveals structure

REPRESENTING THE SYSTEM WORK MODEL

Capturing and representing the system work model in a User Environment diagram gives designers a way to see the whole system and keeps design at the right level.[2] A user interface would be too detailed—it invites the team to get caught up in issues of layout and appearance that can be put off until later, after the base structure is in place. Data flow diagrams show movement and transformation of data intrinsic to the work, not the structure of the system that the user experiences. Structure charts show the components of the system at a higher level of detail than code, but are focused on the structure of the implementation, which is not experienced by the user directly. The

---

[2] For a more detailed discussion of reflection in the design process, see Schon (1983).

same is true for object models: an object hierarchy provides a way to see and structure the implementation, not the user's experience.

Of course, people claim object models can represent anything, and it's true that an object model can represent the parts of a system design. But to be a good design and thinking tool, a model should evoke the thing being designed, making the right issues explicit and concrete. Designers manipulating the model need to feel like they are manipulating the real thing. An object model could

A good model evokes the reality it represents

capture the data in an architect's floor plan—but no architects using such a model would ever feel like they were manipulating space, as they do when they manipulate a floor plan. If the model is too far from the actual design issues, people using it have to make a translation in their heads. So it's not good enough to be able to make a mapping from a modeling technique to the issues for the system work model—a new model is needed to represent the user's experience. An effective model will influence designers' thinking by making the relevant issues jump out, just as work models influence what interviewers see in the workplace.

Such a model won't supplant object-oriented design, of course. In an object-oriented design, the object model keeps the *implementation* consistent—in the object model, developers bring functions from different use cases together into a single object class. They identify the reusable parts that different system components can use. But that's at the implementation level—the object model represents the different parts of the code, invisible to the user. The structure of the system as the user experiences it needs to be kept coherent as well.

THE USER ENVIRONMENT FORMALISM IN THE DESIGN PROCESS

The User Environment Design occupies a place in the design process between storyboards on the one hand, and user interface design and object analysis on the other. It makes the discussion of the system work model tangible by providing a physical representation. In this way it helps to separate the conversation about the system work model from the redesigned work process (represented in storyboards), from the system appearance (represented

Explicit models help keep design conversations separate

TASK-ORIENTED OR OBJECT-ORIENTED?

Is designing with storyboards and User Environment Design task-oriented or object-oriented? On the one hand, it's clearly not object-oriented because the User Environment Design does not focus on identifying common objects as its primary feature. Its most salient concepts are coherent activities—the focus areas—and flow between them. Yet it's clearly not task-oriented either. A User Environment Design prescribes no order, as storyboards do. It shows the parts of the system and their relationships independent of time. Many different stories of use can be walked through a User Environment Design to see how well it supports them just as many different stories of individual actions can take place in a house.

In fact, even in pure object-oriented design from use cases, object modeling does not stand on its own. The purpose of a use case is to tell a coherent story of how the users will work and the system will meet their needs (Jacobson et al. 1992). From this, object modelers can extract the objects and their behaviors. But neither use case nor object model provide a good representation of the system work model. The use case is task-oriented, telling one story of use, for one task, but it doesn't provide a coherent view of the system. The object model gives a coherent view of the system, but not the system the user experiences. Instead, it's a view of the system the developers will implement. It's not customer-centered because it's not focused on keeping the user's work coherent—and rightfully so, since it's an implementation tool. It is supposed to keep the implementation coherent—elegant, evolvable, extensible, and maintainable.

This is true even of so-called object-oriented user interfaces. These reveal to the user only a small proportion of the objects and behaviors of a full object model for the system. Object-oriented user interfaces achieve consistency by presenting objects as identifiable screen artifacts with consistent behavior. But what objects should the system present? How should they be organized? And what behaviors should they have? These are the questions answered by the system work model.

The basic question is, How do designers decide what the objects and behaviors should be to support the user? That's the question answered by the User Environment Design. Rather than base object definitions on use cases, the User Environment Design introduces a coherent model of the system that can be designed, structured, and corrected before object definition starts. In the end, it's neither task-oriented nor object-oriented. By focusing on the structure of work in the system, it's work-oriented and that's what makes it powerful. (Rosson and Carroll [1995] suggest another approach to integrating object-oriented and task-oriented system views.) ❑

by the user interface), and from the internal system structure (represented by the object model). When each conversation has its own physical representation, the design discussion is easier to have. Is the team arguing about how to change the user's work? Then they're standing in front of a storyboard, changing it to reflect their thinking. Are they arguing about how to organize the system to support that work? Then they are modifying the User Environment Design. Are they arguing about appearance and layout? Then they're changing parts of the user interface. Everyone can tell which issues to pay attention to because that's the model the team is updating.

User Environment Designs support the natural alternation between sequential and structural thinking. Storyboards and use cases are sequential; they tell a single series of events in order. The vision, User Environment Design, and object model are structural; they show all parts of the system and how they interrelate, though they focus on new work practice, the system work model, and internal structure, respectively. Each sequential step follows a story of use to work out the details of the

Alternating between sequential and structural thinking drives design details

preceding structure and uncover problems with it, so storyboards help the team work out the details of a vision, and use cases help work out the details of a User Environment Design. Each structural step pulls together the implications of different stories into a coherent system. The designers step back to see how each sequence affects the structure as a whole. So the User Environment Design integrates one system out of multiple storyboards, and the object model integrates one model out of multiple use cases. When a single structure is created, it can be checked for accuracy and completeness—the functions of a User Environment Design and behavior of an object can be reviewed and anything missing added. This continuous process of working out details, integrating, and checking ensures the integrity of the resulting system. Each transformation acts like a structured walkthrough, forcing the team to review all parts of the system from a different perspective (Figure 14.6).

The User Environment Design is created first to support design. It enables the design team to keep the system coherent. But because it represents the structure of the system as the user experiences it, it supports customer-centered project planning. Grouping focus areas that address specific roles identifies subsets of the whole design that sup-

The UED aids planning

port a coherent part of the work and could be delivered together. Identifying focus areas that are closely associated with each other reveals a subset that is appropriate for assignment to an implementation team. Building up a User Environment Design to include external and third-party products creates a strategic design showing what corporate partnerships to create. Building a reverse User Environment

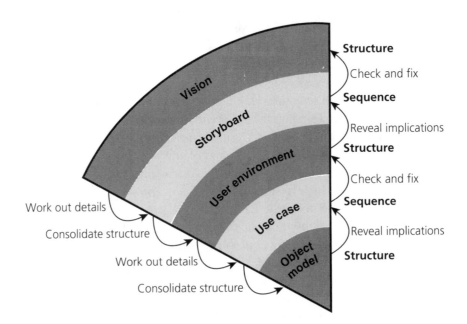

FIGURE 14.6 The progression from design to development. This diagram shows the process of going from work models through systems design to implementation design. It shows the alternation between sequential, story-based thinking and structural, model-based thinking intrinsic to design. The stories build a structure that can be checked for coherence and completeness; the structure drives lower-level stories specifying more detail. Working out the stories reveals holes in the structure defined previously, and putting together the structure reveals inconsistencies in the stories. The stories show a particular instance of using the system; the structure shows how the system can support multiple stories. Contextual Design alternates between the two, providing physical representations all along the way.

model of existing systems identifies duplicated function and holes in the suite. By representing the parts of the system from the point of view of the user's work, engineers can see how their work relates to each other and to the user. And that keeps the whole development process coherent.

One of the challenges of any design process is to keep the design coherent—to maintain the design team's ability to comprehend and operate at the level of the whole system while working on a part. Contextual Design continually returns to a coherent representation that pulls all the detail together. The consolidated work models show the whole customer work, structured and represented along each of the five dimensions. The User Environment model shows the whole system as experienced by the user, with all the parts and their relationships, independent of UI or implementation. The object model shows the whole implementation architecture and how it is organized. Each of these representations is focused on the appropriate issues for its place in the design process, but each represents the whole system coherently. The User Environment Design responds to the work models on one side and drives the object

> *The UED keeps the work coherent by keeping the system coherent*

model, the user interface, and project planning on the other. It's the pivot between customer work and system implementation, making sure that the work as it happens in the system hangs together.

The User Environment Design

15

The goal of the User Environment Design is to present structural issues, making the key considerations salient for keeping the user's work coherent. IT keeps the design team focused on the customer by giving a physical representation to the structure of work that the proposed system will enable for its users. To be a good tool for accomplishing this task, the User Environment formalism organizes the presentation of the system into a structure that supports a natural flow of work.

We saw in the previous chapter that work consists of coherent activities. Each activity is oriented toward accomplishing some intent, requires a certain set of actions to accomplish, and is naturally connected to other activities that the user might choose to switch to, given what they are trying to achieve. By their structure, systems create places that can support an activity if they have the right organization and make the right functions available. The system work model fits the user when it matches the structure of activities and actions that the user needs to accomplish.

Just as any house has a floor plan, no matter how it was designed, any system has a User Environment model implicit within it. Any system can be analyzed, and its underlying User Environment model revealed. We introduced the User Environment Design informally in the previous chapter and showed some models taken from commercial products. To introduce the parts of the User Environment formalism and their definitions, we'll walk through the analysis of another commercial product, Microsoft PowerPoint. As we go, we will show each part of the User Environment formalism and how they build up to a complete model.

Every system has a UED

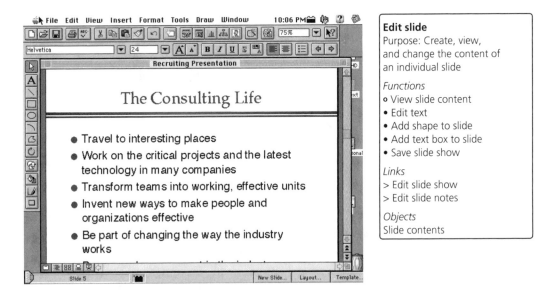

FIGURE 15.1   The main screen of Microsoft PowerPoint and the focus area that represents it. This window creates a place in the system in which to focus on creating, viewing, and changing the content of individual slides. This place is represented on the right, with the work that is done there summarized in the statement of purpose. Functions are available through different mechanisms—toolbar buttons, pull-down menus, the keyboard, and direct manipulation. In the focus area, we show only the functions, with no indication of how they are accessed. As is usual in a model built to analyze an existing product, the functions are high level ("add shape" rather than listing all the different shapes), and the model lists only the primary function in support of the purpose. A model built to design a new product would list every function and every shape designers intend to implement.

Figure 15.1 shows the main window of PowerPoint, a tool for making slide presentations. This window provides a place for creating and editing the content of slides. In the User Environment Design we represent places as *focus areas,* where you focus on doing a certain kind of work. Every focus area has a *purpose,* a succinct statement of the work the focus area supports. If you can't write a single sentence that describes the purpose of the focus area because there are so many different functions doing different things, it's likely that the system is poorly structured. Use the purpose statement to describe everything the focus area does.

This window provides functions that enable doing work in the place—to put rectangles, text boxes, and other slide objects on the slide, color and rotate them, and manipulate them in other ways. Functions are made available through menus, toolbars, keyboard commands, and by direct manipulation. These are alternative UI mechanisms for performing a function; some functions can be accessed all three ways (e.g., to save the presentation, choose "Save" under the "File" menu, click the disk icon on the toolbar, or type CTRL-S). Which mechanism the designers chose to implement for a function matters—a poor UI or

The UED focuses design on coherent work activities and the functions they need

inconvenient access to a function gets in the user's way—but it doesn't change the purpose of the place or the work done there. The UI mechanisms and screen layout are as much a distraction to understanding system structure as rug color would be on a floor plan. So we list the functions once on the right, with no indication of how they are accessed.

The "Edit slide" window also makes available the things the user needs to work on to edit a slide—the slide itself and also text boxes, shapes, lines, and clip art. These objects are collected and organized in the place appropriate for the job at hand—in this case, laid out on the screen to reveal the design of the slide. The focus area captures these work objects as an important part of the definition of the focus area. Later, when the object model is developed, they will be harvested as starting points for the objects.

Some of the function in this window leads to other places. Selecting the small icon at the bottom changes to the slide sorter view. This changes the view and the function available—it is no longer possible to create and edit the content of slides here. Instead, the slide sorter supports viewing a whole presentation in order, changing the order of slides, and controlling the transition from slide to slide. Because the work that can be done is different,

Links between focus areas enable a shift in attention to another activity

the slide sorter supports a new activity in a new place, and we represent it with a new focus area. The function that switched from one to the other is a *link,* shown on the User Environment Design as an arrow (Figure 15.2). You'd expect to find links between focus areas whenever the user might need to switch between the activities they support.

This much of the User Environment formalism will represent 90% of most products. However, there are some additional cases, the

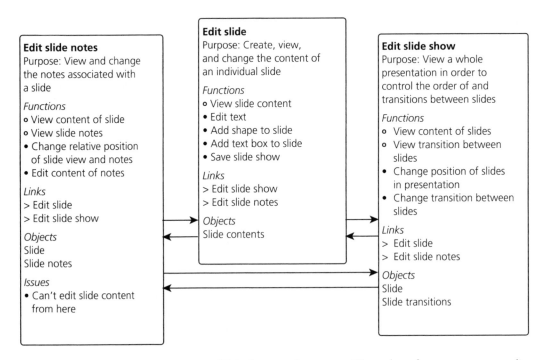

Edit slide notes
Purpose: View and change
the notes associated with
a slide

Functions
o View content of slide
o View slide notes
• Change relative position
  of slide view and notes
• Edit content of notes

Links
> Edit slide
> Edit slide show

Objects
Slide
Slide notes

Issues
• Can't edit slide content
  from here

Edit slide
Purpose: Create, view,
and change the content of
an individual slide

Functions
o View slide content
• Edit text
• Add shape to slide
• Add text box to slide
• Save slide show

Links
> Edit slide show
> Edit slide notes

Objects
Slide contents

Edit slide show
Purpose: View a whole
presentation in order to
control the order of and
transitions between slides

Functions
o View content of slides
o View transition between
  slides
• Change position of slides
  in presentation
• Change transition between
  slides

Links
> Edit slide
> Edit slide notes

Objects
Slide
Slide transitions

FIGURE 15.2 Links between focus areas. These three focus areas support distinct but related activities. They declare that when a user is worrying about the
detailed content of one slide, she is not concerned with the overall structure of the
presentation. Conversely, if she is worrying about the overall presentation, she needs
to see and recognize slide content, but doesn't need to change it there; she's willing to
switch back to the "Edit slide" focus area and lose the context of the whole presentation. This works reasonably well, but on the other side users do need to change slide
notes and slide content together. When developing a slide, we have found that users
naturally develop notes and slide content in parallel, moving information from the
notes to the slide and back as the idea of what is presented shifts. The division of the
work in the current design does not support a fluid movement between notes and
slide content. The User Environment model above shows the connections and reveals
the issue.

most important of which is the *double link.* When the user needs to
do the work of one focus area in the context of another, we show a

*A double link says to keep
one focus area in the
context of another*

double link between the two focus areas. The spell
checker is clearly a separate focus area from the main
slide show—in this focus area, you think about
spelling and dictionaries, not about the overall layout and content of your slide. But on the other

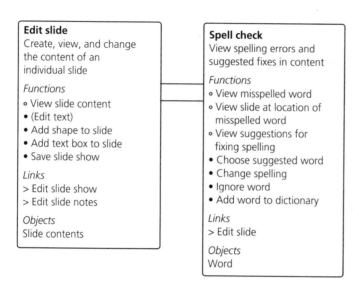

Edit slide
Create, view, and change the content of an individual slide

Functions
○ View slide content
• (Edit text)
• Add shape to slide
• Add text box to slide
• Save slide show

Links
> Edit slide show
> Edit slide notes

Objects
Slide contents

Spell check
View spelling errors and suggested fixes in content

Functions
○ View misspelled word
○ View slide at location of misspelled word
○ View suggestions for fixing spelling
• Choose suggested word
• Change spelling
• Ignore word
• Add word to dictionary

Links
> Edit slide

Objects
Word

FIGURE 15.3 A double link between focus areas. The double link indicates that the work done in the second focus area, spell checking, needs the context of the main focus area and that the user will switch back and forth between the two. Designing the user interface for this is a challenge because the user needs to switch between focus areas without losing her context in either.

hand, it's also closely linked to the "Edit slide" focus area: when you move to the next spelling error, the main window switches to display the slide with the error on it and attempts to position the slide so the error is visible. So we represent the spell checker as a double link to the "Edit slide" focus area (Figure 15.3). This indicates that the two cooperate to support the work, that the user needs to know where they are on the slide while checking spelling and needs to switch back and forth rapidly between the two. (When errors are marked as you type, the function has been merged into one focus area.)

This is a partial reverse User Environment model of PowerPoint, showing the primary parts of the formalism and what they represent in a real product. (See "User Environment Formalism" for a complete definition of the formalism.) Each box or focus area represents a coherent place to do work. The links between places show how the system supports the flow of activities but doesn't prescribe any particular order of work. The double-linked focus areas in Figure 15.3 show how the spell checker is related to the slide view; it says nothing about when the spell checker is run.

USER ENVIRONMENT FORMALISM

Focus area
A focus area collects functions and work objects into a coherent place in the system to support a particular type of work. A function should be necessary to do the work, not to manipulate the UI:

—Supports performing a coherent part of the work
—Named with a simple active phrase
—Lists functions that are needed to do the work
—Lists the work objects that the *user* needs to perform the work
—Numbered for unambiguous references to the focus area

Purpose
Short description of what the focus area does in supporting the work

Functions
Functions are described on the UED with a short phrase. They are written up online with a description of their behavior and justification.

- Functions invoked by the user to do work
o Functions that are automatically invoked by the system as necessary. The user knows these functions exist, but does not invoke them explicitly.
(name) Function clusters that appear in multiple focus areas. This is shorthand for listing all the functions in the cluster. The function cluster name appears between parentheses and is separately defined once to apply to all focus areas.

Links
Links and double links to other focus areas:

> Functions that support links between focus areas. An arrow between focus areas represents the link. The function name may not be the same as the destination focus area name, in which case the name or number of the destination focus area should be given in parentheses.
>> Functions that support *double links* between focus areas. A double line between focus areas represents the double link.

Work objects
The things the user sees and manipulates in the focus area

Constraints
Implementation constraints on the focus area: speed, reliability, availability, form factor (for hardware), etc.

Issues
Open design issues associated with this focus area, UI ideas, implementation concerns, and quality requirements ⇨

Hidden focus areas

Conceptual units of work done by the system that the user knows and cares about, but doesn't have to interact with. Often they automate work that used to be done by a person. Represented as boxes formed of dotted lines, connected to other focus areas with dotted lines.

External focus areas

Conceptual units of work delivered by other teams. External focus areas show how your system works with others to provide coherent support to the customer. ❑

THE REVERSE USER ENVIRONMENT DESIGN

There are two ways to take advantage of the User Environment Design. One is while designing a new system: seeing the structure ensures that the system stays simple and close to the user's needs and helps a team plan how to deliver. We'll show how to do that below. The other is to do what we did with PowerPoint—build a *reverse User Environment Design* to represent a product that already exists.

Building a reverse User Environment Design has a number of uses: to analyze a competitive product, to reveal the structure of multiple systems that need to be integrated, or to represent an existing system version so it can be extended in a new version. Building a reverse User Environment model of an existing system reveals its underlying work model. It reveals what users can think about and do together in the system, and assumptions built into the system about how users work. In the PowerPoint example above, PowerPoint supports changes to notes and changes to the slide content in separate focus areas. This implies that creating notes is an unrelated activity to creating slide content. It doesn't really matter whether the system's designers intended that consciously; that's what's built into the system.

A reverse UED shows your implicit existing system work model

Building a reverse User Environment model can be the first step in designing the next version of an existing system. It's easy for systems to get more unstructured over time—what started out as a reasonable and elegant design turns into a rat's nest of features and connections with no clear structure. Before adding new function, build a reverse User Environment model to see structural issues in the existing system. Modify the design to capture decisions about what to fix. Then you can make storyboards to capture new work practice for the next version to support, and you can use the process we describe below to roll them into the User Environment Design. In this way, you can add function without losing the system's overall design coherence.

When one developer was introduced to the User Environment Design, he started laughing hysterically, then grabbed a piece of paper and started sketching boxes and arrows on it. "I just figured out why users hate our system," he said. "This is what it looks like." He showed us the diagram he had drawn:

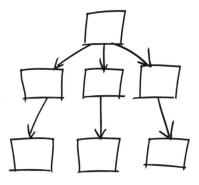

"See? They have to go all the way back up to this top box and then down again to do anything."

Using the reverse User Environment Design to see the structure of competitive products can make it clear to a team what the grounds for competition are. For example, most presentation packages have essentially the same structure at the User Environment level. The three focus areas of outliner, slide sorter, and slide editor are very common. The grounds for competition in presentation packages is at the level of detailed function and UI; the first product to shift the ground through a fundamental improvement in structure or UI paradigm will gain a substantial competitive advantage. Conversely, QuickMail Pro's market message (from their

A reverse UED of your competitor reveals the field of opportunity

marketing literature) is that it offers a base structure different from that of other mail products: "The 'All-in-One' Message window lets you simultaneously view your incoming messages, create and send new messages, and file or sort existing messages." Instead of providing separate focus areas for the in-box, sent messages, and filed messages, it's got one focus area for all three. This will only work if the work practice of users naturally mixes these different activities; otherwise it will be confusing.

The reverse User Environment Design is a good way to step back from a system and get insight into it. Surprising numbers of systems have the hierarchical structure that the engineer recognized in the story above. But the reverse User Environment Design may also reveal the values and assumptions about the work practice built into the existing products. When these are explicit, the team can compare them to the work models representing real customers and decide whether the assumptions built into the current systems work for the market or organization. For example, one team developing a collaborative work tool that allowed anyone to drop in on any conversation realized they were promoting a value of open communication to an extent that might stifle the use of their system.

Discussion during a reverse UED reveals designers' values and assumptions

The reverse User Environment Design gives a team a way to see what the users experience as they move through a system. It's a valuable tool in its own right. But the User Environment Design is also central to designing new systems.

BUILDING THE USER ENVIRONMENT FROM STORYBOARDS

In the design of a new system, storyboarding drives the design of the User Environment. We discussed in the last chapter how design alternates between sequential thinking and structural thinking. Storyboards are sequential and run a single thread; the User Environment Design is structural and reveals how all the threads fit together coherently. Storyboards give a lot of

A good structure suggests and supports unforeseen ways of working

information about a part of the system in the context of a specific use—how that part of the system supports one work task. The User Environment Design lets a team build the single coherent structure that supports multiple different tasks performed by different roles. It's a framework, a structure for doing work that is not constrained to the particular storyboards used to build it. Users will invent new ways to do their work based on the structure in the User Environment Design, if it's designed well.

Separating storyboards from the User Environment Design (and from subsequent user interface design) helps a team separate different kinds of design thought. Storyboards support following a single story of use: "I'm a user sorting my mail. How do I approach it? What do I do?" This is one approach to designing a system. It ensures that the system hangs together from the point of moving through a task, but it tends to hide the relationship to any other tasks the user might do. The User Environment Design supports structural thinking: "What's really going on in this place? Is it supporting a single, coherent activity? Does it provide everything the user needs to do that activity?" With two diagrams, each focused on supporting one kind of thinking well, the conversations can be separated for the team, making them clearer and easier to have.

Separating storyboards from the UED keeps design conversations separate

The User Environment Design is built from storyboards one at a time. Each storyboard contains implications for place, functions, and links in the User Environment Design. After the implications of each storyboard have been incorporated, the team steps back and looks over the whole User Environment Design with an eye to maintaining coherence. They identify focus areas that overlap in purpose and merge them, clean out focus areas that have accumulated extraneous functions, and reorganize the structure so that every focus area has a clear purpose and appropriate links to the rest of the system. (Constantine [1995b] describes building systems from a "use context model," a similar process.)

Storyboards imply the new system structure

A team pulls structural implications out of a storyboard by walking through it cell by cell. Each cell may suggest a new focus area, function, or link in the emerging User Environment Design. Storyboards are pictorial and help a team recall the context and the implications of each cell for the design better than a scenario or other textual description. The team discusses these implications and revises or extends the User Environment Design to capture their decisions.

The sketches that are part of storyboards give designers a way to think in the language most natural to them, while still staying out of the low-level details for as long as possible. The User Environment formalism is a direct representation of the issues for structuring the user's experience of the system. But we've found that teams coming up to speed on the User Environment formalism don't find this new representation a natural form for thinking. They do better thinking and designing in UI sketches, capturing them in the storyboard, and then pulling out the implications for the User Environment. The more they go back and forth between User Environment Design and user interface, the more they start to see the design implications from the User Environment diagram directly, and the more it will work for them not only as a seeing and checking tool, but as a design tool.

> *Moving between storyboards and the UED helps designers see structure in the UI*

Here's how the process works in practice. The storyboard in Figure 15.4 shows the first steps of a user getting help in a new work redesign. The vision implies a mix of hardware and software to implement: the phones are altered to have a "help" button, and the phone system is tied into the computer system so that the call is associated with the office and user where the phone is located. When the call is routed, the first-line helper's phone rings, and at the same time this information is displayed on her screen.

Because the system is a mix of hardware and software, some focus areas in this User Environment represent physical hardware places as well as software screens. In this way the User Environment diagram can be extended to represent the total system delivered to the user: hardware, software, documentation, and other systems. (It won't, of course, represent other aspects of the corporate response such as marketing or services.) The phone acts as a place to do work in an office: the work it

> *The UED can represent hardware and software that the user interacts with*

supports is communicating with others. The help button adds a function to the place: get quick help on system problems. So the implication of the first cell of the storyboard is a new function on an existing hardware focus area in the user's office (Figure 15.5).

FIGURE 15.4   Storyboard for getting help from system management.

The next cell shows how the system acts when the help button is pushed. It's necessary for working out what the system will do, but it isn't part of either the user's experience or the first-line helper's experience; it's entirely behind the scenes. In the next cell, the result of these behind-the-scenes actions is to display information on the first-line helper's screen and ring the telephone. So

The UED shows only what users care about or interact with

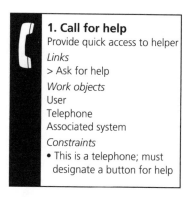

FIGURE 15.5 A focus area representing new functions on the user's phone.

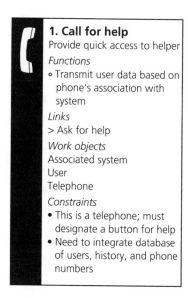

FIGURE 15.6 Function added to an existing focus area.

these actions flesh out the definition of the "help" function; they don't lead to a new focus area (Figure 15.6).

When the screen comes up on the helper's workstation, it creates a new focus area showing the information necessary to work on the user's problem. The information about the user, his system, and any history is displayed immediately, without any explicit request on the part of the helper. This is represented as an automatic function. We choose a name for the focus area that is terse and describes the primary

1. Call for help
Provide quick access to helper

Functions
o Transmit user data based on
  phone's association with
  system

Links
> Ask for help

Work objects
Associated system
User
Telephone

Constraints
• This is a telephone; must
  designate a button for help
• Need to integrate database
  of users, history, and phone
  numbers

- - - ➤

2. Work on user's request
See, work on, and track user's problem

Functions
o See user name and system associated with telephone
o See history of and comments on this problem
• Enter comments on problem or request, including what has
  been tried
• Enter solution to problem
o Update problem history
• Assign self as owner
• Reassign owner (to specified person or to next-level support)
• Cancel problem
o Log ticket into system (when assigned)
o Display time spent on problem (when assigned)
• Mark problem done
• Pause timing
• Restart timing

Links
> See system's history
> Get guru help

Work objects
User
System
Problem
Owner

Issues
• What if the help person isn't there?
• How do people see all their problems?

Roles
• This place will be used by both first-line helper and
  responsible person

FIGURE 15.7   Two focus areas connected by a hidden link. Each focus area collects the functions out of all storyboards needed to support the work of that place. They begin to act as a system specification, organized into clusters that support a coherent work activity.

work it supports: in this case, "Work on user's request" captures the essence of what the place is for (Figure 15.7).

The link between the phone and the new focus area is not an explicit link; neither the user nor the helper move between the phone and the "Work on user's request" focus area. The communication between the two is in the behind-the-scenes work. We show this on the User Environment as a dashed line, showing how the system supports communication between the focus areas.

The storyboard defines additional functions needed by the helper in this place: the ability to turn on and off time charges, assign ownership of problems, and record solutions. We write these functions right into the place. And we add the objects the user works on in this place to the focus area also—the problem report and the user information. Later, when it comes time to build the object model, the functions will define the behavior these objects must support by specifying what to write into the use cases that drive object modeling.

Objects in a focus area reveal the things the user works on

The next storyboard step has the helper looking at detailed system history. At this point, she's not thinking about the overall problem and system anymore; she's thinking about what has happened on the system that might tie into current behavior, either to support or suggest hypotheses. This is a different kind of work from the initial, direct discussion with the user about their problem. The system support for it is quite different—this part of the system is organized around browsing, free-form searching, and locating pieces of history by association. All this implies a new focus area, "See system's history," which is linked to "Work on user's request." Links are like other functions in that the user has to take an explicit action to follow the link; they're different in that the effect they have is to move the user to a new focus area. We find it useful to collect the links together in the User Environment Design so people can see the connections all together.

This decision about when to create a new focus area is critical to the User Environment Design. Focus areas support one part of the work and are organized to support it well. Whenever the user is doing a new kind of work, worrying about a different set of concerns, or engaged in a different style of thought, it implies a new focus area. This generally means that the user should work in any focus area for some amount of time, just as people expect to spend time in a room. It's hard for people to shift their attention from one kind of work to another frequently—the system should not force such a shift unless the work demands it.

A good focus area doesn't complicate or fragment a coherent activity

When rolling storyboards into the User Environment Design, it's the work the storyboard represents that defines the focus areas in the User Environment. The designers of the storyboard were thinking in the UI and may have created subwindows or dialog boxes, but if they don't support a different kind of work, the system doesn't need new focus areas. Conversely, if the storyboard mixes unrelated work in one interface, it implies several focus areas in the User Environment Design. This is the time to clean that up.

Inquiry into multiple storyboards drives the UED

The process of generating a User Environment Design from a storyboard continues in this manner, using the discussion of each cell in the storyboard to identify and capture new focus areas and extend existing focus areas (Figure 15.8). But the User Environment is the structure that supports all stories. After doing the first storyboard, roll in additional storyboards in the same way.

The first cell of the storyboard in Figure 15.9 identifies a place in the system we haven't seen before—a place for seeing all the work assigned to the user. We add it to the User Environment Design. Then the next step defines a place for seeing an existing problem. But when we look at the User Environment Design we already have, we see that "Work on user's request" already allows us to see and work on a problem. Should this cell reuse that focus area or create a new one? This is a question about the appropriate system structure for the work.

The new storyboard suggests a new way of thinking about the system structure. The first storyboard created one place from which to manage all the work of dealing with a problem. That place acted like a control panel or command center, providing access to all the different tools that might help resolve the problem:

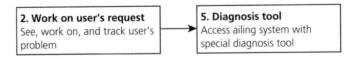

The new storyboard suggests a different approach. Instead of a single command center, the new storyboard breaks out the passive work of seeing the description of the problem and any work done on it to date and documenting any new actions. By breaking the act of working on the problem into a separate cell with a separate UI sketch, the storyboard suggests that access to tools be part of a second focus area:

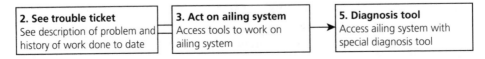

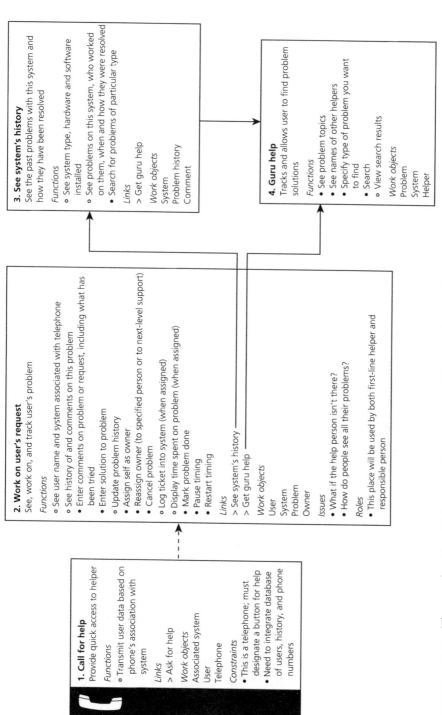

1. Call for help
Provide quick access to helper

Functions
○ Transmit user data based on phone's association with system

Links
> Ask for help

Work objects
Associated system
User
Telephone

Constraints
• This is a telephone; must designate a button for help
• Need to integrate database of users, history, and phone numbers

2. Work on user's request
See, work on, and track user's problem

Functions
○ See user name and system associated with telephone
○ See history of and comments on this problem
• Enter comments on problem or request, including what has been tried
○ Enter solution to problem
○ Update problem history
• Assign self as owner
• Reassign owner (to specified person or to next-level support)
• Cancel problem
○ Log ticket into system (when assigned)
○ Display time spent on problem (when assigned)
• Mark problem done
• Pause timing
• Restart timing

Links
> See system's history
> Get guru help

Work objects
User
System
Problem
Owner

Issues
• What if the help person isn't there?
• How do people see all their problems?

Roles
• This place will be used by both first-line helper and responsible person

3. See system's history
See the past problems with this system and how they have been resolved

Functions
○ See system type, hardware and software installed
○ See problems on this system, who worked on them, when and how they were resolved
• Search for problems of particular type

Links
> Get guru help

Work objects
System
Problem history
Comment

4. Guru help
Tracks and allows user to find problem solutions

Functions
• See problem topics
• See names of other helpers
• Specify type of problem you want to find
• Search
○ View search results

Work objects
Problem
System
Helper

FIGURE 15.8 The complete User Environment Design generated from the first storyboard.

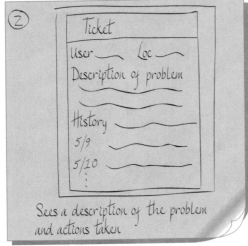

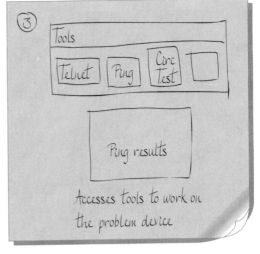

FIGURE 15.9   A second storyboard, in which the system manager starts from a
list of assigned tasks instead of starting by answering the phone.

These are different options for structuring the system. Up to this
point, neither option has been given careful thought. The designers
did what made sense for each storyboard without careful consideration of the implications for the system. Now that the two storyboards
are coming together in the User Environment Design, the team can
have the conversation about which structure would be best for the
work as they have observed it. Should a trouble ticket be like a form,

capturing the whole history of the work that has been done on this problem? That would be a close duplication of a paper ticket, an essentially passive holder of information. Or should a trouble ticket be an active working place bringing together the knowledge and context of the problem with the tools needed to work on it? The User Environment Design helps the team have this conversation with the aid of sketches like Figure 15.9. By removing UI details from the conversation, the User Environment diagram keeps the conversation focused on structure.

In the actual case, the design team decided on the first of the two options and prototyped it with the helpers. The helpers liked having a single command center for dealing with problems but went further: they wanted the interaction with their tools to happen in the same place. And they didn't need to see all the details of the user in that place. The User Environment Design implied by these changes keeps a place to work on the user's

Different storyboards suggest alternate structures to reconcile in the UED

request, but it integrates the tool results into that place through a linked focus area. And the detailed information about the user is moved into a separate focus area, accessible, but out of the way:

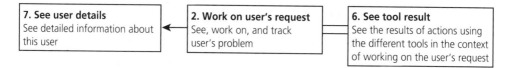

The concepts provided by the User Environment diagram make this discussion easier to have. They focus on the critical question for this level of design: what are the places the system will create, and what work will they support? The different diagrams above support a discussion about what structure fits the user's work best, disregarding UI considerations.

Similarly, these discussions precede any object modeling for the system implementation. If objects were derived directly from the storyboards, there would be no opportunity for this level of structural thinking. Each of the different options above suggests different technical challenges, a different set of use cases, and a different object model. In particular, the third option suggests a use case describing how invoking a diagnostic tool causes that tool to run on the appropriate system and show its results right in the "Work on user's request" place.

<table>
<tr><td>Different UEDs imply
different object models</td><td>Neither of the other two options suggest that use case. By designing the structure of the system work model first, the User Environment Design helps stabilize the design before object modeling starts and limits the amount of rework needed afterwards.</td></tr>
</table>

DEVELOPING SPECIFICATIONS

When you have to work within a software process that expects a software specification, the User Environment Design can take you much of the way. The User Environment Design defines how the new system will behave and organizes its function in a way that makes sense for the user. Based on this, you can drive the different parts of the specification. A typical specification might have the following parts:

Overview: The first part would give an overview of the whole system, its goals, and its basic structure. This is illustrated with a high-level User Environment model—titles, purposes, and links only, as in Figure 14.5. This section introduces the reader to the system and orients them to the parts of the system, showing how the different parts support users' roles and tasks.

Supporting data: This section summarizes the customer data on which the system design is based. It shows key sections of the affinity and consolidated models, reviews the roles that the system primarily supports, names the primary influences that drove the design direction, and summarizes the structure of consolidated sequences for key tasks. Particularly when customer-centered design is new to an organization, it's important to emphasize how a design is built on and responds to concrete customer data.

Functional requirements: This is the basic definition of what the system does. It's organized by focus area. Each section introduces the focus area and describes the work done there. For each function, it names the function and provides a full description of the function's behavior. In this way, it avoids presenting long lists of functions with no organized intent—instead, it's clear how the functions together support particular activities. Objects manipulated in the focus area are named, and constraints and issues are listed. Where the specification includes user interface designs, they are described with the focus area definition.

Nonfunctional requirements: Additional requirements on the system—performance, reliability, maintainability, evolvability, platforms supported, and so on—are listed in their own section. These are collected from the affinity and extended while building the User Environment Design but aren't associated with any particular focus area. They are kept on the side for inclusion in the specification later.

Objects: The objects manipulated in the different focus areas are listed with the focus areas but described once, here. The meaning and usage of the objects across all focus areas are described. This will act as a starting point for later object modeling. Use cases will describe the detailed behavior of the system, and out of that, the behavior of each object can be defined, and additional implementation objects identified. ⇨

External interfaces: External interfaces to the system are described. We'll show in the next chapter how links between focus areas can define interfaces between one system and another. In this part of the specification, these interfaces are collected and described.

It's easy to integrate detailed requirements tracing into this structure when your organization requires it. In each function definition, list the storyboard cells that used that function. Document each storyboard and record the consolidated sequence that you used to define it. List any additional data you used—sections of the affinity, role definitions, or other pieces of consolidated models. Document each consolidated model online, and link it to the individual models from which it was built. Do this, and you'll be able to take any function and walk the steps backwards to the actual customer data that suggested the design of that function. ❏

DEFINING A SYSTEM WITH THE USER ENVIRONMENT DESIGN

The User Environment Design keeps the user's work coherent by holding the whole definition of a focus area in one place. If you have no physical representation, it's too hard to look across a whole system and decide if the parts of it are coherent and where a new function should go. But when the system is concrete in a diagram, it's not hard to scan the purpose and existing function to find the right place for a new extension. When a focus area gets too complex, it's straightforward to review it and related focus areas. What roles does the focus area support? What tasks? For each role, is the focus area reasonable? What's really needed? Using questions like these, designers can rebalance the focus areas and clean up the design.

Within each focus area, the list of functions, links, and constraints summarizes what can happen in that place. As a list, it supports checking the completeness of the focus area—it's easy to scan and check against the issues raised by models and storyboards. Keeping the UI sketches from the different storyboard cells that contributed to a focus area gives additional context: they show what the designers were thinking about when they developed the place. Because they are sketches, they are more concrete, helping designers envision what a system based on this User Environment Design might look like. And

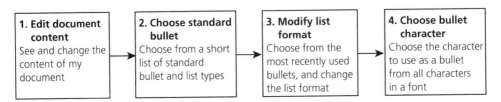

FIGURE 15.10   When a focus area leads to one other focus area, which leads to one other after that, you have a "leggy" User Environment structure. The user will have to go through multiple layers of windows to accomplish a function. This is the structure for defining the bullets in a bulleted list in Microsoft Word. How many different ways are there to choose a bullet? And how many different focus areas do you have to go through before you can choose one? In this case, the focus areas are created by dialog boxes; each dialog box creates its own concern by offering a different interface and different function that the user has to parse and understand. Not every dialog box would be represented as a focus area. Microsoft Word's "Zoom" dialog box is simpler and would be considered part of its parent focus area.

they give UI designers a starting point for designing the presentation of the focus area.

Thinking in terms of focus areas and links tends to keep the basic work of the focus area *in* the focus area, rather than spreading it over several. Thinking in terms of today's user interfaces allows—or encourages—spreading the function across windows, panes, dialog boxes, tabbed dialogs, and other gewgaws. Look at the way MS Word uses three layers of dialog box to specify bullets (Figure 15.10). Thinking in the UI raises worries about constraints of screen real estate and problems of specifying every detail of a function; it's easy to punt and decide to put the function in a dialog box. Thinking in the User Environment Design takes away that excuse—if the function is part of the work of a focus area, it goes into the focus area.

The UED works against proliferation of dialog boxes

Later, when it's time for the UI designer to create a user interface, the User Environment Design will have collected all the different functions from all storyboards and organized them into coherent areas, each focused on one kind of work. It's up to the UI designer to figure out creative ways of making the function available in one coherent place in the interface. This gives the UI designer the most flexibility to be creative—deciding to split a focus area because it will be too hard to design the UI prejudges what the UI design will be able to do.

The sketches from the storyboards offer suggestions for the UI design and show the concepts the storyboard designers intended to reveal. But the UI designer has to decide, for all the storyboards collected into this place, and for all the roles and tasks the place might support, what is the UI appearance that will support the work best. In the above example, the "Work on user's request" focus area has to let the first-line helper see what

The UI designer makes function accessible for all users and tasks

work has been done on a problem and also support the system manager doing the work on the user's system. The User Environment Design specified that they could both take advantage of the one focus area; now the UI design has to support both roles. The first-line helper has an irate user on the phone; he needs a clear and direct interface. But he does want to see the whole history of the problem. The system manager wants powerful access to all the tools, but if that access is provided, she can benefit from the clear and direct interface the first-line helper needs. The UI designer has to consider both roles when designing the presentation and access mechanisms.

This is the ongoing process of extending a design: create a storyboard to work out the implications of a new component to the user's work practice, then roll it into the User Environment Design to see how the system structure can support the work practice you've designed. Storyboards keep the work coherent; the User Environment Design keeps the system coherent. Additional storyboards build up the User Environment Design into a structure that responds to all the multiple tasks and roles the system must support. The resulting User Environment Design shows all the parts together, how they relate, and how they overlap.

DEVELOPING THE OBJECT MODEL

The next task facing the team after developing the User Environment Design (and checking it with users, which we discuss in the next part) is to start the design of the implementation. This is what use cases and object modeling are all about. We will not treat object modeling in depth, but the design work done in storyboards and User Environment Design gives the team the basis they need to design the implementation quickly. ➪

The usual method is to start with use cases and define classes and class hierarchies from them. Going from use case to object model is another example of switching between sequential and structural thinking; the use cases are a story of use, the object model is structural, and (if used) object interaction diagrams are a story again. But, as practiced in the industry, use cases may be very high level, showing a whole task in the work, or low level, showing the accomplishing of a smaller function. And it's always an issue to decide what ought to be specified by the use case anyway.

When building on a Contextual Design project, we incorporate use cases at two points. First, storyboards act like high-level use cases. They show how real users interact with the system to get tasks done. At this level, the storyboard is well grounded in a consolidated sequence and the vision, so there are clear criteria for what should be included. But the storyboard format is more appropriate to this high level of design. Their pictorial nature makes it easy to scan and see the emerging design. And, while use cases include preconditions, postconditions, and exceptions, we've not found it necessary to specify these at this high level.

The User Environment Design provides a high-level structural thinking step that responds to the storyboards. Change the structure or function at this level, and the object model for the implementation will change; merge two focus areas and expand the function of a work object in the User Environment Design, and the corresponding implementation object will take on new responsibilities.

Later, object modeling captures these implications by switching back to sequence-based thinking in low-level use cases. At this level, each use case tells the story of how one function or closely related group of functions operates. The use case is based on storyboards and User Environment Design: the storyboard defines what the user will do, while the User Environment Design defines the function. The use case works out precisely what happens when the user operates these functions, how the system responds, and how the system internals make the designed response possible. They reveal flaws in what went before and drive the next step. Use cases bridge the gap from design of the system work model to design of the implementation.

Similarly, the design team derives events and triggers driving the implementation from the User Environment Design. Whether initiated by the user invoking a function or initiated by the system as indicated by automatic functions, the User Environment Design defines the events that the implementation needs to handle.

Building the User Environment Design as an intermediate step between storyboards and use cases helps ensure that the structure built into the use cases holds together for the user. Until the User Environment structure is stable, there isn't a design to build use cases on—changes at the User Environment level will change what happens in the use cases. Without an explicit representation such as this, the only way to work out structural issues is in the implementation and the UI. The more we can reveal, identify, address, and test these issues with users before starting implementation design, the faster implementation design and coding will go. ❏

USER ENVIRONMENT DESIGN
WALKTHROUGHS

The walkthrough is the final step of building a User Environment Design, and it should never be skipped. It's always done before going on to design a UI or test the design with users. The User Environment Design walkthrough uses principles of good system structure to check the design. Even a careful team will, as they roll more and more storyboards into the design, start to destructure it. A focus area that started out clean will accumulate function until the original purpose gets blurred. Perhaps any individual function could be justified, but taken together they suggest a different work focus that should be separated out. Two focus areas that started clearly distinct will, as function is added to each, start to overlap to the point that the distinction is no longer clear. The team needs the walkthrough as a chance to withdraw from the design, take stock of it, and reorganize what has started to get messy.

You'll see another level of structure when you walk through your design. The design itself suggests new possibilities when you pause to inquire into it. A set of focus areas taken together may imply support for a whole task or role; three focus areas might be consolidated into one addressing the fundamental task more directly; or functions in several focus areas suggest an activity that could be supported directly in its own focus area. It's this

The walkthrough lets you be the groundskeeper redesigning the quad

step of rationalizing the design against the work that will lead to a solid, flexible base structure that supports many different uses.

Walking the User Environment Design also gets the team into position for the next phase of design. It ensures that the whole team is clear on what they intend by the design and how they think it will work. It identifies *test cases*—conditions or design elements that become a focus to test with users in prototypes. In this way it becomes the first step toward iterating the design with users.

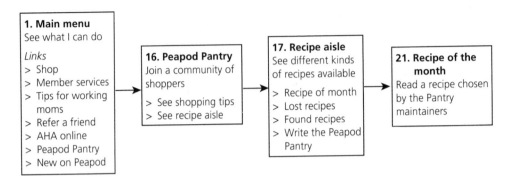

FIGURE 15.11 When a focus area contains no function, only links to other places, you've got a hallway. Here in Peapod are three hallways in succession (1, 16, and 17) before the user can get to doing anything real. System designers frequently create places that have no purpose except to organize access to other places. They are like hallways in a house, where no actual living is done but doors open onto other rooms. Hallways are necessary in houses because of the physical constraints in laying out a house, but in a software system every place can support real work. This kind of structure is often an indication that the designer is carrying over old ways of thinking from non-GUI systems.

PROBING USER ENVIRONMENT DESIGN STRUCTURE

The questions to ask when checking a User Environment Design are similar to those that drove building it:

Are focus areas coherent? Does each focus area support one activity within the overall task? Is that represented by the title and purpose statement? Be suspicious of any focus area that has no purpose. It's often because the team isn't clear on what the purpose is.

Do focus areas support real work? Look for focus areas that are really glorified dialog boxes—they've turned a simple command into a whole subtask (see Figure 15.10). Look for focus areas that group related functions, but that don't support something you might work on. Look for focus areas that don't support a coherent work task, but instead only reveal the data associated with an object in the system.

Are functions correct? Look for functions that are not in direct support of the focus area's purpose. Do they imply a separate activity that should be separated into another focus area?

Are focus areas distinct? Collect the focus areas that support the same part of the work—the same activity, task, or role—and compare them. Are they clearly distinct? Do they, taken together, provide coherent support for this part of the work? Can they be recombined to give a cleaner set of distinctions for doing the work?

Do links make sense? Do they support the work task as you know it from the consolidated and redesigned models? Certain patterns of links and focus areas always indicate trouble (see Figures 15.10 through 15.12). Do any of these patterns appear, and do they indicate problems in the design? (Incidentally, notice the simplified form of focus area used in Figure 15.10, with only title and purpose. This is a useful way to highlight structural issues.)

Is the work supported? Finally, use the consolidated models to refresh your memory, and look at the User Environment Design from the point of view of the different roles and tasks. Does the design work for each different kind of user? Does it account for the issues they care about? Run actual sequences through the model, asking how this user would have done this task given the new system. See if you can make it break down.

Using a walkthrough this way pulls the User Environment Design back together into a structure that makes the user's work coherent. Like a groundskeeper rethinking path layouts, the walkthrough gives you a chance to step back from your design. Check it for fit against the user, for missing parts, and for internal balance. Clean up the structure, and then you can either test it with users or extend it with more storyboards. Or, better yet, do both in parallel—the sooner you get feedback from real users on their design, the better off you are.

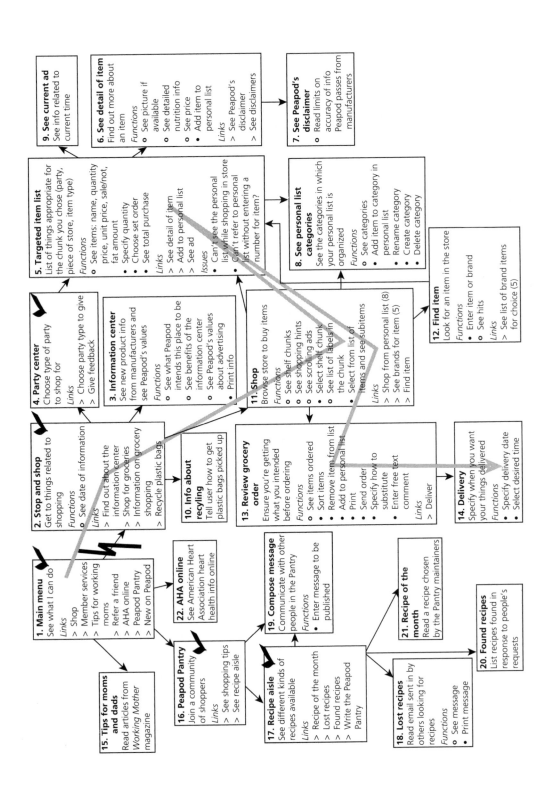

9. See current ad
See info related to current time

6. See detail of item
Find out more about an item
Functions
o See picture if available
● See detailed nutrition info
● See price
● Add item to personal list
Links
> See Peapod's disclaimer
> See disclaimers

7. See Peapod's disclaimer
o Read limits on accuracy of info Peapod passes from manufacturers

5. Targeted item list
List of things appropriate for the chunk you chose (party, piece of store, item type)
Functions
o See items: name, quantity price, unit price, sale/not, fat amount
● Specify quantity
● Choose set order
● See total purchase
Links
> See detail of item
> Add to personal list
> See ad
Issues
● Can't see the personal list while shopping in store
● Can't refer to personal list without entering a number for item?

8. See personal list categories
See the categories in which your personal list is organized
Functions
● See categories
● Add item to category in personal list
● Rename category
● Create category
● Delete category

4. Party center
Choose type of party to shop for
Links
> Choose party type to give
> Give feedback

3. Information center
See new product info from manufacturers and see Peapod's values
Functions
o See what Peapod intends this place to be
● See benefits of the information center
o See Peapod's values about advertising
● Print info

11. Shop
Browse store to buy items
Functions
o See shelf chunks
o See shopping hints
o See scrolling ads
● Select shelf chunk
● See list of labels in the chunk
● Select from list of items and see subitems
Links
> Shop from personal list (8)
> See brands for item (5)
> Find item

12. Find item
Look for an item in the store
Functions
● Enter item or brand
o See hits
Links
> See list of brand items for choice (5)

2. Stop and shop
Get to things related to shopping
Functions
o See date of information
Links
> Find out about the information center
> Shop for groceries
> Information on grocery shopping
> Recycle plastic bags

10. Info about recyling
Tell user how to get plastic bags picked up

13. Review grocery order
Ensure you're getting what you intended before ordering
Functions
o See items ordered
● Sort items
● Remove item from list
● Add to personal list
● Print
● Send order
● Specify how to substitute
● Enter free text comment
Links
> Deliver

14. Delivery
Specify when you want your things delivered
Functions
● Specify delivery date
● Select desired time

1. Main menu
See what I can do
Links
> Shop
> Member services
> Tips for working moms
> Refer a friend
> AHA online
> Peapod Pantry
> New on Peapod

22. AHA online
See American Heart Association heart health info online

16. Peapod Pantry
Join a community of shoppers
Links
> See shopping tips
> See recipe aisle

19. Compose message
Communicate with other people in the Pantry
Functions
● Enter message to be published

21. Recipe of the month
Read a recipe chosen by the Pantry maintainers

20. Found recipes
List recipes found in response to people's requests

15. Tips for moms and dads
Read articles from Working Mother magazine

17. Recipe aisle
See different kinds of recipes available
Links
> Recipe of the month
> Lost recipes
> Found recipes
> Write the Peapod Pantry

18. Lost recipes
Read email sent in by others looking for recipes
Functions
o See message
● Print message

FIGURE 15.12 The Peapod User Environment. A reverse User Environment Design for a shipping commercial product supporting home shopping. This User Environment Design reveals a number of structural issues in the product. The checked focus areas are all hallways, supporting no real work (they have no functions, only links). The gray arrow shows what's required to order one item, suggesting the design is too leggy. And the lightning bolt shows how the recipe/information part of the product is almost totally divorced from the shopping part of the product (only one link connecting the two parts—and that connects two hallways).

This example shows some strategies for analyzing complex real products. In larger products, major subcomponents—such as the "AHA Online" focus area above—often are represented by only the first focus area in the component. This hides the complexity of the component while still revealing the relationships with the larger system. Each focus area only lists four or five primary functions of that focus area, rather than listing them all. Of course, when the User Environment Design is defining the product, such a diagram has to be backed up with a complete definition of the function of each focus area.

Project Planning and 16
Strategy

Because the User Environment diagram shows all parts of the system in relationship to each other, it's a basis for planning as well as a basis for design. Most systems are large enough that they need a team of people to build them and have to be delivered over a series of releases. Most systems don't stand alone; they work together with other systems to support a whole job or business process. It's this collection of systems that taken together must support a coherent work practice. And software development organizations don't care only about individual applications or products—they're often looking for ways to tie their different systems together into a unified strategy for supporting their target market or business. Such a strategy makes the corporate response we discussed in Part 4 possible.

The challenge for project management is to define releases that keep the user's work coherent *and* can be implemented by the people available in reasonable time. Planning coherent releases can take advantage of the User Environment diagram as a representation of the systems, their parts, and their relationships. The User Environment diagram guides planning by breaking the design into natural components, relevant to the customer, that can be considered independently. Whether these components represent a small part of a single product or a complete application in their own right, the User Environment diagram shows what's going on in that component and how it relates to the rest of the system. Based on this, a team can organize and plan their development strategy.

Management challenge: define releases that keep user work coherent

PLANNING A SERIES OF RELEASES

The usual situation with a systems development effort is to envision a larger and more complete system than can easily be delivered in a single engineering cycle. Whether it's a product for sale or an internal system, customers typically don't want to wait years to see the first version. By then, they'll have taken their business to other vendors, or their business will have changed so much that the system will no longer be useful to them anyway. It's not even good engineering to spend years producing the maximal solution—any system will miss the mark to some degree. The sooner there's a version out there, the sooner the team can correct their mistakes and build on the new work practice that customers will invent around the new system.

It's important to envision the bigger picture. It gives you a goal to strive for, a direction to your development. But use the larger vision to

The UED showing the whole system lets you see how to carve it up

define a series of releases, each leading you closer to the vision and each deliverable in a reasonable time frame. Many organizations aim to have the first release out in under a year, even for significant projects. This release sets the customers' first impression of the system and organization that delivered it. The system should make a splash in the market or make a significant contribution to the customers' business. But it also needs to hang together as a coherent way of working. Every function interacts with other functions in the design—it's a waste to do large amounts of work to ship a function and none to ship the other functions that make it useful. The last-minute sessions to decide exactly what will make it into a particular version are the most painful. What's the criteria for choosing what to cut? The last feedback from a user group? The most recent customer to call an account representative on the carpet? Whoever shouts loudest on the engineering team? Teams need a process for deciding what functions are most important for the work of the customer and how to deliver them in chunks that keep the work coherent.

When delivering to an internal client, basing development plans on a long-range vision creates the possibility of integrating the development schedule with the organization's business plans. Each piece of the User Environment Design suggests new roles and new ways of working—as each piece is implemented, the organization can put the process changes in place needed to take advantage of that piece. Keeping the business reorganization and system delivery synchronized keeps the process under control.

When delivering a product to a market, creating a larger vision and delivering to it over a series of releases means you have a coherent market message. Reveal the vision as your strategic direction, and then each release is not only useful in its own right but is also another down payment toward your commitment. Instead of selling individual features, you can sell product directions that address problems people experience in their work. Everyone—marketing, sales, services, and development—can push their work in this common direction.

Focus areas and the clusters of focus areas that together address a common intent are one way of looking at how the functions of a system group into subsets that can usefully be shipped together. In Figure 16.1, the "Select base configuration" and "Find configurations" focus areas together let the user view, search for, and select a configuration to use as the starting point for any changes. These two focus areas work as a unit. It wouldn't make sense to ship one without the other. However, the system could ship without both—developers would then have to type the name of the base configuration directly. This might be reasonable for a first cut at the system.

> *Focus areas work together to support tasks or roles— ship them together*

Another way to prioritize the system is to deliver coherent support for a role, responsibility, or task. The first responsibility of a configuration management system is to support developing code, so the marketing team might decide that the first release has to support developers. "Modify product" is the core focus area for developers, so it had better be included. A minimal release would include just enough other focus areas and functions to support making a change: choosing a base configuration to modify, choosing the specific "parts" to edit, making changes and testing them, and finally packaging up all modifications into a single "change," which is put back in the system.

Once they make the decision what to include in the system, the team makes a *shipping User Environment Design* showing just those focus areas and functions that are intended to be part of this release (Figure 16.2). This shipping design, when all focus areas and functions are fully specified, forms the core of the software specification for this release. By extracting the subset they intend to ship and representing it

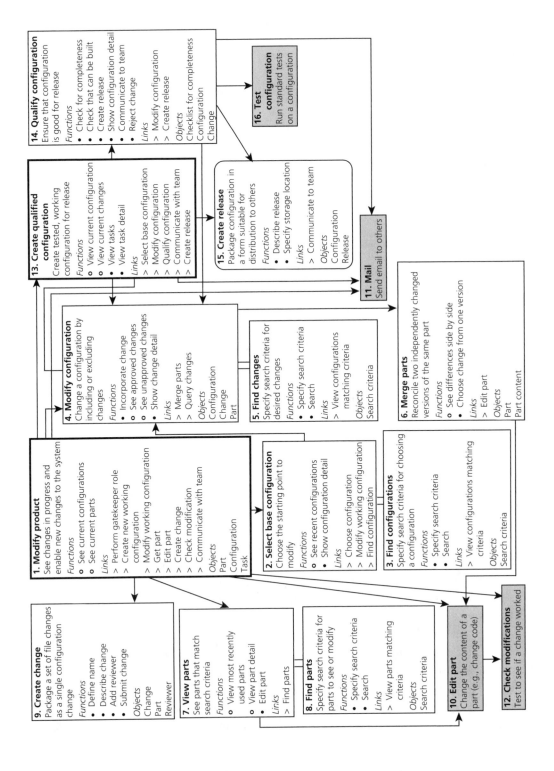

FIGURE 16.1 A User Environment Design supporting configuration management. This design supports two primary roles: Developers, who code changes and extensions to the application, and Gatekeepers, who ensure that any new code is good enough to include in "official" versions. Each specific application version is represented as a "configuration"—the set of specific file versions for that variant of the system. Developers work by selecting a "base configuration" to modify and making their changes as changes to that configuration. When they are done, they package all files they've changed along with the original change order and any assembly instructions and submit that package as a "change." The Gatekeeper can then review and test each change as a coherent unit.

as a User Environment diagram, the team can see whether that subset stands on its own as a self-contained system supporting coherent work. They can validate it, run scenarios through it, prototype it, and test it with users. They can find out both whether it works as a coherent system and whether it works as an interesting release—whether it provides enough to make customers interested in adopting it.

Reviewing the User Environment Design in Figure 16.2 suggests that a cut supporting only development provides only minimal support for one role—hardly a competitive product, and with no extra features for product differentiation. So marketing might decide that supporting the Gatekeeper is a requirement for a viable product. It's a fundamental responsibility of the Gatekeeper's role to review a configuration and decide whether it's good. So there's no point in shipping any of the focus areas supporting the Gatekeeper if the system doesn't include "Qualify configuration." It won't be used by Gatekeepers if it doesn't support that part of the role.

It may not take all the functions of a focus area to support a role.

Ship the functions needed by the role or task you intend to support

Only some of the functions of "Modify configuration" are needed by developers, so if they are the targeted users for a first cut of the system, the other functions could be left out. When a role is the target for a release, looking across focus areas for the core function to support that role reveals what's most important to include.

Finally, because the decision of what to cut is an engineering trade-off that has to account for implementation difficulty, the team can consider alternative presentations of a function or focus area in the UI. The UI can make the function easy or complicated to implement. For those functions core to a focus area or to a role, it may be worth designing a sophisticated UI that makes the operation of the function smooth and easy. But for less central functions that are nonetheless needed to support the work, a bare-bones implementation may be sufficient.

All these ways of looking at how to prioritize a release depend on understanding what the core innovation of the new system is. What is the

Identify your core contribution to your customers and ship that

one key change in people's work practice that the system introduces? Don't look for a feature; look for the key way in which the system makes work different. Look for the key differentiator your product offers over the competition or the core way your system

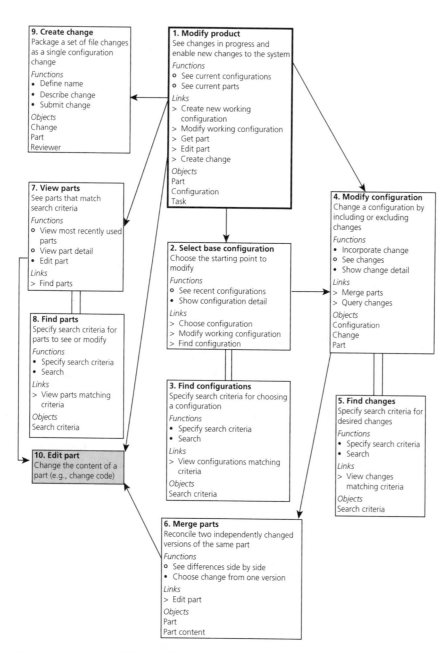

FIGURE 16.2 A shipping User Environment Design: a subset of the configuration management User Environment Design supporting developers.

helps your customers advance their business goals. Once you've identified the key differentiator, ask, What's the minimum subset of the system necessary to introduce that change? The User Environment Design helps to maximize the impact of a new system by showing what part of the system will implement the core innovation coherently. Then you can build on that to support more of the work, more completely.

PARTITIONING A SYSTEM FOR IMPLEMENTATION

Real systems are built by more than one person—by teams working together. If dividing up the system is to be useful, every developer must be free to focus on his or her own part. But any requirements document has holes—developers in front of their machines at 2:00 in the morning will have to make decisions that affect the user. With the User Environment Design, those decisions can be made with the knowledge of how it affects the overall design and other design teams. The User Environment Design organizes requirements to show how the system is structured for the customer. But the User Environment Design also helps manage a project by showing how it can be split up for implementation by teams or individuals working in parallel.

The concepts of the User Environment diagram can help a team keep the coherence of user work during implementation. Assign work purely based on technology or implementation considerations, and each developer may not have a coherent piece of the work to code. That will lead developers to lose the focus on the customer. They can't see how the work is supposed to hang together, so they have no way of knowing if a decision they make disrupts the flow of work or supports it. Each focus area represents a coherent concern. It makes sense to assign whole focus areas together, or sets of focus areas addressing a role or task, so that developers can see one complete piece of the whole. If the User Environment Design can be broken into components, as above, whole components can be assigned together. People can think about and design these coherent units as a piece because they hang together in the system and in the work (Figure 16.3).

The UED maintains work coherence during implementation

An implementation subteam needs a coherent part of the system to design, and focus areas provide such an organizing theme. But a large system will have multiple subteams, and some may be organized around components of the implementation such as common objects or technology components (e.g., the interface to a database). Organizing a project for delivery is a balance between keeping the user's work in the system coherent and keeping the implementation coherent.

For any system to work, the teams focused on implementation components need to understand how they relate to user-visible behavior. A team implementing a reusable component to embed video clips in mail messages, for example, would have to understand how the activities of reading and sending mail are structured so that the reusable component can fit into the work smoothly.

The UED reveals reusable components

It would be important to them to see as many different situations of use as possible, to understand the requirements on the component and how to make it a seamless part of the host system. A team implementing a reusable component to support an underlying database link would need to know what kinds of demands the systems might make on that link.

The User Environment Design reveals how reusable components relate to the system work model and shows who needs to work with whom. A team building an object class to implement a work object from the User Environment Design needs to work with the teams building the focus areas where that work object is used. The teams working on focus areas need to manipulate the objects and have a stake in the design of the class. In the UI, the object is a visible screen artifact and should appear consistently in all parts of the system. The User Environment Design flags all the players who need to be concerned about these elements so they can agree. In this way the whole team—even those working on internals—stays grounded in the user's work. And the User Environment Design provides a map of which development teams need to work together.

Links between focus areas assigned to different subteams show points of integration. A link shows that one part of the product needs to provide access to another part and that the work flows from one part to the other. The parts need to connect technically, so some kind of call or invocation mechanism needs to be provided. This might be through the underlying platform (moving a mouse from one window

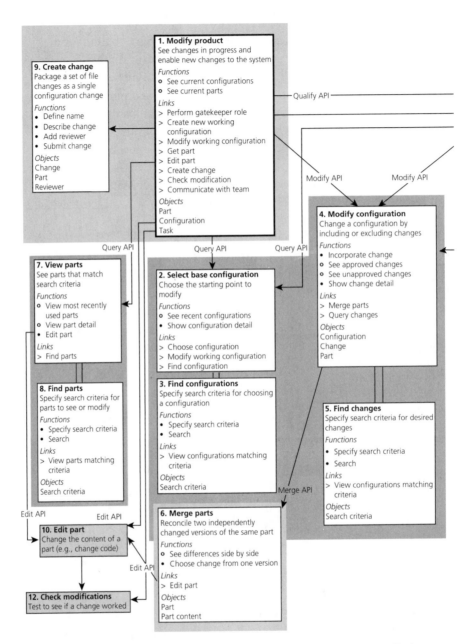

FIGURE 16.3 The configuration management User Environment Design annotated to show implementation details. The different patterns and shading show how the focus areas have been assigned to implementation teams: one team has the Developer's parts, another has the Gatekeeper's, and a third has all the "Find/View result" linked focus areas. Because these focus areas all present the same interaction style, it made sense for one team to implement them all.

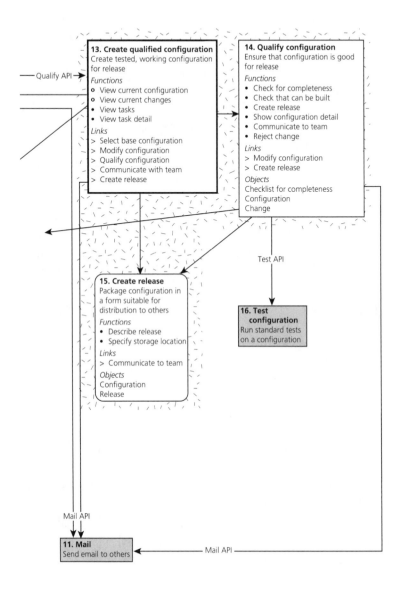

The User Environment Design has also been annotated to show internal application programming interfaces (APIs) that the different implementation teams have to agree on. There will be a standard Query API, for example, that will be consistent across the "View/Find" focus area pairs. This Query API will be used whenever a part of the system wants to present an interface that allows the user to search for and choose an element to work on. Similarly, the User Environment Design shows external APIs that the team has to conform to—the Mail and Edit APIs.

to another), by using standard application integration mechanisms (OLE or CORBA), or through special APIs. But not only do the software components need to access each other, but the user needs to feel like it's one consistent system. It's important that the system have a consistent appearance and behavior across the focus areas that are linked and used by the same people.

Use the UED to help coordinate implementation teams

The User Environment Design helps keep teams from becoming myopic and overfocusing on one situation. The "Modify configuration" focus area is used both by Developers and Gatekeepers. If it were given to the subteam implementing the Developer's part of the system, they could easily overemphasize the Developer as their user. The User Environment Design reminds them they support two roles, two kinds of tasks, achieving two separate intents.

Use the UED to help developers see their part in the whole

UI implementation considerations may also guide the assignment to teams. If several focus areas need a particular technology—such as natural language query mechanisms in "Find configurations" and "Find parts"—it's natural to assign all these focus areas to the same subteam so they can work out the solution once and apply it everywhere needed.

By showing the structure of the system, the User Environment Design provides a map to the implementation. Just as electricians can use a floor plan to talk to carpenters about how to locate the holes inside the walls so that the users can get their outlets where they want them, so the User Environment supports a conversation between the parts of an implementation team about how to deliver the system. It splits up the implementation into coherent units, shows how they relate to each other, and shows how teams focused on internals need to coordinate with the rest of the project. (Hsia et al. [1996] suggests another approach to sectioning a system for delivery.)

COORDINATING A PRODUCT STRATEGY

More and more, both internal organizations and software product companies are shipping sets of applications, each supporting a different aspect of the user's work. More and more, these organizations are looking to tie these point solutions together, so they provide seamless support to the work while still being packaged as separate products. Or they're looking to support a new market or process that they've never addressed before and will need to address with a suite of cooperating applications. This is hard to do, especially when starting from multiple existing applications. It's difficult to put the essentials of each application out next to the others to see how they could relate.

A large User Environment model can show how a set of existing applications combine to support the user's work. Extract such a model as a reverse User Environment Design going application by application. It's usually not necessary to do a full model—representing focus areas, purposes, and flows (as in Figure 14.5) is enough to see the structure without getting overwhelmed. Use a validation walkthrough of the resulting model to look for all the ways your current product set fails to deliver a coherent system work model: all the missing links between components, duplicated functions, missing functions, and inconsistencies. Then collect data on the systems in use to see how the work hangs together in practice. Identify changes to the User Environment model that address the problems. Use the structural principles for a User Environment Design to guide these changes, and use the work models to see where the current design falls down and how to fix it. When you have a new User Environment Design, showing how your existing suite should be modified to provide a coherent solution, you're ready to decide how to change the applications.

A reverse UED ties existing unintegrated systems together

The links between each part of this new design show integration points, where the applications need to share data or support the user's transition from one kind of work to another. The work objects that appear in different parts of the User Environment Design show key points for data integration across the different systems—these are the objects that will need common definitions, common storage, and common UI. Each project can define a plan for moving to the design specified by the User Environment over one or more releases. Build a shipping User Environment Design showing the first release for all projects, and you'll be able to keep them synchronized.

The UED reveals points of integration

Building a systems strategy when there are no existing applications is actually easier. You can design the overall system directly, from storyboards, like a single system with a wide scope. Then use the User Environment Design to identify good places to partition the system into applications. Each application should support a coherent part of the work or role and have clean interfaces with the rest of the system. Once you've partitioned the system, the links across partitions and common work objects identify integration points.

IT shops can use the User Environment Design to identify not only the parts they will build, but also the parts they want to buy from ven-

Drive acquisition from the
specification in the UED

dors. The User Environment defines requirements for the acquisition, showing what it must do, how it must be structured, and how it must fit with the other IT systems. IT development teams have done this—in one case, they designed their desired solution

directly from a vision and storyboards, representing it in a User Environment Design. Then they brought vendors in, showed them the User Environment Design, and invited them to bid on delivering it using their products. The vendors had to prove they could customize their system to support the structure and functions specified in the User Environment Design. They chose the vendor who was most successful at showing that, with reasonable modifications, they could support most of the design the team had specified.

The User Environment is a model that enables the project teams to talk to each other about where system boundaries should lie, how

The UED helps projects
cooperate

to create the bridges between systems necessary to support the work, and how to assign and reuse implementations of common system functions. Teams use their User Environment Designs as an artifact to talk over in coming to an agreement on

the relationship between groups. In one case, two teams laid out their respective User Environment Designs to support their discussions and ended by canceling one of the projects—the diagrams had made the overlap so obvious that they couldn't justify the existence of both.

DRIVING CONCURRENT IMPLEMENTATION

The User Environment Design defines the structure of a part of the overall vision—the part that is instantiated in software (and possibly some hardware). It provides the next level of detail about the vision by working out the system work model for the vision. Just as the vision guides different groups in creating a single corporate response, the User Environment Design guides different groups in delivering parts of the system and associated processes in parallel, yet in coordination:

Planning process: The User Environment Design represents the system work model and can be used to support planning business processes. Once you've worked out the coherent units of work in focus areas, you've also laid out coherent chunks for a business process. Defining the process and defining the User Environment Design go hand in hand. You can walk through the new process to see how it's supported in the system. Out of this, identify problems with the system or process, what training needs to be developed, and how to introduce the new way of working to minimize disruption.

Implementation: The User Environment Design specifies behavior without specifying the user interaction mechanisms. An implementation based on the User Environment Design will be free of bias toward one UI over another. When the UI is designed, it can be hooked to the underlying implementation so that there's a clean separation between the UI-specific code and the code that implements behavior—a cleanly layered implementation. The basic function of the system is defined in the functions and objects of the focus areas. As an additional guide to the implementation, annotate the User Environment Design with implementation constraints—for example, the required speed of following a link or the constraints on size or access time of a focus area.

Documentation: The User Environment Design specifies the function of the system so documentation can start to describe what it does. Furthermore, the specification of coherent focus areas, each with a defined purpose in supporting the work, gives documentation writers a clear structure and motivation to communicate. The User Environment Design reveals opportunities for additional user services, such as help desk support, training seminars, and follow-on consulting, and provides the information needed to plan them.

Test plans: The combination of storyboards and User Environment Design provides the information necessary to start test plans. The storyboards show how the system should work; the User Environment Design provides the formal definition of the functions. It's straightforward to build a test plan that checks these statements of the plan against the actual system.

Because the User Environment Design is focused on the system work model—the system as experienced by the user—it gives a way to structure and think about the system that keeps the system work model coherent. The chunks of the User Environment Design map to chunks that designers need to think about and design as a unit. As such, it's a natural structure for presenting system requirements. Implementation has its own coherence, which will come later and which may be represented in an object model. But the structure of an implementation is less useful for planning a customer-centered project than the structure of the system work model. Thinking about the system work model—the User Environment Design—ensures that the parts of the system and the components that are delivered are coherent from the user's point of view. That's the key value of the User Environment diagram in planning: it ensures you don't lose coherence for the user in the turmoil of getting to the implementation.

> *The UED ensures cross-functional teams deliver a coherent work practice*

MARDELL'S STORY

In the early days of WordPerfect, the founders of the company worked in the same building as their users. It wasn't a problem to stay close to their customers. But as the company grew, developers lost that immediate connection. So the company decided to put together a strategic effort to decide on the direction of the WordPerfect product and recover that immediate sense of the customer.

We put together a team of four or five developers, a marketing person, a documentation writer, a UI designer, and a usability specialist. This was simply not done in the company at the time—design was driven by engineering, with marketing getting involved later. ⇨

We used the complete Contextual Design process in this team to build a picture of our market and design new product directions to address the market better.

The new designs we came up with were well received in the company, but suggested changes beyond WordPerfect itself. So we split into two teams: one focused on broad strategic issues across the product set, and one focused on improvements to WordPerfect. This required both teams to refocus and redefine their mission.

I led the team focused on WordPerfect. We found that the most important parts of the process for us were interviewing, sequence model analysis, visioning, and paper prototyping. The strategic team continued to use the User Environment Design to show the company's different products and how they related to each other. But we had the strategic direction from the first round: we were focused on developing one product and concentrated on one focus area, WordPerfect's editing window. We didn't need the User Environment Design for that.

As we worked with the process, we recognized that it was a backbone for understanding the customer that could incorporate different activities. We started to use it less rigidly than we had. We decided we weren't creative enough and started to incorporate other techniques to expand the possibilities in our visioning. We found that our customer insight helped us make better use of enhancement requests in our customer feedback database because we understood more of the context of a request. We did a teardown of the current WordPerfect product and competitors to find places for improvement. And we analyzed other kinds of products for ideas as well.

Early on, we had a choice whether to focus on short-term improvements or long-term new directions. Since we did have critics in the early days, we decided we had to show concrete results. We developed specific ideas, prototyped them in paper and in code, and got them into WordPerfect 6.1. When these features were the ones reviewers and customers picked out as being the important innovations of the product, our credibility went way up.

Though we conceived of our ideas as integrated product directions addressing whole themes in the customer's work, we found it easiest to communicate them to developers as features. We would select features to push out together, to address some aspect of the customer's work. We did a lot of one-on-one work with developers, showing them prototypes of a new idea and taking them along on customer visits. (We've tried to make sure every developer goes on at least one customer visit.) We transfer ownership of the idea to the developer—they get credit for refining it and making it real.

WordPerfect's been sold now—several times—but that was an amazing team, and the ideas we developed are still important to the product. ❑

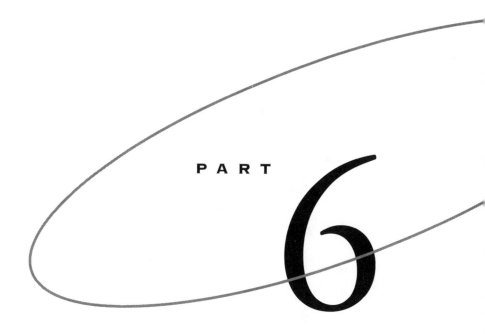

Prototyping

Prototyping as a Design Tool

17

We call this a customer-centered process, but it's been quite a few chapters since talking to customers was the main activity (not counting any customers on the design team). The activities covered in the last few parts have focused on the customer—understanding how they work as individuals and the common structure of their work, visioning new ways for them to work, and designing those ways into a software system. These activities keep the customer's work practice coherent and use customer data as the final arbiter. And the consolidated models and vision suggest holes in the team's knowledge of the customer, which they fill through additional interviews. But it's now time to get direct customer feedback again.

One of the difficulties with explaining any process is that each part of the process must be described in turn, and the explanation itself takes up time. The description unrolls the process and lays it out, making it possible to see and examine each part, but also making the process appear more sequential than it is. In fact, the period from the beginning of consolidation to the first pro-

> *The goal: continuous iteration and extension*

totype interview should be no more than a month, even for complex systems, and the team gathers additional data to fill gaps in their understanding and inform the vision during this time. For smaller projects, this period may be as short as a week or two. The point we have now reached in the process is the norm for a design team: with a base understanding of their customers and a target vision for their design, they extend and iterate their design with customer feedback. Iterating with prototypes is a design tool ensuring that the team builds the right system, that the structure fits the user's work, that the detailed structure internal to a focus area works, and that the user interface is usable and reveals the structure clearly. Teams that get bogged down in design are usually those that have lost touch with their customers—that aren't going back out to interview or test prototypes on a regular basis.

The most basic attribute of a customer-centered process is that the customers are the final arbiters of what works and what doesn't. When

The customer is the final arbiter of the design

you create a design, captured in a User Environment diagram, that design is really a claim about what will work for the user. The claim is that this particular system simplifies the user's work, overcomes pain, or otherwise improves their work practice. So, how do

we test this claim? How do we find out where the design falls short and how to improve it? How do we communicate the design to users in a form that they can respond to—in a form that helps people see the consequences of different design decisions and react to them clearly?

THE DIFFICULTY OF COMMUNICATING A DESIGN

Most of the approaches commonly used to communicate a new design downplay the difficulty of communicating a design. Think

Demos and specifications can't evoke work practice

about it—it's a conceptual nightmare. Consider presenting a demo of the proposed new system to potential customers in a conference room: they must view the product's user interface, understand from the interface and the verbal description what the

product does and how it is structured, apply that implicit structure to their own work practice (which is also unarticulated, as we established in Chapter 2), envision how their work practice will be restructured in the presence of the new system, imagine themselves living in this new way, and decide whether they like it. Then, if they don't, they have to imagine some better way to work, transform it into implications for the design, and express those implications clearly to the designers. The task is overwhelming. It's no wonder most people complain about an icon that confuses them, comment on the color, and ask about one or two key features they care about.

Requirements specifications fare no better. Most are text; most break the system down into categories that relate to the system, not the user (all reliability requirements together, for example). Even when the first level of organization is by UI component, their textual and list-based nature tends to present features in isolation. It's hard even for designers to see how a feature relates to other parts of the design; internal users reading the requirements for sign-off find it even harder. Requirements specifications are less approachable than a demo and make it no easier to imagine the impact that the proposed system will have on users' work. They may have their place in specifying exactly what's in the system, but they aren't a good way to communicate a design.

The challenge: communicate the experience that a new system will offer

Talking to the customers with models has a similar set of drawbacks. Process models or object models introduce a new language, which must be learned and understood by the users if they are to participate in the discussion at all. The models represent either facts about their work or the new system. But their work is unarticulated, and the models represent it in a strange and unfamiliar language that offers no touchstones to their experience. In Contextual Design, we don't even try to talk to customers with our work models, unless we're building systems for an internal business partner, and they have an interest in representing their own work practice explicitly. Then the work models become a tool for the whole department to think about how they work and maintain an ongoing conversation about how they might improve it. When customers think models are a tool for them to manage their business, they can learn to use them in the way that designers use them; otherwise it's too hard for them to see how they map to reality.

Models introduce a new language for customers to translate

Other forms of communication such as use cases and scenarios attempt to communicate more of the context of use. These methods tell stories of how people will work in the new system, so they communicate better than a model or specification. However, each scenario can only tell one story out of the many the system must support. And they all suffer from the same basic drawback: most customers have only an unarticulated knowledge of their own work and cannot check a proposed design against their own experience unaided. They can react to such a story at the level of "I hate that" or "I love that," so scenarios can help test the marketing pitch. They'll help answer the question, "What matters to the customer?" but not "How should the system be structured for them?" To provide that level of feedback, customers need not just an artifact but an event, a process that will allow them to live out their own work in the new system and articulate the issues they identify.[1] Without such a process, it doesn't matter how many signatures are on the requirements document—there's no guarantee that the specified system will solve any real problems.

INCLUDING CUSTOMERS IN THE DESIGN PROCESS

The problem for this point in the design process is to get feedback from customers on the detailed structure of the proposed system—on

Scenarios test the customer's response to the story

whether the system work model fits. Getting good feedback from customers is made more complicated because we don't just want "yes" or "no" answers. We want to explore possibilities and create new alternatives. In fact, we want to co-design the system with the users. In Part 1, the question was how to make

the customers the best masters of apprentices possible; now the question is how to make them the best co-designers. We'll draw heavily on the same principles that drove Contextual Inquiry for the answer.

The team's design needs testing with customers who haven't been members of the team. The obstacles to making these customers co-

The challenge: make customers strong co-designers

designers are real and have to be faced head-on: First, no one articulates their own work practice as an ordinary thing. It would be nice if the users could give three concrete reasons why a design should be changed; usually they can only say that the design just feels wrong. The design process needs to create a

way of interacting that helps them articulate the issues. Second, customers have not spent time studying all the users of the proposed system. (Even when customers are on the team, we interview them and follow them around to help them articulate how they work.) What this

---

[1] This is, of course, the core insight of Participatory Design (PD) practice, and much of PD research is looking for better ways to make "living out the work" more real.

means is that any customer testing a prototype can only respond to it from their own point of view. Third, customers aren't technologists—they don't know the range of possibilities that technology could support. They may be either unrealistic or excessively cautious as a result. And they don't know what it takes to make a design hang together. And why should they, after all? It's their job to do their job, not design systems. (For a discussion of these issues and a range of techniques for overcoming them, see Wixon and Ramey [1996].)

And yet it's absolutely critical that these customers, immersed and steeped in their own work, be made a powerful partner with the design team, so they have real influence over the design. It's the customers who will have to live with the new system. If it's an internal system, they have a right to say how the work they do will change. If it's a commercial product, it won't be bought if it doesn't meet people's real needs. And unless it works well for customers, both internal and commercial systems will fail. So the challenge for design is to include them in the process to iterate, refine, and extend the initial design concept put together by the team.

The starting point is an initial design concept. *Any* prototyping process starts from an initial prototype, which designer and user refine. It's always easier to renovate an existing design than to start from a totally blank slate. But because prototyping is iterative, it's hard to make fundamental changes to the initial concept, so you want to be sure the first cut addresses the right issues. It's also easier to renovate if you're starting with something reasonably close to what you want. Parts 1–5 were about how to get to a good starting point—all the effort that went into understanding the customer's work and needs ensures that your initial design is addressing the right problems and has a reasonable structure. Now, we need to get the details right.

> *A prototype defines limits on what will be co-designed*

USING PAPER PROTOTYPES TO DRIVE DESIGN

In Contextual Design, we borrow the idea of rough mock-ups from Participatory Design by introducing very rough prototypes in paper to start the co-designing with users. The goal of the prototype is not to provide a demo; prototypes are a prop in a contextual interview, enabling the user to play out the experience of living with the new

*Put the customer's real
data in the prototype*

system. By acting out their real work in the proto-type, customers can make their unarticulated knowl-edge explicit. Fleshing out the prototype with the customers' own data and work situations gives them the touchstones they need to put them in the experi-ence of doing the work. And their interaction with the designer/inter-viewer lets them explore different technical possibilities. The designer knows technology and provides options, which the user considers, matches to their experience of the moment, and discusses why one alternative fits and another doesn't. It's another application of Contex-tual Inquiry—using the prototype in the real work context keeps the discussion grounded, the partnership leads to co-design, together cus-tomer and designer interpret work issues, and the prototype gives them focus.

Prototypes act as a language for communicating between user and designer. Instead of introducing a new language, a prototype builds on

*Let the customer do real
work in the paper system*

users' own experience using computers. A prototype enables them to interact with the proposed system as they would with any system and to respond in a lan-guage that is immediately relevant to them. "I think *this* should happen when I click *here*," they say, unaware that they have just redesigned a focus area on the User Envi-ronment Design—but the designer can tell because they can see how the comment relates to structure and can investigate the issue if it chal-lenges the design.

To look at structure, the first prototypes are always paper. Paper is eminently practical and meets the primary need: it makes it possible

*Paper invites conversation
about structure*

to express the structure of the system and makes it hard to overfocus on user interface detail. When a window is drawn by hand, it's pretty clear that icon design, precise layout, and fancy direct manipula-tion are not the important points. When users inter-act with paper, they aren't distracted by fancy user interfaces; they have to focus on structure. Even house architects, who aren't con-strained by writing code, prefer to communicate their first ideas to clients as sketches rather than finished drawings. (See "Readings and Resources" for a range of approaches to paper prototyping.)

PROTOTYPING AND USABILITY TESTS

The goals of prototyping in Contextual Design are very different from the goals of a traditional usability test, and the two techniques complement each other. Usability tests typically seek to measure users' performance on set tasks to ensure they can be done reasonably efficiently. The techniques are different because the goals are different and the kind of information being elicited is different. Usability tests tune a user interface at the tail end of design, to clean up any rough edges or unnecessary difficulty in understanding or interacting with the interface. It's not a goal of traditional usability tests to discover a better system structure or to discover that this isn't an important task at all. In fact, these issues get in the way—usability professionals are constantly frustrated at being asked to fix major structural problems through last-minute Band-Aids. By the tail end of design, it's simply too late to decide that your system addresses the wrong problem. Recognizing this, usability professionals are moving to be involved earlier in the life cycle and are using more contextual techniques in which the user does their own work task. The more they do this, the more they get involved in the design of the whole system, not just the final tailoring. ❏

The very nature of a paper prototype invites change. When the user gets to a window in the prototype and says, "But now I need to do *this*," it's easy to add the function right on the window. It's easy to invite users into a discussion of what they need, why they need it, and which of several alternatives would better meet their need. It's easy to move into co-design of the system. The user

Hand-drawn paper prototypes invite change

is discussing his or her own work, in the context of doing it, and manipulating the system interfaces that will help to do it. A running prototype couldn't be changed immediately to track the conversation. Interviewer and user would have to talk about design alternatives with no support, or by sketching them—on paper.

We've discussed the advantages of understanding work for deciding what to build, but there's a whole layer of detailed requirements that users simply can't communicate except when they're working with an actual design. It's natural to develop requirements in layers, just as an architect works out the overall layout of the house before deciding where the closets go. The vision was the first layer of design, defining the overall corporate response. We worked out the details of the vision in storyboards,

Rough prototypes focus detailed requirements gathering

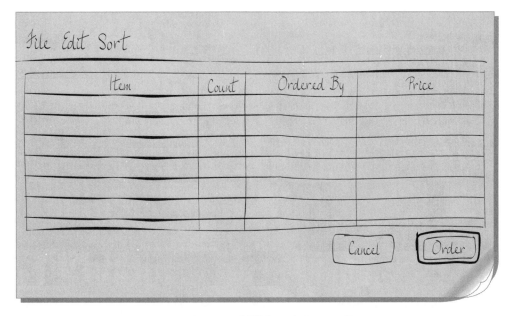

FIGURE 17.1   A proposed UI for ordering supplies.

but we needed additional data (the consolidated sequences and issues from the models) to build them. The User Environment Design pulled together the parts of the system into a single diagram to work out their relationships. But now we need an additional level of detailed customer data to work out exactly what will happen in each focus area.

A first level of requirement might be, "The ordering system should make it possible to batch orders from several people." But a *complete* specification would give intricate detail: "Orders from several people will be organized in rows, grouped by person or item ordered, with who requested the item, the item description, and price visible on the screen, and movement from order to order will be supported by the TAB key..." (Figure 17.1). Ignoring the difficulty of communicating this much detail precisely, how are the designers to get these details right? How can they determine exactly what information the user needs to see? If it's a new system (the customers currently don't batch orders from different people), they can't use existing work practice as a guide. Customers can't tell them what

Prototypes make it possible to test work practice that doesn't yet exist

they will need in a system that they haven't experienced. The only way to get this level of specification right is to work it out in the context of the specific design. Prototyping in paper lets the team complete the detailed design without committing anything to code.

Then, once designer and user are working together on a new system prototype, it becomes possible to take the next step in design. When a system is entirely new, putting it in place will change the user's world in unpredictable ways. Not until users have worked with the system and understood the possibilities it creates can they start to restructure their world around it. Movies are *not* filmed theater—but until people had experience

Prototypes reveal future possibilities resulting from the new system

with the new medium, they could not see how to move beyond theater. Word processing is *not* typing—but the first editor was jokingly called the "Expensive Typewriter" by its creators because they weren't sure they had created anything really new. Not until word processors were part of the workplace could anyone see how profoundly they would change work and redefine the role of professionals and secretaries along the way. Until spreadsheets were in use, no one could tell that they would become an important way to present data and that formatting would matter. As people take advantage of new systems, they change their work practice in ways the designers may not foresee. If designers can find out about this *emergent work practice* before the design is complete, they can support it directly. Lotus 1-2-3 became successful by recognizing the emergent work practice that VisiCalc did not support. Recognize the emergent work practice yourself, before your competition does, and you can leapfrog a whole generation of products. Interviews with paper prototypes are the first step toward seeing these issues.

The first round of interviews reveals the basic structure of work and needs for the new system. The new system is designed in response to the current work structure. But working through a prototype of the new system, pretending to do real work, and discussing the interaction of the system with the work reveals issues that would otherwise remain invisible. Together, user and designer can

The trick: using real work pushes co-design

explore how the system will impact the work and how work is likely to change in the future as a result. There's a chance of designing the system to account for these changes.

Prototyping as a communication tool

In Chapters 2 and 5, we discussed the need to build a partnership with the customer organization, especially for IT departments. What's been missing until now has been concrete activities that build day-to-day communication and trust. What's needed is not just a formal agreement on deliverables but the sense among the customers that the development organization understands their problems and will produce useful software.

The continual involvement of users is an important way to achieve this trust. Prototype interviews excite and interest users—they can see progress, they can talk directly to developers, and they can see how their responses shape the design. It's immediately clear that the design team is listening. This can cause its own problems—one team had to ensure everyone in their customer department was interviewed to handle the interest and excitement—but surely these are better problems to have than mistrust and contempt. The interest and involvement generated by the sessions leads to easier acceptance and adoption of the system when it comes time to roll it out. And for commercial products, it's a good way to find out if a design works and if it generates excitement among the people who try it. It's also a great sales point for commercial product developers to work out the design with their users—after one set of interviews, one customer had their internal company newsletter do a piece on how well their vendor was listening. Another customer, when asked, said they would pay three times the price marketing thought was possible because they understood the potential impact on work practice.

Co-design over a prototype builds trust with customers

The prototyping process not only brings the users into the design process, but it changes the design process itself. The customers, remember, are the final arbiters in a customer-centered process. But that's not an achievable goal unless bringing them into the process is fast and easy. We regularly mock up a design alternative in paper on one day and test it with users on the next. We have results and are ready to rethink the design within

Rapid iteration mediates arguments within the design team

two days. It's possible to go through multiple iterations, trying out many different ideas, in the course of a week. There's no time for people to get overly invested in one design alternative and no reason to argue for any length of time over two alternatives. It's almost always faster to take the alternatives to users and try them out. Most arguments in a design team come about because the team really doesn't have the data to make an informed decision. Paper prototyping reduces the cost of getting data so low that the team can depend on having it and makes getting data so fast that no one has time to get overly invested in a feature. (Moll-Carrillo et al. [1995] and Lundell and Anderson [1995] offer case histories of this kind of rapid iteration.)

From Structure to User Interface

18

A paper prototype tests the structure captured in a User Environment Design by talking to users through the medium of a user interface. Because the initial intent of the prototype is to test structure, the UI should be a fair representation of the underlying structure. Making the translation from User Environment Design to user interface is a necessary part of the prototyping process.

We'll discuss how to map from User Environment Design to UI in this chapter, but we will not try to cover how to design a good UI. Creating a good UI is its own design problem and is covered extensively in other books. What we care about is that the interface presents the User Environment Design cleanly, so we don't fragment the work in building the UI and we provide a fair test of the structure. The UI should hang together as an interface, conform to any guidelines for the UI platform, and be a fairly straightforward translation of the User Environment Design. The team may choose to put some extra effort into designing the interface, so they can test some of their UI ideas as well. But a clean presentation of the structure is the first priority.

USING THE USER ENVIRONMENT DESIGN TO DRIVE THE UI

The User Environment Design is the user interface designer's specification. It tells the UI designer how to organize the interface, what functions should be available, and where to put the functions. But it leaves open how the interface should work—the underlying user interface paradigm, the interaction style, and the appearance. When the first prototypes are built, the User Environment Design may also leave open low-level design details, such as exact content and order of fields in a list. It's best to work out these details directly with the user in front of a prototype. UI designers use the User Environment Design as a guide and also draw on the work models to inform their design. The affinity collects issues, including issues with using tools; the physical model shows what's placed where and suggests what should be most accessible and apparent in the UI; and artifact models show the conceptual structure and intents that should be reflected (but not slavishly followed) in the UI. Storyboards not only collect UI ideas for different system components, but give UI designers a sequence of work steps to test their design against.

The UED is the UI designer's specification

Like any good specification, the User Environment Design does not determine how to design the user interface. It leaves even the choice of technology open, whether command line, character-cell, windows and mice, or something else. The hardware platform, operating system, and UI technology determine UI style; the User Environment Design defines the structure and function to implement. It's up to the UI designer to make creative use of the technology to get the UI out of the user's way so they can focus on work, not the tool. Then the prototyping interview will test not only the system structure but the first level of the UI, too.

MAPPING TO A WINDOWING UI

Here's an example of how a User Environment Design might turn into a user interface. The "Select base configuration" focus area in Figure 18.1 specifies that the user should be able to see, sort, and choose from a list of configurations and get details on a configuration in the list. It also says there should be a close link to the "Find configuration" focus area, which allows for creating a new list of configurations that match a specified criteria. This pair of focus areas could be realized on any base platform, but Figure 18.2 shows a windowing implementation, and Table 18.1 shows the appropriate mapping.

Every user interface technology offers a unique set of advantages and drawbacks. One of the challenges of UI design is to overcome the particular drawbacks of a platform. Windowing interfaces offer the possibility

> **2. Select base configuration**
> Choose the starting point to
> modify
>
> *Functions*
> o See recent configurations
> • Show configuration detail
>
> *Links*
> > Choose configuration
> > Modify working configuration
> >>Find configuration

FIGURE 18.1   Part of the User Environment Design supporting configuration management, first introduced in Chapter 16.

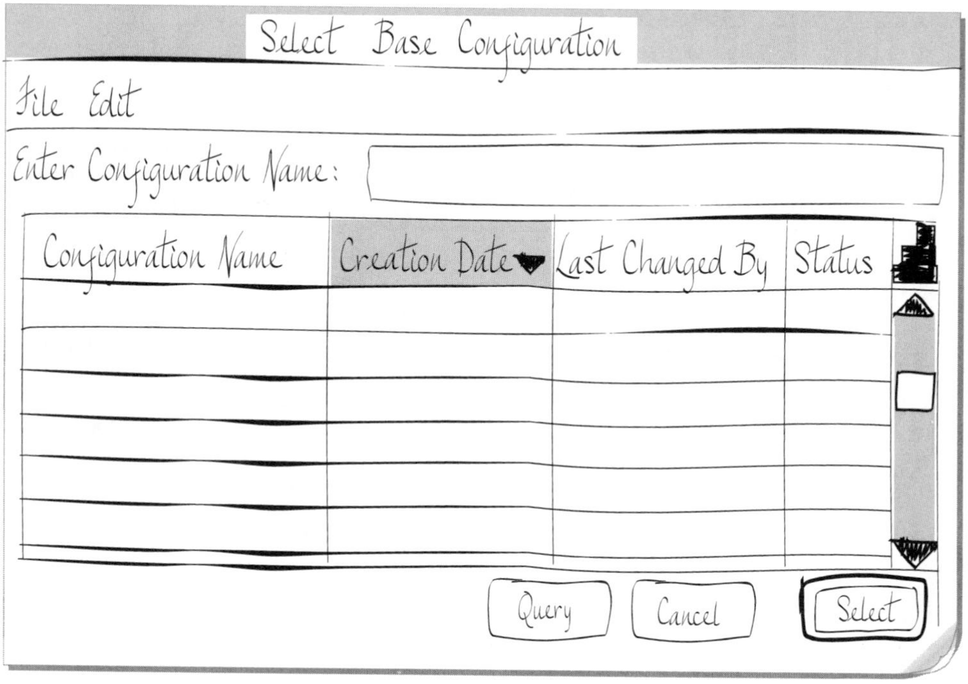

FIGURE 18.2   A windowing implementation of the configuration management User Environment.

of great transparency because all options and changes are visible at once—but some aspects of the interface are cumbersome. The design in Figure 18.2 goes to some effort to make it as easy as possible to select a

USER ENVIRONMENT COMPONENT	WINDOWING EQUIVALENT
Select base configuration (focus area)	The "Select Base Configuration" window is devoted to displaying a list of configurations, sorting, and choosing from them.
View recent configurations (automatic function)	The "Select Base Configuration" window comes up with the most recent configurations listed by default.
Enter and choose configuration name (link)	Text entry field in the "Select Base Configuration" window. Input focus is given to this field when the window first comes up. If the user types a name and presses RETURN, the system will select the configuration (if it exists) and close the window. This supports choosing a configuration by name quickly.
Choose configuration (link)	Double-clicking on a configuration in the list chooses the configuration and closes the window.
Sort by name or date (function)	Clicking on the Configuration Name or Creation Date column header changes the sort order to name or date, respectively. A small triangle at the right end of the column headers indicates forward or reverse sort order; clicking on it toggles to the opposite order.
Find configuration (double link)	The Query button on the window brings up a floating window that allows the user to enter criteria for matching configurations. As new criteria are entered, the list in the "Select Base Configuration" window changes in real time to reflect the matching configurations.

TABLE 18.1   Mapping to a windowing UI.

single configuration by name. The user clicks on the button that brings up a dialog box, types the name, and hits RETURN without even having to wait for the window to draw on the screen, in a good implementation. Nevertheless, the nature of a windows interface is that a window has to come up to present the text entry field, and anytime a windowing UI does this, it will disrupt work. (Some products

Every UI technology has its characteristic strengths and weaknesses

find creative ways around the problem—MS Word 5 on the Mac would steal part of the horizontal scroll bar for text entry. This bent the UI style rules, but minimized disruption to the work flow.)

Designing the UI introduces new functions that are specific to manipulating the UI and so don't appear on the User Environment Design. Selecting a configuration and sorting the list are required by the User Environment Design and are handled in the UI by the standard mechanisms of double-clicking to select and (the somewhat less standard) clicking on column heads to specify sort order. But "scroll up," "scroll down," and "select" aren't User Environment functions at all—they are just ways of manipulating the UI and are not fundamental to the work the system supports. They should be designed to stay out of the user's way.

Most focus areas end up being windows in a windowing UI, but that's not the only way to do it. The User Environment Design only specifies that the function in a focus area be presented as a coherent chunk: that can be done by putting the function in a pane or segmenting a larger window in some other way. Some successful products (Claris Emailer or M.Y.O.B.) make the most important focus areas tabs in a tabbed dialog box and put secondary focus areas in windows accessible from the different tabs (Figure 18.3). Tabs in dialog boxes are problematic because each tab creates its own focus area whether you want it to or not, but when a tab is *intended* to act like a focus area, the interface can work well.

A focus area defines a set of functions to be kept together

MAPPING TO A COMMAND-LINE UI

We presented the mapping to the windowing interface first because it's most direct. But the same User Environment Design can be implemented in other user interface styles. As an example of a *very* different style, Figure 18.4 shows how a command-line interface might represent the same User Environment Design.

This mapping of a User Environment Design to a command line shows another way to deliver the basic intent of the specification (Table 18.2). Here, the "Select base configuration" focus area is a subsystem. By relisting the configurations automatically after each command that affects the current list, the design ensures that the user

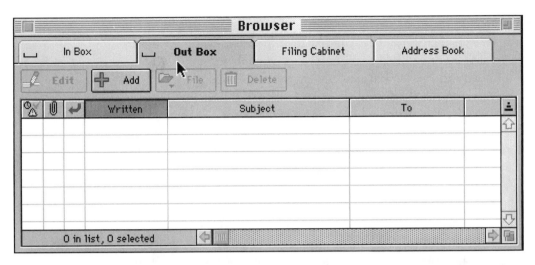

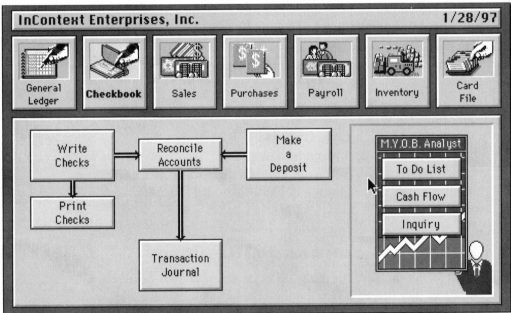

FIGURE 18.3   Claris Emailer and M.Y.O.B., two products that use tabs or tab-like buttons to organize access to their primary focus areas.

always knows what is going on and fills the requirement of the "see current list" automatic function. But it's more cumbersome than the windowing implementation.

```
CM> SELECT BASE CONFIGURATION
1. CONFIG1  8-AUG-96    JOHN SMITH
2. CONFIG2  7-AUG-96    JANE DOE
3. CONFIG3  6-AUG-96    SAM SPENCE
SELECT CONFIGURATION> SELECT 2
CONFIGURATION CONFIG2 SELECTED
CM>
```

FIGURE 18.4   A command-line implementation of the configuration management User Environment.

USER ENVIRONMENT COMPONENT	COMMAND-LINE EQUIVALENT
Select base configuration (focus area)	SELECT BASE CONFIGURATION puts user into a mode that allows searching and specifying a base configuration.
View recent configurations (automatic function)	SELECT BASE CONFIGURATION responds by listing the 10 most recent configurations immediately. This fulfills the requirements for an automatic function, allowing the user to select from the list immediately.
Enter and choose configuration name (link)	SELECT BASE CONFIGURATION <NAME> identifies the desired configuration by name. The intent of this function as defined by the User Environment Design is to make it as fast as possible to choose a configuration when the name is known. Command lines excel at this immediate action to function.
Choose configuration (link)	SELECT <N> and SELECT <NAME> let the user choose a configuration from the current list either by ordinal number in the list or by name.
Sort by name or date (function)	SORT BY [REVERSE] {NAME | DATE} allows the user to choose a sort order for the list, sorting in either forward or reverse order, by name or date. The command-line system responds by relisting the current selected configurations in the new order.
Find configuration (double link)	FIND [CONFIGURATIONS] WITH [NAME = <PATTERN>] . . . chooses a set of configurations to view based on criteria

⇨

TABLE 18.2   Mapping to a command line.

USER ENVIRONMENT COMPONENT	COMMAND-LINE EQUIVALENT
Find configuration (double link) *continued*	provided by the user. Each query command is prefaced by FIND and puts the user back into the SELECT BASE CONFIGURATION subsystem, listing the newly selected configurations automatically. Command lines don't support context well, but this scheme gives the user a way to access the query function quickly without leaving the focus area, which is the basic intent of a double link.

TABLE 18.2   *continued*

The two forms of the "select base configuration" function—with and without a configuration name—provide an economical way to select a specific configuration quickly or begin a search for the right configuration. This overloading of the command is appropriate to command-line interfaces, and the possibility of such overloading is one reason why command lines can be terse and direct. Windows interfaces have no equivalent—we saw above how the windowing design had to separate the two functions and pop up a text entry window to do the same thing.

The UI introduces additional functions to manage the interface

The command line is at a disadvantage in dealing with the list of configurations. You can't point and click in a command line, so how will selection be supported? This design numbers the list and allows choosing both by number (for brevity) and by name (to support recall). These are appropriate options for a command-line user interface style. They don't appear on the User Environment Design because they address issues unique to this UI design. Similarly, the user interface designer will have to decide what to do when the list is too long (over 10 or so). Should the list just scroll? Should there be another layer of function to display the list a screenful at a time? These are questions about working with the constraints of this particular user interface and are decided at this level.

MAPPING TO UI CONTROLS

When mapping function in the User Environment Design to controls in a windowing UI, there remains the question of how to decide what kind of control to use. The different options for making a function available in a windowing user interface are not equivalent. Functions can be implemented through a pull-down menu, a button, direct manipulation, or a command key. Which mechanism will work best for a particular function depends on the nature of the function with respect to the work of the focus area. Who the user is, what role they are playing, and what influences them in the cultural model will all affect what makes an acceptable influence. Doctors and medical technicians both update patient records—but doctors are more pressed for time and will tolerate less complexity from their computer systems. The UI for a system supporting both would have to work for both user populations. It's up to the UI designer to understand the work context and map the function in a style that supports the intent of the focus area and fits with the people who will use it. UI designers have a number of options for presenting a function, none mutually exclusive. Some distinctions between ways of presenting functions can be useful:

Different styles for presenting functions support different usage

In your face: A button, whether on a toolbar or directly on a window, is in your face. It's always present and it always takes up screen real estate (unless you allow the user to redefine the interface by reconfiguring toolbars). They're easy to find because they give a direct visual clue to their existence. In Chapter 15, we discussed core functions, the functions that are central to the work of a focus area. It's often a good idea to implement core functions with mechanisms that put the function in the user's face. Making these functions easy to find and access is worth the drawback of using up screen real estate on them. Also look at the physical model to see what users chose to put in front of them—those things represent the concerns users care about, so functions related to those concerns are good candidates for putting in the user's face.

In your fingers: A command key is the fastest and least distracting way to invoke a function for expert users. Even multiple keys can be struck like one if they're familiar enough. Moving the hand to the mouse, positioning it over the right button, clicking, and returning the hand to the keyboard is always a greater distraction than typing CTRL-B. But a command key is entirely invisible; all but the most common will be used only by power users. When mapping critical functions, frequent functions, or functions that are available across many focus areas, command keys are appropriate. They're also appropriate when the function needs to fit seamlessly into the work flow—when users are concentrating on the work in front of them and want to invoke the function without thinking about it. CTRL-B for "Bold" is a great command key—it's consistent across every tool that edits text and it doesn't interrupt the user's thought.

Direct manipulation: Direct manipulation is as invisible as a command key. But direct manipulation functions suggest themselves through the physical metaphor of a windowing user interface. Users think they can drag around icons on the desktop, so it's natural to move files by dragging them between folders. The physical and artifact models will suggest what things are moved around, their structure, and operations on them. Direct manipulation works well when it maps obviously to the physical metaphor and it provides a convenient way to access the function. The work objects in each focus area are natural candidates for manipulable objects in the interface; functions that interact with them are good candidates for direct manipulation.

Available when needed: Pull-down menus make a whole additional range of function available. This function is neither totally available, like the in-your-face function, nor is it totally hidden. It's like the artifacts on the physical model that are moved away behind the user. It's a reasonable choice for the function you need for completeness, but which isn't core to the work of the focus area. The work models—especially models of workplaces and artifacts—will suggest what can be put out of the way or out of sight. Functions related to these or similar objects can be put out of the way on menus. In the User Environment Design, functions that address the same intent within a focus area are clustered together—it makes sense to put them on the same toolbar or same pull-down menu.

In a dialog: Finally, some functions need additional information from the user, so the UI designer has to invent a way to get it. The easiest way is usually through a dialog box. It's safe to assume that a dialog box that does not represent a focus area always disrupts work to some degree—look at how inserting a page break from the "Break . . ." dialog box in MS Word 6 disrupts the flow of work in a way that having "Page Break" directly on the menu did not. Once a dialog box has too many controls, it creates the experience of a new focus area by sheer complexity. Experienced users may learn to ignore irrelevant parts of the box—as 90% of users ignore 90% of the print dialog box 99% of the time—but others will have to stop and parse the information in the box. That makes dealing

Good UI design lets the user focus on an activity in a single place

with the box its own type of work and therefore its own focus area. Taking another example from Word, look at the difference between creating a table from the toolbar button and creating a table from the table dialog box. The button fits directly into the flow of editing—it's appropriate when the user is just inserting a table as part of the flow of editing. The separate dialog requires that you read, understand, and manipulate a new interface. It's appropriate when the user is thinking about the structure and appearance of the table as a design problem. For the cleanest mapping, try to keep all functions in the focus area's window. Avoid dialog boxes that don't map to focus areas.

A PROCESS TO DESIGN THE UI

Getting the UI right is an important part of the design process. Good user interface designers experience the User Environment Design as giving them freedom. Rather than being asked to reinvent the product in the user interface, they are given a clear specification for what goes into the design. The specification is full of hints and implications—automatic functions, potential focus areas, and double links all suggest user interface options that will implement the intent of the designers. But the specification does not overspecify the user interface. It leaves a broad field open for creativity. Even if the UI designer is on the team, separating the User Environment Design allows them to concentrate on structure, then focus on UI as its own task.

Whatever approach is used to design the UI, it builds on the information in the User Environment Design and work models. A few principles help UI design fit it into the overall Contextual Design process.

Follow a defined process: It's possible to approach the UI design task much like visioning—sketch several alternative approaches to the

UI, evaluate them with positives and negatives, and synthesize a single UI theme from the best of the alternatives. Just as the vision captured a single, comprehensive response to the work situation, a UI vision captures a unified response to the User Environment Design. It ties the system together at the UI level. However you approach UI design, take advantage of the affinity and models—review them for issues and concepts to inform the UI.

Base your design on the work models: The consolidated work models help guide UI design. The flow model shows the different roles and individuals that use the system; consistency and common mechanisms are most important for those parts of the system that support the same role and individuals. The artifact models show how people break up the work into chunks—design the UI to fit those chunks to make it more comprehensible. Sequences show how one step and task follows on another—running them through the UI reveals problems in interacting with the system. The cultural model shows how the users think of themselves—use color, packaging, and style to match your users' self-image. The vision shows how the system hangs together, and the storyboards walk through specific sequences of use. The UI designer can take advantage of them all.

Keep conversations separate: Remember that every new step in a design process sheds light and uncovers flaws in the previous step. As soon as the UI designers try to make a focus area real in an interface that works, they'll discover missing functions and structures that simply can't be made to work. At this point, separating conversations becomes critical: knowing whether the point under discussion hinges on UI, system work model, or customers' work practice and sticking to it makes all the difference to resolving disagreements amicably. By this point in the design process, a good Contextual Design team will automatically identify the conversation they are in and go stand in front of that model.

When working on the UI reveals a problem in the User Environment Design, the team decides whether to go back and fix it or not. If it's just a question of a missing function, and adding the function in no way changes the purpose or scope of the focus area, it's easy to note it and go on. But you may find that the basic structure of the User Environment Design doesn't work. You may find that adding the function changes the scope of the focus area beyond its current definition. In these cases it's best to go back and rethink the User Environment

Design. Use the physical props to help you here. Your sketch of the user interface holds the user interface design conversation, and your User Environment model holds that conversation. Move between the two physically as you discuss the different issues, and you'll focus your team better on the question at hand. (Constantine [1994b] discusses how to support movement between phases in the development process.)

Move between storyboards, UED, and UI as you raise and address issues

The User Environment Design and storyboards are the primary guide in working out the UI—the User Environment because it gives the structure to make it real and the storyboards because they capture alternative UI ideas and show sequential histories of use. Other models give additional guidance in working out the details of the user interface. When it's done, the result is an interface that presents a coherent system work model to the user and is ready to be mocked up in paper.

Iterating with a Prototype

19

The only reason for building a paper prototype is to support the conversation between user and designer about how to modify the proposed system to fit the user's work better. To do this well, the prototype must be easy to build, represent the user interface well enough to communicate it to a user, and be easy to modify in the field to support the design conversation. The process in Contextual Design is to validate the User Environment Design to ensure it's consistent; design a UI that represents the User Environment and mock it up in paper; interview customers using the paper mock-up in their own work context; interpret those interviews in the design team; make changes to User Environment Design and UI to respond to the issues; and repeat until the design stabilizes.

The original work on low-fidelity mock-ups was done at Aarhus University (Ehn and Kyng 1991). Since then, many others have modified the basic concepts to software (Muller 1991). Our approach builds on the concept of a low-fidelity prototype, but puts it in the context of a contextual interview in which the prototype can be tried out, discussed, and modified in partnership with the user.

BUILDING A PAPER PROTOTYPE

Ease of building is a primary requirement of paper prototypes. Remember that part of the goal is to make it easy to try out design options with users; if it's too hard to build the prototype, people will be less willing to use them as design tools. Off-the-shelf stationery

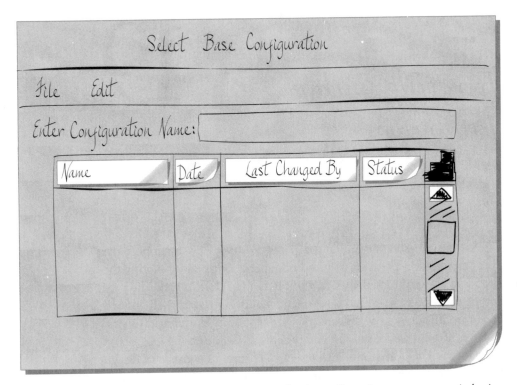

FIGURE 19.1   A paper prototype for the configuration management windowing UI. The column headers and triangle to set sort order are on separate pieces of paper to suggest that they are clickable. The real UI might make them three-dimensional. The blank list will be filled in during the interview with configurations the user works with.

supplies, especially Post-its in all their varieties, are the basic components of a paper prototype (Figure 19.1).

The key for a successful prototype is to put everything that might have to move during the interview on its own Post-it. This includes pull-down menus, buttons, and the objects of a direct manipulation interface. The interviewer will write in the content of the interface with the user's own data during the interview, so any example content should be on a removable sheet. The interviewer will take extra sheets to write the new contact on.

If the system mixes hardware and software, use other kinds of props in addition to the paper mock-up. Pens make good bar code scanners, pen boxes make good PDAs, and stationery boxes make good laptops.

Post-its on the laptop and PDA boxes represent their interfaces. Use these whenever the form factor of the physical device matters.

The final paper prototype represents the structure and the behavior of the proposed user interface. It's rough and handwritten, but legible—the user needs to be able to read it. The prototype should cover the whole system. Focus areas that aren't worked out yet are a blank Post-it with a title bar in the prototype. This gives enough structure to discuss the place with the user should it be wanted. Organize the paper so that all the parts for a window are together, with extra parts that appear on demand on a separate sheet. Put the windows in order of expected use, and you're ready for an interview.

A good paper prototype is clean but looks like it can be changed

BUILDING A PAPER PROTOTYPE

The screen: Use a 9 × 12-inch sheet of card stock as the background to represent the screen. This gives you a slightly rigid base to the prototype, which is useful when manipulating the parts in the field. The slightly larger size gives you more flexibility in laying out a complex prototype.

Windows: Use an $8^1/_2$ × 11-inch sheet of paper or the largest size Post-it as a window. The larger size lets you lay out a more complex window but also occupies most of your card stock screen (much as real windows do). In the interview, watch for issues caused by multiple overlapping windows.

Decorate windows with a title bar and any permanent contents. Draw a menu bar and write in the names of pull-down menus. Draw scroll bars if any.

Pull-down menus: The name of the pull-down menu goes on the window because it's always visible. The contents of the menu go on a 2 × 3-inch Post-it. Write the name of the pull-down menu at the top. In the interview, keep the menu to one side, and put it on the window when the user clicks on it in the menu bar to simulate pulling it down. Any pull-right submenus go on their own Post-its—you'll pull them out when needed in the same way.

Tool palettes and button bars: If they are permanent, draw the space for them on the window but put each tool or button icon on its own Post-it (cut these small by hand). In the interview, you'll want to talk about what needs to go on the bar or palette, and having them on their own Post-its makes it easier to reconfigure them. It also makes them appear more manipulable and inviting to press.

If you're designing a floating palette, put the whole thing on its own 2 × 3-inch Post-it. Either draw the tools on it directly, or put them on their own small Post-its if you want to design exactly what goes on the palette. ➪

Radio buttons, check boxes, controls: Draw right on the window.

Dialog boxes: Use smaller-sized Post-its for these—3 × 3-inch or 3 × 5-inch. Treat them just like windows, drawing on permanent content and using separate Post-its for things that may change.

Window contents: For most windows, the bulk of the contents will be the user's own data—the information she would expect to see if she were using the application in her own work. It's okay to fill in dummy data while building the prototype to work out what the screens will really look like, but take a blank version to the interview. When you're there, you'll tailor it to them.

Special techniques: The more interesting your design is, the more you'll want to extend these basic techniques to represent your design. Drag-and-drop is easy if you put the element you want to drag on its own Post-it, so the user can pick it up and move it. If you want to represent an overlay of information—like annotations on a document—cut overhead transparency film and draw and stick Post-its on it. If you're designing a tabbed interface, use Post-it flags to represent the tabs. Play with the medium. Anything that represents your intent and isn't too complicated to create or use is fair game. ❑

Running a prototype interview

A paper prototype interview is very similar to a contextual interview in attitude, but very different logistically. The mechanics of handling the paper prototype make it a different kind of interview to run. But like a contextual interview, the attitude is one of inquiry, probing into the reasons for the user's actions and generating a sense of shared discovery, co-interpretation, and co-design. The same principles that guide Contextual Inquiry guide a prototyping interview.

Context

In a contextual interview, you stay grounded by staying close to the ongoing actions and real past events of the user's work. You can't do real work in a paper prototype, but you can stay grounded in real events. Either replay a real past event, or alternate between doing a real task and replaying it in the prototype:

User: *I like this "change" concept you have. Keeping all the parts of a logical change together is a big problem for us.*

Designer: *When was the last time you ran across that?*

U: *Just last week, when I was putting in a bug fix to our system.*

D: *Let's replay that situation in the prototype. What were the different parts of the system you had to change?*

U: *Well, there was the bug report; then there were two modules, PROA.C and PROB.C; and there was my description of the change that we're all required to do.*

D: (writing furiously) *Like this?*

U: *Right.*

D: (putting the list on the prototype in the right place) *Okay, let's do it.*

The designer writes new data into the prototype to show the data associated with the real event. This keeps users interacting with the prototype, either touching and changing it themselves or telling the designer how to manipulate it. Don't let users drift into generalities—if they start talking about what they would like in a system, pursue a real story to see how the changes would play out. As they act out the story, invent fixes to the system to support them better. One design team working on a portable device drove around with their user. When she bought gas, she said, "And now, I pay for it with this thing," and she pretended to plug it into the pump. Having the device in her hand, it was easy to invent new uses for it.

> *Follow a single case— don't do a demo*

PARTNERSHIP

The partnership between user and designer is around co-design of the prototype. As the user works with the prototype, both user and designer will discover problems. When the user raises problems or suggests different ways to do things, the designer modifies the prototype to represent the suggestion. The designer also gives design options to the user by suggesting several alternative solutions to a problem they've run into.

There will often be points where the user's expectations don't match what the designer intended: "Oh, that 'change' thing lets me submit a change proposal, right?" In such cases, always pursue the user's interpretation first: "Right, what do you think would happen?" Start co-designing this new possibility immediately. You're not committed to the design that you and the user come up with, but by exploring it you can find out what they are thinking.

Users are never wrong: change the prototype to meet their expectations

You may discover a whole new issue or approach that you hadn't thought of before. You'll take the design you work out back and integrate it properly later—or at least the ideas underlying the design. Once you've explored this other avenue and come to a natural stopping point, you can return to the prototype you designed: "That was interesting. But remember back here, when you first saw this 'change' thing? Suppose I told you it kept the parts of a change you make together?" This is also the right way to handle the user's design ideas. If they are limited by their experience or skills—if everything they suggest is a tabbed dialog box or a menu—pursue their idea until you see what they are trying to get at. Then you can draw on your wider range of options to come up with cleaner or more inventive solutions. In this way, you'll see both what the user had in mind and, when you share them, his reaction to your ideas. You'll also give the users more technology ideas that they can incorporate and apply themselves.

INTERPRETATION

When the user reacts to some aspect of the prototype or to the designer's ideas, the goal is to find out what they expected and why the prototype or suggestion doesn't match. It's okay to discuss their ideas. It's important to understand what they want and why, not just the specific idea they propose (Figure 19.2).

Find out why a design does or doesn't work for the work

User: *This list of what's changed in this configuration isn't useful. I need to see the exact files, not just the developer's description attached to each change.*

Designer: *That tells you whether to trust the change?*

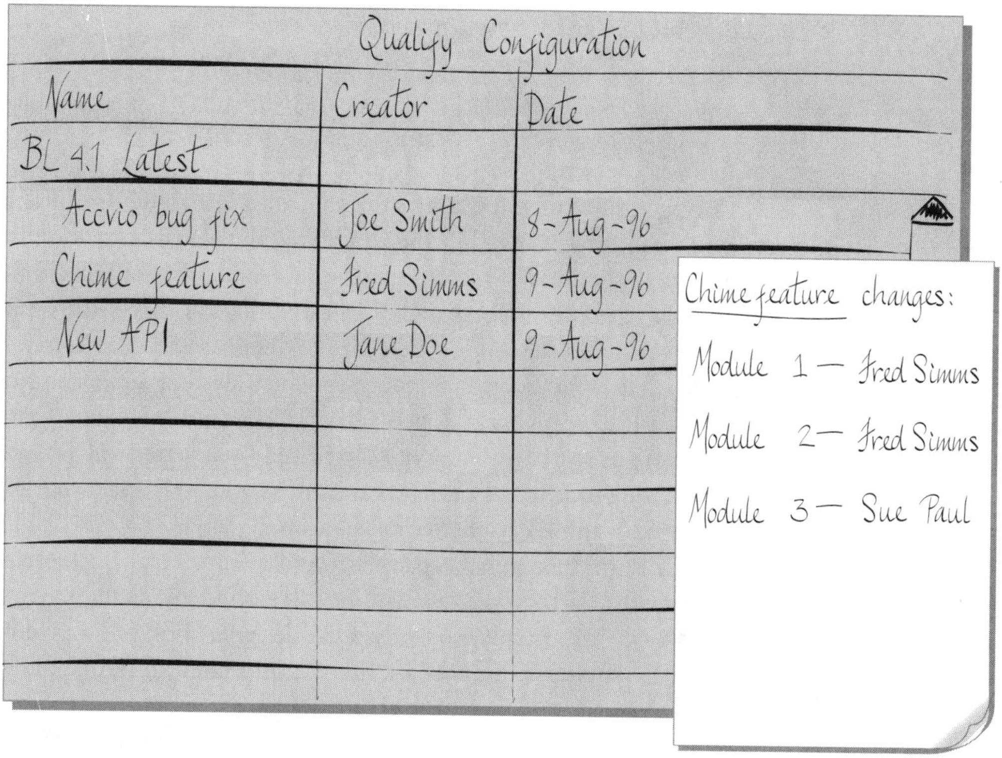

FIGURE 19.2 A paper prototype of the "Qualify Configuration" focus area.

U: *Right. If I'm surprised by what files they've touched, or if they've touched a couple of modules that are real complex, I know to be careful.*

D: *So how might you fix it?*

U: *Well, I don't know . . . Maybe double-click to see a list of contents?*

D: *That could work. Or we could give you a little triangle like Macintosh's finder. Click the triangle and see what's in the configuration. Or we could add an area to see contents and update it when you pass the mouse over a change—*

U: *I like that. That way I can scan up and down looking for who changed a particular module or get a fast look at everything that's changed. Let's do that.*

D: *You need to see exactly who changed what?*

U: *Oh yeah. Some of our modules are real rat's nests. If they weren't changed by the one or two people I trust, I'll be real careful of them.*

In every case, you're looking to understand the structure of the user's work and how it matches the prototype, but you'll be talking in the language of the UI. So in this example, designer and user talk about "double-click" and the "little triangle." But the solution they settle on is the one that matches the work. The data the designer will take home is structural—that what matters to the user when looking at a changed configuration is to see what changed and who changed it. The particular UI idea might work, or it might be replaced by a better way of seeing into a configuration. As long as the user's intent is met, the UI designer is free to think up a better mechanism.

It's important that you keep open to the user's reaction (verbal and nonverbal) and that you be willing to respond by changing the prototype promptly. One designer took out a prototype with two alternative interfaces, one of which (her favorite) merged two focus areas in the User Environment Design and was based on a calendar. When that one was placed in front of the first user, she visibly recoiled and said, "Oh no, I don't want that—that's much too complicated." On another project, one user was given an interface that simply didn't match what she was trying to do. She did her best to make it fit her job, but it wasn't until the designer created a new window (and new focus area, though the designer didn't say so) that the prototype started to click.

Nonverbal reactions showing that users are overwhelmed or frustrated reveal excessive complexity

FOCUS

As we discussed above, the User Environment Design represents the team's claim that this system will improve the user's work practice. The focus of a prototyping interview is to test that claim and fix the system when it's wrong.

Keeping to this focus is hard because it's easier for people to assimilate changes and see them as a minor adjustment than to recognize a challenge to the basic structure or assumptions of the system. It's important for the designer to be looking not for validation, but for the ways in which the system fails. Taking this attitude makes it more likely that designers will recognize a fundamental challenge.

The User Environment Design gives designers a way to listen that also makes it easier to break existing assumptions. With the User Environment Design behind them, designers can tell whether a suggested change affects only the UI or whether it's really challenging the structure of the system. When the User Environment Design was created and when the prototype was reviewed, designers identified specific tests to check for during the interview (we'll discuss this more below). Where the team considered alternative designs, the prototype tests the chosen option; if the user has problems with it, the designer can design in the alternative on the fly and see if it fares better.

Focus on testing structure first: ignore pure UI problems

Finally, focus keeps the conversation on the right level of design. Early in the process the prototypes test structure, not the UI. If the user suggests changes to the UI—a new icon, a different word—the designer just writes them in. They don't need to be discussed—they aren't in the focus—but the user does need to be heard. Later, when the prototypes are intended to test the UI, the designer will discuss and suggest alternative UI mechanisms. The same is true if the entire focus of the project is to clean up an existing product's UI—the prototyping interviews will focus on UI issues from the beginning.

THE STRUCTURE OF AN INTERVIEW

Interviewing around a paper prototype has very much the same structure as a normal contextual interview. The difference is that after the initial discussion, you move to working with the prototype.

SETUP

Prototype interviews, like any Contextual Inquiry, need to be set up in advance so that everyone knows what to expect. Users can be people who the team has talked to already or entirely new users—it's usually best to do a mix. Interview two or three customers with a prototype, then review the feedback from them and redesign the prototype before going out again. If you continue to bring in new users, the pool of customers interviewed over the course of the project will continue to grow. In this way, some large projects have worked with 50–100 users over the course of the project.

It's especially important to make sure a prototype interview is set up with the right roles and that they are doing the work the prototype supports. The user needs to have current or recent examples of doing the work that they can replay in the system, or there's no way to test the prototype with them. In setting up the interviews, find out what the users are doing, and make sure the work you care about is covered.

Don't run prototype interviews with people who don't do the work

For the team, the designers who will interview need to be familiar with the User Environment Design and the paper prototypes. Review the prototype as a team and identify *tests*—issues that the prototype will test because of the way the prototype was designed. Perhaps the designer put lots of buttons and other interface components on the screen—then you'll find out if the user is prone to being overwhelmed. Perhaps the designer added a strong visual element that separates what should be one focus area into two—then you'll test whether dividing the focus area works. Whatever the issues are, note them along with the design choices you decided to test in developing the User Environment model. These will refine your focus for the interviews.

INTRODUCTION

Start by introducing yourself and the focus of your design, including the kind of work the design supports. It's not necessary to describe the design itself at this point. You just want to start the user thinking about the kind of work you'll want him to do.

Then find out about the user, the work they do, and the particular tasks they have to do or have done recently. At this point you're looking for a *hook* to get you into the prototype. You're looking for all the different situations, current or in the recent past, that your system would support. You may not find one; it's possible that this person simply isn't doing the work you support right now. But that's rare if the interviews are well set up. Usually, you'll find a

Introduce the "Let's pretend" situation

couple of situations that are good candidates for re-creating or doing for the first time in the prototype.

TRANSITION

Once you've found a set of appropriate situations to re-create, choose one to start with and transition to the prototype interview. Bring out the prototype and introduce it. Give a brief summary of the screen they start with: "Here's a window that lets you choose a configuration of the system to base your development on." Do *not* do a whole walkthrough of the window. As you introduce it, write in the specific data for the user—get the names of the configurations they might actually have seen given the work they've done. If they have no configuration management system, so they never created or named configurations explicitly, talk to them about how they have organized their development. Look for ways in which the configuration concept would have been useful to them, and agree on the configurations they would have created in their recent development. Name them, and write them into the prototype.

Map new concepts to the user's experience and data

The amount of discussion needed to introduce the system depends on how much change you're introducing to the work: if it's small, you can go right into the prototype; if large, you'll have to introduce your approach. "This product organizes the software development process by tracking the different modules, keeping developers from getting in each other's way, and making stable versions of the whole system as the basis of development and for release. What's unique about it is that, instead of treating every modification to a file as independent, it treats all the modifications that accomplish a single fix or implement a single feature as one change." That would be sufficient to introduce the customer to what you're building.

Don't give a demo of the new system

THE INTERVIEW

Once you have the prototype out and ready, move the user into interacting with it. If you're reproducing a recent event, suggest that he do his work in the prototype, and you'll play CPU, making the system work like it should. Or get them to start interacting with the prototype by inviting them to explore, describing what they see and what they think it will do. Change the mock-up as they run into problems: add and redesign parts to fit their needs. Give them a pen so they can modify parts of the prototype themselves. Some users will dive right into doing their work; others will want to poke around and explore the different parts of the system. Let them follow whichever style is natural for them.

If the user asks for an explanation of some part of the system, you can give them a one- or two-sentence description. This is an important place to listen for the "no." If you get a blank stare and have to keep elaborating on the explanation in hopes that they will get it, you have a concept that doesn't work. If your user can't figure out what a "configuration" is, or can't understand how they might use it to organize their development, it's too big a mismatch with their current practice to be useful. Adopting the system will require huge amounts of retraining.

Be the online help: one or two sentences only

Always run prototype interviews in pairs; it's too hard to try and manage the prototype, interact with the user, and keep notes at the same time. The notes of a prototype interview are critical to reconstructing it with the team later—it will be hard to recover the sequence of events from just the prototype, and an audiotape misses too much. It usually works best to assign one person to be notetaker while the other runs the interview and manipulates the prototype. It's usually not necessary to videotape the interview. Video can be critical if you are communicating back to a design team that is not going on their own customer interviews and doesn't really understand them. Video can also be critical if you are looking at problems in the detailed interaction with the UI. Otherwise, we've found the extra effort of videotaping gets in the way of rapid and frequent prototyping.

While running the interview, if you're replaying a past event, keep referring to that event to keep the interview grounded. Ask how the user would expect the system to respond, and when he says something you didn't expect, design on the fly, extending the design you have and pulling in parts from other focus areas when they're useful (Figure 19.3).

Ground the interview by replaying specific events

Designer: *So how did you decide what configuration to use as the base for fixing the bug that day?*

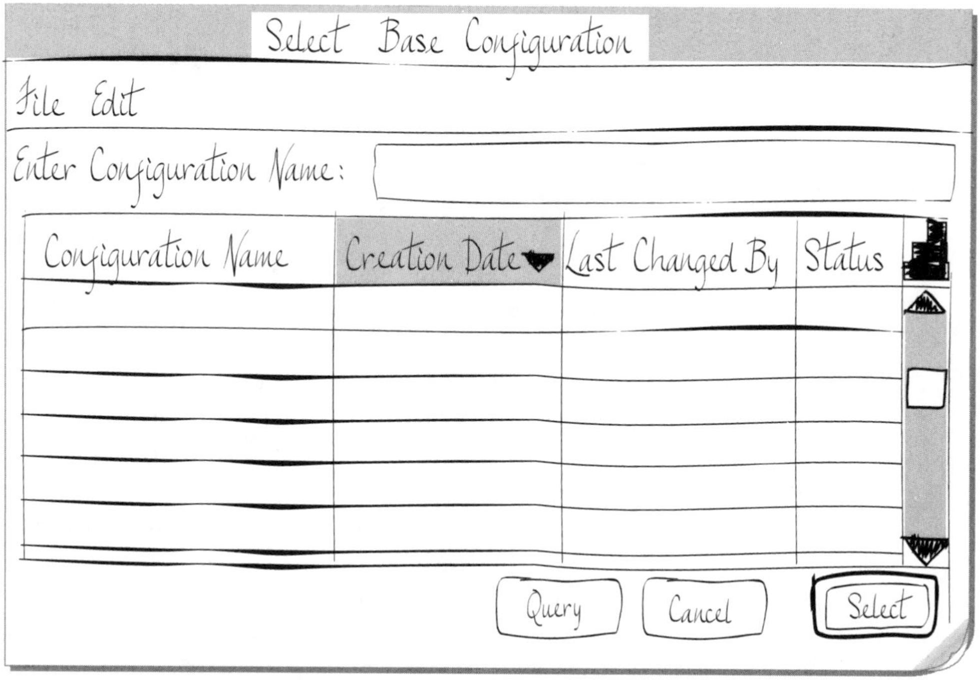

FIGURE 19.3 A paper prototype of the "Select Base Configuration" focus area.

User: *Oh, I just used V5. That's the version the bug was reported against, so I started there.*

D: *Okay, here's our interface to let you specify the base configuration. What do you do?*

U: *I guess I type the name in here.* (Indicates the text entry field)

D: *Go ahead.*

U: (Writes "V" with a pen on the field) *Now what happens?*

D: *What would you expect?*

U: *Probably the list changes so it's just the configurations that begin with "V."*

D: *Oh. Okay, that's what happens.*

U: (Writes "5") *There's only one "V5," so now I hit the "Okay" button and I'm done.*

D: *Didn't you show me you also had a V5.1?*

U: *Oh yeah. Well, the exact match should show up first on the list and be selected, so I can still just press "Okay."*

This isn't the design that was originally intended—the team didn't think about using the "name" field as a simple query filter—but it fits with the design. The user assumes an "Okay" button rather than pressing RETURN or "Select," and the designer doesn't bring it up—that's a user interface question that isn't in her focus right now. This is an example of following a user's design to see where it goes. At this point the designer could back the user up and suggest the original design: "Suppose I told you that this is just a text entry field for choosing a configuration by name?" That would allow her to test the team's design after seeing what the user had in mind.

But the designer won't return to her team only with a UI tweak. What she's discovered challenges their User Environment Design:

Use the UI conversation to see structural issues

should there be a "Find configuration" focus area separate from the "Select base configuration" focus area at all? The user's idea suggests that some level of quick query can and should be integrated right into "Select base configuration." Perhaps there's no need for "Find configuration." It makes sense as a separate focus area only if querying is so complicated that just forming the query is a separate kind of work. Do users ever really need to form such complicated queries, especially if all they are doing is choosing one configuration to work with? So our designer moves the interview forward by discussing the need for real queries and probing for how this user specifies configurations—looking for cases when a simple search by name would not work. Because she is in the User Environment Design conversation with the team, it's easy to guide the interview to answer questions about structure.

WRAP-UP

The final wrap-up of a prototype interview is a simple summary of the key points that came up during the interview. Summarize the points, and if it's useful, summarize any parts of the prototype you didn't get to for a quick reaction. But this won't be contextual data, so don't spend a lot of time on it. Finally, check the emotional aspect. Ask: Does he like it? Would he buy or recommend buying it? How much would he pay for it? You're not looking for a real committed figure here. You're looking for a sense of how valuable they think the system really is and also the unarticulated expectations and threshold fig-

> *Check the sales point: do they love it?*

ures that lie behind how they think about cost. You'll get a response that incorporates any excitement generated by the interview—by playing with and manipulating the design. In this way, the response is better grounded than you might get from a focus group or demo.

This is the general pattern of a prototype interview. If you're tracking an ongoing task rather than replaying an old one, the user will alternate between doing some real work and then redoing it in the prototype, but otherwise the pattern is the same. Designer and user discuss the prototype, using the task to drive the conversation. From time to time they elaborate on some idea of the user's, then come back to the prototype as

> *Don't create scripts—let the user's real work be the script*

designed. The designer uses her knowledge of the User Environment Design and technology to drive the interview. If you can recognize when the user is challenging some aspect of the User Environment Design, you can probe for details immediately, instead of having to wait for another interview.

Later in the design process, when you trust the structure in the prototype, concentrate more on the user interface and on enforcing the limits of a real system. When the user tries to do something the design doesn't allow, instead of taking it as an opportunity for co-design, act like a real CPU: beep at him. See if he can figure out how to make the system work given the limitations you're building in.

Follow the task the user is doing or re-creating until it's done or has moved beyond the scope covered by the prototype. Then choose another situation to follow that will exercise any parts of the prototype that haven't been touched yet. Usually, you won't get to all the parts of the prototype and that's okay; end the interview after two or three hours and save the rest of the prototype for the next user.

THE INTERPRETATION SESSION

The last part of a prototype interview is parallel to a contextual interview: the interviewers bring the data back to a design team and replay the interview for them so that everyone can see what happened and offer their different perspectives. This interpretation session is focused narrowly on identifying the issues raised by the interview.

Issues are captured on Post-its by the recorder, one point per Post-it. Points to capture are any new aspects of work practice that haven't been seen before, validations of design elements that worked for the user as designed, problems that got in the user's way, places where the structure of the system didn't help him get his work done, and any user interface validation and problems.

Most of the data from an early prototype interview will be structural issues for the User Environment Design. Capture these and stick them directly to the affected part of the User Environment Design. There will be some issues for the user interface, even though this is not the primary focus—the issues are captured and can be dealt with as the interface is refined. Any issue that has to do with presentation, layout, or wording is a UI issue. There will also be some issues for the work models. These include any points that capture new aspects of work practice that aren't properly represented on the existing models. Rather than try to update the models in the meeting, it's easier to capture the issue and stick it right to the model in question. If there's any disagreement about where an issue goes, move it upstream—put it on the User Environment Design in preference to the UI and on the work models in preference to either. This whole session is good practice in separating conversations, as each conversation has its own model and its own place on the wall.

Use the models and the UED to organize findings

Throughout the interpretation session, the primary task is to see behind the user's reaction to the UI to understand the work issue. If the user was overwhelmed, was that because the focus area wasn't clean, the design didn't match his work, or was the UI for that part of the system unnecessarily complex? Examine the user's actions and words to understand what his reaction meant to the design.

ITERATION

When a design has been tested with two to four users, it's time to iterate it. The issues raised by the users are grouped so related issues can be addressed together. Changes to work models may affect the User Environment Design, and changes to the User Environment may affect the user interface, so the first issues to deal with are those related to the work models—move forward from there. No one wants to spend hours on some aspect of the user interface, only to discover later that a change to the User Environment Design obviates that whole part of the interface.

For the work models, collect the issues from all users for each type of model. Organize them to see what they imply for the model. Extend it with any new aspects of work practice that came from this interview: new roles or flows between roles, new strategies, new influences, or new structures in the physical environment. If this new data affects the focus of the design, you'll deal with it as part of

> *Address work issues first, then UED, and then UI*

addressing the User Environment Design; otherwise, it becomes part of your permanent representation of your customer population.

Then turn to the User Environment Design. First consider whether any of the work model changes affect the design, and if so identify which parts they affect. Then look across the data from all the users and ask what the primary structural issues are. Look for ways to redesign the overall system to address these issues. Then start working on sets of issues part by part, starting with the parts that are involved in the most important and far-reaching issues. Collect the issues across all users for each of those parts, and consider how to redesign them to address the issues and the new information from the models. Use the storyboards to help you think through particular tasks in the changed system. Go on from section to section of the User Environment Design until you've addressed all the issues you need to. You may decide that some issues are at too low a level of detail to bother with yet or affect some part of the system that is too peripheral. There's no point in spending a lot of time to get a part of the design right if it's only going to be cut later. Work to get the overall system stable, then prioritize what to ship, and then do the details.

Restructuring the system tends to pull it apart as a system, so finish with a validation pass to reorganize it and pull it back together again. Clean up the loose ends, and make sure the design is reasonably clean.

Finally, roll the User Environment changes forward into a redesign of the user interface. First look for broad issues that affect the whole interface: Did the base metaphor work? Were your interaction mechanisms usable? Were there consistency issues to address? Decide what to do about these issues. If you'll change the base metaphor, do it first, before addressing any of the particular issues. Then move from focus area to focus area, collect the user interface parts that represent a focus area and the issues associated with them, and redesign the interface to deal with the issues and User Environment changes together.

COMPLETING A DESIGN

This is the iterative, customer-centered process of Contextual Design. As you expand your design to address more and more of your vision,

Maintain regular customer contact to keep yourselves moving forward

the process will change and flex to accommodate new issues. The core design may be quite stable, but when you move to address a new area of work, you'll collect much more basic work practice data. You may need to switch to capture a set of work models in the middle of the interview. You may capture sequences for a task that you were never able to observe until this point. Then the interview will move back to the prototype, and your interpretation session will go back to primarily capturing issues.

But you're always using the prototype to drive customer visits and keep the team grounded in real customer data. Returning to the customer every 10 days to two weeks keeps the team focused and moving forward; in our experience, lack of regular contact with customers is a primary reason teams lose focus and break into arguments with each other. A prototyping approach to design keeps you going.

This iterative design process continues until the team is sure it has a workable design. Usually after two to three iterations of a part of the

When structure stabilizes, move to testing UI directly

User Environment Design with customers, that part begins to stabilize. The number of structural issues, which are recorded on the User Environment Design, fall off, and the UI issues start to predominate. This is your signal that the structure is pretty much right. Move to testing primarily the UI while simultaneously extending the prototype to test the structure of another part of the system. The part that has stabilized can be moved simultaneously to implementation design and code. Prioritize what parts of the system to deliver, as we described in Chapter 16, and build a shipping User Environment Design for the next release. This becomes your working specification.

When you move through a design in this way, you can be confident that you've understood the requirements and the appropriate system structure. Development of the system can proceed through the implementation and testing of running code in much the same way that we've tested prototypes. This maintains the customer contact while implementation progresses. The iterative prototyping process merges with an iterative implementation process that coordinates all the parts of the team to deliver on the vision.

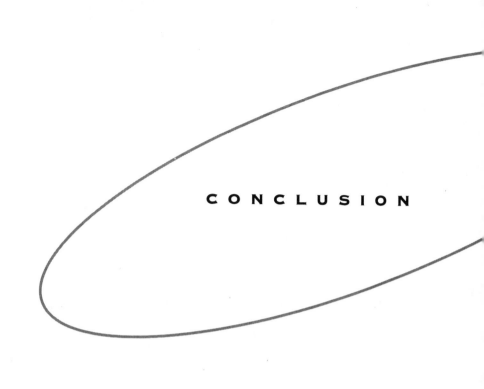

CONCLUSION

Putting It into Practice

20

No process works for every problem, in every organization, for every team structure. In fact, the first job of a design team is to design the process that will enable them to collaborate in gathering data, designing a system, and producing the result.

This is as true for Contextual Design as for any other process. The special contribution of Contextual Design is that it offers a complete set of techniques, guiding design from gathering initial data about what matters to make, to defining the system function and structure that works for the customer. Each technique is a placeholder for discussing a particular set of issues about designing for the customer in a real organization. If you're defining a front-end design process, the steps of Contextual Design suggest the thought steps you need to cover, in a framework that hangs together. You can alter or substitute steps that achieve the same intent, add new techniques to put more emphasis on a step, or remove steps you believe are irrelevant to your particular problem. In this way, Contextual Design can be a backbone for designing customer-centered processes. (Constantine [1996] and Hefley and Romo [1994] offer other ways to fit customer-centered approaches into the software engineering process.)

> *Contextual Design can be a template for designing your design processes*

THE PRINCIPLES OF CONTEXTUAL DESIGN

Contextual Design is grounded in principles of what it takes to drive design thinking, what makes for good customer data, and what's going on in teams and organizations to ensure that the design process works. Just as the principles of Contextual Inquiry redesign the inquiry situation, you can use the principles of Contextual Design to redesign the entire design process. In the spirit of a consolidated sequence model, we've revealed the intents of each part of Contextual Design in Table 20.1. The principles on which the process is based fall into three categories: using customer data, running the team, and driving design thinking. We've discussed these techniques throughout the book but will summarize them here.

THE PRINCIPLE OF DATA

Ground all design action in an explicit, trustworthy understanding of your customers and how they work. Without a clear understanding of your customers, based on real events rather than anecdotes, and captured explicitly, you have no criteria for deciding on one action or design decision over another. At every point in the design process, ask what data is needed to justify one decision over another and what the best way is to gather that

Decide what data you need to make a decision and how to get it

data. But customers cannot tell you the important aspects of their own work practice because they are implicit and unrecognized. To gather trustworthy data, use a process that reveals the unarticulated aspects of work. Contextual Inquiry reveals the hidden aspects of work practice; paper prototyping reveals how a particular design plays out in the real work context. To ensure that the data can be trusted, set up the situation to make the customer the best teacher possible. This means basing interactions on the customer's own work situation, where they are the expert, and communicating with them in their own language.

Data on customer work practice will always be complex because work practice is complex, so gathering data necessarily includes mechanisms for handling that complexity. Use a concrete representation of the customer data to reveal how the work hangs together as a whole.

Use representations that reveal both the common structure that applies across customers and also the unique variation that your design will have to account for. And that representation should effectively highlight those aspects of work that are most critical to be considered during system design.

Gathering customer data is only worthwhile because it helps make design decisions. We aren't gathering random data about people in the world; we're using the data to drive our design processes. All data is gathered for a purpose, and that purpose sets your focus as a team. It will tell you what matters to make, how to structure your system, and how you are doing as you design and build it. The data is the continuing ground for design, and it drives continuous iteration of your ideas. By providing an external check on the design, it alleviates arguments in the team.

> *Ask: what will you design differently if you have this data?*

THE PRINCIPLE OF THE TEAM

Design is done by people, and managing people is an important part of any process. Anytime you can build on people's natural design processes, you're better off. In design discussions, understand what conversations people are trying to have and make them explicit. Are they asking about what's true for the customer? What would make a good design? What's implementable? Maintaining control of a meeting is now an important skill. Give each conversation a time to happen and a tangible representation. Use the representation to keep the team focused on the right conversation, and put off other conversations to the appropriate time. Capture off-topic issues, so the people raising them know they are heard and so the team can be sure they are not lost. Define and manage the roles and procedures so everyone knows how to behave.

> *Running a meeting is an important design skill*

Drawings representing the customer work practice and the system work model help manage the design conversation and keep the design coherent, but they also manage communication within and beyond the team. The external representation enables you to check your thinking for errors and omissions, share it with others, and communicate it to the larger organization. Building the representation together allows you to include others in the thinking process, so the final

	INTENTS		
STEP	**CUSTOMER DATA**	**DESIGN THINKING**	**TEAM AND ORGANIZATION**
Contextual Inquiry	• Gather detailed data needed for design • Discover implicit aspects of work that would normally be invisible	• Put technical experts in the customer data • Stimulate the recognition of implications for design	• Build the team through shared experiences • Collect concrete data to resolve conflicts
Interpretation sessions	• Use whole team's perspective to see what matters in the work • Capture all aspects of one customer's work efficiently	• Manage the flood of insight from all team members • Capture design ideas as they come • Share preliminary design ideas to start cross-pollination	• Bring multiple perspectives to bear on the data • Teach team members the perspectives of other organizations • Keep everyone engaged in processing the data
Work models	• Create a coherent representation of work practice • Record actual user data to check the system • Distinguish between opinions and real data	• Reveal aspects of work that matter for design • Capture elements of work in a tangible form	• Feed market stories, scenarios, and planning • Create a culture in which concrete data is the basis for making decisions
Affinity diagram	• Organize data across all customers to reveal scope of issues • Provide a review of the data prior to consolidation and visioning • Identify holes in the data	• Push from point fixes to systemic solutions • Introduce inductive thinking • Allow individuals to develop their response to the data • Share design ideas without evaluation	• Drive consensus about what the data means • Make data easy to share • Make key customer issues stand out • Create the first step toward corporate knowledge of their customer
Work model consolidation	• Create one statement of the customer population • Show common structure without losing variation across customers	• Reveal implications for design through dialog with each model	• Create a map of customer population for planning, sharing, and reuse • Make it possible to validate understandings with customers

▷

TABLE 20.1   The key intents of Contextual Design.

| | INTENTS | | |
STEP	CUSTOMER DATA	DESIGN THINKING	TEAM AND ORGANIZATION
Vision	• Respond to the data with new work practice designs • Shift the team's focus from tools to work practice	• Create a coherent response by reacting to the data rapidly • Generate divergent options before deciding on one • Separate evaluation from generation of ideas	• Develop design ideas together as a team • Defuse ownership in ideas
Storyboards	• Redesign work practice, not technology • Ground redesign in consolidated data • Ensure redesigned work practice hangs together	• Work out details of vision sequentially • Let designers think in the UI without committing to it	• Create a public representation of a task for sharing and checking • Enable parallel design work in small teams
User Environment Design	• Design the user's experience of the system to be coherent • Allow different user scenarios to be checked in the system	• Make the system work model explicit • Show relationships between parts of the system • Find errors in system structure before coding • Drive later object modeling • Separate out the UI conversation	• Make the system structure explicit and sharable • Show the relationship between systems • Provide a tool for planning and coordinating multiple systems and teams • Provide a high-level specification
Paper prototyping	• Check system structure and user interface with customer • Let the customer communicate in their own language • Get an additional layer of detailed data about actions within the system • Check sales point of potential products	• Provide a fast way to check design alternatives • Learn to separate UI from structural implications	• Create and test ideas quickly to prevent overattachment • Ensure a shared understanding of what customers find valuable • Share ideas in terms that customers and management can understand

TABLE 20.1 *continued*

design reflects the expertise of the whole team. Contextual Design incorporates a set of diagramming techniques that support the conversations we've found most useful: what the work practice of the customers is, what the new work practice is, how a user will perform a specific task in the new system, and what the system work model is. If you need to introduce additional conversations, introduce new techniques to represent them.

The people you include in a design process determine the kind of design you get. If you want a corporate response to the customer's whole work that can drive all parts of your company, put together a cross-functional design team—a team with members only from marketing, or engineering, or any other function, will emphasize solutions they can implement. Make sure you have a mix of skills on the team, but especially the skill of seeing design implications in people's everyday work practice. This may not be the strength of your best engineers. Look for it everywhere in your organization (documentation people often have the mix of technical and customer knowledge that makes them strong here).

Be cross-functional: team skill set determines the scope of the design

Effective team design depends on being able to manage design meetings. Define the roles you need to make the discussion work, and put people in the roles who can play them well. Give the team a clear process to follow, so they don't have to spend their time arguing about what they are doing as well as what they are building.

THE PRINCIPLE OF DESIGN THINKING

Support the needs of design thinking itself. A design process naturally alternates between working out a piece of design sequentially, then stepping back and considering the whole design as a structure. Any sequential design step wants a following step to look at the whole and check for appropriate structure, consistency, and completeness. Once the structure is good, the natural next step is to work out the next level of detail sequentially. This alternation between doing and reflecting keeps the design moving forward while remaining coherent. Use the appropriate formalism or drawings to capture the key issues for each step. The successive transformations act like a walkthrough of the design; they force your team

Support the natural alternation between doing and reflecting

to walk through the whole design and restate what they mean, finding holes and inconsistencies in the process.

The system you design is a whole and needs to fit together as a whole, or it won't provide coherent support for your customers' work. Define your design process to start by making the work issues real for the team so they can create new solutions. Then lead your team from focusing on individual features to thinking about how the design works as a whole. Use the appropriate representation

Push systemic thought throughout the process

of the design (such as the User Environment model) to show it as a whole and to make issues real so the team can envision solutions to them. Let developers working on a part use this representation to see how their part relates to the rest of the design. The right representation guides the design conversation and manages the complexity of the design by representing it appropriately. It shows the whole design in a form that the team can comprehend and manipulate.

BREAKING UP DESIGN RESPONSIBILITIES ACROSS GROUPS

These considerations drove the structure of Contextual Design. Use them to help guide any tailoring of the design process you do to fit your own project and organizational structure. Below, we discuss some different project situations and how Contextual Design might be adapted to them. The roles driving system design are very similar from organization to organization (as we learned in Part 3), but they'll be mapped to different job functions in your organization, and each mapping will lead to different communication and interpersonal problems. Design the process to recognize and ameliorate these problems, but remember there's no perfect organizational structure. You're always balancing role isolation against role strain.

Just as consolidated sequences break into activities that are common across whole customer populations, systems design breaks into activities that are common across organizations we've worked with. The activities we've seen are finding out what matters in the customer population, deciding how to respond at a high level, deciding how to structure the system to fit its users, choosing how to ship in coherent releases, and doing the implementation (we're focused on the front-end process, so we collapse all the parts of implementation into one).

The big difference across organizations is in how they map the natural activities of design to job functions. In old-time engineering-driven organizations, engineering initiated projects and marketing tried to find the market for them. More typically, marketing decides what a product would be based on customer contact and decides how to respond, and engineering determines how to structure the system. This is also the typical split between systems analysts or internal customers and developers in IT organizations. Whatever the formal definition of roles, it's rare to find a development organization that really only codes to a specification they are given, with no extensions—in fact, we've never worked with one. At the end of the process, usability has to figure out how the system is doing in fitting to the users' work.

The way the activities of design are split across job functions determines the kind of problems you will have. When a separate group decides how to respond to the customer work situation, they then have to convince development that they know what they're talking about when they say what to build. But the design response comes from knowing what's possible with technology, so some level of engineering knowledge is required even if the job is given to systems analysts or marketers.

How you break design activities across groups determines what problems you have

Conversely, developers still need to know and have contact with their customers because they have to know the structure of the work to design the structure of the solution. Creating a middleman to do analysis—a customer who focuses on communicating to engineering or an engineer who takes the job of learning about the customer—doesn't meet the need for combining customer and technical knowledge to envision new solutions. Even with a mix of customer and technical knowledge on the team, the design still has to be communicated to the larger development team that will build it—the need for communicating a design to another group doesn't go away.

Communicating a design or handing off responsibility between groups is always a danger point. The next group never understands everything you understand, they always have questions you didn't think of, and their different focus means they need additional data you never collected. So don't think of communication happening primarily through any sort of document. Linear text never communicates the feel for why a design element matters. It's too hard to see all the context and implications of different decisions. It's even hard to really describe all the functions of a system in enough detail to code.

Don't create role isolation— plan activities to generate shared perspectives

So look for ways to create events and partnerships that make the work and the reasons for decisions real. Communicate the consolidated models and the vision in addition to the User Environment Design. Take developers out on customer visits so they understand the context at a visceral level (this is probably the single most powerful technique for changing developers' perspective). Build a living online specification with hot links between data, storyboard, User Environment focus area, and functional specification. Build online prototypes that demonstrate the behavior you want. Treat the communication as one element of an ongoing relationship, not as a handoff.

Splitting the process up across groups also alters the different groups' perceptions of time. Expecting engineering to gather customer data, when they currently don't, always looks like additional overhead, no matter how much they need the data and how much time they lose by not having it. On the other hand, anything marketing and analysts do is invisible to engineering. One team suggested that moving the task of gathering data to marketing would reduce the time the process takes. It's an illusion, of course—it takes just as long in end-to-end calendar time, but the part engineering would have to do would be shorter.

Fitting customer-centered design into your organization works best when you consider and account for the division of responsibilities that already exists. When groups recognize how the process can help them achieve their goals and meet their needs, they are more likely to welcome the change. Marketing and analysts will be more excited by the front end of the process, as will usability and UI designers; engineering will like the tail end, including prototyping. Fit the way you use the process to the organization and the specific project you undertake.

Addressing different design problems

There are a number of different ways that design problems present themselves in organizations. Each kind of problem needs a different design approach, appropriate to the scale and time frame of the problem. Here are a few of the most common kinds of problem we've seen and how we've altered Contextual Design to address them. (See Coble et al. [1997] and Wixon and Ramey [1996] for experience reports on using contextual methods.)

We have a base level ready to test. Is it okay? What are the top 10 issues we should fix? In this case, no one wants to hear that they are designing the wrong product. A huge investigation would be inappropriate—either it will be a waste of time because it will confirm what everyone is doing, or it will suggest doing something very different, which will be threatening because there isn't time to do anything very different. A design process that answers a question people aren't ready to ask isn't successful. Success comes from influencing what the organization is delivering.

In this case, try stripping Contextual Design down to evaluate just the specific design. Use contextual interviews to see how people use the current system or prototype, with a focus on how the system gets in their way or interferes with their work. Interpret the interviews and capture notes, but build no work models. At most, capture low-level sequences to see problems and intents in how users interact with the system. Build an affinity to organize findings, and use it to identify the key issues to address in this version.

Gather data on point fixes when that's all anyone can respond to

Such a process could be run by a small group—perhaps usability experts—on behalf of a larger design team. It doesn't support the team in actually working out any of the issues, but does use customer data to get a quick check of an existing design and direction on how to fix it. In a week, the small team could collect and analyze data from four to eight customers—which is enough for a first cut at issues to fix.

I've already started development. Am I okay? In this case, work has started. Some part of the UI has been designed; some part of the code has been written. Now you want to know if you're on track.

It is possible to start Contextual Design in the middle. Start with a reverse User Environment model of your existing user interface to see its structure. Just doing the model may reveal a set of issues you want to address, and it will enable you to see structural issues in prototypes. Then mock up the system in paper and prototype it with users. Review the issues raised in an interpretation session, evaluate their importance, and feed the ones that have to be fixed back to development. When the current version is released, do regular Contextual Inquiries to build up models of the customer, and redesign the system based on the reverse User Environment Design.

> *Do a reverse UED and paper mock-up interviews*

Such a process can be run by a small subteam—two to four UI designers, usability engineers, and developers could do it within two weeks as a quick status check and midcourse correction.

We need to redesign our existing product. How can we rework it to address the customers' issues better? In contrast to the prior case, this design team is expecting to do some redesign. They aren't just looking for point problems to fix; they're looking for how best to improve an existing system. Usually they're at the beginning of a release cycle, but the time allotted to the release is relatively short.

Design a process that incorporates the critical structural elements of Contextual Design. Do contextual interviews and interpretation sessions, capture notes, but don't build flow or cultural models. These models show the larger work context and reveal how to expand the system scope or design other continuous systems. You're not doing that in this project—you're improving the system in the scope it has—so you don't need these models. Instead, build sequence, artifact, and physical models to see how the system interacts with the users' world structurally.

> *Use models that show a big view of the work when you're affecting the whole work*

Rather than do formal consolidations, use the sequences to generate scenarios of use. These scenarios make a composite of the customers you interviewed to tell the story of a typical user. Build an affinity, and use the affinity, scenarios, and models to brainstorm issues and design responses. See work structure by looking for natural clusters of work and artifacts in the physical model. Look for data used in artifacts. Run a visioning session based on key issues you identify, build up the design response, build storyboards based on the scenarios, and go right to UI design and paper prototyping. Artifacts guide the layout and presentation of the UI. Use the structural thinking behind the

User Environment Design to help organize the UI, but don't build a User Environment diagram explicitly.

This process gets you as quickly as possible from seeing the data to organizing a design response. When it's not a goal to create a new kind of system, but to create the next iteration on a system that already exists, it's an appropriate way to use the process. Such a process could be run in about two months by a small group of four to six, drawn from engineering, UI design, usability, and marketing. Eight to fifteen customer interviews would give enough data.

What new thing should we create in the world? This question is asked in different ways by different teams. Perhaps the team has been given the mandate to rethink an internal business process. Perhaps marketing has asked the team to invent a new product for a given market. Perhaps a version of the system exists, but the team wants to reinvent the market and so recapture the competitive edge.

In these cases, you want the full Contextual Design process as we've laid it out in this book. The models reveal the work practice of

Use the whole process when you need to set strategic direction

the whole customer population and make it possible to invent wholly new approaches. Because you see how the work ties together across roles and tasks, you can invent a strategy for supporting the work coherently with multiple systems. The User Environment Design organizes your response, just as the consolidated work models organize your understanding of the customer. It drives all aspects of implementation, including object-oriented design of the software. If you want to evolve an existing system, use a reverse User Environment Design to see the structure of the existing system and build on it. And expect to collect and incorporate more customer data into your consolidated work models. They are your picture of the customer population and will continue to be useful over the next few years.

This process could be run by a marketing team or by a mixture of engineering and marketing or systems analysts. A team driven by marketing might stop after the vision, identifying requirements on the system, services, and market message, but leaving it to engineering to structure the system. Though Contextual Design projects have been completed in five weeks, a big strategy like this will take at least four months to develop the User Environment Design and prototype it. And because of all the organizations that have to buy in, it usually requires a larger team of six to eight. Larger teams require more management; consider getting an external facilitator if you need a larger team.

How can we tie our products or applications together? This is the question asked by organizations that have developed many independent systems over the years, only to discover that they don't add up to complete support for the customers' work practice. The goal is both to integrate the independent systems, match them better to the customers' needs, and extend them to support more of the work domain.

In this case, use the full Contextual Design process, but precede it with a reverse User Environment model of the existing systems, capturing primary focus areas, purpose, and key functions only. This gives you a base understanding of what you have and starts the conversation of how you can fit the various systems together. But integrating the systems right, so that they provide seamless support of the work, depends on understanding the

> *Do a reverse UED and full Contextual Design to find old and new issues*

work they will support, and that's what the Contextual Design portion of the project provides. When you get to designing the system response to the work, instead of starting from scratch, start from the high-level reverse User Environment model you built. Modify it to fit the work better, and you'll both specify an integration strategy and address the worst mismatches between your systems and your customers' work. With a redesigned User Environment in place, each application team can redesign their own part to fit, using the Contextual Design process to get detailed data on their own customers' work practice.

Like any strategic project, such a project requires participation from the affected parties, particularly the different systems that will be integrated. Expect a team of six to eight to take at least four months.

In each of these cases, start with the design problem the team is facing and pull together the parts of the process that address that problem. Beware of including too much of the process—you'll make the process take longer and drive the team to consider high-level issues they can't really address. But look at the intents behind each part of the process to ensure you do include all the parts you need. And pull in additional techniques if

> *The nature of the design problem determines the best design process*

you need them. One team with a strong need to innovate decided they were getting stale and pulled creativity-enhancing techniques into the brainstorming part of the process. (They used "scenario modeling" to help them expand the possibilities they came up with.) You might use Participatory Design techniques, such as futures workshops and metaphors workshops (Kensing and Madsen 1991), during brainstorming and visioning to include the customers in the design process. A BPR project might use high-level process maps to show the whole business process across departments, with consolidated sequences showing how each task in the process is done. Or you might include more formal UI design techniques and usability methods at the end of the process. In this way, you'll build on the basic framework of Contextual Design to create a customer-centered process that meets your specific needs.

TEAM STRUCTURE

Whatever the design problem, you'll have to deal with the structure of the team doing the work. Managing a design team of 15 people is a very different problem than trying to specify a system with only two analysts. It's always best to include multiple perspectives and have cross-functional representation on the team, but given your organizational structure, achieving that goal may be hard.

When the whole project is small (four to six people), doing the front-end design can be the full-time job of the team. When the team is large, it doesn't make sense for the whole team to work on the design together—instead, assign a smaller group to act for the team. Whether it's one or two analysts defining a system that a larger group will code, a single marketer studying the market and defining a product direction for an engineering team, or a few designers specifying a system to build, these few people will work out the system that a larger number of people will code later. Be aware that these teams will feel intense pressure to keep the coders busy. If their design isn't complete in time, the coders will finish whatever they are working on and either quit working or start building with no data or design. And the relationship between the small design team and the larger group of coders is often tricky—coders get used to being the ones who have final say over what goes into the design.

Design a process to fit the size of the team

The small group can have *core* and *adjunct* members. Core members devote most of their time (60–80%) to the project and are primarily responsible for it. Adjunct members devote less time (30–50%) but are involved in working sessions every week. People who want to be part of the process but can't devote the time can be adjuncts. Adjunct members expand the team with additional perspectives and more manpower throughout the process. Inviting people from the larger team to participate in design activities is an important part of the small team's strategy for communicating the customer data and their designs.

When you're operating with very tight resources, consider sharing people across projects. If you have a team of one or two and need additional people to build your affinity, invite them in for a day—then help them out with theirs when they need people. Review each other's data and give each other design ideas. In this way, you not only get the people you need, but you also cross-fertilize data and design ideas across projects. You can still do all the parts of the process with one or two people, but it will take longer. Even though the man-hours don't go up, the clock time does, and that affects how people perceive the process. When you have multiple projects addressing the same work domain—the same internal department or external market—pool your resources. Develop one set of models for the whole customer population, and use them to drive all the projects. Build up a single User Environment Design to show how the different systems interrelate.

Build one set of models for multiple projects when resources are tight

Sometimes the initial team is responsible for less of the design. You're a marketing team that is only supposed to understand the market and decide what kind of product to sell, or you're a data-gathering team that is supposed to report to the larger team that makes the real decision about what to build, or you're a business analyst that has to decide what the business department needs. In these cases, you'll need an explicit transition from the data-gathering team to the engineering team. Run the transition by walking the engineering team through the affinity and consolidated work models as described in Part 4, then vision together. Remember: anytime you vision with a group, they have to be thoroughly grounded in the data first. They have to know it, and they

Use a transition process to pull in other people's ideas and their buy-in

have to believe it's valid. Once they've done the vision, the engineering team can work it out using the User Environment Design or their own process. This kind of transition is a good way to bring in the customer when you're designing an internal system. It allows customers and designers to look at and react to work issues together and design process and technical solutions together.

Before trying to run a transition process, clean up the consolidated models and affinity. This is a good point to get them online. A graphical language communicates by shape, color, relative size, arrangement on the page, and white space. If the models are too messy or poorly arranged, they won't communicate well. You're introducing people who aren't familiar with the models to a new set of concepts—they'll do better if they don't have to make sense of messy models.

When a small team does the design, it's important that the larger group understand what the data is and where it came from. The whole group has to feel involved and committed to the whole process. Otherwise, they'll decide that the design team is locked in their ivory tower, doesn't understand the real issues, and doesn't understand what it really takes to deliver a product. Keep lines of communication open so this doesn't happen. A useful goal is that every developer should go out on at least one customer interview. They can accompany the interviewer, and you can go over the interviewing rules with them ahead of time (have them read Chapter 3 on interviewing principles). When they understand where the data comes from, they'll have more confidence in the resulting design.

Maintaining a strategic customer focus

If you choose, the consolidated models can become a reusable resource over time, especially if you put them online. As the investigation and design team gathers additional data, filling in holes and expanding their understanding to new roles and tasks, they'll extend the models with this new information. When the engineering team ships a product and comes up for air, ready to think about what to do next, the models remind them of who the customer is and all the parts of their work that the system doesn't address yet. If the investigation team is

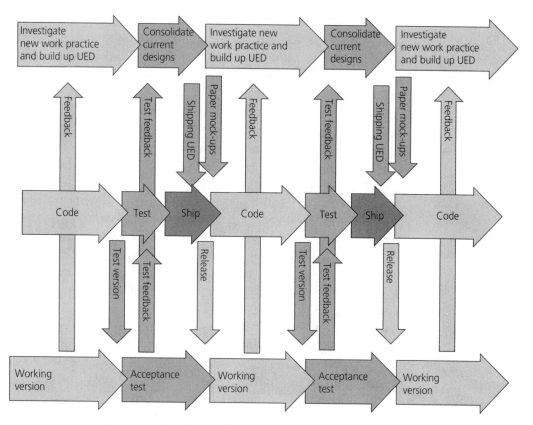

FIGURE 20.1 One way to handle the "feed the coders" problem. An ongoing team, which might include marketing, business analysts, and designers, continues to develop the high-level design, while the engineering team builds the previous version. When they're ready to do the next phase, the design team decides what part of the design is the right thing to ship next, ties up the loose ends, and drops out a specification for it (including a shipping User Environment Design and paper prototypes).

separate from the engineering team, they can expand and extend the models while the engineering team codes a release. They'll be ready with new insights and designs when a release goes out (Figure 20.1).

If, on the other hand, the investigation and coding teams are the same, the models help maintain a conversation about strategy and how to support the customer population. It's hard to maintain an ongoing conversation about strategy—the day-to-day distractions of getting a system built always seem more critical. But it is possible to take

Consolidated models help maintain a strategic focus

time out to look at an organization's strategy—for example, by scheduling a week every few months for focusing on strategic issues. When
you do this, the consolidated models, affinity, and long-term User
Environment Design together hold the strategic conversation. They
show who the customer population is, what their issues are, and how
the team is responding with a coherent system. The team can collect
data, if needed, to determine whether there have been changes in the
work practice that they need to respond to, whether their strategic
direction still makes sense, and whether they are on target for delivering to that strategy.

You can choose whether to start growing the work models from a
broad or narrow focus. Starting with a broad focus covers a wide variety of roles, work situations, and demographic variants quickly. However, it requires a lot of time up front to develop this high-level information, and it's easy to get overwhelmed by the scale of the problem.
It's also possible to develop the larger view over time. Start with the
focus needed to drive a specific project. As you do more projects,
reuse and add on to the data collected by the first project. From time
to time, you can gather a little data from very different situations just
to check your data. One team went to Japan and the military to get as
different a perspective on the work they were supporting as possible.
In this way you build up an understanding of the whole market without ever having to gather large amounts of information that aren't
immediately applicable to a single project. There is some risk in
designing from more limited data, and you won't see the whole diversity of the customer population immediately, but building up the data
this way can be a viable option.

HANDLING ORGANIZATIONAL CHANGE

It would be nice if everyone in an organization would cheerily adopt
new processes without any kind of resistance. It would be nice if the
same process would always work for everybody. In practice, that's never
the case. People are invested in their current ways of doing things. They
know what their process is and how to work it; they have the skills to
do it. They feel successful and don't want to hear how they could do

things better. Or, if they are not successful, they often feel too much under the gun to be open to new processes. Adopting a new process is hard because people have to rethink the ways they do things and take on new procedures without any guarantee that they'll be happier.

Any company has a core consisting of the products that the company was built around and that make a lot of the company's money. Then there are the outlying parts of the company, developing newer, unproven products. It's common for the outlying parts of a company to adopt a new approach first. They are less invested in standard ways of doing things, want to create something new, and haven't built up a tradition of how to do things —in fact, they are often reacting against the core company's traditions. These outlying groups are often the first to try new techniques and processes. Only after the techniques have proved themselves do they start to be adopted by more central parts of the company.

Change happens from the outside in and from the bottom up

As the new processes move into the core of the company, there will be more resistance, and the processes will be modified and adapted to the company's culture and approach. Techniques will be picked out and put into the context of the existing process; techniques will be renamed and reworked to fit with the organizational structure. People decide redesigned sequences are too hard and do storyboards instead—but they achieve the same intent. People decide not to draw a User Environment Design explicitly but lay out their UI windows and draw links between them so they can see their system's structure. People adopt Contextual Inquiry as a standard part of development while strenuously denying they are doing anything new. Changes of this sort are inevitable—you should expect to reevaluate and iterate the process continually as it spreads through an organization. But don't lose the core of the process as you go. It's not okay to talk only to your own salespeople or customer representatives instead of to customers directly. It's not okay to design with no data at all. Look at the intent of each technique in the process, and maintain that intent within your organizational context.

If you're trying to introduce new techniques to the organization as an individual contributor, recognize the difficulty of making change and work from the bottom up (Allen 1995). Don't try to start on the most important project your organization has; start with a small, focused problem. Start with a friendly team that wants to try new

things. Start with individual techniques—interviewing, for example—
and build up from there into more of the complete design process.

Every project tests the credibility of a new approach

Make an ally of a friendly manager and ensure that person knows what you're doing to introduce the techniques. Get a design room and paper it with customer data to increase visibility and curiosity. Remember that everything you do will add to the credibility of the new approach or destroy it. Make sure you start with something you can be successful at. And don't get too evangelistic. People don't like to be preached at.

If you're introducing new processes as a manager, recognize that the new ways of working will call on different skills—they will change the job that people do. Some people won't like this. Engineers tend to go into software because they like inventing cool things, coding them up, and shipping them. Some will decide it's okay for someone else to do the work of understanding the customers and designing for them—the engineer will code whatever they design because his interest and challenge is in designing the implementation. Others won't like to be constrained, won't be happy in the new organization, and will ultimately leave.

Other forms of resistance will show up, too. Usability experts are often the champions of contextual techniques because they are tired of

Include the people who might think their roles are being usurped

being asked to apply Band-Aids to broken products. But when they aren't driving the change, they may object to others redefining their work for them. Usability experts are comfortable with lab techniques and quantitative measurements; moving to qualitative field techniques may be a big change. IT departments may find that the identified customer representatives don't like developers talking to customers directly—put them on the team so they don't feel left out of the loop. And IT departments that place developers in the customer organization may find that they like doing quick fixes to each problem as it comes up. It doesn't require a lot of planning and the rewards are immediate. Moving to a process that expects them to look at the whole department's work may seem like overhead with no immediate return.

On the other hand, you want to look for the people who may not have stood out in the past, but who will be able to pick up and excel at the new skills. We've found that people such as those in documentation who have not stood out in traditional development have insight into work practice, are able to interview and see design implications, and can build up a vision for a synthetic corporate response. These people will move into more prominent positions as their skills become more desirable. Expect some organizational disruption as people search for the right new role for themselves.

Because a customer-centered process puts design up front, people's initial reaction will be that it takes longer. Talk about what true time costs are—there's a lot of deciding, arguing, redeciding, and deciding again when there's no real data to base decisions on. Remember that a customer-centered process will replace some of the requirements specification work you currently do. Show how the deliverables of Contextual Design feed or replace the deliverables expected of your teams. And do as one manager does when people tell her it will take too long to get customer data: she asks, "When do you need the results by?"—and then manages the process to deliver results to that date.

Try to measure the true costs of not designing from data

There are some real time sinks inherent in customer-centered approaches that you can do something to overcome. For commercial companies, setting up customer visits can be time-consuming when there are no procedures or organization in place for it. There may be an existing organization that can take on the role—marketing might do it, or you may be able to build on your process for recruiting field test sites or usability test users. Your sales and marketing organization, or your internal customer representative, may adopt the attitude that access to the customers is their responsibility and keep the design team away. Management can change attitudes by stating the expectations for adopting customer-centered design. (Wilson et al. [1997] has a further discussion of the practical difficulties of achieving greater user involvement.)

Get logistical problems out of people's way

Introducing change to an organization is possible, either as an individual contributor or as a manager. But from either position, you have to deal with the reactions people will have and the roadblocks they will put in the way. Recognize the issues and deal with them as they come up to make change happen. Measure your success not by how far you are from the end state you can imagine, but by the change you've introduced in people's daily work practice. Every new technique or expectation you put in place is a success. If your teams now expect to gather customer data when before they did not, it's a success even if they aren't gathering as much or using it as well as you would like. And remember that changing an organization takes time—two years to introduce a new technique into an organization so that it becomes part of the culture.

DESIGNING THE DESIGN PROCESS

We've discussed customer-centered design all through this book— how to understand the customer and design to their needs. Underlying all these conversations has been the assumption that the design process itself is a topic for design. The ability to see, manipulate, and design a process for delivering systems is a fundamental skill for anyone trying to change the way an organization works. Throughout this book we've discussed the underlying rationale for the different parts of Contextual Design, both to show why it has its current structure and to guide you in adapting it to your needs.

Designing your design process is just another exercise in customer-centered design. Your users are the people who make it possible to create a system: engineers, marketers, analysts, documentation people, usability people, and others. The organization they are a part of, their attitudes toward the design task, and the way they approach the job are all elements of their work practice that you must account for. Just as with any design, you are looking for the optimum match to this work practice—the maximum improvement to their way of working that they can successfully adopt. And you'll be patient because you know that true transformation happens over successive steps, each one incremental, but adding up to radical changes in the way people work.

Create an organization that knows how to manage its own processes

As you introduce new processes, you have the opportunity to create process awareness in your organization. Continuous evaluation and iteration of the processes you use will make the processes people use a topic of conversation. And that will liberate people by giving them control over the processes they live in.

Contextual Design is the result of such an inquiry into the process of systems design. It balances the need of an engineering organization to produce a result in a given time frame against the need of the design team to really understand their customers and how they work. It provides a structure concrete enough that people know what to do when they come into work in the morning, but with freedom enough for people to be creative. Take it, adapt it, and try it out on your own problems. Your competitors are using processes like this to develop their new systems. You can, too.

KAREN AND INGRID'S STORY

Last year a small pharmaceutical research lab in our company asked for a team to design some software to run their work process. This lab was new, and many of the people we were supporting had only been doing the work a few months. Because they did not have established ways of working, they were open to our investigating how they did their jobs and ways their work could be changed. However, the team and the lab were both on a tight schedule. We needed to deliver a working system in three months.

As two of our company's trained experts in Contextual Design, we were excited and a bit overwhelmed by this opportunity. Part of our strategy for getting the Contextual Design finished quickly was to have several team members who were already trained in Contextual Design. We had two developers who were already fully trained, two who were not trained (and whom we only minimally trained), and a project leader who participated fully in the training. Two of our customers were also involved peripherally and received some training.

The system would have only four direct users, and we interviewed all of them. The customers learned a lot about their jobs through the interviews and consolidations. We consolidated some of the data with the users so they would understand where the data and designs came from and could participate in visioning the new system.

To reduce the time necessary for the Contextual Design process, we consolidated only three models—the affinity, the flow model, and the sequences. We then visioned and made redesigned sequence models (which were a precursor to storyboards). Based on these, we built a User Environment Design for the new system. Our users got very excited about the User Environment Design. They found they could see their work process in this model and could see how the system would support the process and the different roles in the organization. In fact, the managers of the lab had a number of conversations about their work practice while walking the User Environment model.

The UI design and object modeling went forward in parallel once we had the User Environment Design in place. For the UI, we built paper prototypes and did three rounds of testing (UI interviews) on them before moving to online prototypes. We used the redesigned sequences and User Environment Design to develop use cases, using the focus areas on the ⇨

User Environment to identify potential objects. We kept the User Environment Design and use cases synchronized pretty well until we got to coding.

The customers are excited and involved and used our data to help them see how to improve their own processes. Their new system actually eliminated a large portion of the work one person was doing. She spent a lot of time reformatting files as part of analyzing them. Now, she can do this analysis directly and spend this saved time on other projects.

For this focused project, the process took us eight weeks full-time, from initial data gathering through the object modeling and UI design. The Contextual Design portion took only five weeks. ❑

Afterword

We said in Chapter 5 that any domain of knowledge tends to generate words that communicate the thoughts and concepts important to that domain. These words become the vehicle for communication between people, but they also frame and limit what we think.

Our own field is full of such words: usability engineer, software developer, human factors engineer, user interface designer. When we use these concepts to help us identify and promote the skills necessary to deliver useful systems, they serve us well; but when they lead us to balkanize our organizations, separating the functions into groups focused only on their own part of the problem, they become stumbling blocks.

I started in this industry as a liaison between customer service and engineering. From this position I learned firsthand how different the two points of view are and how difficult it is to bridge the gulf. There is no good way to explain to an extremely competent database expert why his technically sophisticated three-phase commit algorithm is simply beside the point given the reality of specific customer needs. Even when there's a clear need to introduce new ways of working, making change happen is another story. People are helpless to adopt new ways of working unless they know of available alternatives and have the skill to put them into action. My first development work was on data dictionaries, which had (at the time) the distinction of being almost the only point of integration between development tools. Consistent use of the dictionary would make or break the integration among tools, but no one had any idea how to get the different groups to agree. I naively took the problem on and had no trouble generating interest in solving the problem—in fact, I ended up with representatives of 14 teams in a room and not the least idea what to do with them. The idea that an engineer should learn how to manage a room as a basic tool of the trade was foreign to the expectations of the time, as it is still.

Just as our language tends to compartmentalize our organizations, so it tends to compartmentalize the development process itself. "Requirements analysis," or "needs analysis"—whatever term is currently fashionable—splits the initial task of determining what a system will be from the rest of development. In doing so, it gives developers a reason for thinking "It's not my job. It's marketing's job—or the analysts' job—or the customers' job to tell us what they want." But it's not a job that can be done in isolation. Black-box design is a useful implementation strategy but not a good approach to organizational design. We need development expertise involved in understanding the customer's problems, and we need the other functions involved in understanding how to turn the solution to these problems into a system structure that works for the user.

Much of the work that Karen and I have done together has focused on how to put the techniques, process tools, and interpersonal tools into the hands of project teams so that they can solve their own problems. Contextual Inquiry hit me at just the right time—I had recently completed a round of customer visits for a product I was working on, using traditional interviews and discussions, so I recognized the idea as stunningly obvious on the one hand and yet totally foreign to the accepted way of gathering product requirements on the other. But I wasn't interested in the technique to give it away—as a project leader, I wanted it for myself and my team, and I wanted to build it up into a rational way of designing products. So we've always approached the process not as an add-on, or a tool for those with specialized expertise, but as a way to get the basic job of design done.

We've had to learn along the way that what makes a process rational differs from organization to organization and from team to team. Whether you're designing what you'll do for the next hour or how you'll run a two-year project, you can't get out of process design. Contextual Design is the raw material for designing a workable process. We've had the privilege of working with teams that learned how to manage and reinvent their own processes, picking up the customer-centered techniques while inventing and integrating new approaches and techniques along the way. We've distributed some of their stories throughout the book. These teams have taught us what is possible, and for that, we are grateful.

Hugh Beyer

Readings and Resources

PERSPECTIVES ON THE CUSTOMER-CENTERED APPROACH

There are many people writing about a customer-centered approach to systems design, some focusing on contextual techniques, some looking at larger issues. Here are a few different perspectives on the topic and the issues.

Constantine, L. 1995a. *Constantine on Peopleware.* Englewood Cliffs, NJ: Prentice Hall.

Greenbaum, J., and M. Kyng, eds. 1991. *Design at Work: Cooperative Design of Computer Systems.* Mahwah, NJ: Lawrence Erlbaum Associates.

Grudin, J. 1990. "Interface." *Proceedings of the Conference on Computer-Supported Cooperative Work,* October 7–10, Los Angeles, CA, p. 269. New York: ACM

Kapor, M. 1991. "A Software Design Manifesto: Time for a Change." *Dr. Dobb's Journal* 172: 62–68 (Jan).

Landauer, T. 1996. *The Trouble with Computers.* Cambridge, MA: MIT Press.

Norman, D. A., and S. W. Draper, eds. 1986. *User Centered System Design.* Mahwah, NJ: Lawrence Erlbaum Associates.

Potts, C. 1995. "Invented Requirements and Imagined Customers: Requirements Engineering for Off-the-Shelf Software." *Proceedings of the International Symposium on Requirements Engineering,* pp. 128–130. New York: IEEE Press.

Rasmussen, J., A. M. Pejtersen, L. P. Goodstein. 1994. *Cognitive Systems Engineering.* New York: John Wiley & Sons.

Winograd, T., ed. 1996. *Bringing Design to Software.* Reading, MA: Addison-Wesley.

PHILOSOPHICAL BACKGROUND

Though it's not necessary to understand the techniques, Contextual Design is based on philisophical and psychological principles that guide how to gather effective data and how to use that data to build an understanding of what to design. For those who are interested, here are some of the fundamental works that shed light on Contextual Design.

Fowler, T. 1876. *The Elements of Inductive Logic,* 3d ed. Oxford: Clarendon Press.

Glaser, B., and A. Strauss. 1967. *The Discovery of Grounded Theory: Strategies for Qualitative Research.* Chicago: Aldine Publishing Company.

Goffman, E. 1959. *The Presentation of Self in Everyday Life.* Garden City, NY: Doubleday.

Hutchins, E. 1995. *Cognition in the Wild.* Cambridge, MA: MIT Press.

Nardi, B. 1996. *Context and Consciousness: Activity Theory and Human-Computer Interaction.* Cambridge, MA: MIT Press.

Polanyi, M. 1958. *Personal Knowledge: Towards a Post-Critical Philosophy.* Chicago: University of Chicago Press.

————. 1967. *The Tacit Dimension.* London and New York: Routledge & Kegan Paul.

Whiteside, J., and D. Wixon. 1988. "Contextualism as a World View for the Reformation of Meetings." *Proceedings of the Conference on Computer-Supported Cooperative Work,* September 26–28, Portland, OR, p. 369.

Winograd, T., and F. Flores. 1986. *Understanding Computers and Cognition.* Norwood, NH: Ablex.

APPROACHES TO WORK MODELING

Modeling the way people work for the purpose of design is a problem as old as software engineering. Here are some approaches to representing work that others have taken.

Clement, A. 1990. "Cooperative Support for Computer Work: A Social Perspective on the Empowering of End Users." *Proceedings of the Conference on Computer-Supported Cooperative Work,* October 7–10, Los Angeles, CA, p. 223. New York: ACM.

Easterbrook, S. 1993. "Domain Modeling with Hierarchies of Alternative Viewpoints." *Proceedings of the 1993 IEEE International Symposium on Requirements Engineering,* January 4–6, San Diego, CA, p. 65. Los Alamitos, CA: IEEE Computer Society Press.

Hughes, J., J. O'Brien, T. Rodden, M. Rouncefield, and I. Sommerville. 1995. "Presenting Ethnography in the Requirements Process." *Proceedings of the Second IEEE International Symposium on Requirements Engineering,* March 27–29, York, England. Los Alamitos, CA: IEEE Computer Society Press.

Jackson, M., and P. Zave. 1993. "Domain Descriptions." *Proceedings of the 1993 IEEE International Symposium on Requirements Engineering,* January 4–6, San Diego, CA, p. 56. Los Alamitos, CA: IEEE Computer Society Press.

Johnson, P., et al. 1988. "Task-Related Knowledge Structures: Analysis, Modeling and Application." In *People and Computers IV,* eds. D. M. Jones and R. Winder, pp. 35–62. Cambridge; New York: Cambridge University Press.

Suchman, L. 1989. *Plans and Situated Actions. Cambridge: Cambridge University Press.*

Suchman, L., ed. 1995. "Representations of Work." *Communications of the ACM/Special issue* 38(9) (Sep).

Yu, E. 1993. "Modelling Organizations for Information Systems Requirements Engineering." *Proceedings of the 1993 IEEE International Symposium on Requirements Engineering,* January 4–6, San Diego, CA, p. 34. Los Alamitos, CA: IEEE Computer Society Press.

CUSTOMER-CENTERED DESIGN AS PART OF SOFTWARE DEVELOPMENT

Understanding customers and designing for them is just one part of the overall systems lifecycle. It has to fit into the overall work of software development and has to fit the organizations that design and build software. The following readings discuss how customer-centered techniques fit into the larger context.

Beyer, H. 1993. "Where Do the Objects Come From?" *Software Development '93 Fall Proceedings,* August, Boston, MA.

Bustard, D., and T. Dobbin. 1996. "Integrating Soft Systems and Object-Oriented Analysis." *Proceedings of the Second International Conference on*

Requirements Engineering, April 15–18, Colorado Springs, CO, p. 52. Los Alamitos, CA: IEEE Computer Society Press.

Constantine, L. 1996. "Usage-Centered Software Engineering: New Models, Methods, and Metrics." *Proceedings of the 1996 International Conference on Software Engineering: Education & Practice,* January 24–27, Dunedin, New Zealand: New Zealand Computer Society.

Goguen, J. 1996. "Formality and Informality in Requirements Engineering." *Proceedings of the Second International Conference on Requirements Engineering,* April 15–18, Colorado Springs, CO, p. 102. Los Alamitos, CA: IEEE Computer Society Press.

Hefley, W., and Romo, J. 1994. "New Concepts in Engineering Processes for Developing Integrated Task Environments." *Proceedings of the IEEE 1994 National Aerospace and Electronics Conference* (NAECON 1994).

Hefley, W., et al. 1994. "Integrating Human Factors with Software Engineering Practices." *Proceedings of the Human Factors and Ergonomics Society, 39th Annual Meeting,* Nashville, TN, October 24–28, pp. 315–319. Santa Monica, CA: Human Factors and Ergonomics Society.

Holtzblatt, K., and H. Beyer, eds. 1995. "Requirements Gathering: The Human Factor." *Communications of the ACM/Special issue* 38(5) (May).

Hughes, J., J. O'Brien, T. Rodden, M. Rouncefield, and I. Sommerville. 1995. "Presenting Ethnography in the Requirements Process." *Proceedings of the Second IEEE International Symposium on Requirements Engineering,* March 27–29, York, England. Los Alamitos, CA: IEEE Computer Society Press.

Rosson, M., and Carroll, J. 1995. "Integrating Task and Software Development for Object-Oriented Applications." *CHI '95 Conference Proceedings,* May 7–11, Denver, CO, p. 377. New York: ACM.

Sommerville, I., T. Rodden, P. Sawyer, R. Bentley, and M. Twidale. 1993. "Integrating Ethnography into the Requirements Engineering Process." *Proceedings of the 1993 IEEE International Symposium on Requirements Engineering,* January 4–6, San Diego, CA, p. 165. Los Alamitos, CA: IEEE Computer Society Press.

Approaches to paper prototyping

Creating rapid, low-fidelity prototypes in paper and cardboard has a history and literature derived from the Participatory Design movement. Here are some discussons of paper prototyping and Participatory Design in general.

Kyng, M. 1988. "Designing for a Dollar a Day." *Proceedings of the Conference on Computer-Supported Cooperative Work,* September 26–28, Portland, OR, p. 178.

Muller, M. 1991. "PICTIVE—An exploration in participatory design." *Human Factors in Computing Systems CHI '91 Conference Proceedings,* pp. 225–231.

Muller, M., and S. Kuhn, eds. 1993. "Participatory Design." *Communications of the ACM/Special issue* 36(4) (Jun).

Schuler, D., and A. Namioka, eds. 1993. *Participatory Design: Principles and Practices.* Mahwah, NJ: Lawrence Erlbaum Associates.

Wulff, W., S. Evenson, and J. Rheinfrank. 1990. "Animating Interfaces." *Proceedings of the Conference on Computer-Supported Cooperative Work,* October 7–10, Los Angeles, CA, p. 241. New York: ACM.

Case histories

Here are some case histories that use contextual techniques and customer-centered design on different practical problems.

Moll-Carrillo, H., G. Salomon, M. Marsh, J. Suri, and P. Spreenberg. 1995. "Articulating a Metaphor through User-Centered Design." *CHI '95 Conference Proceedings,* May 7–11, Denver, CO, p. 566. New York: ACM.

Lundell, J., and S. Anderson. 1995. "Designing a 'Front Panel' for Unix: The Evolution of a Metaphor." *CHI '95 Conference Proceedings,* May 7–11, Denver, CO, p. 573. New York: ACM.

Coble, J., J. Karat, and M. Kahn. 1997. "Maintaining a Focus on User Requirements throughout the Development of Clinical Workstation Software." *CHI '97 Conference Proceedings,* March 22–27, Atlanta, GA, p. 170. New York: ACM.

Wilson, S., M. Bekker, P. Johnson, and H. Johnson. 1997. "Helping and Hindering User Involvement—A Tale of Everyday Design." *CHI '97 Conference Proceedings,* March 22–27, Atlanta, GA, p. 178. New York: ACM.

Wixon, D., and J. Ramey, eds. 1996. *Field Methods Case Book for Product Design.* New York: John Wiley & Sons.

References

Allen, C. D. 1995. "Succeeding as a Clandestine Change Agent." *Communications of the ACM6* 38(5).

Beyer, H. 1993. "Where Do the Objects Come From?" *Software Development '93 Fall Proceedings,* August, Boston, MA.

———. 1994. "Calling Down the Lightning." *IEEE Software* 11(5):106.

Boas, M., and S. Chain. 1977. *Big Mac: The Unauthorized Story of McDonald's.* New York: The New American Library.

Boehm, B. W. 1976. "Software Engineering." *IEEE Transactions on Computers* 25(12):1226–1241.

Brassard, M. 1989. *Memory Jogger Plus.* Methuen, MA: GOAL/QPC.

Bustard, D., and T. Dobbin. 1996. "Integrating Soft Systems and Object-Oriented Analysis." *Proceedings of the Second International Conference on Requirements Engineering,* April 15–18, Colorado Springs, CO, p. 52. Los Alamitos, CA: IEEE Computer Society Press.

Carlshamre, P., and J. Karlsson. 1996. "A Usability-Oriented Approach to Requirements Engineering." *Proceedings of the Second International Conference on Requirements Engineering,* April 15–18, Colorado Springs, CO, p. 145. Los Alamitos, CA: IEEE Computer Society Press.

Carter, J., Jr. 1991. "Combining Task Analysis with Software Engineering for Designing Interactive Systems." In *Taking Software Design Seriously,* ed. John Karat, p. 209. New York: Academic Press.

Catledge, L., and C. Potts. 1996. "Collaboration during Conceptual Design." *Proceedings of the Second International Conference on Requirements Engineering,* April 15–18, Colorado Springs, CO, p. 182. Los Alamitos, CA: IEEE Computer Society Press.

Chin, G., Jr., M. Rosson, and J. Carroll. 1997. "Participatory Analysis: Shared Development of Requirements from Scenarios." *CHI '97 Conference Proceedings,* March 22–27, Atlanta, GA, p. 162. New York: ACM.

Clement, A. 1990. "Cooperative Support for Computer Work: A Social Perspective on the Empowering of End Users." *Proceedings of the Conference on Computer-Supported Cooperative Work,* October 7–10, Los Angeles, CA, p. 223. New York: ACM.

Coble, J., J. Karat, and M. Kahn. 1997. "Maintaining a Focus on User Requirements throughout the Development of Clinical Workstation Software." *CHI '97 Conference Proceedings,* March 22–27, Atlanta, GA, p. 170. New York: ACM.

Constantine, L. 1992. "Getting the User Interface Right: Basic Principles." *Software Development '92 Fall Proceedings,* September, Boston, MA.

———. 1994a. "Persistent Usability: A Multiphasic User Interface Architecture for Supporting the Full Usage Lifecycle." In *OzCHI 94 Proceedings,* eds. S. Howard and Y. Leung. Melbourne.

———. 1994b. "Up the Waterfall." *Software Development* 2(1) (Jan).

———. 1995a. *Constantine on Peopleware.* Englewood Cliffs, NJ: Prentice Hall.

———. 1995b. "Essential Modeling: Use Cases for User Interfaces." *ACM interactions* 2(2) (Apr):34–46.

———. 1996. "Usage-Centered Software Engineering: New Models, Methods, and Metrics." *Proceedings of the 1996 International Conference on Software Engineering: Education & Practice,* January 24–27, Dunedin, New Zealand: New Zealand Computer Society.

Curtis, B., and B. Hefley. 1992. "Defining a Place for Interface Engineering." *IEEE Software* (Mar):84–86.

———. 1994. "A WIMP No More: The Maturing of User Interface Engineering." *ACM interactions* 1(1):22–34.

Daley, E. 1977. "Management of Software Development." *IEEE Transactions on Software Engineering* 3(3):229–242.

Davis, A. 1993. *Software Requirements: Objects, Functions, and States.* Englewood Cliffs, NJ: Prentice Hall.

Denning, P., and P. Dargan. 1996. "Action-Centered Design." In *Bringing Design to Software,* ed. T. Winograd, p. 116. Reading, MA: Addison-Wesley.

Easterbrook, S. 1993. "Domain Modeling with Hierarchies of Alternative Viewpoints." *Proceedings of the 1993 IEEE International Symposium on Requirements Engineering,* January 4–6, San Diego, CA, p. 65. Los Alamitos, CA: IEEE Computer Society Press.

Ehn, P. 1988. *Work-Oriented Design of Computer Artifacts.* Falkoping, Sweden: Gummessons. International distribution by Almqvist & Wiksell International; also Coronet Books, Philadelphia, PA.

Ehn, P., and M. Kyng. 1991. "Cardboard Computers: Mocking-it-up or Hands-on the Future." In *Design at Work,* eds. J. Greenbaum and M. Kyng, p. 169. Mahwah, NJ: Lawrence Erlbaum Associates.

Fisher, B. A. 1980. *Small Group Decision Making,* 2d ed. New York: McGraw-Hill.

Fowler, T. 1876. *The Elements of Inductive Logic,* 3d ed. Oxford: Clarendon Press.

Glaser, B., and A. Strauss. 1967. *The Discovery of Grounded Theory: Strategies for Qualitative Research.* Chicago: Aldine Publishing Company.

Goffman, E. 1959. *The Presentation of Self in Everyday Life.* Garden City, NY: Doubleday.

Goguen, J. 1996. "Formality and Informality in Requirements Engineering." *Proceedings of the Second International Conference on Requirements Engineering,* April 15–18, Colorado Springs, CO, p. 102. Los Alamitos, CA: IEEE Computer Society Press.

Goguen, J., and C. Linde. 1993. "Techniques for Requirements Elicitation." *Proceedings of the 1993 IEEE International Symposium on Requirements Engineering,* January 4–6, San Diego, CA, p. 152. Los Alamitos, CA: IEEE Computer Society Press.

Gomaa, H. 1983. "The Impact of Rapid Prototyping on Specifying User Requirements." *ACM SIGSOFT Software Engineering Notes* 8(2) (Apr).

Grandin, T. 1996. *Thinking in Pictures: And Other Reports from My Life with Autism.* Garden City, NY: Doubleday.

Greenbaum, J., and M. Kyng, eds. 1991. *Design at Work: Cooperative Design of Computer Systems.* Mahwah, NJ: Lawrence Erlbaum Associates.

Grudin, J. 1990. "Interface." *Proceedings of the Conference on Computer-Supported Cooperative Work,* October 7–10, Los Angeles, CA, p. 269. New York: ACM.

Hansen, A. 1997. "Reflections on I/Design: User Interface Design at a Start-up." *CHI '97 Conference Proceedings,* March 22–27, Atlanta, GA, p. 178. New York: ACM.

Hauser, J. R., and D. Clausing. 1988. "The House of Quality." *Harvard Business Review* 66(3): 63–73.

Hefley, W. E. 1993. "The Cobbler's Children: Applying Total Quality Management to Business Process Improvement, Information Engineering and Software Engineering." *ACM Software Engineering Notes* 18(4): 19–25.

———. 1996. "Usability Trends in Government." Keynote address at NIST Symposium on Usability Engineering: Industry-Government Collaboration for System Effectiveness and Efficiency, Gaithersburg, MD, February 26.

Hefley, W., and Romo, J. 1994. "New Concepts in Engineering Processes for Developing Integrated Task Environments." *Proceedings of the IEEE 1994 National Aerospace and Electronics Conference (NAECON 1994).*

Hefley, W., et al. 1994. "Integrating Human Factors with Software Engineering Practices." *Proceedings of the Human Factors and Ergonomics Society,* 39th Annual Meeting, Nashville, TN, October 24–28, pp. 315–319. Santa Monica, CA: Human Factors and Ergonomics Society.

Holtzblatt, K., and S. Jones. 1995. "Conducting and Analyzing a Contextual Interview." In *Readings in Human-Computer Interaction: Toward the Year 2000 2d,* eds. R. M. Baecker, J. Grudin, W. A. S. Buxton, S. Greenberg. San Francisco: Morgan Kaufman. p. 241.

Holtzblatt, K., and H. Beyer, eds. 1995. "Requirements Gathering: The Human Factor." *Communications of the ACM/Special issue* 38(5) (May).

Hsia, P., C. Hsu, D. Kung, and L. Holder. 1996. "User-Centered System Decomposition: Z-Based Requirements Clustering." *Proceedings of the Second International Conference on Requirements Engineering,* April 15–18, Colorado Springs, CO, p. 126. Los Alamitos, CA: IEEE Computer Society Press.

Hughes, J., J. O'Brien, T. Rodden, M. Rouncefield, and I. Sommerville. 1995. "Presenting Ethnography in the Requirements Process." *Proceedings of the Second IEEE International Symposium on Requirements Engineering,* March 27–29, York, England. Los Alamitos, CA: IEEE Computer Society Press.

Hutchins, E. 1995. *Cognition in the Wild.* Cambridge, MA: MIT Press.

Jackson, M., and P. Zave. 1993. "Domain Descriptions." *Proceedings of the 1993 IEEE International Symposium on Requirements Engineering,* January 4–6, San Diego, CA, p. 56. Los Alamitos, CA: IEEE Computer Society Press.

Jacobson, I., M. Christerson, P. Jonsson, and G. Övergaard. 1992. *Object-Oriented Software Engineering: A Use Case Driven Approach.* Reading, MA: Addison-Wesley.

Johnson, P., et al. 1988. "Task-Related Knowledge Structures: Analysis, Modeling and Application." In *People and Computers IV,* eds. D. M. Jones and R. Winder, pp. 35–62. Cambridge; New York: Cambridge University Press.

Kapor, M. 1991. "A Software Design Manifesto: Time for a Change." *Dr. Dobb's Journal* 172:62–68 (Jan).

Kawakita, J. 1982. *The Original KJ Method.* Tokyo: Kawakita Research Institute.

Keil, M., and E. Carmel. 1995. "Customer-Developer Links in Software Development." *Communications of the ACM* 38(5):33–44.

Keller, M., and K. Shumate. 1992. *Software Specification and Design.* New York: John Wiley & Sons.

Kelley, D., and B. Hartfield. 1996. "The Designer's Stance." In *Bringing Design to Software,* ed. T. Winograd, p. 116. Reading, MA: Addison-Wesley.

Kensing, F., and K. H. Madsen. 1991. "Generating Visions: Future Workshops and Metaphorical Design." In *Design at Work,* eds. J. Greenbaum and M. Kyng, p. 155. Mahwah, NJ: Lawrence Erlbaum Associates.

Kyng, M. 1988. "Designing for a Dollar a Day." *Proceedings of the Conference on Computer-Supported Cooperative Work,* September 26–28, Portland, OR, p. 178.

Landauer, T. 1996. *The Trouble with Computers.* Cambridge, MA: MIT Press.

Long, J., S. Hakiel, B. Hefley, L. Damodoran, and K. Y. Lim. 1994. "Guilty or Not Guilty? Human Factors Structured Methods on Trial." *Human Factors in Computing Systems—CHI '94 Conference Companion, Boston, MA,* April 24–28, pp. 181–182. New York: ACM.

Loucopoulos, P., and V. Karakostas. 1995. *System Requirements Engineering.* New York: McGraw-Hill.

Lubars, M., C. Potts, and C. Richter. 1993. "A Review of the State of the Practice in Requirements Modeling." *Proceedings of the 1993 IEEE International Symposium on Requirements Engineering,* January 4–6, San Diego, CA, p. 2. Los Alamitos, CA: IEEE Computer Society Press.

Lundell, J., and S. Anderson. 1995. "Designing a 'Front Panel' for Unix: The Evolution of a Metaphor." *CHI '95 Conference Proceedings,* May 7–11, Denver, CO, p. 573. New York: ACM.

Martin, C. E., W. E. Hefley, D. J. Bristow, and D. J. Steele. 1992. "Team-Based Incremental Acquisition of Large-Scale Unprecedented Systems." *Policy Sciences* 25:57–75.

Martin, J., and J. Odell. 1992. *Object-Oriented Analysis and Design.* Englewood Cliffs, NJ: Prentice Hall.

McClelland, I., B. Taylor, and B. Hefley. 1996. "User-Centered Design Principles: How Far Have They Been Industrialised?" *ACM SIGCHI Bulletin* 28(4):23–25.

McMenamin, S., and J. Palmer. 1984. *Essential Systems Analysis.* Englewood Cliffs, NJ: Yourdon Press.

Moll-Carrillo, H., G. Salomon, M. Marsh, J. Suri, and P. Spreenberg. 1995. "Articulating a Metaphor through User-Centered Design." *CHI '95 Conference Proceedings,* May 7–11, Denver, CO, p. 566. New York: ACM.

Moore, G. 1991. *Crossing the Chasm: Marketing and Selling Technology Products to Mainstream Customers.* New York: HarperBusiness.

Muller, M. 1991. "PICTIVE—An exploration in participatory design." *Human Factors in Computing Systems CHI '91 Conference Proceedings,* pp. 225–231.

Muller, M., and S. Kuhn, eds. 1993. "Participatory Design." *Communications of the ACM/Special issue* 36(4) (Jun).

Muller, M., R. Carr, C. Ashworth, B. Diekmann, C. Wharton, C. Eickstaedt, and J. Clonts. 1995. "Telephone Operators as Knowledge Workers: Consultants Who Meet Customer Needs." *CHI '95 Conference Proceedings,* May 7–11, Denver, CO, p. 130. New York: ACM.

Nardi, B. 1996. *Context and Consciousness: Activity Theory and Human-Computer Interaction.* Cambridge, MA: MIT Press.

Norman, D. A., and S. W. Draper, eds. 1986. *User Centered System Design.* Mahwah, NJ: Lawrence Erlbaum Associates.

Orr, J. 1986. "Narratives at Work—Storytelling as Cooperative Diagnostic Activity." *Proceedings of the Conference on Computer-Supported Cooperative Work,* December 3–5, Austin, Texas.

Polanyi, M. 1958. *Personal Knowledge: Towards a Post-Critical Philosophy.* Chicago: University of Chicago Press.

———. 1967. *The Tacit Dimension.* London and New York: Routledge & Kegan Paul.

Potts, C. 1995. "Invented Requirements and Imagined Customers: Requirements Engineering for Off-the-Shelf Software." *Proceedings of the International Symposium on Requirements Engineering,* pp. 128–130. New York: IEEE Press.

Pugh, S. 1991. *Total Design.* Reading, MA: Addison-Wesley.

Rasmussen, J., A. M. Pejtersen, L. P. Goodstein. 1994. *Cognitive Systems Engineering.* New York: John Wiley & Sons.

Rheinfrank, J., and Evenson, S. 1996. "Design Languages." In *Bringing Design to Software,* ed. T. Winograd, p. 77. Reading, MA: Addison-Wesley.

Rosson, M., and Carroll, J. 1995. "Integrating Task and Software Development for Object-Oriented Applications." *CHI '95 Conference Proceedings,* May 7–11, Denver, CO, p. 377. New York: ACM.

Rumbaugh, J., M. Blaha, W. Premerlani, F. Eddy, and W. Lorensen. 1991. *Object-Oriented Modeling and Design.* Englewood Cliffs, NJ: Prentice Hall.

Schon, D. 1983. *The Reflective Practitioner.* New York: Basic Books.

Schuler, D., and A. Namioka, eds. 1993. *Participatory Design: Principles and Practices.* Mahwah, NJ: Lawrence Erlbaum Associates.

Sommerville, I., T. Rodden, P. Sawyer, R. Bentley, and M. Twidale. 1993. "Integrating Ethnography into the Requirements Engineering Process." *Proceedings of the 1993 IEEE International Symposium on Requirements Engineering,* January 4–6, San Diego, CA, p. 165. Los Alamitos, CA: IEEE Computer Society Press.

Suchman, L. 1989. *Plans and Situated Actions.* Cambridge: Cambridge University Press.

———, L., ed. 1995. "Representations of Work." *Communications of the ACM/Special issue* 38(9) (Sep).

Sumner, T. 1995. "The High-Tech Toolbelt: A Study of Designers in the Workplace." *CHI '95 Conference Proceedings,* May 7–11, Denver, CO, p. 178. New York: ACM.

Terwilliger, R., and P. Polson. 1997. "Relationships between Users' and Interfaces' Task Representations." *CHI 97 Conference Proceedings,* March 22–27, Atlanta, GA, p. 99. New York: ACM.

Whiteside, J., and D. Wixon. 1988. "Contextualism as a World View for the Reformation of Meetings." *Proceedings of the Conference on Computer-Supported Cooperative Work,* September 26–28, Portland, OR, p. 369.

Wilson, S., M. Bekker, P. Johnson, and H. Johnson. 1997. "Helping and Hindering User Involvement—A Tale of Everyday Design." *CHI 97 Conference Proceedings,* March 22–27, Atlanta, GA, p. 178. New York: ACM.

Winograd, T., and F. Flores. 1986. *Understanding Computers and Cognition.* Norwood, NH: Ablex.

Winograd, T., ed. 1996. *Bringing Design to Software.* Reading, MA: Addison-Wesley.

Wirfs-Brock, R. 1993. "Designing Scenarios: Making the Case for a Use Case Framework." *SmallTalk Report* (Nov–Dec).

Wixon, D., and J. Ramey, eds. 1996. *Field Methods Case Book for Product Design.* New York: John Wiley & Sons.

Wulff, W., S. Evenson, and J. Rheinfrank. 1990. "Animating Interfaces." *Proceedings of the Conference on Computer-Supported Cooperative Work,* October 7–10, Los Angeles, CA, p. 241. New York: ACM.

Yourdon, E., and L. Constantine. 1979. *Structured Design.* Englewood Cliffs, NJ: Prentice Hall.

Yu, E. 1993. "Modelling Organizations for Information Systems Requirements Engineering." *Proceedings of the 1993 IEEE International Symposium on Requirements Engineering,* January 4–6, San Diego, CA, p. 34. Los Alamitos, CA: IEEE Computer Society Press.

Index

About the Authors

Together, Karen Holtzblatt and Hugh Beyer are founders of InContext Enterprises, specializing in process and product design consulting. This company works with major players in the shrink-wrap software industry, high-tech hardware design firms, and IT organizations, helping them develop product designs and product strategies and introducing customer-centered design into their organizations.

Before founding InContext, Hugh Beyer and Karen Holtzblatt collaborated on customer-centered design of integrated CASE systems and a strategy for integration of proprietary and third-party tools. At this time, they developed and refined the Contextual Design approach through working with 20 development teams to implement aspects of the integrated environment.

Hugh Beyer has designed and developed software for 16 years. In Digital Equipment Corporation's customer service organization, he managed the introduction and support of new information management products and worked with engineers to understand the impact of their products on customers.

He was a principal architect and developer for Digital's leading entity-relationship repository system. After the successful introduction of the repository product, Beyer pioneered the definition of object-oriented repositories with a standard object model for integration and later built a customizable windowing interface to this repository system. He applied object-oriented analysis and design techniques to define one of the first repository-based I-CASE environments in the industry; the implementation of this strategy forms the basis for Digital's current repository architecture.

As Digital's representative on national and international standards bodies, Beyer introduced ATIS, an object-oriented repository standard based on Digital's experience. He was primarily responsible for the adoption of this proposal by ANSI for the national standard and as the U.S. position to the ISO.

Karen Holtzblatt has designed products and processes for the past 10 years as a consultant to the computer industry and as an engineer at Digital Equipment Corporation. She developed the Contextual Inquiry approach to gathering field data on product use in a postdoctoral internship with John Whiteside and Digital's Software Usability Engineering (SUE) group. She was subsequently hired as a consultant to Digital to train the SUE group in the use of these processes for product evaluation and development, allowing the SUE group to become involved in the initial definition of new products, in addition to enhancing their ability to affect the usability of already developed products. She also consulted with Lotus, evaluating their documentation evaluation processes and making recommendations on using Contextual Inquiry practices to improve their documentation.

Ms. Holtzblatt joined Lou Cohen's quality group at Digital, where she worked on the VAX 9000 control panel, the VAX cluster console, integrated CAD, system management products, transaction processing products, and a representation of the work of Digital's High Performance Systems. During this time she linked her field data-gathering processes to quality processes such as QFD and Pugh Matrixes. She also initiated the inclusion of customers in the QFD process. Today starting the QFD process with Contextual Inquiry is institutionalized within Digital.

As a member of the quality group, Karen Holtzblatt and Sandra Jones developed the first Contextual Inquiry course, which has now been delivered to thousands of people around the world. Contextual Inquiry and work modeling have been taught for the last five years as a Computer-Human Interaction (CHI) conference tutorial. Contextual Design techniques have been presented as part of the design curriculum at the Software Engineering Institute at CMU, Stanford, and the University of California at Irvine.

Holtzblatt has over 15 years of teaching experience both in industry and as an associate professor of psychology. She holds a doctorate in applied psychology from the University of Toronto.